I0130483

Exploring Initiative and Referendum Law

Researching ballot measures can be one of the most daunting types of legal research. *Exploring Initiative and Referendum Law: Selected State Research Guides* offers legal researchers an easy-to-use guide that provides thorough overviews of I&R (initiative and referendum) laws within twenty-three states. This unique resource provides state-specific guidance about both forms of I&R law, those state laws permitting I&R, and those state laws enacted as a result of the I&R process. Any legal researcher beginning a project or needing to know just where to go for the right resources will get helpful general and specific information on practical research strategies and resources.

Up to now, finding the literature to research the state-specific history of a law passed by initiative or referendum has been extremely difficult. This book fills this gap by providing top researchers with brief overviews of the individual state processes while providing important primary and secondary sources, including Web sites. The guide's chapters are separated alphabetically by state for fast and easy reference. Annotated bibliographies of books, articles, and Web sites are provided, along with instructions about what documents one can expect to find on the Web, and how to use free databases.

Because of this useful volume's unique focus, the book may well become an essential resource for law librarians, attorneys, law faculty, law students, and Political Science scholars.

This book was published as a special issue of *Legal Reference Services Quarterly.*

Beth Williams is Reference Librarian, Arthur W. Diamond Law Library, Columbia University School of Law. As a member of the Columbia Law Library Reference Department, she teaches legal research to first-year law students every fall and participates in teaching seminars in Advanced Legal Research and International Legal Research each spring semester. She holds appointments as Lecturer in Law at Columbia Law School and as Lecturer in Information and Archive Management at Columbia University.

Exploring Initiative and Referendum Law

Selected state research guides

Edited by Beth Williams

Routledge
Taylor & Francis Group

LONDON AND NEW YORK

First published 2009 by Routledge

2 Park Square, Milton Park, Abingdon, Oxon OX14 4RN
711 Third Avenue, New York, NY 10017, USA

Routledge is an imprint of the Taylor & Francis Group, an informa business

First issued in paperback 2016

Copyright © 2009 Edited by Beth Williams

Typeset in Times by Value Chain, India

All rights reserved. No part of this book may be reprinted or reproduced or utilised in any form or by any electronic, mechanical, or other means, now known or hereafter invented, including photocopying and recording, or in any information storage or retrieval system, without permission in writing from the publishers.

Notice:
Product or corporate names may be trademarks or registered trademarks, and are used only for identification and explanation without intent to infringe.

British Library Cataloguing in Publication Data
A catalogue record for this book is available from the British Library

ISBN13: 978-0-7890-3792-3 (hbk)
ISBN13: 978-1-138-96939-1 (pbk)

CONTENTS

Preface   ix

Introduction to Researching Initiative and Referendum Law:
General Strategies and Resources   1
  Beth Williams

1   Alaska Initiatives and Referenda   15
    Tina S. Ching

2   Arizona Initiatives and Referenda   21
    Tina S. Ching

3   Researching Initiatives and Referendums in Arkansas   31
    Joseph A. Custer

4   Researching Colorado Ballot Measures   51
    Goldie Burton

5   Researching Initiatives and Referendums:
    A Guide for Florida   63
    Elizabeth Outler

6   Initiative and Referendum Process in Idaho:
    A Research Guide   79
    Kristin M. Ford

7   Illinois Initiatives and Referenda   89
    Shannon L. Malcolm

8   Researching Initiatives and Referenda: A Guide for Maine   97
    Christine I. Hepler

9 Democracy's Harvest: Resources for Massachusetts Voters'
   Initiatives and Referendums   113
   Spencer E. Clough

10 Initiatives and Referenda in Michigan: A Research Guide   137
   Tammy R. Pettinato

11 Researching Initiatives and Referendums:
   A Guide for Mississippi   147
   Stacey A. Lane

12 Researching Initiatives and Referenda: A Guide for Missouri 163
   Margaret McDermott

13 Researching Initiatives and Referendums:
   A Guide for Big Sky Country–Montana   177
   Lisa Mecklenberg Jackson

14 Researching the Initiative and Referendum
   Process in Nebraska   205
   Patrick J. Charles

15 Researching Initiatives and Referenda:
   A Guide for Nevada   223
   Thomas R. Boone

16 Powers Reserved to the People: A Guide for Researching
   Initiatives and Referendums in North Dakota   231
   Rhonda R. Schwartz

17 Researching Initiatives and Referenda: A Guide for Ohio   257
   Sara A. Sampson

18 Researching Initiatives and Referenda:
   A Guide for Oklahoma   265
   Patricia R. Monk

19 Researching Oregon Initiatives and Referendums   273
   Beth Williams
   David Dames

20 Researching Initiatives and Referendums:
   A Guide for South Dakota   287
      Candice Spurlin

21 Utah Initiatives and Referenda: A Research Guide   299
      Connie Strittmatter

22 Researching Washington State Initiatives
   and Referendums   309
      Beth Williams

23 Initiatives and Referenda in Wyoming   321
      Debora Person
      Tawnya Plumb

   Index   337

Preface

This project began as a paper written while I was a law librarianship student at the University of Washington in 2004-2005. Trying to decide on a seminar paper topic, I asked myself, *what kind of reference question scares me the most*? Though I had long since stopped worrying about *every* kind of reference question under the consummate tutelage of the Gallagher Law Library Reference Staff, the answer was still immediately obvious to me: state legislative history. Yikes. There was something uniquely opaque to me about conducting state legislative histories, much of which was born out of the paucity of documents available in Washington State.

What could be worse than compiling a legislative history for a Washington State law? Easy: researching the history of a law passed outside the legislative system, without even the hope or promise of documents generated regularly by government bodies, i.e., a law passed via initiative or referendum. No bill versions, no committee reports, no legislative debates, no bill jackets, no nothing. How might one craft an argument concerning the intent of a law when there was literally no legislative intent behind its passage? How could historical context be gleaned without any legislative record of the law prior to its passage? What documents might one reasonably expect to find when searching for the context and meaning of such a law?

A quick glance at the literature revealed almost nothing that might help a legal researcher simply trying to trace the history of a law passed via initiative or referendum. Nothing, that is, except for an excellent article written by Tobe Liebert called "Researching California Ballot Measures," originally published by the *Law Library Journal* in 1998. This is exactly the kind of piece I'd had in mind, and more; but what about all the other states possessing initiative and referendum powers? I originally planned to write a similar paper about researching I&R in the remaining Western States. I quickly discovered the foolishness of this overreaching, and ultimately confined myself to Washington and Oregon.

Upon submitting a copy of my seminar paper (affectionately known by UW grads as the "Penny Paper") to *Legal Reference Services Quarterly* for publication, I was greeted with a slyly tempting offer. Sure, *LRSQ* would publish the paper as is, but wouldn't it be better to solicit articles from the remaining I&R states and publish a special double issue in order to fill this gap in the literature all at once? Much to my surprise the offer suggested that I solicit and edit the additional twenty-plus articles. Having just moved cross-country for the second time in 12 months, started a new job in a new career, and drowning in a sea of grading 90 weekly first-year legal research homework exercises, once again, the answer seemed obvious: how could I say no?

If the offer to coordinate this project was a surprise, the response to my call for contributors was nothing short of astounding. I had no idea that I could interest more than a handful of people to write about this subject, but I was thoroughly gratified to learn that the intellectual curiosity of the people in this great profession is at least equal to their generosity of spirit. I am so grateful to all those who offered to contribute, as well as those who worked with me so diligently on this project. My most sincere thanks to Professor Mike Chiorazzi, editor of *LRSQ*, for giving me this wonderful opportunity. I must also thank my friends and colleagues at the Columbia University Arthur W. Diamond Law Library for their encouragement and support, particularly Silke Sahl, for her thoughtful comments and suggestions. My special thanks goes to all the staff of the Gallagher Law Library at the University of Washington School of Law, and to Penny Hazelton, in particular, whose unselfish and boundless love for this profession infects everyone lucky enough to meet her. Finally, thanks to my husband, Matt, for making all good things possible.

Beth Williams

Introduction to Researching Initiative and Referendum Law: General Strategies and Resources

Beth Williams

INTRODUCTION

By virtue of either state constitution or statute, twenty-four states grant the people the power to propose new law and to enact it directly by popular vote–bypassing altogether the state legislative body–otherwise known as the initiative process.[1] Many of these same states also provide the people with another significant power: the right to propose a popular vote on whether to accept or reject laws that were previously enacted by the state legislature, otherwise known as the popular referendum.[2]

These powerful rights are in no way new: most states adopted an I&R process during the first two decades of the previous century. Nor has this subject been ignored by scholars; much ink has, and continues to be, spilled decrying, applauding, and analyzing these principles.

From a research perspective, however, there is precious little guidance about initiatives and referendums.[3] The articles in this collection aim to fill this gap for legal researchers, providing guidance about both forms of I&R law: (1) those state laws permitting I&R, which I will call *first order I&R*, and (2) state laws enacted as a result of the I&R process, or *second order I&R*.

Researching *first order I&R* law–constitutional and statutory provisions that create each state's unique I&R rights, administrative regulations governing how those rights may be exercised, and case law that arises from these elements–is, for the most part, a traditional exercise in statutory research. Though the tools and techniques one must use in order to find these laws are not unfamiliar to the seasoned legal researcher, they can be complicated by the fact that states often differ dramatically in both the process of initiating ballot measures and in the types of measures available. Of the twenty-seven states that have some form of initiative or popular referendum, the processes may permit the enactment of statutes, constitutional amendments, or in some states, both–all with their own unique technical requirements regarding signatures, the timing of filing, etc. To further complicate matters, not only are each state's laws permitting I&R unique, initiative and referendum powers also exist within hundreds of county and city codes.[4]

Moreover, if traditional legal research is typically a challenging, sometimes methodical, sometimes creative skill, then researching *second order I&R* law, i.e., initiatives and referendums themselves, is the extreme case. There are no customary roadmaps to finding information about these odd, but often significant, entities, unless and until they become law. However, questions may arise at every stage of the life of a ballot measure: Where did it come from? Who drafted it? Who supported it? Who opposed it? How many votes did it get? Who challenged it in court? Where is it codified? If we were dealing with a traditional piece of legislation, these questions would be much easier to answer–though the assertion that conducting a legislative history is easy gives me some pause. The documents describing the pedigree of particular legislative bill–for example, previous versions of the bill, transcripts of committee hearings, and, if one is very lucky, committee reports revealing the express intent of the legislative body passing the bill–simply do not exist for ballot measures. In other words, the deliberative process that is purposefully transparent in the life of law enacted by the legislative branch is often nothing more than vapor for ballot measures.

There is simply no one research source or strategy that adequately encompasses this expansive subject. The articles that follow in this collection offer state-specific guidance for researchers seeking an understanding of both *first* and *second order I&R* law in twenty-three states[5] possessing the initiative power. In many cases, these articles provide recommendations for general sources that will assist researchers focused on their particular state. The information that follows below offers some general strategies and resource recommendations for legal researchers beginning a project, for those intending to compare state systems, and for those who may not need individual state materials. The sources are listed from the general to specific: beginning with dictionary definitions, moving on to legal encyclopedias and an almanac, then periodicals and periodical indexes, session laws and annotated codes, digests, and Internet resources. Finally, a selective, annotated bibliography of important books on this subject is included to help begin any I&R research project.

DEFINITIONS

Initiatives, Generally

An initiative is generally defined as an "electoral process by which a percentage of voters can propose legislation and compel a vote on it by the legislature or by the full electorate."[6] That is, the initiative is the peoples' power to adopt laws or to amend the state constitution independently of the state legislature. Twenty-four states have some form of the initiative process.[7]

There are two forms of initiatives: direct and indirect. A direct initiative permits citizen-proposed constitutional amendments or statutes to be placed directly on the election ballot for the people's approval or rejection.[8] In the case of direct initiatives, the state legislature has no role in the process. Sixteen states provide for constitutional amendment by direct initiative, and sixteen states permit the adoption of law by direct initiative.[9]

An indirect initiative permits citizen-proposed constitutional amendments or statutes to be submitted to the state legislature for review during a regular legislative session.[10] If the legislature fails to act on the proposal, the original petition will in most cases be submitted subsequently to the people for approval or rejection in the next general election. Be aware, however, that state procedures vary under these circumstances. Two states–Massachusetts and Mississippi–permit constitutional amendment by indirect initiative; seven states currently permit statutes to be passed by indirect initiative.[11]

Referendums, Generally

A referendum is the "process of referring a state legislative act, a state constitutional amendment, or an important public issue to the people for final approval by popular vote."[12] In other words, the referendum power permits citizens to reject laws or amendments proposed by the state legislature. Like initiatives, there are two general forms of referendums: popular and legislative.[13]

A popular referendum permits the people to petition for a general vote on whether to accept or reject specific legislation enacted by the legislature through a citizen-sponsored petition.[14] Though there is no national referendum process, twenty-four states permit popular referendums.[15]

A legislative referendum is when the state legislature, an elected official, state appointed constitutional revision commission, or other government agency or department submits propositions (constitutional amendments, statutes, bond issues, etc.) to the people for their approval or rejection.[16] All 50 states require that constitutional amendments proposed by the legislature be submitted to popular election via legislative referendum for approval or rejection.[17] Because legislative referendums are not citizen-sponsored, they are generally excluded from discussions about direct legislation.

ALMANACS AND ENCYCLOPEDIAS

Holliday, Beth, B. "Initiative and Referendum." *American Jurisprudence 2d* 42 (2000): 489-532.

   Though not state-specific, this article contains good general background information for the novice I&R researcher. As always, the citations contained in this *Am Jur* article are nearly as good as the encyclopedic treatment. References include members of the family of *American Jurisprudence* publications, e.g., *Pleadings and Practice Forms* and *Legal Forms*, both of which contain chapters under the West topic/subject heading "Initiative and Referendum."

Macy, J. E. "Power of Legislative Body to Amend, Repeal, or Abrogate Initiative or Referendum Measure, or to Enact Measure Defeated on Referendum." *American Law Reports 2d* 33 (1966): 1118-1134.
This is the broadest ALR annotation on the subject of I&R, though it is worth noting that there several annotations on more specific subjects involving ballot measures, e.g., zoning. This annotation contains citations to significant legal challenges to ballot measures in all relevant states and a discussion about the power of a legislature or municipal government to restrict ballot measures at various stages in the I&R process. Updates through 2005 are incorporated into the electronic version available on WESTLAW.

Waters, M. Dane. *Initiative and Referendum Almanac*. Durham, North Carolina: Carolina Academic Press, 2003.
This book is an ideal reference resource for I&R reference information. Waters is the founder of the Initiative & Referendum Institute at the University of Southern California (see Web site information *infra*). This Almanac provides comprehensive information about the history of I&R in the United States. The book also includes the following: statistics comparing statewide I&R usage; scholarly articles on a variety of subjects, including judicial and legislative issues affecting the I&R process, and subject analyses of I&R usage on, for example, tax issues, campaign finance, and drug policies; a draft model of I&R legislation; a 70-page comprehensive listing of all statewide initiatives since 1904; and individual state-by-state histories and overviews for those states that have provisions for initiatives and/or referendums. The state-by-state guides include charts of all statewide initiatives up to 2001 and the full text of constitutional and statutory provisions permitting I&R, where applicable. The individual state chapters and the comprehensive list of all statewide initiatives alone make this resource a goldmine for I&R research. The charts contained in these chapters provide the year of passage or failure for initiatives by measure number, subject matter, and brief description–all of which make finding the codified version of these laws much easier. This book is the closest thing to one-stop-shopping for practical I&R information

currently available. The only drawback to this wonderful resource is currency: all references to statutory and case law must be updated by the diligent legal researcher.

PERIODICALS AND PERIODICALS INDEXES

Articles provide one of the most reliable sources of information about particular ballot measures. Newspapers, law reviews, bar journals, non-profit research, and civic organizations often publish articles that help supplement the paucity of documentation associated with initiatives and referendums. Electronic access to these kinds of articles is discussed throughout the *Internet Resources* section below. However, there are other commercial periodical indexes that provide access to articles on this subject that should be consulted when conducting a thorough search for I&R information. The following is a brief description of how to use several particularly valuable print and electronic periodical indexes. Note that these indexes are expensive commercial products, typically available only via a library's subscription.

Current Law Index. The print version of the *Current Law Index* uses the subject "Referendum" to index articles about ***both*** initiatives and referendums. The subject index fails to list preferred terms for either "Initiative" or "Ballot Measure," though a broader search under the subjects "Election Law" or "Voting" may also be fruitful.

Expanded Academic. *Expanded Academic* is a multidisciplinary electronic index also published by Thomson Gale. Coverage includes major newspapers, political magazines (e.g., *The Nation, Time,* and *The New Republic*), library journals, academic journals in history and political science, and some major law reviews. Like *LegalTrac* and the *Current Law Index, Expanded Academic* uses the subject "Referendum" to index articles about ***both*** initiatives and referendums. Some of the options listed under the main subject "Referendum" are links to subdivisions, e.g., individual countries and states, and topics, e.g., zoning. Related subjects are also provided.

Index to Legal Periodicals and Books. In contrast to the *Current Law Index,* the *Index to Legal Periodicals and Books* (ILP) uses the subjects "Initiative and Referendum" and "Direct Democracy" to index articles, though it is not immediately clear how a distinction is drawn between these two subjects. ILP also conveniently uses individual state and country subheadings under "Initiative and Referendum." ILP is available on LexisNexis (File-name: ILP, from 1978 through current) and on WESTLAW (Database identifier: ILP, from August 1981 through current). There are scores of law review articles on specialized subjects, e.g., limitations on I&R subject matter (especially the single subject rule, appropriations and expenditures, and repeat measures), passage requirements (including signature gathering and the "supermajority" requirement), and judicial review that may be found efficiently and effectively by using this specialized periodical index.

LegalTrac. *LegalTrac* is Thomson Gale's electronic version of the *Current Law Index*. This version, though, adds coverage of some legal newspapers and legal newsletters. Like the *Current Law Index*, *LegalTrac* indexes articles about ***both*** initiatives and referendums under the subject heading "Referendum." The electronic version contains a list of subdivisions and a list of related subjects–both of which are useful. It also appears that some relevant articles are indexed under the subjects "Legislative Histories–Research" and "Ballot–Research."

PAIS International. *PAIS International* provides indexing and abstracting for scholarly journals, books, articles in books, some government publications and other resources, with a particular emphasis on political science academic journals. Newspapers and newsletters are not indexed. The preferred term, according to the thesaurus, for both "Initiative" and "Direct Legislation" is simply "Referendum." For the best results, search in the advanced search mode by using "Referendum" as a subject heading–called "Descriptors" in this index–and then narrow the search by adding state names or other key terms.

ProQuest. An all-purpose, partially full-text database, this resource is particularly useful to I&R legal researchers due to its collection of newspaper articles, which can be a significant source of information on initiatives and referendums past and present. Contains coverage of major U.S. newspapers, including *The New York Times*, *The Boston Globe*, *The Wall Street Journal*, *The Detroit News*, *The Los Angeles Times*, *The Denver Post*, the *Chicago Tribune* and the *St. Louis Post-Dispatch*, and other I&R state-based newspapers.

SESSION LAWS & ANNOTATED CODES

Laws concerning state initiative and referendum processes may often be searched using both the session laws and codified laws of that state. Publishers typically index "Initiative and Referendum" subject headings for *first order I&R* laws. Unfortunately, that subject heading does not include or cross-reference to *second order I&R*, i.e., the substantive laws passed by the I&R process, and no known published session law or code set indexes ballot measures either by popular name or by number. Therefore, researching the codified versions of laws that began as initiatives and referendums when only the popular ballot title or number is known will require interim steps. If the I&R subject is known, then these subject indexes may be more useful, though that will not always be the most efficient way to find the appropriate code sections for legislation passed by initiative or referendum.

Many session laws contain lists of statewide ballot measures passed during the previous election, and they ultimately must contain the text of those measures that did pass alongside the text of legislative bills that were signed into law. Though consulting the legislature's session laws may seem initially counterintuitive to the I&R researcher, these publications are often excellent resources to consult for both current and historical information.

DIGESTS

Digests provide subject access to published case law. Digests specifically tailored to finding state case law are published by West Thomson. For that reason, it is useful to review the organization of West's indexing system as it relates to initiatives and referendums. *West's Analysis of American Law* is the comprehensive outline of West's main subject headings or "Topics," and sub-headings, called "Key Numbers" in West's indexing system. A review of that outline reveals that "Initiatives and Referendums" are not assigned their own topic in West's system. Initiatives and referendums are sub-headings under other main topics, primarily "Statutes," though there are a few relevant key numbers also scattered in various places under other topics. However, "Initiatives" and "Referendums" are separately indexed in the Descriptive Word Index volumes of all West digest sets. In order of importance, the best key numbers to review for finding case law on this subject are:

- Statutes–key numbers 301-327 for initiatives and key numbers 341-367 for referendums;
- Constitutional Law–key numbers 9-9(3);
- Municipal Corporations–key numbers 46, 49 and 108-108.8;
- Elections–key numbers 175, 184 and 189;
- Counties–key number 55; and
- Mandamus–key numbers 74-74(5).

INTERNET RESOURCES

The difficulty of finding documents in this research area is somewhat tempered by the abundance of information on the Web. I&R sponsor Web sites, government Web sites, non-profit research centers, and online newspaper archives: all of these contain important information for researching initiatives and referendums and placing them in a meaningful context.

Nevertheless, the information that is available on the Web is, at best, scattershot. The following is intended to be a guide through that maze of information on this topic currently available on the Web. The sites are listed in order of importance for I&R legal researchers. Though all of the information on the Web could potentially be gone tomorrow, it is my hope that these sites will continue to build their Web archives with valuable historical materials, securely and permanently.

Initiative & Referendum Institute, *at* http://www.iandrinstitute.org. The Initiative & Referendum Institute at the University of Southern California Law School is a non-profit research and educational organization founded in 1998 to study how the I&R process has been used in this country. Though there is no secret about where they stand politically on the role of I&R in a democratic society, the organization provides a tremendous amount of educational information through their Web site and publications. This is an ideal starting place for I&R research on the Web. The site contains information about the I&R process in every state, including **brief analytical treatments** of the state processes, PDF documents of **constitutional and statutory provisions**, **statistical charts** of historical usage in each state, **guides** to undertaking the process in each state, and **links to state Web sites**. There are also recommendations for **print resources, reports** on previous elections, **handouts**, and **links to other educational and political organizations** in the United States and Europe specializing in this topic.

National Conference of State Legislatures, *at* http://www.ncsl.org.
The National Conference of State Legislatures is a bipartisan advocacy organization serving legislators and their staffs with research and technical assistance since 1975. The site contains much of the information available on other sites described above, including **titles, descriptions** and **sponsor information**. However, this site also has a very useful **searchable ballot measures database** at http://www.ncsl. org/programs/legman/elect/dbintro.htm. The database permits searching by state, subject, year, election type and/or measure type. Though the dates available to search go back to 1970, coverage from that date is not complete for every state. It appears that coverage of most state I&R information goes back to 1990. It is particularly useful to be able to search by subject. Unfortunately, the search function does not permit searching all available years, so if you undertake a subject search in all states, it must be repeated for each individual election year. The caution about currency and accuracy also holds for this Web site–i.e., all references to legal authority should be verified and updated using other, preferably official, sources.

LLRX.com's Research Roundup: Federal and State Elections Resources, *at* http://www.llrx.com/columns/roundup31.htm.
The free Web journal LLRX.com features a frequently updated Research Roundup article on Federal and State Elections Resources. This is a useful **index of Secretary of State and/or Elections Divisions Web sites**, along with a brief description of the information you can expect to find on those sites. The majority of primary information about state law is likely to be found from these Web sites, along with the text of pending and recent ballot measures.

Ballot Initiative Strategy Center, *at* http://www.ballot.org.
Initially founded as an arm of the People for the American Way, the Ballot Initiative Strategy Center is a non-profit organization that seeks to use the initiative process to "further the goals of the labor and progressive community by developing a proactive, national strategy to advance progressive ballot measures." The organization publishes **reports** analyzing election results, digests **news stories** covering I&R issues, and lists **state-by-state election results** on ballot measures, all of which are quite useful to researchers.

Project Vote Smart, *at* http://www.vote-smart.org.

Project Vote Smart is a non-profit, nonpartisan Web site dedicated primarily to providing "unbiased and accurate campaign information" to the American people. The site contains a considerable amount of information on ballot measures by state from the 1996 to 2006 elections. Click on the heading "My State" then "Ballot Measures" and choose your state of interest: there is a ballot measure **number and title**, a **summary**, **election results**, and, for some states, the **official arguments for and against** the measure. The information contained here conveniently duplicates much of the information often found in state Voter's Guides, and may be more accessible than those archived materials, depending upon your location.

SELECTED BIBLIOGRAPHY

Braunstein, Rich. *Initiative and Referendum Voting: Governing through Direct Democracy in the United States*. New York: LFB Scholarly Publishing, 2004.

Braustein presents an unusually neutral treatment of I&R in this slim volume. The narrative briefly describes the historical foundations of direct democracy, but the book's aim is more pragmatic than scholarly. The chapters are brief and contain a number of illustrative tables and charts. This is a very good place to go for a snapshot of I&R history and current issues.

Cronin, Thomas E. *Direct Democracy: The Politics of Initiative, Referendum and Recall*. Cambridge, Massachusetts: Harvard University Press, 1989.

This was the first major work on the subject of I&R by a political scientist and it is still probably the best-known and most widely respected monograph on the subject. A large body of political science I&R scholarship grew in the wake of this work. Cronin's position is reasonably objective, and his prose is both clear and pleasant to read. This volume also contains an excellent bibliography.

Ellis, Richard J. *Democratic Delusions: The Initiative Process in America*. Lawrence, Kansas: University Press of Kansas, 2002.

Richard Ellis, Mark O. Hatfield Professor of Politics at Willamette University in Oregon, writes about what he calls widespread naïve beliefs that are often accepted regarding the I&R process. His goal is to persuade readers to approach the initiative process critically, with at least as much skepticism as is currently aimed at legislatures. While making this argument, Ellis provides a very good historical sketch of the national use of I&R throughout the twentieth century.

Matsusaka, John G. *For the Many or the Few: The Initiative, Public Policy, and American Democracy.* Chicago: The University of Chicago Press, 2004.
Matsusaka, Professor of Business and Law at the University of Southern California School of Law, is currently the President of the I&R Institute at USC. *For the Many or the Few* uses empirical analysis to examine the impact of initiatives and referendums on government tax and spending. This method makes for some extremely compelling arguments against those characterizing the I&R process as the "tyranny of the majority."

Schmidt, David D. *Citizen Lawmakers: The Ballot Initiative Revolution.* Philadelphia: Temple University Press, 1989.
Despite its age, this remains an incredibly timely and useful research resource, still cited by legal and political science scholars alike. Much of the data appearing on the I&R Institute Web site comes from Schmidt's historical telling of the rise and fall and rise again of the I&R movement in America.

Smith, Daniel A. and Tolbert, Caroline J. *Educated by Initiative: The Effects of Direct Democracy on Citizens and Political Organizations in the American States.* Ann Arbor: The University of Michigan Press, 2004.
A brief but engaging look at how the initiative process educates citizens, special interest groups, and political parties. The authors offer up the initiative process as a response to Robert Putnam's call for increased civic engagement in his book *Bowling Alone.* Includes an appendix with some selected statistics about the use and impact of initiatives on elections primarily between 1970 and 2000; a bibliography and index are also included.

Waters. M. Dane, ed. *The Battle Over Citizen Lawmaking: An In-Depth Review of the Growing Trend to Regulate the People's Tool of Self-Government: The Initiative and Referendum Process.* Durham, North Carolina: Carolina Academic Press, 2001.

Dane Waters, President of the Initiative and Referendum Institute at the University of Southern California Law School, presents a series of articles written by different authors, each promoting the idea that the growing trend towards legislative regulation of the process is damaging to the system and the people's power. Of particular interest to researchers are both Anne Campbell's chapter on the single-subject rule for ballot initiatives and each of the chapters in section three regarding legal challenges to the regulation of initiatives and referendum process. Waters also includes several appendices, including a list of important court cases relating to the I&R process, a list of requirements to place an initiative on the ballot, and an annotated list of major initiative regulations since 1998.

NOTES

1. Those states permitting the initiative process are Alaska, Arizona, Arkansas, California, Colorado, Florida, Idaho, Illinois, Maine, Maryland, Massachusetts, Michigan, Mississippi, Missouri, Montana, Nebraska, Nevada, North Dakota, Ohio, Oklahoma, Oregon, South Dakota, Utah, Washington, and Wyoming. In the interest of convenience, I will often refer to initiatives and referendums as "ballot measures," "direct legislation," or simply "I&R."

2. With the exception of Florida, Illinois, and Mississippi, the same states permitting the initiative process also permit the popular referendum. Kentucky, Maryland and New Mexico also have the popular referendum process.

3. The only such legal research tool I am aware of is Tobe Liebert's *Researching California Ballot Measures*, 90 L. Lib. J. 27 (1998). An updated version of this article appears as Chapter 5 in Daniel W. Martin's *Henke's California Law Guide* (Matthew Bender 2004).

4. In some cases, the state-specific articles in this collection mention local initiative processes. However, county and city I&R legal research is generally beyond the scope of this project.

5. California is the only initiative state not represented here, *see ibid.* Liebert's work was, in many ways, a model for the articles appearing here and could not be improved upon, hence the omission of California in this collection.

6. *Black's Law Dictionary* 799 (8th ed. 2004).

7. M. Dane Waters, *Initiative and Referendum Almanac* (2003) at 12. Note also that eighteen states permit constitutional amendment by initiative, and twenty-one states permit the adoption of statutes by initiative. In both the *Almanac* and on the Initiative and Referendum Institute Web site (http://www.iandrinstitute.org, discussed at length *supra*), Waters provides a plethora of useful statistics, often in easy to read chart form. I will provide a small sampling of those statistics here in the interest of putting the I&R system in a national context.

8. M. Dane Waters, *The Battle Over Citizen Lawmaking: An In-Depth Review of the Growing Trend to Regulate the People's Tool of Self-Government: The Initiative and Referendum Process* (2001) at 261.

9. Waters, *supra* note 7, at 12.

10. Waters, *supra* note 8, at 261.

11. Waters, *supra* note 7, at 12.

12. *Black's Law Dictionary* 1307 (8th ed. 2004).

13. A brief word about vocabulary seems in order for those of you who cringe at the use of the term "referendums." Please take heart: The Oxford English Dictionary prefers the term referendums, while acknowledging the minority preference for the plural form "referenda." *See The Oxford English Dictionary* vol. XIII, 466 (2d ed., Clarendon Press 1989).

14. Waters, *supra* note 8, at 261.

15. Waters, *supra* note 7, at 12.

16. Waters, *supra* note 8, at 261.

17. *Id.*

Alaska Initiatives and Referenda

Tina S. Ching

INTRODUCTION

This article is intended to be used as a starting point for those researching initiative and referendum issues for the state of Alaska. A brief history of I&R in Alaska is followed by an overview of the process. The piece concludes with an annotated list of resources to begin research into Alaska I&R.

HISTORY OF I&R IN ALASKA

Alaska adopted a limited initiative and referendum process at statehood in 1959 amid much debate. Despite the fact that most of the Western States had already adopted a version of the initiative and referendum by the time the Alaskan delegates met to draft their constitution, some of the members of Alaska's Constitutional Convention were not immediately convinced that direct legislation was a necessary component for their constitution.[1] In the end, the members of the convention approved the initiative and referendum process, but not without several restrictions.

Some of those restrictions have affected the implementation of approved measures. For instance, the constitution does not allow the people to make appropriations or amend the constitution using the initiative and referendum. The people of the State of Alaska have voted several times on issues related to moving the State capitol from Juneau, beginning with the first Alaskan initiative in 1960.[2] In 1974, a measure was passed to move the capitol. However, because a move would require money to be allocated to the cause and the legislature did not make any appropriations for the move, the measure was eventually repealed.[3]

BASICS OF ALASKA'S I&R PROCESS

Direct legislation via the initiative and referendum is reserved for the people of Alaska through the Constitution of Alaska.[4] The procedure for using the I&R process is set out in the Alaska Constitution,[5] Alaska Statutes[6] and Alaska Administrative Code.[7]

There are several steps that must be taken before a petition appears on a ballot. First, an application must be filed with the Lieutenant Governor.[8] The application includes the contact information for the three primary sponsors of the initiative, a refundable $100 deposit, and the text of the proposition.[9] The proposition must only cover one subject and cannot deal with issues such as appropriations or create courts.[10] The application must also be accompanied by a collection of at least 100 signatures of voters who are considered sponsors for circulation purposes.[11]

The application is then reviewed by the Lieutenant Governor, the Department of Law and the Division of Elections.[12] Once the application is certified, the Division of Elections prints 500 petition booklets.[13] Circulators use these booklets to gather the required number of signatures.

The booklet includes information such as the text of the proposition, a summary of the bill written by the Department of Law, a statement of costs and space for signatures.[14]

Within one year, the sponsors must file the petition with the required number of signatures.[15] A number of qualified signatures equal to at least 10 percent of the votes in the previous general election must be gathered.[16] Signatures from at least three-fourths of the house districts in the state are also required.[17] In addition, sufficient signatures equal to at least seven percent of the votes cast in the previous general election within that district are required.[18] The Lieutenant Governor provides the amount needed in each district on the elections Web site.[19]

Within 60 days of filing, the Lieutenant Governor will review the petition.[20] The committee will be informed whether the petition was filed properly and in which election the proposition will appear.[21] If the petition is properly filed, then the $100 deposit is refunded.[22]

LOCATING ALASKA I&R MATERIALS

The best place to begin researching Alaskan I&R materials is the State of Alaska Division of Elections Web site, available at http://www.gov.state.ak.us/ltgov/elections/. The site not only provides a summary of Alaska's I&R laws, but it also includes information on filing a petition, the status of petitions filed and sponsors' contact information. While the site itself is not particularly well organized or intuitive to navigate, it does contain a substantial amount of valuable information about I&R which should satisfy most research needs.

General Information

State of Alaska Division of Elections, *Initiative, Referendum and Recall Information*, at http://ltgov.state.ak.us/elections/petitions/irr.php.
The Division of Elections does a good job of breaking down the statutes and regulations and explaining the provisions clearly, with references to the applicable laws.

Waters, M. Dane, *Initiative and Referendum Almanac*, 38-49 (Carolina Academic Press 2003).
Waters provides a brief description of how I&R has been used in Alaska, followed by a list of statewide initiatives from statehood to

2000, a reproduction of the relevant laws and the basic initiative process steps.

History of I&R in Alaska

Alaska Statutes, vol. 11 (Lexis 2006).
    Anyone with access to a law library that has a set of the *Alaska Stat-
utes*, published by the Alaska Legislative Council and annotated and
printed by LexisNexis, will find near the end of volume 11 a section
on initiatives. This section lists all of the propositions from the first
initiative in 1960 to the publication date (as of this article it includes
ballot measures appearing in the 2006 election). It also includes a
summary of the proposal and if available, the disposition, where it
was codified, when it became effective and any cases that directly relate to the proposal.

State of Alaska Division of Elections, *Alaska's History of Ballot Issues
and Petitions,* at http://www.ltgov.state.ak.us/elections/inithist.htm (last
visited May 5, 2007).
    This page includes prior initiatives and referendums (election date,
title and ballot language, votes for, and votes against); a list of proposed measures that did not make it to the ballot (year and subject); a
list of rejected applications (year and subject); a separate list of constitutional amendments that have been on the ballot (election date,
title and ballot language, votes for and votes against); bonding propositions; advisory votes, propositions and other questions on Alaska's
ballots (election date, title and ballot language, votes for and votes
against).

Minutes of the Daily Proceedings, Alaska Constitutional Convention
(Alaska Legislative Council, 1965).
    The Minutes are either found as a six part print set or on micro-
fiche. There is an index available, though it does not appear to be
readily available outside of Alaska. The minutes lay out the discussion amongst the committee members about the issues surrounding
I&R and how the process should be administered.

Victor Fischer, *Alaska's Constitutional Convention* 79-81 (University
of Alaska Press, 1975).
    If you do not want to read through the Minutes of the Daily Proceed-
ings, this resource may be for you. Fischer summarizes the over 100

pages of discussion during the Constitutional Convention on initiative and referendum in four concise pages.

Miscellaneous Resources

M. Katheryn Bradley and Deborah L. Williams, *"Be it enacted by the people of the state of Alaska . . ." A Practitioner's Guide to Alaska's Initiative Law*, 9 Alaska L. Rev. 279 (1992).
  This article begins by briefly discussing the steps to filing a petition and then proceeds to a discussion of how the Alaskan courts have treated I&R issues. Because the article was published in 1992, it does not include changes that have been recently made due to amendments to the statutes, particularly the 2004 and 2005 amendments, or recent cases. However, the authors do an excellent job of summarizing the issues and analyzing past court cases dealing with the initiative and referendum.

Sen. Dave Donley with Douglas Baily, Mara Mallory, Ted Popely, & Matthew Roskoski, *Bess v. Ulmer–The Supreme Court Stumbles and the Subsistence Amendment Falls*, 19 Alaska L. Rev. 295 (2002).
  The authors in this article take an in depth look at the Alaska Supreme Court case *Bess v. Ulmer* in which the court makes the distinction between a constitutional amendment and revision.

Rachael Downey, Michelle Hargrove & Vanessa Locklin, *A Survey of the Single Subject Rule as Applied to Statewide Initiatives*, 13 J. Contemp. Legal Issues 579, 580-581 (2004).
  A very brief discussion about how the Alaska courts have interpreted the single subject rule with regard to initiatives.

NOTES

  1. *See Minutes of the Daily Proceedings, Alaska Constitutional Convention* 931 (Alaska Legislative Council, 1965).
  2. St. of Alaska Div. of Elections, *Moving the Capital: A History of Ballot Measures*, http://www.ltgov.state.ak.us/elections/capmove.htm.
  3. 1981 Alaska Sess. Laws 54.
  4. Alaska Const. art. XI.
  5. *Id.*
  6. Alaska Stat. §§ 15.45.010-15.45-720 (Lexis 2006).
  7. Alaska Admin. Code tit. 6, §§ 25.240 and 245 (2007).

8. Alaska Const. art. XI, § 2; Alaska Stat. § 15.45.020 (Lexis 2006).

9. Alaska Const. art. XI, § 2; Alaska Stat. § 15.45.030 (Lexis 2006).

10. Alaska Stat. § 15.45.040 (Lexis 2006).

11. Alaska Const. art. XI, § 2; Alaska Stat. § 15.45.030 (Lexis 2006).

12. St. of Alaska Div. of Elections, *Initiative, Referendum and Recall Information*, http://ltgov.state.ak.us/elections/petitions/irr.php (last updated July 18, 2006).

13. *Id.*

14. Alaska Stat. § 15.45.090 (Lexis 2006).

15. Alaska Stat. § 15.45.140 (Lexis 2006).

16. *Id.*

17. *Id.*

18. *Id.*

19. St. of Alaska Div. of Elections, *supra* n. 12.

20. Alaska Stat. § 15.45.150 (Lexis 2006).

21. *Id.*

22. Alaska Stat. § 15.45.020 (Lexis 2006).

Arizona Initiatives and Referenda

Tina S. Ching

INTRODUCTION

With 19 measures in the November 2006 general election, voters in Arizona claimed the distinction of having the longest ballot in the nation.[1] The measures covered issues ranging from an increased minimum wage to smoking rights to immigration. Most of the measures that appeared on the poster-sized ballots resulted from the direct initiative process–where members of the public or organizations filed for and circulated petitions to place the measure on the ballot–while several of the measures were placed on the ballot by the Arizona State Legislature. However, even with the widespread use of initiatives and referenda in Arizona, there are limited sources of information. Depending on the purpose of research, especially if one is looking for information on older elections, there will be a few places to obtain that information.

This guide offers some direction about where information can be located, whether looking up information on past I&R, on filing an initiative or referendum, or trying to find information on a proposition in an upcoming election. After a very brief history of how the I&R system began in Arizona, I will give an overview of the process, and describe some of the major resources that will help a researcher begin their quest for information on I&R in Arizona.

HISTORY OF THE ARIZONA SYSTEM

For those interested in politics, Arizona's history with the initiative and referendum is a fascinating chronicle beginning prior to statehood.[2] There were a couple promising pushes to permit the I&R process while Arizona was still a territory. The legislature of the territory of Arizona, strongly influenced by labor unions, passed an I&R bill in 1899 but, ironically, it was vetoed by the Governor.[3] In 1909, a direct legislation bill was introduced, but the bill died in the house.[4]

By the time the Enabling Act of 1910 allowed Arizona to form a constitution to join the Union, the debate was not over whether there should be an initiative and referendum process, but rather what percentage of signatures would be required for petitions.[5] After much debate during the constitutional convention, the Arizona Constitution, including provisions for initiatives and referenda, was finally approved.[6]

Since the first initiative in 1912, when women were given the right to vote, Arizonan voters have seen over 200 measures on ballots–making it one of the most widely used direct legislation systems in the United States.

BASICS OF ARIZONA'S I&R PROCESS

While members of the Arizona State Senate and the House of Representatives have legislative authority, according to the Arizona Constitution, the people have initiative power.[7] In addition, the Arizona Revised

Statutes discuss the particulars of the form, circulation and filing of initiatives and referendums.[8] These laws provide for direct initiatives, popular referenda, and legislative referenda, allowing the people of Arizona the ability to create statutes and amend the constitution.

Before circulating a petition to obtain signatures, a form must be filed with the Secretary of State including information such as a brief description and text of the proposed law.[9] The petitioner must do this to obtain a petition number that must be located on all signature sheets.[10] Petition numbers beginning with a "C" are measures that if passed would amend the constitution. Petition numbers beginning with an "I" would add or amend the Arizona Revised Statutes if passed. In the case of a measure placed on the ballot by the legislature, the identifier begins with an HCR or SCR.[11] While voters generally ignore the identifier and better know the measure by its ballot number or title, the identifier can be helpful in finding legislative history for these resolutions.

Next, petitioners must obtain signatures. The constitution dictates how many signatures are required for an initiative to appear on the ballot. For constitutional amendments, the number of signatures must equal fifteen percent of all votes cast for Governor in the last general election.[12] For statutes, the number of signatures needed equals ten percent of the votes cast for Governor.[13] Each petition sheet must have a place on it indicating whether the circulator is paid or is a volunteer. If it is not indicated, then the entire page of signatures will be deemed invalid.[14] When circulating, the signature sheets must be attached to the full text of the measure.[15] Petition circulators must also sign an affidavit stating that they are qualified to be a registered voter.[16] Once the sheets are turned in, the Secretary of State uses a random sampling method to verify the signatures.[17] The county recorder must also certify the signature sheets.[18] If enough signatures have been collected, then the measure will appear in the Publicity Pamphlet and ultimately on the ballot.

The Publicity Pamphlet is one way the Secretary of State's office distributes information about the measures. It is an official State publication that includes the measure's title, full text, form in which it appears on the ballot, arguments for and against the measure, legislative council analysis, and fiscal impact statement. The pamphlet is mailed to every household with a registered voter. Anyone can write a statement for or against the measure, but for it to be printed in the Publicity Pamphlet, a $100 fee is required and the statement cannot exceed 300 words. The State also holds open hearings for the public to obtain information about and discuss the measures. The hearings are held in at least three different counties prior to the election.[19] The schedule of hearings can be found on the Secretary of State's Web site.[20]

The measures that appear on the general election ballots receive a new number, generally known as the ballot number. Measures assigned numbers in the 100s are proposed constitutional amendments, initiatives affecting statutes begin in the 200s, referenda affecting statutes begin at 300 and then are consecutively numbered in the order in which they were filed with the Secretary of State.[21]

Measures or amendments that are approved in the general election are printed with the laws that are enacted in the next legislative session.[22] Once an initiative or referendum has been approved by the electorate, the Governor cannot veto it and the legislature cannot repeal it.[23] The legislature can amend an initiative or divert funds created or allocated by an initiative only if it furthers the purpose of the measure and at least three fourths of each house vote to amend the measure.[24]

LOCATING ARIZONA MATERIALS

Most I&R researchers (whether in or outside of Arizona) will be happy to know that most information can be found in the comfort of their own homes via the Internet. The information available includes recent publicity pamphlets, news coverage on the most recent general election, the Arizona laws on I&R, and limited historical information. For information on elections older than 1990, researchers will likely have to contact the Arizona State Archives or the Secretary of State's office. Some resources may also be available at the Arizona State University and University of Arizona libraries, though most of the I&R resources are for use in the library only and will be difficult to obtain out of state.

Official Documents

Arizona Secretary of State, at http://www.azsos.gov/.
   The Arizona Secretary of State's Web site provides a wealth of information on initiatives and referenda. Most I&R information can be found at http://www.azsos.gov/election/IRR/. The link to the "Initiative, Referendum & Recall Handbook" is an electronic version of the laws pertaining to Arizona's initiative, referendum and recall. The "Ballot Measure Information" link provides information on the most recent election. Most valuable is a PDF of the Publicity Pamphlet that includes the full text of all measures and the arguments for and

against it. In addition, the site has a schedule of town hall meetings that are open to the public. These meetings allow the public to discuss and obtain information about measures on the ballot. Information on all applications (including ones that did not make the ballot) is available including the petition serial number, the title, sponsor contact information, description, the application date, due date and the number of signatures required. Notifications of Contributions to Ballot Measure Committees are also available. Information on older ballot measures is also available online on the Secretary of State's Web site back to 1992 at http://www.azsos.gov/election/PreviousYears.htm. For elections back to 1998, the publicity pamphlet is located under the "Miscellaneous Election Information" link. For the election years 1992, 1994 and 1996, the information is located under the "Ballot Propositions" link. Election results are also available online back to 1974.

Arizona State Legislature, at http://www.azleg.state.az.us/.
The constitutional provisions and statutes on initiative, referendum and recall are available at the Arizona Legislature's Web site. Bill information, which may be helpful for research on legislative referenda, is available online back to the Forty-second Legislature (1995). While the Legislative Council analyses on ballot measures and fiscal impact analyses from the Joint Legislative Budget Committee are available in the publicity pamphlets, they may also be made available on the legislature's Web site. The 2006 Legislative Council analyses can be found in both Word and PDF versions at http://www.azleg.state. az.us/2006_Ballot_Proposition_Analyses/. Fiscal Impact Analyses back to 2000 are available at http://www.azleg.gov/jlbc/06fisnotes.htm.

Arizona I&R History

Fitzgerald, William Richard. *Trends in the Use of the Initiative and Referendum in the State of Arizona 1912-1948* (M.A. thesis, Ariz. St. U. 1949).
This master's thesis, only available at the Arizona State University Library, examines the use of I&R in Arizona. It uses the information to examine how I&R has influenced electorate participation. While the span of years covered is outdated, limiting its usefulness, it groups measures by topic and discusses trends in voting in Arizona's first decades of statehood.

Leshy, John D. *The Arizona State Constitution: A Reference Guide* (Greenwood Press 1993).
   This guide discusses each section of the Arizona Constitution. Particularly useful is the in depth examination of the provisions related to I&R as well as the commentary, analysis, and references to case law.

Roush, Russell Brown. *The Initiative and Referendum in Arizona: 1912-1978* (Ph.D. dissertation, Ariz. St. U., 1979).
   This valuable resource takes an extensive look at I&R going back to popular lawmaking in ancient Greece and Rome. Roush discusses the history and legal basis of the initiative and referendum in Arizona. Various statistics are available on all referred and initiated proposals between 1912 and 1978. The dissertation is available at the University of Arizona and Arizona State University.

The Records of the Arizona Constitutional Convention of 1910 (John S. Goff ed., Sup. Ct. Ariz. 1991).
   This is an invaluable resource for those looking to investigate the origins of the initiative and referendum in Arizona. It contains an index to subjects making it fairly painless to find discussion of I&R during the convention. Looking up "initiative and referendum" will direct the researcher to the relevant pages. Be warned, however: the number of pages where it was discussed could fill a short novel.

Todd, Charles Foster. *The Initiative and Referendum in Arizona* (M.A. thesis, U. Ariz., 1931).
   This thesis is perhaps the most comprehensive discussion of the history of the initiative and referendum in Arizona. It contains references to letters and personal interviews with those directly involved in creating the process. In addition, it refers to historical resources that may be helpful to those interested in the origins of the Arizona processes. The thesis is available at the University of Arizona, Arizona State University and the Arizona State Archives.

Local News

Local news sources are generally good resources for an upcoming election or a look back at the most recent election. These resources, while an excellent resource for the most recent election, do not generally maintain their special election Web pages for older elections. Be aware that some of the links listed here may not work in the future, but the sources that are listed will more than likely continue to cover future elections.

Arizona Capitol Times, at http://www.azcapitoltimes.com/.
The *Capitol Times* focuses on government and political issues in Arizona with an emphasis on the State legislature's activities. 2006 election coverage is available at http://www.azcapitoltimes.com/ group.cfm?sect=election2006 though, to access it, you must be a subscriber.

Arizona Daily Star, at http://www.azstarnet.com/.
The *Daily Star* covers news in the Tucson area. Archives are available online back to 1991 for purchase through Newsbank.

Arizona Republic, at http://www.azcentral.com/news/election/ballot/ ballot.html.
The *Arizona Republic* covers news for the Phoenix area and has coverage on the most recent election including stories on the ballot initiatives. The paper also provides its own voting recommendations. Older articles are available on the site for purchase through Newsbank.

Horizon, at http://www.azpbs.org/horizon/index.asp.
Horizon is an Arizona public affairs show on local Public Broadcasting Service station KAET. Selecting "Elections" under the "Topics" menu will result in transcripts for recent shows. There are several shows on propositions. Some shows also have video and audio available including Windows Media and Quick Time video files on each of the propositions. A list of links for the 2006 election can be found at http://www.azpbs.org/vote2006/watch.htm#props.

KJZZ, at http://kjzz.org/news/arizona/archives/200607/ballotmeasures.
This National Public Radio station based out of Tempe, Arizona has made available MP3 files of its show *Here and Now* when ballot measures were discussed for the 2006 election. The Web site also has a list of the ballot measures with a brief description of the measures, including information on funding.

Miscellaneous Resources

Hodgkinson, Randall L. *Executive, Legislative, and Judicial Power Over Direct Legislation in Arizona*, 23 Ariz. St. L.J. 1111 (1991).
This article discusses the constitutional basis for Arizona's I&R and the Governor's power to veto measures that have been passed.

Hodgkinson also discusses the legislature's power to repeal or amend passed measures as well as the judiciary's power to review measures that have been approved by the electorate.

Initiative and Referendum Institute–*Arizona*, at http://www.iandrinstitute. org/Arizona.htm.
This Web site includes a history of I&R in Arizona, an explanation of the direct initiative process (specific to the 2002 election), and other very useful links.

Kilmark, Jeffrey Allan. *Government Knows Best? An Analysis of the Governor's Power to Veto and the Legislature's Power to Real or Amend Voter Enacted Initiative and Referendum Petitions in Arizona*, 30 Ariz. St. L.J. 829 (1998).
Kilmark explains the I&R process in Arizona and proceeds to analyze the Governor's and Legislature's powers to alter measures that have been approved by the electorate. The article concludes with possible alternatives to the current system.

National Conference of State Legislatures, *Initiative and Referendum Database*, at http://www.ncsl.org/programs/legismgt/elect/dbintro.htm.
Also called the "Ballot Measures Database," this Web site allows users to search measures by state, topic, year, type of election and measure type. It has basic information on initiatives and referenda back to the general election of 1914. However, be aware of some of the information: It is not comprehensive and may not be accurate. For instance, it does not include information on the measures from the 1912 general election, and for at least one proposition, it had an incorrect status listed.

Project Vote Smart, *Arizona Ballot Measures*, at http://www.vote-smart. org > My State > Ballot Measures > Arizona.
This Web site has information on Arizona ballot measures back to 1996 including the title, summary, and whether it passed or failed.

Waters, M. Dane. *Initiative and Referendum Almanac*, 49-72 (Carolina Academic Press 2003).
This invaluable I&R resource gives a brief overview of Arizona's history with the initiative and referendum followed by a handy chart listing the measures voted on since I&R was first used in 1912. It includes the year, the measure number (if available), the type, subject

matter, a brief description and whether it passed or failed. The relevant sections of the Arizona Constitution and statutes are reproduced followed by "The Basic Steps to Do an Initiative in Arizona." The appendix includes information on the 14 measures that appeared on the November 2002 general election ballot.

NOTES

1. *See e.g.* National Conference of State Legislatures, *Ballot Measures Preview 2006,* at http://www.ncsl.org/statevote/06ballotpreview.htm.

2. For a more substantial treatment and analysis of the history of I&R in Arizona, please consult one of the resources listed under "Arizona I&R History" as an extensive discussion is beyond the scope of this guide.

3. Charles Foster Todd. *The Initiative and Referendum in Arizona*, 10 (M.A. thesis, U. Ariz., 1931).

4. *Id.* at 13.

5. *Id.* at 28.

6. Arizona became a state on February 14, 1912.

7. The source of the initiative and referendum powers originate from Arizona constitution article 4 discussing legislative powers and article 21 dealing with amendments to the constitution.

8. Ariz. Rev. Stat. Ann. §§ 19-101 et seq.

9. Ariz. Rev. Stat. Ann. § 19-111(A).

10. Ariz. Rev. Stat. Ann. § 19-121(A).

11. "H" indicates that the resolution originated in the House and the "S" indicates origination in the Senate.

12. Ariz. Const. art. IV, § 1 (2) and (7).

13. *Id.*

14. Ariz. Rev. Stat. Ann. § 19-102.

15. Ariz. Rev. Stat. Ann. § 19-121(A).

16. Ariz. Rev. Stat. Ann. § 19-112(D).

17. Ariz. Rev. Stat. Ann. § 19-121.01(B).

18. Ariz. Rev. Stat. Ann. § 19-121.02.

19. Ariz. Rev. Stat. Ann. § 19-123(D).

20. *Arizona Secretary of State*, at http://www.azsos.gov/.

21. Ariz. Rev. Stat. Ann. § 19-125(B).

22. Ariz. Rev. Stat. Ann. § 19-127.

23. Ariz. Const. art. IV, § 1 (6)(A)-(B).

24. Ariz. Const. art. IV, § 1 (6)(C)-(D).

Researching Initiatives and Referendums in Arkansas

Joseph A. Custer

INTRODUCTION

Researching initiatives and referendums in the State of Arkansas has become easier through use of the Internet, which provides an excellent medium for voters to gain information on ballot measures. The ubiquitous caveat remains, however, regarding Internet information: It can be fleeting and, in the case of unofficial Web sites, very dubious.

The statewide vote on initiatives during 1996-2005 exceeded the record of the previous decade, which had more than doubled initiatives voted on in the 1970s.[1] Advocates argue that the increase in the number of initiatives on the ballot is beneficial because citizens can use this tool to create new laws and reforms that state legislatures are unwilling or unable to enact. Cynics are quick to point out the frustrations associated with the process. State legislatures struggle with signature fraud, non-disclosure of initiative campaign finances, and lack of debate and deliberation.[2] Other large concerns regard lack of representative minority interests and the simple "yes or no" format. Many argue that the simple format oversimplifies or confuses voters about the complex issues involved in many initiatives. Often there is no issue exposure to expert analysis and balanced competing needs and considerations.[3]

In this environment, it is important–now more than ever–that all voters be given every opportunity to research proposed initiatives and referendums. This article is a reference guide to research resources available to the Arkansas citizens wanting to become better informed on initiatives and referendums for their State.

EARLY HISTORY OF ARKANSAS INITIATIVES AND REFERENDUMS

The earliest reported effort in Arkansas to put a State constitutional amendment establishing the initiative and referendum[4] process to a vote was in the early 1890s. "Men who connected with the General Assembly at the time declared that the resolution was greeted with jeers and laughter and when put to a vote reserved only one vote–that of the Senator who introduced it."[5]

The second effort came in late 1905, but the resolution never reached a vote.[6] Just one month after it was introduced, the Arkansas General Assembly adjourned *sine die* without giving the matter further attention.[7]

Senator E. R. Arnold of Clark County still was not discouraged. In 1909, on the second day of the General Assembly Session, he reintroduced the same I&R proposal defeated previously. Now, backed by out-of-state leaders from the Progressive movement, newly elected Democratic Governor George W. Donoghey and Williams Jennings Bryon, the job was finally done. This determined group drove the first initiative and referendum amendment through the Arkansas legislature on September 5, 1910. Five days during the summer of 1910, Bryon rode the rails with Governor Donoghey, covering 1,750 miles, giving 55 speeches to numerous, impressive gatherings across Arkansas.

When asked about his part in the Arkansas fight over the initiative and referendum campaign, Bryon responded:

> About three years ago or four, I will not attempt to state positively which, I made a speech before the legislature of your state, at the invitation of the legislature. I, at that time, spoke in favor of the initiative and referendum. Some one had introduced a bill in the legislature providing for the submission of this amendment . . . I mention this to you to show you that I advocated this amendment in Arkansas before your legislature was ready to submit it . . .[8]

The Arkansas Gazette predicted upon hearing of Bryon's trip to the state:

> When his speeches have been finished we suspect several thousand people will leave actually burning with impatience to get to the polls and vote for the amendment.[9]

That prediction appeared to be on the mark. A very large affirmative majority was tallied: 92,781 to 38,648.[10]

WHAT HAPPENED AFTER 1910?

It took several years after 1910 before initiatives and referendums gained much strength in Arkansas. Initiatives and referendums were routinely challenged by the Arkansas Supreme Court on legal technicalities. Finally in 1925, an appeal to the Arkansas Supreme Court reversed an earlier 1920 decision that, at the time, had dealt another supreme blow to I&R in Arkansas (overturning the voter-approved 1920 I&R constitutional amendment).[11]

A very circuitous route was taken in the 1925 *Brickhouse* case which gave I&R provisions teeth in Arkansas. Tom J. Terral, the newly elected Governor, took full advantage of an extremely rare occurrence. The regular Arkansas Supreme Court justices had to dismiss themselves due to the facts of *Brickhouse*. Ben B. Brickhouse was the mayor of Little Rock, and had been restrained by Circuit Judge Marvis Harris from issuing municipal bonds. The tribunal stated that the municipal bond amendment of 1924 was not legally adopted by popular vote. The issue really came down to whether a majority consisted of the total popular vote that cast votes for candidates or rather, just the number of voters who specifically voted on the amendment. Two other amendments were passed in the same manner in 1924. One of the other two amendments provided for an increase in the number of Arkansas Supreme Court justices, from 5 to 7. The Arkansas Constitution, Article VII, Section 20 provided:

> No judge or justice shall preside in the trial of any cause in the event of which he may be interested, or where either of the parties shall be connected with him by consanguinity or affinity, within such degree as may be prescribed by law; or in which he may have been of council or have presided in any inferior court.[12]

Thus, with the self-imposed dismissal, the judges gave way to the Governor's individually picked, special court. Although the means were messy, the end product justified the confusion. A majority of the special Arkansas Supreme Court reversed *Brickhouse*, thus validating the 1920 I&R constitutional amendment. The decision made it possible for voters to go to the polls and vote a constitutional amendment up or down, regardless of what percentage of the total popular vote cast ballots on the candidates. Those who did not vote on the amendment would not have any effect on the outcome. The 1920 amendment, now the law in Arkansas, had been drafted in such a clever and precise manner as to clear up any confusing and conflicting interpretations in the 1910 amendment, i.e., majority vote needed. This made it much harder for the regular Arkansas Supreme Court to make imaginative rulings. Any amendment that had been passed by a majority of the affirmative vote on amendments since the 1920 I&R amendment was immediately made law.

The specific, clear language in the superseding I&R amendment of 1920 reads as follows:

> Majority–Any measure submitted to the people herein provided shall take effect and become a law when approved by a majority of the votes cast upon such measure, and not otherwise, and shall not be required to receive a majority of the electors voting at such elections.[13]

With the issue of "majority" finally resolved, Arkansas moved on. Several I&R measures have been passed over the years. The voting trend generally approves of measures for general welfare, while defeating measures aimed to assist minorities.

The voters' interpretation of general welfare was largely in touch with the Southern mood at the time. For example, in 1928 voters in Arkansas enacted a regressive initiative to ban the teaching of evolution in public schools.[14] In 1930 Arkansas enacted a measure to require Bible-reading in public schools.[15] On the other hand, Arkansas voted for an initiative to increase workers' compensation in 1938.[16]

Regarding minority rights, the early record of I&R resolutions in Arkansas is as bleak as any Southern State. Voters continually overturned efforts to eliminate the poll tax, which was finally abolished in 1964.[17] In 1956, Arkansas voters–with 56% of the affirmative vote–passed an initiative requiring the use of any constitutional means possible to block school integration.[18] Recent Arkansas history since the 1960s shows a more favorable trend of voters using I&R enactments to truly support minority interests.

SELECTED CASE LAW

The following list provides selected Arkansas case law related to initiative and referendum issues.

Porter v. McCuen, 310 Ark. 674, 839 S.W.2d 521 (1992).

Provisions authorizing direct popular participation in law-making should be liberally construed so as not to restrict its use.

Case also holds that the title of an amendment does not have to contain a synopsis. However, it should be complete enough to convey an intelligible idea of the scope and impact of the proposed law.

Plugge v. McCuen, 310 Ark. 654, 841 S.W.2d 139 (1992).

A preamble should not be included in the title of a ballot in Arkansas where the preamble is not part of the text of the proposed initiative, referendum or amendment.

Tindall v. Searan, 192 Ark. 173, 90 S.W.2d 476 (1936).

Given the hierarchical supremacy of state law over enactments of local government units, the people of a county cannot, under initiative and referendum authority, validly enact provisions which are contrary to a general state law.

Hanson v. Hodges, 109 Ark. 479, 160 S.W. 392 (1913).
Arkansas state legislation to be emergency measures are immune from the initiative process.

Jumper v. McCollum, 179 Ark. 837, 18 S.W.2d 359 (1929).
Legislative declaration of emergency used for purpose of exempting a measure from the operation of the referendum as final and conclusive.

Gregg v. Hartwick, 292 Ark. 528, 731 S.W.2d 766 (1987).
Deannexation of land deemed proper proposition for initiative or referendum.

Moorman v. Priest, 310 Ark. 325, 837 S.W.2d 886 (1992).
Reorganization of city government deemed proper proposition for initiative or referendum, such as changing the number of wards or changing the number of representatives in each ward or district.

This case also found that courts may consider the validity of proposed legislation in cases where the proposed referendum sought to be removed from the ballot is in direct conflict with state statute. In addition, the Court ruled that whether an ordinance is subject to initiative or referendum is a judicial question.

Stilley v. Henson, 342 Ark. 346, 28 S.W.2d 274 (2000).
Resolution of the sales or use tax rates deemed proper proposition for initiative or referendum.

Cochran v. Black, 240 Ark. 393, 400 S.W.2d 280 (1966).
Housing authority was and could have been legally dissolved or terminated by initiative ordinance number 1, adopted by the vote of the people.

Terral v. Arkansas Light and Power Co., 137 Ark. 523, 210 S.W.2d (1919).
Public utility rate change found subject to initiative or referendum.

Tomlinson Bros. v. Hodges, 110 Ark. 528, 162 S.W.2d 64 (1913).
The power of initiative and referendum is not extended beyond "general county and municipal business."

Scroggins v. Kerr, 217 Ark. 137, 228 S.W. 2d 995 (1950).
The power of initiative and referendum is usually restricted to legislative ordinances, resolutions or measures.

Greenlee v. Munn, 262 Ark. 663, 559 S.W.2d 928 (1978).
The power of initiative and referendum is not extended to administrative action.

Gregs v. Hartwick, 292 Ark. 528, 731 S.W.2d 766 (1987).
The test of what is legislative and what is an administrative proposition, with respect to the initiative or referendum, depends on whether it is one to make new law or to execute law already in existence. If new law, it is legislative. If executing a law already in existence, it's considered administrative. An annexation was construed as municipal legislation and a law to which referendum power applied.

Summit Mall Company, LLC v. Lemond, 355 Ark. 190, 132 S.W.3d 725 (2003).
Allowed referendum to be applied to planned commercial district rezoning.

Camden Community Development Corp. v. Sutton, 339 Ark. 368, 5 S.W.3d 439 (1999).
Held recommendation of rezoning and city boards' rejection of rezoning recommendation were administrative acts not subject to referendum. Court ruled that rezoning ordinance may not be subject to initiative and referendum measures but must be adopted in accordance with statutory procedures.

SELECTED ARKANSAS STATUTES

The following selected statutes from the Arkansas Code are provisions relating to initiative and referendums.

1. *Signing of Petition–Penalty for Falsification* Ark. Code Ann. § 7-9-103.
2. *Form of Initiative Petition–Sufficiency of Signatures* Ark. Code Ann. § 7-9-104.
3. *Form of Referendum Petition–Sufficiency of Signatures* Ark. Code Ann. § 7-9-105.
4. *Required Attachments to Petitions* Ark. Code Ann. § 7-9-106.
5. *Procedure for Circulation of Petition* Ark. Code Ann. § 7-9-108.
6. *Voter Registration Signature Imaging System* Ark. Code Ann. § 7-9-124.

7. *Initiative and Referendum Generally* Ark. Code Ann. § 14-14-914.
8. *Initiative and Referendum Requirements* Ark. Code Ann. § 14-14-915.
9. *Judicial Jurisdiction over Initiative and Referendum* Ark. Code Ann. § 14-14-916.
10. *Initiative and Referendum Elections* Ark. Code Ann. § 14-14-917.

SELECTED SECONDARY MATERIALS

Monographs and dissertations provide research with valuable background information on initiatives and referendums.

Beard, Charles A. and Birl E. Schultz. *Documents on the State-Wide Initiative, Referendum and Recall.* New York: The Maxmillan Co., 1912.
Includes good description of the first Arkansas initiative and referendum constitutional amendment passed in 1910.

Book of States. Lexington, KY: Council of State Governments, 1935-.
An annual reference book. In the 2006 edition, tables 6.9 through 6.18 deal with initiatives and referendums. Tables 6.19 through 6.21 deal with recalls.

Butler, David and Ramney, Austin, eds. *Referendums: A Comparative Study of Practice and Theory.* Washington, D.C. American Enterprise Institute, 1978.
States that only 7.5 percent of constitutional initiatives are measures to regulate business and labor. One of these constitutional initiatives was passed by Arkansas in 1944 to prohibit union membership as a precondition for employment (succeeded with 55 percent yes).

Cronin, Thomas E. *Direct Democracy: The Politics of Initiatives, Referendum, and Recall.* Cambridge, Harvard University Press, 1999.
In chapter eight, "Direct Democracy and its Problems," author writes about the lack of sensitivity majorities at the ballot box may have regarding minorities. Unfortunately, Arkansas has some history of this and it was displayed again in 1986. A measure was placed on the State ballot forbidding public funding of abortions and making the protection of unborn children official state policy. The Arkansas Supreme Court intervened striking the measure from the ballot stating the wording was inaccurate and misleading.

Dunning, Archibald Williams. *Studies in Southern History and Politics.* New York. Columbia University Press, 1914.

> Discusses the fact that no Southern State had adopted the recall as of 1914, and only Arkansas had adopted direct legislation through initiative and referendum.

Gaffney, Edward McGlynn. *Two Cheers for Popular Sovereignty and Direct Democracy: Historical Reflections.* Paper prepared for democracy symposium. Williamsburg, VA, 2002.

> Table 2 in book rates the states by historical use of direct democracy. Arkansas ranks seventh with .95 initiatives on the ballot per year.

Piott, Steven L. *Giving Voters a Voice: Origins of the Initiative and Referendum in America.* Columbia, MO: University of Missouri Press, 2003.

> Each state in which proponents conducted an active campaign to win adoption of direct legislation is studied in detail. The book analyzes the crucial roles played by individuals who led the movement to empower voters by enabling them to enact or veto legislation directly, and reveals the arguments, the stumbling blocks, and political compromises that are often slighted in generalized overviews. Each state, including Arkansas, possessed its own political dynamic.

Initiative and Referendum Petitions: A Guide for Sponsors and Canvassers. Little Rock, AR. Published by the Arkansas Secretary of State, Election Division.

> A biannual distributed to the full Arkansas State Documents Depository. Helpful instrument for the general public interested in the petition process in Arkansas.

Oberholtzer, Ellis Paxson. *The Referendum in America: Together with Some Chapters on the History of the Initiative and the Recall.* New York. C. Scribner, 1911.

> Discusses how initiatives voted on by male voters of Arkansas townships were the final authority in how school lands were sold. Discusses other various Arkansas historical referendums such as the choice of county seats, school finance, local option liquor laws and fence laws.

Persily, Nathaniel and Anderson, Melissa Cully. *Regulating Democracy Through Democracy: The Use of Direct-Legislation in Election Reform Law*. University of Pennsylvania Law School, 2005.
    Paper discusses how in 1996 Arkansas voters approved an initiative to lower contribution limits from $1,000 to $100 for legislative races. The courts later struck it down.

Reaves, Robert Gibbs. *Amending the Arkansas Constitution by the Initiative Process*. Dissertation at University of Arkansas, 1948.
    Well-researched dissertation that does a good job at explaining the convoluted early years of initiatives and referendum in Arkansas.

Schmidt, David D. *Citizen Lawmakers: The Ballot Initiative Revolution*. Philadelphia, Temple University Press, 1989.
    In chapter one, "History," author writes that Arkansas and Colorado were the only states during the depression era to pass an initiative to increase workers compensation.

Tarr, Alan G. ed. *Constitutional Politics in the States: Contemporary Controversies and Historical Patterns*. Westport, CT. Greenwood Press, 1996.
    Chapter five discusses the Arkansas Supreme Court's place in Arkansas school finance and direct democracy.

Tarr, Alan G. and Williams, Robert F. eds. *State Constitutions for the Twenty-first Century*. Albany. State University of New York Press, 2006.
    Discusses the role of the American Independent Party in passing the first I&R referendum by constitutional amendment in 1910.

Thomas, David Y. *The Initiative and Referendum in Arkansas Come of Age*. Fayetteville, University of Arkansas, 1933.
    Author states there were radical and conservative referendums adopted from 1910 through 1932. The most radical were prohibition (defeated in 1912), free textbooks (defeated in 1912), and the child-labor law (adopted in 1914). The most conservative were the anti-evolution law (adopted in 1920) and reading the Bible in public schools (adopted in 1930).

2006 Initiative and Referendum: Facts and Information for the 2006 General Election. Little Rock, AR. Published by the Arkansas Secretary of State, Election Division.
    Biannual election publication that has helpful fact sheet, local measures section, petition form, frequently asked questions section, sample signature section and sample petitions.

Waters, M. Dane. *The Initiative and Referendum Almanac*. Durham, NC: Carolina Academic Press, 2003.

This almanac, which is part of the Initiative and Referendum Institute's Citizen Lawmaker Series of Educational Tools, lists the basic steps involved in establishing an initiative in Arkansas.

ADDITIONAL SELECTED SECONDARY MATERIALS

Legal encyclopedias, A.L.R. annotations, law review articles and other periodicals can help the researcher learn more about initiatives and referendums in the state of Arkansas. The following list of selected materials provides an indication of each item's usefulness.

Board of Trustees of the Leland Stanford Junior University, *Limitations on Initiative and Referendum*, 3 Stan. L. Rev. 497 (1951).

Discusses the unique practice in Arkansas of allowing the whole State to vote on matters affecting only one locality. The article argues that this Arkansas provision is clearly inconsistent with the purpose of initiative and referendum.

Thomas M. Carpenter, *In Whose Court is the Ball? The Scope of the People's Power of Direct Legislation*, 28-SPG Ark. Law. 35 (1994).

Twenty-four states now have an initiative and referendum measure for state government. In Arkansas, this authority is extended to local government.

Corpus Juris Secundrum, 82 C.J.S. *Statutes* §§ 108-144 (1999 & Supp. 2006).

Legal encyclopedia article provides a good introduction to initiatives and referendums. For example, Section 110 states that legislative power is vested in the legislature and the people under initiative and referendum constitutional provisions; this right of the people cannot be abridged by the legislature.

Thomas B. Cotton, *The Arkansas Ballot Initiative: an Overview and Some Thoughts on Reform*, 53 Ark. L. Rev. 759 (2000).

This article explains the initiative process in Arkansas from the first stages of drafting to the final popular vote on the initiative.

Elana Cunningham Wills, *Tearing Down Brickhouse: Could Judicial Demolition of Brickhouse v. Hill Prompt a New Arkansas Constitution?*, 54 Ark. L. Rev. 19 (2001).
 The Supreme Court, if it overruled *Brickhouse*, could render continued piece-meal amendments of the Arkansas Constitution infeasible, and prompt much needed constitutional reform. Of course, the Court could overrule *Brickhouse* and make its decision prospective only. The decision would apply only to the amendment before the Court and to those voted on subsequently. Prospective application may be the most likely outcome of overruling *Brickhouse*, but it is interesting to explore the possibility of the retroactive application of such a decision.

Elizabeth Garrett and Daniel A. Smith, *Veiled Political Actors and Campaign Disclosure Laws in Direct Democracy*, 4 Election L.J. 295 (2005).
 In several states, prior to the advent of electronic disclosure for contributions and expenditures on ballot campaigns, groups involved in ballot campaigns that wanted anonymity could shield their identities by relying on the slow process of making disclosure records available to the public. Three states with the initiative process (Arkansas, Montana, and Wyoming) do not provide campaign finance data on ballot measures via the Internet. A "major weakness" of the disclosure laws in Arkansas, Wyoming, and several other states "is that the filing schedule allows last minute contributions and independent expenditures to be hidden from voters until after the election." See Campaign Disclosure Project, Grading State Disclosure 28 (2004), available at http://campaigndisclosure.org/gradingstate2004/gsd04printreport.pdf (quotation in context of Arkansas, but there are similar findings for Arizona, Wyoming and other states).

Beth Bates Holliday, *Initiative and Referendum*, 42 American Jurisprudence 2d §§ 1-53 (2000 & Supp. 2006).
 Strong legal encyclopedic introduction to initiatives and referendums.

Kurt G. Kastorf, *Logrolling Gets Logrolled: Same-Sex Marriage, Direct Democracy, and the Single Subject Rule*, 54 Emory L.J. 1633 (2005).
 During the 2004 election, Georgia was one of eleven states to allow voters to weigh in on whether its State constitution should exclude gays and lesbians from marriage. The drafters of the Georgia proposal, like those of Arkansas, Kentucky, Michigan, North Dakota, Ohio, Oklahoma, and Utah, went further than simply adopting a

restrictive definition of marriage. The proposed amendment also restricted couples in civil unions from obtaining any of the benefits of marriage, banned state courts from recognizing the judgments of other states, and carved out an exception to the Georgia court system's subject matter jurisdiction.

J. R. Kemper, *Adoption of Zoning Ordinance or Amendment Thereto as Subject of Referendum*, 72 A.L.R.3d 1030 (1976).
This annotation collects the cases in which the courts have been called upon to resolve the issue of whether or not the power of referendum may properly be employed by the electors of a municipality to approve or reject a zoning ordinance, or an amendment thereto, previously passed and adopted by the council or other legislative body of such community.

Kurtis A. Kemper, *Constitutional Validity of State or Local Regulation of Contributions by or to Political Action Committees*, 2003 A.L.R.5th 21 (2003).
This annotation collects and analyzes the state and federal cases discussing the constitutional validity of state or local regulation of contributions by or to political action committees (PACs). Included in the annotation are cases in which provisions of statutes or regulations specifically applicable to PACs are challenged as well as cases in which statutes or regulations, while containing provisions specifically applicable to PACs, are challenged as a whole and a PAC is among the challenging parties.

Calvin R. Ledbetter Jr., *Adoption of Initiative and Referendum in Arkansas: The Roles of George W. Donaghy and William Jennings Bryan*, 51(3) Ark. Historical Q. 199-223 (1922).
Arkansas voters approved the 1910 State constitutional amendment on the initiative and referendum. Support came from the Farmer's Union, the Democratic Party, and Governor George W. Donaghy. Bryan stumped the State in favor of the amendment.

Joseph Lubinski, *The Cow Says Moo, the Duck Says Quack, and the Dog Says Vote! The Use of the Initiative to Promote Animal Protection*, 74 U. Colo. L. Rev. 1109 (2003).
Not every anti-cruelty proposal will succeed. The lone animal defeat in 2002 occurred in Arkansas, where voters rejected an attempt to make animal cruelty a felony. Arkansas' proposed Animal Cruelty

Act would not have automatically made animal cruelty a felony, but instead would have given prosecutors the discretion to charge a person either with the old misdemeanor or the new felony. Opponents of the measure, as in other elections, attempted to paint the initiative as just the first of many attempts by radical animal activists to limit human rights by creating rights for animals.

Supporters of stronger anti-cruelty laws pointed to studies that suggest animal abuse is often a prelude to violence against humans. Supporters further noted that thirty-seven other states already had felony animal cruelty statutes on the books. The *Arkansas Democrat-Gazette* endorsed the measure, writing that it was put on the ballot to prevent knowing, malicious, deliberate, extreme acts of cruelty–like cock-fighting, dog-fighting, and torturing of animals. The paper also stressed the measure was not put on the ballot by some out-of-state animal rights organization, but instead reached the voters through the signatures of 87,000 Arkansans. Voters weren't convinced, however, and defeated the measure handily: 462,549 to 281,334.

The margin of defeat seemed surprising to many. After the election, there was speculation that opposition to the measure did not stem from a concern about the effects of the proposal itself, but was instead simply "a crude demonstration of raw political power" on the part of the measure's opponents. The initiative, looked at through this lens, was not just a vote on animal cruelty–it was a message to animal protectionists to take their cause elsewhere. The measure's supporters, Citizens for a Humane Arkansas, spent $294,775, while opponents, Arkansans for Responsible Animal Laws, spent an equivalent $289,231. Despite the relatively modest campaign spending, animosity between proponents and opponents nonetheless forced them to make the money (and its sources) an issue in the campaign. Thus, even measures that might find popular support in some areas of the country must be carefully crafted in more conservative areas likely to resist animal protection reform. In such circumstances, careful management of the campaign is key.

J. E. Macy, *Power of Legislative Body to Amend, Repeal, or Abrogate Initiative or Referendum Measure, or to Enact Measure Defeated on Referendum*, 33 A.L.R.2d 1118 (1954).

The question dealt with is how far the power of a legislature or municipal council to enact measures on a subject is suspended by action of the electorate with which those measures would conflict. Mainly, the questions arise under conventional initiative and referendum provisions, but cases are included under provisions for referendums on particular questions, where the problems are the same.

Jennifer Modersohn, *Constitutional Law–First Amendment Rights of Direct Democracy Participants versus the State's Interest in Regulating the Election Process. Buckley v. American Constitutional Law Foundation, Inc. 119 S. CT. 636*, 22 U. Ark. Little Rock L. J. 105 (1999).
Like the attempt to eliminate property taxes in Arkansas, controversial issues are often the focus of direct democracy campaigns. Confronted with numerous state imposed regulations, the active participants of direct democracy are sometimes forced to defend their fundamental rights, including the First Amendment right of free speech.

Stephen B. Niswanger, *A Practitioner's Guide to Challenging and Defending Legislatively Proposed Constitutional Amendments in Arkansas*, 17 U. Ark. Little Rock L.J. 765 (1995).
There are two different ways to propose constitutional amendments to the voters in Arkansas. One method permits the people of the State to propose amendments through the initiative process. Amendment VII to the Arkansas Constitution provides the requirements for the initiative process. The other method permits the General Assembly to propose amendments and submit them to the electorate for approval or rejection. Article XIX, Section 22 of the Arkansas Constitution provides the requirements for the process by which the General Assembly proposes amendments. This comment discusses the history of the constitutional provision governing legislatively proposed amendments and attempts to demonstrate why amendments proposed by the General Assembly should be subject to some of the same legal propositions that govern initiated amendments under Amendment 7 of the Arkansas Constitution. In particular, the requirements for ballot titles and popular names in amendments initiated under Amendment 7 should be applicable to ballot titles and popular names in amendments proposed by the General Assembly under Article XIX, Section 22.

Steve Sheppard, *Intelligible, Honest, and Impartial Democracy: Making Laws at the Arkansas Ballot Box, or Why Jim Hannah and Ray Thornton were Right About May v. Daniels*, 2005 Ark. Law Notes 123 (2005).
There is a long-standing tension in America between the ideals of direct democracy and the rule of law. In its simplest form, rule by

democracy requires that the majority gets what it wants, but the rule of law requires not only respect for certain procedures but also, as we know it today, respect for those who would oppose the majority. Nowhere in Arkansas law does one see this tension as clearly as in our perennial disputes over ballots for initiatives proposing new statutes or constitutional amendments. Initiatives have been used to enact state-wide and municipal laws since 1925.

H. A. Wood, *Character or Subject Matter of Ordinance Within Operation of Initiative and Referendum Provisions*, 122 A.L.R. 769 (1939).
This annotation is concerned with the question of what ordinances or municipal enactments by their nature or subject matter are within the operation and purview of initiative and referendum provisions. A liberal interpretation is taken of the term "ordinances," so cases are included involving resolutions and other forms of municipal enactment, where the question has arisen as to the applicability of initiative or referendum provisions.

SELECTED LEXISNEXIS AND WESTLAW DATABASES

LexisNexis (a Reed Elsevier division) and Westlaw (Thomson West) are two premier, fee-based, legal research databases. Below are selected databases that might prove helpful to the researcher.

LexisNexis Selected Library and File Names

Bills (full text): ARK; ARTEXT
Cases (state): ARK; ARCTS
Cases (state and federal): ARK; ARMEGA
Constitution: ARK; ARCNST
Law Review: ARK; ARKLR
Statutes (annotated): ARK; CODE

Westlaw Selected Database Identifiers

Bills (full text): AR–BILLTXT
Cases (state): AR–CS
Cases (state and federal): AR–CS–ALL
Journals and Law Reviews combined: AR–JLR
Statutes (annotated): AR–ST–ANN

SELECTED WEB SITES

Electronic resources can assist the researcher a great deal. Emphasis on Arkansas.

Arkansas Constitution at http://www.sos.arkansas.gov/ar-constitution/ arconst/arconst.htm.
   The Constitution of Arkansas is available as a PDF document on this Web site.

Arkansas Ethics Commission at http://arkansasethics.com.
   Includes the *Rules of Campaign Finance & Disclosure* at http:// arkansasethics.com/rules/Campaign_Finance_and_Disclosure.doc.

Arkansas General Assembly at http://www.arkleg.state.ar.us.
   This site provides information about the Senate and House, Senate/House calendars, legislators and committees, research sources and a new research publications link.

Arkansas State Government at http://www.state.ar.us/.
   The official Web site to the State of Arkansas. A true state government portal for all Arkansas state government, with links to education, government, living, state facts, tourist information, working, and directories for agencies, forms, and online services.

Arkansas Governor at http://www.governor.arkansas.gov/.
   This site includes Executive Orders and Proclamations, the Governor's Initiatives, the Governor's Proposed Budget, and links to the State directory, agency information and constitutional officers.

Arkansas Supreme Court at http://courts.state.ar.us/courts/sc.html.
   Provides access to Arkansas Supreme Court and Arkansas Court of Appeals opinions by hand-down date, by party name and date, or by full-text search; opinions are usually available on the date handed down (HTML and WordPerfect formats). Links to corrected opinions and parallel citations also available.
   Arkansas court rules, administrative orders, Arkansas Judicial Code, and regulations/rules of related commissions/entities are searchable by keyword. Click on "Recent Arkansas Court Rules and Administrative Orders" link to access a reverse-chronological listing, by hand-down date, of the per curiam orders by which the court

rules, administrative orders, etc., were adopted or modified. Search Arkansas Supreme Court and Court of Appeals dockets by case number or party name. Updated daily.

Ballot Measures at http://www.votesmart.org/election_ballot_measures.php?src=mystate.
The Project Vote Smart Web site has compiled a list of ballot measures for each state. Voters can read the text of the initiative and find links to sites of supporters and opponents.

Election Reform Information Project at http://www.electionline.org.
Gives updates from around the nation on election reform activities.

Initiative & Referendum Institute at http://www.iandrinstitute.org.
This Web site is recommended as one of the best online resources for information about initiative and referendum processes in all fifty states.
    For Arkansas, the site includes a history of the initiative and referendum process; indicates which processes are available in Arkansas (the initiative, the popular referendum, and the legislative referendum); provides information on the elections; provides an initiative historical listing; provides the basic steps to undertake an initiative campaign in Arkansas; provides relevant constitutional and statutory provisions; and provides links to the Arkansas Secretary of State's initiative and referendum history and election results.

League of Women Voters at http://www.lwv.ogr.
The site includes links to projects, to actions, to voter information; searchable by state.

National Agricultural Law Center at http://www.nationalaglawcenter.org.
The National Agricultural Law Center serves as an agricultural and food law information center affiliated with the National Agricultural Library. Its Web site, developed by the University of Arkansas, provides access to Center publications and serves as a gateway to agricultural law resources on the Internet. The Center maintains an agricultural and food law collection in the Young Law Library at the University of Arkansas School of Law, adds cataloging to the agricultural database, AGRICOLA, and prepares and disseminates research bibliographies. In addition, the Center participates in the online agricultural reference network AgNIC.

National Conference of State Legislators at http://www.ncsl.org. The site includes state legislature Internet links, with links to all state legislatures, searchable by content area, e.g., bills, constitution, issue reports, legislators, etc. The site also includes a ballot measures database, searchable by state, topic area, year, election, and measure type.

Secretary of State, Election Division at http://www.sosweb.state.ar.us. Election Laws of Arkansas (compilation of election laws); Election Calendar; Candidate Information Handbook; Initiative & Referendum Petitions booklet and Arkansas Directory of Elected Officials.

State Board of Election Commissioners at http://www.state.ar.us/sbec/. Running for Public Office handbook; Training for Election Officials and Election Commissioners; ADA Compliance and accessibility reports and Voting Systems–Approval of Voting Systems in Arkansas.

NOTES

1. Matsusaka, John G.; *Direct Democracy and Electoral Reform*, chapter seven of *The Market Place of Democacy*. Washington DC. Brookings Institution (2006).
2. Ibid.
3. Ibid.
4. Hereinafter "I&R."
5. *Arkansas Gazette* (LR) January 23, 1909.
6. Reaves, Robert G.; *Amending the Arkansas Constitution by the Initiative Process*. PhD. Dissertation, University of Arkansas, 1948, at 26.
7. Ibid at 28.
8. *Arkansas Gazette*, September 11, 1910.
9. *Arkansas Gazette*, August 24, 1910.
10. Reaves at 48.
11. *Brickhouse v. Hill*, 167 Ark. 513 (1925).
12. Repealed by Ark. Const. Amend. 80, § 22(A), effective July 1, 2001.
13. Const. Amend. No. 7 (1920).
14. Schmidt, David; *Citizen Lawmakers: The Ballot Initiative Revolution*, Philadelphia. Temple (1989).
15. Ibid.
16. Ibid.
17. Ibid.
18. Ibid.

Researching Colorado Ballot Measures

Goldie Burton

INTRODUCTION

The initiative and referendum inspire both passionate adherents and detractors among those who study government. For the researcher, they present special challenges. Ballot measures follow their own rules and processes, and leave behind a different set of documents than laws produced entirely by a state legislature and Governor. This guide is intended to streamline the research process for anyone tracking the origin and progress of an initiative or referendum in Colorado by identifying both the documents one can normally expect to find and where they are available.

HISTORY OF THE INITIATIVE
AND REFERENDUM IN COLORADO

Colorado adopted the initiative and referendum process in 1910.[1] In 1912, for the first time ballot measures proposed through the initiative and referendum processes were passed into law. Sixty-nine initiated ballot proposals have been adopted by Colorado voters since 1912. Most of these have amended the State constitution rather than the statutes.[2]

The constitution also provides for a popular referendum. It is rarely used because the General Assembly began in 1910 to attach a "safety clause" to all laws, immunizing them from popular referendum. A safety clause recites that the law is "necessary for the immediate preservation of the public peace, health, or safety," the exclusion from referendum provided for in the Colorado State Constitution.[3] The Colorado Supreme Court has consistently upheld the validity of safety clauses.[4] The legislature must refer constitutional amendments to the citizens to approve and it may refer statutes, although it has rarely used this option.

Since 1980, the legislative research and drafting offices of the General Assembly review proposed initiatives and advise the proponents of any perceived problems.[5] Since 1995, a single-subject rule limits the scope of initiatives. The Ballot Title Setting Board ("the Title Board") determines whether a proposal violates this rule. Its decision may be reviewed by the Colorado Supreme Court through an expedited appeal process.

Colorado's use of the initiative has increased, especially in the last forty-one years. In their definitive book on the Colorado Constitution, Oesterle and Collins note that, of the 23 most significant amendments to the constitution, 15 were added by initiative since 1966 "in a pattern of increasing length and frequency."[6] The Colorado Legislative Council's *Digest of Initiated and Referred Constitutional and Statutory Amendments Since 1912* shows the bulk of all successful initiatives have passed since 1966, a period considerably shorter than the preceding 54 years of the availability of the initiative and referendum.[7]

COLORADO'S INITIATIVE AND REFERENDUM PROCESS

The Office of Legislative Legal Services Counsel ("the Office") and Legislative Council ("the Council") currently serve as technical consultants on the language of all initiated ballot measures. Their recommendations are not binding. Public review, along with the jointly-prepared comments of the Office and the Council, occurs at a meeting scheduled no more than two weeks after the submission of the proposal to the Council. The meeting is open to the public, though it is not an opportunity for the public to speak. If the proponents choose to amend the proposal following the meeting, they must submit the revised proposal to the Council, triggering a second meeting no more than two weeks from the date of resubmission. The Council will cancel this second meeting if the Council and the Office have no additional comments.[8]

When this review and comment process is complete, the Secretary of State receives the proposed act.[9] The Secretary of State then convenes the Title Board to set a title and submission clause for the measure. The Title Board is composed of the Secretary of State, the Attorney General and the director of the Office.[10] In addition to setting the title and submission clause, the Title Board determines whether the proposal violates the single-subject rule. If the Title Board concludes that the proposal contains more that one subject, it will not set a title.[11]

Proponents of a proposal found to violate the single-subject rule may remove the offending language and resubmit it directly to the Title Board, but substantial revisions require submission to the Council for additional review and comment meetings. Objections to decisions of the Title Board can be filed as direct appeals to the Colorado Supreme Court. This expedited process ensures that conflicts over the language of a proposed measure are resolved before the election.[12]

When the title is set, the Secretary of State sends the proponents the final title and submission clause. If the proponents object to the outcome, they may file a motion for rehearing with the Secretary of State. If they are not satisfied with the results of the re-hearing, they may file an appeal with the Colorado Supreme Court.[13]

Once they are satisfied, proponents then submit a proof of their petition to the Secretary of State for approval before they may print or publish petitions. If no motion for rehearing has been filed within the time allowed, the Secretary of State will then approve or disapprove the format of the petition within forty-eight hours.[14] Petitions must be submitted within six months of the Title Board's decision and no later than three months before a statewide election. Specific requirements govern the format of the petitions, in addition to the collection of signatures. The rules require a warning to be placed at the head of the petition, each section of which must be printed on a form created by the Secretary of State.[15] The warning states that it is against the law for anyone to sign a petition if he or she is not a registered elector or has already signed a petition for the same measure.

The United States Supreme Court struck down a statute prohibiting payment to petition circulators[16] but other strictures remain, including that the petition circulators must be electors themselves. According to the statutes, if petition circulators are paid, they must wear a badge that reads "PAID CIRCULATOR"[17] and the payments must be reported as expenditures under the Colorado Constitution, the Colorado Statutes and the Secretary of State Rules Concerning Campaign and Political Finance.[18] Notwithstanding an extant Colorado statute, on its Web site the Colorado Secretary of State advises that the statutory language requiring circulators to wear badges has been invalidated by a United States Supreme Court decision.[19]

To earn a place on the ballot, the proponents must collect the number of signatures equal to five percent of the votes cast for the office of the Secretary of State at the previous general election.[20] The Secretary of State verifies the signatures by random sampling of either five percent or four thousand signatures, whichever is greater.[21] If the Secretary of State extrapolates from the sample that ninety percent or less of the required signatures are valid, the petition is deemed insufficient. If the random sample verification establishes that the number of valid signatures totals one hundred ten percent or more of the number of required signatures of registered eligible voters, the petition is deemed sufficient.[22] If the number deemed valid falls between ninety-one and one hundred and nine percent, the Secretary of State orders the examination and verification of each signature.[23]

WHERE TO LOCATE DOCUMENTS
RELATED TO COLORADO I&R RESEARCH

The documents helpful for researching legislation adopted through the initiative and referendum process include the Council's *Ballot Proposal Analyses* (also called "the Blue Book"). These are available from 1998 on the Web in English and Spanish at http://www.state.co.us/gov_dir/leg_dir/lcsstaff/. Other years are available in print at the University of Colorado Norlin Library's Government Publications Department and the William A. Wise Law School Library. The University of Denver Westminster Law Library, the Colorado Joint Legislative Library, the Colorado State Archives, the Colorado State Publications Library and the Colorado Supreme Court Library also have the Blue Book for most, if not all, years of its publication. Contact information for the libraries and other organizations mentioned in this section is available below under the "Further Contacts" heading.

The *Colorado Session Laws* from 1910-present can be found in both academic law libraries mentioned above and at the Colorado Supreme Court Library. Abstracts of Votes Cast are available for all years at the Colorado Joint Legislative Library and for most years from the Colorado Secretary of State, the Colorado Supreme Court Library, the Colorado State Publications Library, and the Colorado State Archives. Of course, if the election of interest occurred in 1996 or more recently, this information is available on the Web site of the Secretary of State, at http://www.elections.colorado.gov/DDefault.aspx?tid=398&vmid=101. Taped recordings of the comment and review meetings are only available through the Colorado Secretary of State and the Colorado Joint Legislative Library.

Newspaper articles published contemporaneously with a ballot measure may speak to the motives of its sponsors, as well as those of the opposition. Historical Colorado newspapers are collected on microform at Norlin Library and at the Denver Public Library. Material produced between 1920 and 1990 by the Colorado League of Women Voters is archived at Norlin Library, documenting the League's positions on many issues voters have faced.

Biographical information on sponsors may be found in the Colorado State Archives, the Stephen H. Hart Library, the Western History Collection of the Denver Public Library, the Colorado Joint Legislative Library, the Archives at Norlin Library and the Special Collections Department at the University of Denver's Penrose Library. All of these libraries have information on various influential individuals.

Pending ballot measures often provoke sufficient controversy to be discussed in journal articles. The Colorado legal community might voice its opinion in the state bar journal, *The Colorado Lawyer*. Likewise, the Denver Bar Association publishes *The Docket*. Academics who focus on Colorado may publish in scholarly journals such as the *University of Colorado Law Review* or the *Denver University Law Review*. Both law schools have other journals, as well. In addition to electronic databases that carry law reviews, these periodicals are available in print in the two Colorado law schools' libraries, as well as the Colorado Supreme Court Library.[24]

SELECTED BIBLIOGRAPHY
OF STATE SPECIFIC SECONDARY MATERIAL

While a ballot measure will have a specific subject and, thus, its own topically-related articles and Web sites, the following sources are relevant to most, if not all, research projects related to initiatives or referenda.

Collins, Richard B. & Oesterle, Dale A., *Structuring the Ballot Initiative: Procedures that Do and Don't Work* 66 U. Colo. L. Rev. 47, 64 (1995).
This article presents an authoritative critique of the specific mechanisms of the ballot measure and direct democracy, acknowledging the both strengths and weaknesses of both. The authors focus on Colorado's initiative procedures in Section IV.

Colorado Legislative Council, Colorado General Assembly, *Colorado Ballot Proposal Information* (available at http://www.state.co.us/gov_dir/leg_dir/lcsstaff/balpage.htm).
This page includes links to: instructions for putting initiatives on the ballot; a complete digest of all past initiated and referred constitutional and statutory amendments in Colorado; and non-partisan analyses of ballot measures going back to 1998.

Colorado Office of Legislative Legal Services, Colorado General Assembly, Colorado Legislative Drafting Manual ch.12 (available at http://www.state.co.us/gov_dir/leg_dir/olls/LDM/12.0_The_Initiative_Process.pdf).
This Web site explains the role of the Legislative staff in reviewing drafts of ballot measures, giving the constitutional and statutory requirements on the initiative process. It provides a link to the rules promulgated by the Legislative Council governing initiatives. It explains the review and comment process, and gives writing tips to those drafters who wish to avoid some common pitfalls of legal drafting.

Colorado Office of Legislative Legal Services, Colorado General Assembly, Colorado Legislative Drafting Manual app. G (available at http://www.state.co.us/gov_dir/leg_dir/olls/LDM/20.0_Appendix_G.pdf).
This Web site contains a description, with accompanying illustrations, of the writing and corrections arising from a review and comment hearing, and an explanation of the legal importance of clear writing. It gives detailed style guidelines, some of the legal issues arising from ambiguity in written law and summaries of judicial

interpretations of the law governing submission of ballot initiatives in Colorado.

Colorado Office of Legislative Legal Services, Colorado General Assembly, *Memorandum Regarding the Use of Safety Clauses* (available at http://www.state.co.us/gov_dir/leg_dir/olls/PDF/USE%20OF%20SAFETY%20CLAUSES.pdf).
    Legislative Legal Services must, by law, ask legislators whether they wish to include a safety clause. This memo explains the use and meaning of the "safety clause" for the benefit of these legislators when answering that question.

Colorado Secretary of State, *Initiative and Referendum Election Resources* (available at http://www.elections.colorado.gov/DDefault.aspx?tid=175).
    This Web site provides links to the documents connected with Title Board Hearings (e.g., agendas, filings and results) for the current year, and links to other resources for proponents of ballot measures and voters.

Colorado Secretary of State, *Initiative and Referendum Procedure and Guidelines 2007-2008* (available at http://www.elections.colorado.gov/WWW/default/Initiatives/2007-2008_init_ref_manual.pdf).
    This 49-page guide addresses in detail the procedures governing placement of a measure on the ballot. In layman's terms it gives the constitutional and statutory requirements, along with the citation to the controlling constitutional or statutory section. It sets forth format requirements and provides a form for petitions, and a checklist for tracking the steps of the process and the relevant deadlines. For the year given, it provides a schedule of significant deadlines for processing initiatives.

Colorado Secretary of State, *Prior Years Election Information* (available at http://www.elections.colorado.gov/DDefault.aspx?tid=398&vmid=101).
    This Web site gives the election results by county from 1996.

Initiative and Referendum Institute at the University of Southern California, *Colorado* (available at http://www.iandrinstitute.org/Colorado.htm).
    This Web site promotes the use of ballot measures as a means of democratic government. It provides instructions for initiating a ballot measure and links to relevant statutes and constitutions for all states that have the initiative and referendum to assist would-be proponents

of ballot measures. It also gives a history of the use of initiatives and referenda for each state.

Oesterle, Dale A & Collins, Richard B., *The Colorado State Constitution: A Reference Guide* (Greenwood Press 2002).
The definitive work on the Colorado Constitution is a scholarly but accessible book. It is organized by Article of the Constitution; Section 1 of Article V is devoted to the initiative and referendum.

Polhill, Dennis, *Are Coloradans Fit to Make their own Laws? A Common-Sense Primer on the Initiative Process* (available from http://www.iandrinstitute.org/Studies.htm).
This issue paper argues for the importance and legitimacy of the initiative process and direct democracy, in general. Appendix B is a recap of Colorado ballot issues from 1912-1995.

FURTHER CONTACTS

Colorado Historical Society
Stephen H. Hart Library
1300 Broadway
Denver, Colorado 80203
http://www.coloradohistory.org/chs_library/library.htm
Email: Research@chs.state.co.us
Phone: 303-866-2305

Colorado Joint Legislative Library
State Capitol Building
Room 048
200 East Colfax
Denver, Colorado 80203-1784
http://www.state.co.us/gov_dir/leg_dir/lcsstaff/
Phone: (Molly Otto) 303-866-4011
Phone: (Gay Roesch) 303-866-4799

Colorado Secretary of State
Elections Division
1700 Broadway
Denver, Colorado 80290
http://www.elections.colorado.gov/DDefault.aspx?tid=175
Email: sos.elections@sos.state.co.us
Phone: 303-894-2200

Colorado State Archives
1313 Sherman Street, Room 1B20
Denver, Colorado 80203
http://www.colorado.gov/dpa/doit/archives/
Email: archives@state.co.us
Phone: 303-866-2358

Colorado State Publications Library
201 East Colfax, Room 314
Denver, Colorado 80203
http://www.cde.state.co.us/stateinfo/
Email: spl@cde.state.co.us
Phone: 303-866-6725

Colorado Supreme Court Library
B112 State Judicial Building
2 East Fourteenth Avenue
Denver, Colorado 80203
http://www.state.co.us/courts/sctlib/
Email: library@judicial.state.co.us
Phone: 303-837-3720

Denver Public Library
Central Library
10 West Fourteenth Avenue Parkway
Denver, Colorado 80204
http://www.denverlibrary.org
Email: dplref@denverlibrary.org
Phone: 720-865-1111

Government Publications
http://www.denverlibrary.org/research/government/index.html
Phone: 720-865-1711

Western History and Genealogy
http://history.denverlibrary.org/
Phone: 720-865-1821

University of Colorado Norlin Library
184 UCB, 1720 Pleasant Street
University of Colorado
Boulder, CO 80309-0184
http://ucblibraries.colorado.edu/norlin/
Email: libweb@colorado.edu
Phone: 303-492-8705

Government Publications
http://ucblibraries.colorado.edu/govpubs/index.htm
Email: govpubs@colorado.edu
Phone: 303-492-8834

Archives
http://ucblibraries.colorado.edu/archives/index.htm
Email: arv@colorado.edu
Phone: (David Hays) 303-492-7242

University of Colorado William A. Wise Law School Library
402 UCB, Wolf Law Bldg., Rm. 223A
2450 Kittredge Loop Road
Boulder, CO 80309-0402
http://www.colorado.edu/Law/lawlib/
Email: lawlib@colorado.edu
Phone: 303-492-3522

University of Denver Penrose Library
2150 East Evans Avenue
Denver, Colorado 80208
http://library.du.edu/
Email: reference-1@du.edu
Phone: 303-871-2905

Special Collections and Archives
http://library.du.edu/About/collections/SpecialCollections/index.cfm
Email: archives@du.edu
Phone: 303-871-3428

University of Denver Westminster Law Library
2255 East Evans Avenue
Denver, Colorado 80208
http://www.law.du.edu/library/
Email: refdesk@law.du.edu
Phone: 303-871-6206

NOTES

1. 1910 Colo. Laws 11 (Extraordinary Session).
2. Colorado Legislative Council, Colorado General Assembly, *Digest of Initiated and Referred Constitutional and Statutory Amendments Since 1912* (available at http://www.state.co.us/gov_dir/leg_dir/lcsstaff/research/Ballot_Hist_Defs.htm).

3. Colo. Const. art. V, § 1(3).

4. *Cavanaugh v. State*, 644 P.2d 1, 8 n.6 (Colo. 1982), cert. denied, 459 U.S. 1011 (1983); *Van Kleeck v. Ramer*, 156 P. 1108 (Colo. 1916); *In re Sen. Res. No. 4*, 130 P. 333 (Colo. 1913).

5. Colo. Const. art. V, § 1(5).

6. Dale A. Oesterle & Richard B. Collins, *The Colorado State Constitution: A Reference Guide* 119 (Greenwood Press 2002).

7. *Supra*, n. 2.

8. Colo. Rev. Stat. § 1-40-105 (2006); Colorado Legislative Council, Colorado General Assembly, *Steps for Placing an Initiated Proposal on the Statewide Ballot* (available at http://www.state.co.us/gov_dir/leg_dir/lcsstaff/initiative.htm).

9. Colo. Rev. Stat. § 1-40-105(4) (2006).

10. Colo. Rev. Stat. § 1-40-106 (2006).

11. Colo. Rev. Stat. § 1-40-106.5 (2006).

12. Colo. Rev. Stat. §1-40-107 (2006).

13. Colo. Rev. Stat. § 1-40-107(2) (2006).

14. Colorado Secretary of State, *Initiative and Referendum Procedures and Guidelines* 6 (available at http://www.elections.colorado.gov/WWW/default/Initiatives/2007-2008_init_ref_manual.pdf).

15. *Supra*, n.14 at 22.

16. *Meyer v. Grant*, 486 U.S. 414 (1988).

17. Colo. Rev. Stat. § 1-40-112 (2006).

18. Colo. Rev. Stat. § 1-40-121 (2006).

19. *Supra*, n. 14 at 8 (referring to *Buckley v. Am. Const. Law Found., Inc.*, 520 U.S. 182 (1999).

20. Colo. Const. art. V, § 1(3).

21. Colo. Rev. Stat. § 1-40-116 (2006).

22. *Id.*

23. *Id.*

24. Links to Denver University Law Review and the School's four other legal journals are available at http://www.law.du.edu/journals/. Links to the University of Colorado Law Review and its two other journals are available at http://www.colorado.edu/law/students/journals.htm.

Researching Initiatives and Referendums: A Guide for Florida

Elizabeth Outler

INTRODUCTION

The primary source of direct legislation in Florida is the constitutional amendment by initiative. There never has been a statutory initiative or popular referendum process in Florida. The Florida Constitution requires a referendum to approve issuance of state bonds, and of course the legislature may choose to submit laws to the voters for approval. The referendum process is so rarely used, and so unlikely to be driven by popular will, that any discussion of direct democracy in Florida must focus almost exclusively on the initiative process for amending the State constitution.

THE INITIATIVE PROCESS FOR AMENDING THE STATE CONSITUTION

History

Florida has had six constitutions over its history as a state. The document currently in effect is referred to as the Revised Constitution of 1968. Florida's first constitution was approved by the electors in 1839, when Florida was still a territory, and remained in effect when Florida became a state in 1845. Florida's participation in the Confederacy does not seem to have a noteworthy place in the popular memory, but it was the third state to secede from the United States in 1861. Consequently, Florida was not represented in the Congress from January 1861 to June 30, 1868. Three state constitutions were ratified during this period–the "war" or "Confederate" constitution of 1861, an early Reconstruction constitution in 1865 that was not accepted by Congress, and the Reconstruction Constitution of 1868 that finally allowed Florida to be readmitted to the Union. Another major constitutional revision was ratified in 1885, and this constitution, though heavily amended over its history, remained in effect until 1968.[1]

The Revised Constitution of 1968 was necessary to "modernize the administrative structure of the state, change provisions for local government," and accomplish reapportionment.[2] The legislature had repeatedly failed to address the need for reapportionment, despite significant population changes in the state and the federal attention to enforcing civil rights laws. The need for constitutional change became more urgent after the United States Supreme Court decided *Reynolds v. Sims,* in which it held that state constitutional provisions for apportionment that did not accomplish a system of "one man, one vote" were invalid.[3] In 1965 a

Constitutional Revision Commission was established, and by the time it had a document ready to submit to the legislature in 1967, another Supreme Court decision, *Swann v. Adams*, had directly invalidated Florida's apportionment law and required new districts to be drawn and new elections held.[4] The new legislature that reconvened later that year was particularly receptive to the new constitution, and approved it with few changes.[5] The document was approved by the people of the State of Florida in 1968. With amendments, the 1968 constitution remains the underlying framework of Florida constitutional law today.

It is in the 1968 constitution that the primary source of direct democracy in Florida first appeared, namely, the initiative method of amending the constitution. The recalcitrance of the legislature about amending the constitution to accomplish reapportionment, a crisis which lasted close to twenty years, prompted the Revision Commission that drafted the 1968 constitution to add the ability to amend the constitution without the participation of the legislature. Chesterfield Smith, the chair of the 1968 Revision Commission and the person most directly responsible for the major features of the redrafted document, reportedly stated that he believed the new provisions for amending the constitution were the most important things that were added.[6] The first time an initiative amendment appeared on the ballot was in 1976, to require public officials to disclose their assets and other financial information, and it was approved. From the information available on the Web site of the Division of Elections, twenty-six initiatives have made it to the ballot since then, with more than eighty-four percent approved. Voters saw and approved five initiative amendments in 2002, and six in 2004, which was the largest total to date. As a result of the perceived rise in the number of initiative petitions, and the apparent high chances of success for those that reach the ballot, a constitutional amendment (originating in the Florida Legislature) to increase the votes required to pass an initiative-sponsored amendment was approved by the voters in November 2006. Now, instead of a simple majority, an initiative-sponsored constitutional amendment must receive at least sixty percent approval in order to succeed.

Process

Core Requirements

The process for amending the constitution by initiative petition can be long and difficult, due to the numbers of signatures that must be acquired and the stringent review of the petition by the Florida Supreme

Court. The Web site of the Division of Elections, an office of the Florida Department of State (http://election.dos.state.fl.us/initiatives/index.shtml) has information about the process for filing initiative petitions, including the calculation of the number of signatures required to certify a petition for the ballot at the next general election.[7] The authorization and the minimum requirements for the initiative method of amending the constitution are found in Article XI, Section 3 of the Florida Constitution. Two basic requirements are stated there, namely, the so-called single subject rule, and the number of signatures required to get an initiative on the ballot. As mentioned above, a third requirement, sixty percent approval by the voters, is a legislative amendment approved in November 2006.

The Single Subject Rule

The single subject rule is that any citizen-sponsored "revision or amendment, except for those limiting the power of government to raise revenue, shall embrace but one subject and matter directly connected therewith."[8] The single subject rule has been the death of many initiative petitions, and strongly pro-direct democracy organizations like the Initiative and Referendum Institute at the University of Southern California School of Law have complained that the rule is "outrageously stringent."[9] It is true that only the initiative method of amending the constitution is subject to this limitation; the legislature has no such restriction in proposing constitutional amendments. However, the single subject rule has a long history in Florida constitutional law in a similar standard applied to the legislature's power to enact laws.[10] The legislative single subject rule existed in the 1885 constitution, and many laws have been invalidated due to its requirement.

The seminal case for the Florida Supreme Court's application of the single subject rule to initiative petitions is *Fine v. Firestone*.[11] In that case, the court explained that it will stringently apply the single subject rule to its review of initiative petitions because unlike legislative proposals, there is no filtering process for the drafting of the language, and no opportunity for debate or public hearing. In addition to discerning whether the text of the proposed amendment embraces more than one subject, the court will consider how a proposed amendment would affect other articles or sections of the constitution. The court also unequivocally stated that a severability clause in a petition cannot cure a violation of the single subject requirement. The only exception to the single subject rule is stated in the constitution: initiative amendments to limit the government's taxing power are not subject to the rule. This exception was added by an initiative amendment in 1994, largely in response to *Fine v. Firestone.*

Signatures

The second basic requirement is the total number of signatures required. This calculation is described in the constitution as follows:

> [A] number of electors in each of one half of the congressional districts of the state, and of the state as a whole, equal to eight percent of the votes cast in each of such districts respectively and in the state as a whole in the last preceding election in which presidential electors were chosen.[12]

The grand total currently required is 611,009, according to the Division of Elections Web site. The Web site also breaks down the totals required for each individual congressional district.[13]

Step-by-Step Process

Step One–Registration of Sponsor and Approval of Petition Form. As stated above, the Division of Elections Web site is an excellent starting point for citizens needing information about the process.[14] The main statutory sources governing the process of filing an initiative petition are Section 100.371, which prescribes the procedure for placement on the ballot, and Section 101.161, which prescribes the required wording for initiatives and referenda on a ballot. The first step is to register a political committee with the Division of Elections.[15] Any political committee must file a "statement of organization" with the Division of Elections prior to collecting money or signatures.[16] A "political committee" is defined to include "the sponsor of a proposed constitutional amendment by initiative who intends to seek the signatures of registered electors."[17]

The sponsor of an initiative petition must then submit the text of the proposed amendment and the form for collecting signatures to the Division of Elections for approval.[18] The approval of the petition and form must take place before gathering any signatures. The standards for sufficiency of a petition and signature form are laid out by Section 101.161, Florida Statutes, and Rule 1S-2.009 of the Florida Administrative Code. There must be a ballot title, not exceeding fifteen words, "by which the measure is commonly referred to or spoken of," and a ballot summary, "an explanatory statement, not exceeding 75 words in length, of the chief purpose of the measure."[19] Rule 1S-2.009 prescribes that the size of the form must be a minimum of three by five inches, and a maximum of eight and one-half by eleven inches. The form must be clearly and conspicuously titled at the top, "Constitutional Amendment Petition Form," and must contain the ballot title and summary, followed by the full text of the amendment being proposed, including the article and section being created or amended. The form must contain adequate space for the signee to write his or her name, legal residential street address, city, county, date of birth, signature, and date of signature. Only one signature is permitted per form, and a form that allows for multiple signatures will not be approved.[20]

Step Two–Gathering and Certifying Signatures. After approval, petitioners may begin gathering signatures, which remain valid for a period of four years from the date of signature. The required number of signatures overall and from any given congressional district may be acquired from the Division of Elections, which calculates the requirement based on the total number of registered voters who cast ballots in the preceding presidential election. Again, this information is available on the Division of Elections Web site.[21] When a threshold of ten percent of the required signatures have been gathered, from at least one-fourth of the congressional districts in the state, the petitioner may submit them for certification in order to begin the process of placing the petition on the ballot.[22] The sponsor must submit signatures to the appropriate Supervisors of Elections for each county in which signatures are collected.[23] There is a fee for verification of ten cents per signature, or the actual cost of verification of each signature, whichever is less; however, a sponsor may submit an affidavit that such a fee would be an undue burden on the sponsor in order to have the fee waived.[24] The Supervisors of Elections in each district verify the signatures and submit their reports to the Division of Elections, which provides a letter to the Secretary of State confirming that the sponsor has met the threshold to begin the review process. Then, the Secretary of State must immediately submit the petition to the Attorney General and the Financial Impact Estimating Conference.[25]

The Financial Impact Estimating Conference (FIEC) was made necessary by Article XI, Section 5(c) of the Florida Constitution, which was added by legislative amendment in 2002 and directed the legislature to enact laws to provide a statement to the voters of the "probable financial impact" of any initiative amendment that appears on the ballot. The FIEC consists of four members, one from the Executive Office of the Governor, one from the Office of Economic and Demographic Research, and one each from the professional staffs of the House of Representatives and the Senate, and all members should have "appropriate fiscal expertise in the subject matter of the initiative."[26] The FIEC is tasked to analyze the financial impact of the proposed amendment, including any "estimated increase or decrease in revenues or costs to state or local governments."[27] The group must provide an opportunity for proponents and opponents of the initiative to submit information to them, and any meetings must be noticed and open to the public.[28] The FIEC has forty-five days to complete its analysis and draft a "clear and unambiguous financial impact statement, no more than 75 words in length," and submit it to the Attorney General.[29] This financial impact statement will appear on the ballot, following the ballot summary.[30]

Step Three–Supreme Court Review. Within thirty days of receiving a certified amendment proposal from the Secretary of State, the Attorney General must petition the Florida Supreme Court for "an advisory opinion regarding the compliance of the text of the proposed amendment or revision with s. 3, Art. XI of the State Constitution and the compliance of the proposed ballot title and substance with s. 101.161."[31] While there is no statutory requirement that the Attorney General forward the financial impact statement to the Supreme Court for review, the court has adopted Florida Rule of Appellate Procedure 9.510, which directs the Attorney General to indicate in his petition for review of the proposed amendment the date by which the financial impact statement will be forwarded to the court, if the statement is not included with the petition.

The Court's review of an initiative petition is limited to two issues: (1) whether the petition complies with the single subject rule, and (2) whether the proposed ballot title and summary are clear and unambiguous.[32] Other than the single subject inquiry, the Court does not judge the merits of the proposed amendment. The single subject standard was laid down by the court in *Fine v. Firestone*, and is usually reiterated as "a logical and natural oneness of purpose."[33] This analysis includes a determination of whether the proposed amendment will affect more than one function of government, or more than one section of the constitution.

Step Four–Placement on the Ballot. If the petition survives Supreme Court review, it awaits placement on the ballot for the general election.[34] A "general election" is held each even-numbered year in November.[35] The sponsoring committee continues to submit signatures for verification until the required total for ballot placement is reached. Each signature must be submitted to the Supervisor of Elections for the county in which the signee is a registered voter. The Supervisors of Elections verify the signatures and submit their certifications to the Division of Elections. As of January 1, 2007, this process will be done electronically in a statewide voter registration system.[36] The Division of Elections determines whether the required number of signatures has been reached. The deadline for placement on the ballot for a general election is 5:00 p.m. on February 1 of the year in which the general election is held. Once the required number of signatures has been obtained and verified, the Secretary of State issues a certificate of ballot position.[37]

REFERENDA

The referendum is rarely used in Florida, and when it does appear, it is usually for a special law, e.g., limited geographical scope.[38] There is also the bond referendum, which has a constitutional source, but this too seems to happen extremely rarely.[39] Article VII, Section 11(a) declares that:

> State bonds pledging the full faith and credit of the state may be issued only to finance or refinance the cost of state fixed capital outlay projects authorized by law, and purposes incidental thereto, upon approval by a vote of the electors.

This does not include so-called revenue bonds, which finance projects that would pay for themselves (e.g., a toll bridge);[40] consequently, state capital projects for which bonds are issued are styled as revenue bonds, avoiding the requirement of voter approval.

FINDING DOCUMENTS RELATED TO FLORIDA INITIATIVES AND REFERENDA

The two best sources for information about initiative petitions and associated documents are the Division of Elections Web site (http://election. dos.state.fl.us/initiatives/index.shtml), and another Web resource, entitled *Florida's Constitutions: The Documentary History*, preserved by the Florida State University College of Law along with its Web archive of documents for the 1997-98 Constitution Revision Commission.[41] Other than the Division of Elections Web site, there have been no published guides or other information resources found that instruct or make recommendations about the process. There are several organizations, mentioned below, whose mission includes attention to election issues and the initiative process, but none are focused on fostering citizens who need assistance either with the process of proposing an initiative or with researching one. However, these groups may have useful information, and their Web sites are listed below in the selected bibliography.

Included below is a selected bibliography of other resources that might be useful for researchers attempting to find information about the citizen initiative process in Florida, or to locate historical documents related to initiatives or referenda.

Selected Bibliography

Florida Laws Governing Initiatives and Referenda

Florida Constitution

> Article XI, Section 3 (Amendments by Initiative)
> Article XI, Section 5 (Amendment or Revision Election)
> Constitution, Article VII, Section 11 (State Bonds; Revenue Bonds)
> Most of the initiative amendments that have been added to the Florida Constitution are found in Article X (the "Miscellaneous" article).

Florida Statutes

> Section 15.21–Initiative Petitions (Secretary of State)
> Section 16.061–Initiative Petitions (Attorney General)
> Section 100.371–Initiatives; Procedure for Placement on Ballot
> Section 101.161–Referenda; Ballots

Florida Administrative Code

> Rule 1S-2.009–Constitutional Amendment by Initiative Petition
> Rule 1S-2.0091–Constitutional Amendment Initiative Petition Submission Deadline, Verifying Electors' Signatures

Court Opinions

Note: If one is attempting to retrieve a comprehensive list of cases for historical research, a combination of keyword searching and digest searching is suggested.

West Digest System

> In *West's Florida Digest 2d* (and on Westlaw) a great percentage
> of the court opinions reviewing initiative petitions can be found
> using Constitutional Law, key number 9(1). However, this is not a
> perfect solution for finding a list of such cases for two reasons;
> first, not all such cases were indexed with headnotes, and second,
> this key number is not exclusive to review of initiative petitions.

Electronic Searching

> The statutory requirement that made the process of the advisory
> opinions automatic was enacted in 1986, so the petitions that were
> proposed before then had to be challenged if there was to be a review
> by the courts. Since 1986, the court's opinions are more uniformly
> captioned, e.g., "Advisory Opinion to Attorney General re: . . . ,"
> which makes keyword searching for them easier.

Internet Resources

**Division of Elections, Florida Department of State, Initiative Petition
Process**, available at http://election.dos.state.fl.us/initiatives/index.
shtml.

> The section of the Division of Elections' Web site that is devoted to
> initiatives is very helpful. It has a database of the titles and text of all
> the initiative petitions that have been filed, including the names and
> contact information of their sponsoring organizations, their status
> (active, closed, defeated, passed, removed, or withdrawn), the num-
> ber of signatures that have been verified (including a breakdown by
> district), and dates of significant activity, as well as the Supreme
> Court's ruling (for petitions that get that far). The Web site also has a
> section instructing citizens about steps in the process if they wish to
> file a petition themselves.

> The Division of Elections is the only authoritative resource for the
> petitions that are active and ongoing in the pursuit of signatures. If the
> Web site did not exist or were inaccessible, this information would be
> available via a public records request. The database is also an excellent
> resource for historical information about nearly all the initiative petitions
> that have been filed. There are some gaps in the historical coverage,

however. The very first initiative amendment in 1976 does not appear in the database. Additionally, there were three initiative petitions for the 1978 election that did not receive enough signatures and never made it to a ballot, and the text of these petitions is not available from the Division of Elections Web site.[42] Lastly, before 1988, sponsorship information for the various initiative petitions appears to be unavailable, with all such sponsors labeled "Initiative Committee Before 1988," for which there is no information in the database.

Division of Elections, Florida Department of State, Election Results, available at http://election.dos.state.fl.us/elections/resultsarchive/index.asp.
Election results since 1978 are available on this web page; this database is useful for identifying what items appeared on the ballot at each election (although the text does not appear, only the title), and what the vote totals were. For information about what appeared on the ballot before 1978, one would have to contact the Division of Elections or the State Archives.

Jo Dowling, Florida's Constitutions: The Documentary History, available at http://www.law.fsu.edu/crc/conhist/.
This is a compilation or bibliography to aid in historical research (through 1998), and it seems to be the only one that exists. This bibliography lists all of the amendments to the 1968 constitution, including the text of all initiatives that received review from the Supreme Court, whether or not they made it to the ballot (with the exception of the two 1978 failed initiatives mentioned above), and whether or not they were successful. In addition, it includes citations to all of the court opinions reviewing initiative petitions, and it seems to be the only comprehensive source for this list of court opinions. There is no other straightforward, sure-fire way of finding all such opinions in general. For these reasons, the *Documentary History* is quite a gift to the researcher.

State Library and Archives of Florida, Florida Department of State, available at http://dlis.dos.state.fl.us/library/.
The State Library and Archives Web site provides access to the online catalog for the Florida Documents Collection, which includes documents provided to the library by state agencies. There is also

contact information for the reference librarians at the State Library, who can be very helpful resources.

Bureau of Archives and Records Management, available at http://dlis. dos.state.fl.us/barm/fsa.html.

This is the separate Web site for the State Archives, which also has an online catalog allowing users to search what is available. The Reference Unit at the Archives will provide some research assistance as well, and contact information is available on the Web site.

Books

Talbot D'Alemberte, *The Florida State Constitution: A Reference Guide* (Greenwood Press 1991).

Written by a former governor of Florida, this guide is part of a series of reference guides for state constitutions. It recounts the history of Florida's constitutions, and gives a section by section analysis and explanation of the constitution (as it existed in 1991, when the book was published) including citations to significant cases. The discussion of the section governing the initiative amendment process is succinct but helpful, though dated. The book also contains an extensive bibliography.

Florida's Politics and Government (Manning J. Dauer ed., 2d ed., University Press of Florida 1984).

The editor of this book was the pre-eminent political science scholar in Florida for many decades, and played a role in the adoption of the 1968 Revised Constitution. This book is a collection of chapters by the leading scholars of Florida politics and history, with chapters focusing specifically on the history of the state, the constitution, and the legislature, among many other topics. Chiefly useful for historical perspective because of its age, this book is significant because it was edited by Manning Dauer, who also authored the chapter on the constitution.

Government and Politics in Florida (Robert J. Huckshorn ed., 2d ed., University Press of Florida 1998).

This book is essentially a revised and updated version of Florida's Politics and Government, listed above. Like that book, it is primarily useful for historical research and context.

Pamphlets

Public Information Clearing Service, University of Florida, Civic Information Series
This series of pamphlets was published by the University of Florida from 1950 to 1988. These were published to give voters information about proposed amendments to the state constitution, and only include information about those that actually appeared on a ballot. The pamphlets do not necessarily reproduce the language of a proposed amendment, but do explain the purpose and likely effect, and present arguments pro and con. The complete series is available at the University of Florida and Florida State University libraries. Other Florida libraries have items from this series, and they have been found in other university library collections around the country.

Legal Periodical Articles

P. K. Jameson & Marsha Hosack, *Citizen Initiatives in Florida: An Analysis of Florida's Constitutional Initiative Process, Issues, and Alternatives*, 23 Fla. St. U. L. Rev. 417 (1995).
This article presents a brief history of the Florida constitution and describes the initiative amendment process including the standard of review applied by the Supreme Court. It surveys the constitutional and statutory initiative processes in other states and compares those with Florida. The article concludes, among other things, that a statutory initiative process would benefit Florida because so many proposed initiative amendments address subjects that are inappropriate for the constitution.

Joseph W. Little, *Does Direct Democracy Threaten Constitutional Governance in Florida?*, 24 Stetson L. Rev. 393 (1995).
Professor Little recounts the history of the initiative amendment and decries the abuse of the State constitution by repeated amendments with non-constitutional subject matter. He notes that the legislature and the Constitutional Revision Commission have been guilty of the same sort of transgressions. He argues for two solutions: a statutory initiative process so that citizens will have a proper avenue for their lawmaking petitions, and a rule governing constitutional content to prevent further inappropriate constitutional amendments by all parties.

Robert M. Norway, *Judicial Review of Initiative Petitions in Florida*, 5 Fla. Coastal L. J. 15 (2004).

This article is a very detailed examination of the initiative process, focusing particularly on the role of the Florida Supreme Court. This would be a good article both for researchers and for citizens involved in the process.

Jim Smith, *So You Want to Amend the Florida Constitution? A Guide to Initiative Petitions*, 18 Nova L. Rev. 1509 (1994).

This is a very short and readable guide to the process of the initiative amendment. It is now somewhat dated, but still functions well as an introduction.

Organizations

As stated above, none of these organizations have compiled any historical documents, nor do they provide guidance for either proposing an initiative or researching one. However, these groups are very interested in issues surrounding the initiative process and may be sources of information for those issues.

Florida Public Interest Research Group (PIRG)–http://floridapirg.org/
League of Women Voters of Florida–http://www.lwvfla.org/

NOTES

1. Manning J. Dauer, *Florida's Politics and Government* (2d ed., U. Press of Fla. 1984).
2. Robert J. Huckshorn, *Government and Politics in Florida* 3 (2d ed., U. Press of Fla. 1998).
3. *Reynolds v. Sims*, 377 U.S. 533 (1964).
4. *Swann v. Adams*, 385 U.S. 440 (1967).
5. Dauer, *Florida's Politics and Government* at 95.
6. Talbot D'Alemberte, *The Florida State Constitution: A Reference Guide* 13 (Greenwood Press 1991). In addition to the citizen initiative process, the Florida constitution also requires a Constitutional Revision Commission to be convened every twenty years, and allows for the people to call a Constitutional Convention to consider the redrafting of the entire constitution. The recommendations of a Revision Commission or Constitutional Convention do not require legislative review, but rather are submitted directly to the people for approval.
7. Div. of Elections, Fla. Dept. of State, *Initiative Petition Process*, http://election.dos.state.fl.us/initiatives/index.shtml.

8. Fla. Const. art. XI, § 3.

9. Initiative & Referendum Inst. at the U. of S. Cal., *Florida*, http://www.iandrinstitute.org/Florida.htm.

10. Fla. Const. art. III, § 6.

11. *Fine v. Firestone*, 448 So. 2d 984 (Fla. 1984).

12. Fla. Const. art. XI, § 3.

13. Div. of Elections, Fla. Dept. of State, *Initiative Petition Process–Congressional District Requirements*, http://election.dos.state.fl.us/initiatives/congres.shtml.

14. Div. of Elections, *supra* n. 7.

15. Fla. Stat. § 100.371(2) (2006).

16. Fla. Stat. § 106.03(1)(a) (2006).

17. Fla. Stat. § 106.011(1)(a) (2006).

18. Fla. Stat. § 100.371(2) (2006).

19. Fla. Stat. § 101.161(1) (2006).

20. Fla. Admin. Code r. 1S-2.009 (2006).

21. Div. of Elections, Fla. Dept. of State, *Congressional District Requirements*, http://election.dos.state.fl.us/initiatives/congres.shtml.

22. Fla. Stat. § 15.21(3) (2006).

23. The process by which the Supervisors of Elections are to verify signatures is provided in the Florida Administrative Code. Fla. Admin. Code r. 1S-2.0091 (2006).

24. Fla. Stat. § 99.097(4) (2006).

25. Fla. Stat. § 15.21(3) (2006).

26. Fla. Stat. § 100.371(5)(b)2 (2006).

27. Fla. Stat. § 100.371(5)(a) (2006).

28. Fla. Stat. § 100.371(5)(b)1 (2006).

29. Fla. Stat. § 100.371(5)(b)3 (2006).

30. Fla. Stat. § 100.371(5)(c) (2006).

31. Fla. Stat. § 16.061(1) (2006).

32. The court's standard of review is succinctly stated in *Advisory Opinion to the Attorney General re Florida Marriage Protection Amendment*, 926 So. 2d 1229, 1233 (Fla. 2006).

33. *Fine v. Firestone*, 448 So. 2d 984, 990 (Fla. 1984).

34. If a petition is rejected by the court, the process ends. If the sponsor wishes to continue, it must re-draft its proposal and start the process over from the beginning.

35. Fla. Stat. § 100.031 (2006).

36. Fla. Admin. Code r. 1S-2.0091 (2006).

37. *Id.*

38. For example, in 2000, a referendum on Chapter 00-480, Laws of Florida, was presented to the voters of Manatee and Sarasota Counties. Division of Elections, *Election Results*, http://election.dos.state.fl.us/elections/resultsarchive/index.asp. The law provides for appointment of board members of the Sarasota-Manatee Airport Authority. 2000 Fla. Laws ch. 2000-480.

39. Evidence of only one bond referendum since 1968 has been found. See Clement H. Donovan & Manning J. Dauer, *Proposed Amendments to the Florida Constitution and Bond Referendum, Nov. 7, 1972 Election* (Pub. Administration Clearing Serv., U. of Fla., Civic Info. Series No. 53, 1972).

40. Fla. Const. art VII, § 11(d).

41. Jo Dowling, *Florida's Constitutions: The Documentary History*, http://www.law.fsu.edu/crc/conhist/.

42. *Florida's Constitutions: The Documentary History* has the text for the "Tax Cap–Poston" initiative but states that no known copy of the text for the other two 1978 initiatives exists. *See* http://www.law.fsu.edu/crc/conhist/1978amen.html.

Initiative and Referendum Process in Idaho: A Research Guide

Kristin M. Ford

INTRODUCTION

The initiative and referendum process in Idaho allows the citizens of Idaho to enact new or amend existing Idaho statutes (but not the Idaho Constitution), completely bypassing the Legislature, or in the case of the referendum, allows citizens to disapprove and void an act of the Legislature. The process for an initiative or referendum is nearly identical. Twenty electors' signatures are required to accompany a proposed initiative or referendum to the Secretary of State's office. The Attorney General reviews the petition and issues an advisory Certificate of Review to the petitioners, who are free to accept or reject the Attorney General's recommendations. If the petitioner wishes to proceed, the Attorney General provides ballot titles. The petitioner then must collect signatures from 6% of qualified electors, whose signatures are verified by county clerks. The Secretary of State receives the petition and verified signatures, and prepares the ballot with the initiative language. The Secretary of State is also responsible for printing and mailing Voter Pamphlets which contain not only the text of the initiative but also arguments for and against the initiative which have been written by voters. If the measure receives a simple majority approval by the voters, the governor issues a proclamation that the measure is law and thereafter the measure has the same force and effect as a law passed by the Legislature. *See* Idaho Code 34-1801 et seq.

HISTORY

The state of Idaho was just twenty-one years old when Idaho lawmakers passed Senate Joint Resolution 12 in 1911, a resolution to amend the Idaho Constitution to authorize an initiative and referendum process for its citizens. Idaho voters approved the constitutional amendment at the general election in 1912.

Article III, section 1 of the Idaho Constitution provides:

SECTION 1. LEGISLATIVE POWER–ENACTING CLAUSE–REFERENDUM–INITIATIVE. The legislative power of the state shall be vested in a senate and house of representatives. The enacting clause of every bill shall be as follows: "Be it enacted by the Legislature of the State of Idaho."

The people reserve to themselves the power to approve or reject at the polls any act or measure passed by the legislature. This power is known as the referendum, and legal voters may, under such conditions and in such manner as may be provided by acts of the legislature, demand a referendum vote on any act or measure passed by the legislature and cause the same to be submitted to a vote of the people for their approval or rejection.

The people reserve to themselves the power to propose laws, and enact the same at the polls independent of the legislature. This power is known as the initiative, and legal voters may, under such conditions and in such manner as may be provided by acts of the legislature, initiate any desired legislation and cause the same to be submitted to the vote of the people at a general election for their approval or rejection.

The foregoing provision provides the language of the constitutional section as it read after the 1912 amendment, with the struck-out clause showing the language deleted by a 1980 amendment to the Idaho Constitution. 1980 Senate Joint Resolution 112 has been the only change made to Idaho's constitutional provisions regarding initiatives and referenda since 1912.

The constitutional amendment provided that the "conditions" and "manner" of the initiative and referendum process would be determined by acts of the Legislature, which took 21 years to agree upon. In 1933, a new chapter was added to the Idaho Code setting forth the procedures by which Idaho citizens could propose and enact laws via the initiative process, and could approve or reject laws passed by the Legislature via the referendum process. These procedures today are found in Chapter 18 of Title 34 of the Idaho Code (available on the Legislature's web page at http://www3.state.id.us/idstat/TOC/34018KTOC.html).

The right of referendum was exercised for the first time in 1936, when voters rejected a law imposing a 2% sales tax. Interestingly, this first referendum is the only instance of Idaho voters rejecting a law through referendum in Idaho history. The right of initiative was first exercised in Idaho in 1938, creating the Idaho Fish and Game Commission. Since that time, thirty additional initiative or referendum measures have appeared on the ballot in general elections. A complete historical listing of these measures can be found on the Idaho Secretary of State's Web site, available at http://www.idsos.state.id.us/elect/inits/inithist.htm.

The remainder of this guide will aim to assist the researcher interested in learning more about the general initiative and referendum process (hereafter "I&R") in Idaho, as well as how to research specific I&R measures. Finally, I will share some of my favorite resources for multi-state research on I&R issues.

RESEARCH RESOURCES
FOR GENERAL IDAHO I&R INFORMATION

Idaho Secretary of State

The Idaho Secretary of State's Office is the richest resource for information on Idaho initiatives and referenda, both in terms of the general process and in terms of specific measures. This office condenses the Idaho statutes on the I&R process to a helpful step-by-step procedure, available on their Web site at http://www.idsos.state.id.us/elect/inits/initinst.htm. This overview includes pertinent deadlines and provides citations to the appropriate sections of Idaho Code, so this may be the best starting point for gaining an overview of the entire I&R process. Their instructions also alert potential petitioners to the fact that one provision of Idaho Code regarding signature collection has been found unconstitutional, so even though the language still appears in the Code, it is not enforced.

Legislative History

One way to gain additional background and insight into the evolution of the I&R process in Idaho is to research the legislative history of not only the Idaho constitutional amendments, but the enactment and subsequent amendments to the statutory laws regarding the I&R process. To do this, examine the history lines which follow the pertinent constitutional provisions or statutes in the Idaho Code volumes published by Lexis/Michie or else by Thomson West (Note: as of the date of this writing, Thomson West provides history lines only for the statutes and not for the Idaho Constitution). Here you will discover when a section was first enacted and each time it was later amended. Legislative history records, including statements of purpose and legislative committee minutes, are available from the Idaho Legislative Reference Library from 1960 forward, but are not available online until 2003. While the original 1933 enactment of I&R procedural requirements predate the available legislative history records, later amendments do have historical records available. In addition to the constitutional provision cited earlier, I suggest examining Idaho Code 34-1801 through 34-1823 for general state-wide ballot procedures, Idaho Code 50-101 (first enacted in 1967) for city-wide I&R procedures, and Idaho Code 31-717 (first enacted in 1977) for county-wide I&R procedures.

Law Review Articles and Journals

Cathy R. Silak, *The People Act, the Courts React: A Proposed Model for Interpreting Initiatives in Idaho*, 33 Idaho L. Rev. 1 (1996).
   Written by former Supreme Court Justice Cathy R. Silak, this article offers not only an overview of the I&R process in Idaho, but also an interesting comparison of citizen-enacted law versus legislature-enacted

law and a discussion of the resulting statutory construction principles to be applied by the Idaho judiciary. The Idaho Law Review is available at the Idaho State Law Library and the University of Idaho Law Library, as well as through electronic databases such as Westlaw.

Brian Kane, *If the Citizens Speak, Listen: Idaho's Local Initiative Process*, The Advocate (Idaho State Bar), March 2007, at 17-19.
Discusses significant cases and suggests revisions to the law.

Significant Court Cases

These cases and others from the Idaho Reports are available at the Idaho State Law Library, the University of Idaho Law Library, and the Idaho Legislative Reference Library.

City of Boise City v. Keep the Commandments Coalition, 143 Idaho 254, 141 P.3d 1123 (2006).
Overruled earlier Idaho Supreme Court decisions by holding that an initiative that had not yet been voted upon was not ripe for the Court's review, since it was only a proposal and had not become law.

Idaho Coalition United for Bears v. Cenarrusa, 342 F.3d 1073 (9th Cir. 2003).
Held that Idaho Code 34-1805 requiring that I&R petitions must contain a number of signatures from six percent of qualified voters in each of at least half of the state's counties violated the Equal Protection Clause and was therefore unconstitutional.

Gumprecht v. City of Coeur d'Alene, 104 Idaho 615, 661 P.2d 1214 (1983).
Held that use by a city of the initiative process was an impermissible method of enacting local planning and zoning ordinances, as it attempted to bypass the comprehensive state statutory planning and zoning procedures.

Dredge Mining Control-Yes!, Inc. v. Cenarrusa, 92 Idaho 480, 445 P.2d 655 (1968).
Held that the term "legal voter," with respect to those who may sign initiative petitions, means a registered voter and not merely someone who is qualified to be a registered voter.

Lukins v. Curtis, 64 Idaho 703, 136 P.2d 978 (1943).

Held that a law passed by initiative is on equal footing with a law passed by the legislature, and as such is equally capable of being subsequently amended or repealed by the state legislature. This became a hot topic in recent years when the Idaho Legislature repealed term limits that had been enacted by voter initiative. However, when the matter was put to referendum, voters narrowly approved the Idaho Legislature's decision to repeal term limits.

RESEARCH ON SPECIFIC I&R BALLOT MEASURES

The researcher of the rare Idaho referendum measure (there have been only four in Idaho's history!) may examine the legislative history of the legislation which is the subject of the referendum, in the same way that the legislative history of any bill may be done. However, researching the history of a referendum *after* it leaves the legislature, or researching the history of an initiative which has never touched the Legislature's process, requires resort to other materials.

Certificates of Review. Since 1995, the Idaho Attorney General's Office has been publishing their Certificates of Review of initiative petitions in the annual volume of Attorney General Opinions and Guidelines. They occupy a separate section of the volume and are indexed by Title/Description and also by Idaho Code or constitutional citation. These volumes are available in the Idaho State Law Library, the Idaho Legislative Reference Library, the Idaho State Historical Society, the University of Idaho Law Library and other Idaho university libraries, and some major public libraries like the Boise Public Library. The Certificates of Review are also available from 1995 forward on the Idaho Attorney General's Web site and may be accessed in three ways: chronologically, by topic index, or through keyword searching (available at http://www2.state.id.us/ag/ops_guide_cert/index.htm). To review older certificates of review, contact the Idaho Secretary of State.

Voters Pamphlets. Another important resource in researching a ballot initiative is the Voters Pamphlet published by the Idaho Secretary of State. The Voters Pamphlets contain not only the text of the proposed laws, but also contain arguments for and against the initiative submitted by the various groups. These documents are available on the Idaho

Secretary of State's Web site from 1998 forward at http://www.sos. idaho.gov/elect/inits/initinfo.htm. Older voter pamphlets are available at the Idaho Secretary of State's office, the Idaho State Historical Society, and from the libraries of all of the Idaho universities.

Special Publications. For some popular or controversial initiatives, additional materials by special interest groups, universities, and governmental entities, published both pre- and post-election, may also be available at the university libraries and the Idaho State Historical Society. For example, my random searches in library catalogs turned up materials on the 1% property tax initiative, and an anti-gay rights initiative.

Newspapers. For the truly dedicated, one could also search the newspaper archives for the relevant time period to find editorials, letters and ads regarding an upcoming initiative. The Idaho State Historical Society, the Boise Public Library and the Idaho university libraries all archive copies of the Idaho Statesman on microfiche or microfilm, as well as other Idaho newspapers. If your initiative is of recent vintage, you may also be able to search a newspaper's archives on its Web site.

MULTI-STATE RESOURCES

Frequently, the question arises, how do OTHER states do X? Here are some of my favorite resources for those handy-dandy wonderful time-saving state-by-state comparison charts.

University of Southern California's Initiative & Referendum Institute, available at www.iandrinstitute.org.
The Initiative & Referendum Institute is one of the best resources for multi-state information on initiatives and referenda and will doubtless be mentioned in every state's I&R research guide. While the commentary may be less than impartial, the Web site does provide a great deal of useful information by state, including the constitutional and statutory provisions, initiative steps, historical listing of initiatives and links to the state elections office. In addition, the multi-state charts on particular initiative topics are very useful. This is a site not to be overlooked!

National Conference of State Legislatures, *Initiative and Referendum in the 21st Century: Final Report and Recommendations of the NCSL I&R Task Force* **(2002).**
This book adopts the opposite tenor in commentary and recommendations from the I&R Institute, but also provides very handy state-by-state charts on state initiative requirements such as initiative subject restrictions, state agency review of initiatives, circulation periods, signature requirements, supermajority passage requirements, etc. Most legislative libraries own this book, and it is also available for download on the NCSL Web site.

The National Conference of State Legislatures, available at www.ncsl.org.
NCSL also provides a wealth of additional information on their Web site regarding state initiatives, including current and recent ballot measure tracking. Just choose the "State and Federal Issues" link, then choose the "Issue Areas A-Z," then scroll down and click on "Elections, Campaigns and Redistricting." From there, click on "Initiatives and Referendum" in the left hand panel, and you will find some great research resources!

Council of State Governments, *Book of the States,* **300-323 (2006).**
This annual volume also provides state-by-state charts on state initiative and referendum requirements, including topics such as deadlines, fiscal disclosures, and penalties. This book is available from many college and public libraries in Idaho, as well as the Idaho State Historical Society and the Idaho Legislative Reference Library.

CONTACT INFORMATION FOR IDAHO RESOURCES

Boise Public Library
715 S. Capitol Blvd
Boise, Idaho 83702
Phone: 208-384-4076
http://www.boisepubliclibrary.org

Idaho Attorney General
700 W. Jefferson Street
P.O. Box 83720
Boise, Idaho 83720-0010
Phone: 208-334-2400
http://www2.state.id.us/ag

Idaho Legislative Reference Library
P.O. Box 83720
Boise, Idaho 83720-0054
Phone: 208-334-4822
http://www.legislature.idaho.gov/research/referencelibrary.htm

Idaho Secretary of State
700 West Jefferson
Boise ID 83720-0080
Phone: 208-334-2300
http://www.sos.idaho.gov

Idaho State Historical Society
2205 Old Penitentiary Road
Boise, Idaho 83712
Phone: 208-334-2682
www.idahohistory.net

Idaho State Law Library
451 W. State Street, Boise
Idaho 83702
Phone: 208-334-3316
http://www.isll.idaho.gov

University of Idaho Law Library
P.O. Box 442324
Moscow, Idaho 83844-2324
Phone: 208-885-6521
http://www.law.uidaho.edu/library

Illinois Initiatives and Referenda

Shannon L. Malcolm

OVERVIEW

Initiatives and referenda tend to be lumped together in Illinois' primary, and even many secondary, resources under the term "questions of public policy,"[1] but I will retain the distinct terminology for clarity's sake, since both procedures are used in Illinois, and which procedure is used has legal significance. The outcomes of initiatives and referenda in Illinois are legally binding if, and only if, a statute or the constitution expressly so provides.

Illinois has an initiative process, but initiatives remain widely unused because they are difficult to initiate and not very meaningful even when successful. Excepting initiatives to make limited amendments to the constitution, statewide initiatives in Illinois are advisory only; their outcome does not bind the legislature, which has regularly ignored whatever advice they may have contained over the past century. As of this writing, Illinois' electorate has only passed one statewide initiative: an amendment to the constitution reducing the number of the legislature from 177 to its current 118 in 1980.

There are no statewide referenda in Illinois, but local referenda are fairly common. Local initiatives may also occur, but are least common of all, and are usually more properly considered back door referenda than true initiatives. Back door referenda are referenda wherein the electorate determines whether to accept or reject an ordinance already passed by the local government.[2] Their outcome has the force of law and legally binds the government. They are fairly common in Illinois, and are required before local governments can take certain actions. The relatively new constitution (adopted in 1970) establishes one of the strongest home rule systems of any state, and makes these local referenda and initiatives the fundamental means for a municipality (county, city, township, etc.) to decide whether or not it will implement home rule, as well as for a host of other decisions at the local level (whether to annex territory to a district, alter taxes, make certain expenditures, etc.).

For all local initiatives, a petition is required and must be filed with local election officials no less than 78 days prior to the election at which the initiative will be voted upon. For all local referenda, the ordinance (for a backdoor referendum) or resolution (for a standard referendum) must be passed no less than 65 days before the election at which the referendum will be voted upon. These deadlines apply to both advisory and statutorily mandated initiatives and referenda unless the relevant statute instructs otherwise.[3] I have omitted the more spurious details regarding petitions (sheet sizes and bindings, circulators' affidavits, etc.)

in this article for brevity's sake. When references are made to percentages of the electorate, note that the percentage of the electorate is calculated based upon the number of votes cast in the most recent gubernatorial election–not based upon the number of currently registered voters–unless otherwise noted.[4]

CONSTITUTIONAL AMENDMENTS

Although as of this writing it has never been done, voters can amend the constitution by initiative during a general election, but any such amendments may only alter the structure and procedure of the legislature. Initiatives to amend the constitution, like statewide advisory initiatives, can be placed on the ballot by filing with the secretary of state a petition signed by 8% of the electorate.[5] The Secretary of State must publish all proposed constitutional amendments, along with arguments supporting and opposing them, in each county's newspaper and mail a pamphlet containing this information to each postal address in Illinois.[6] The *Chicago Tribune* and other newspapers are therefore an excellent resource, not only for media coverage of any proposed amendments, but also for the text of the amendments themselves.

ADVISORY INITIATIVES & REFERENDA

In 1901 Illinois' legislature passed a law that allowed voters to petition for questions to be put on statewide or local ballots. The law required a petition signed by 10% of all registered voters in a municipality for a question to appear on the ballot in a local election, or 25% of all registered voters for the question to appear on the ballot in a statewide election. In either case, the results were advisory only; the original act refers to such measures as "an expression of opinion by electors on questions of public policy."[7] The law also required election officials to place such questions on the ballot for whatever general or special election the original petition designated, and no more than three such questions could appear on the ballot for any single election; otherwise acceptable petitions for advisory referenda submitted to the Secretary of State will not be accepted if three have already been duly filed for any given election.[8] In 2003, the law was again amended so that statewide advisory initiatives require only 8% of the number of electors who voted in the most recent

gubernatorial election, a significant decrease from the previous requirement of 10% of all registered voters.[9]

Advisory initiatives can also be placed on local elections' ballots.
Such initiatives require petitions signed by at least 8% of the electorate in the municipality for which the question is to be submitted and,
as mentioned earlier, must be filed with the local election officials,
instead of the secretary of state.[10] Advisory referenda can also be
placed on the ballot of a local election by resolution of the governing
body.[11]

Ironically, the earliest advisory initiatives requested a meaningful,
binding, statewide initiative process to replace the toothless act of 1901.[12]
Illinoisans passed statewide advisory initiatives calling for a binding
initiative process twice–in 1902 and 1910; both initiatives passed by an
overwhelming majority, and both were completely ignored by the legislature.[13] The message was clear: politicians were more than willing to
accept voters' direct input, but not necessarily to pay attention to it. As
one might expect, petitions to place such advisory questions on the
ballot became less common over time. There remains today no way to
enact statutes in Illinois via either initiatives or referenda, but ordinances and some administrative decisions by local governments use
both processes.

BINDING INITIATIVES & REFERENDA

In Illinois, as with so many other states, some municipal ordinances,
particularly those involving the issuance of bonds and/or other fiscal
matters, are subject to statutorily mandated backdoor referenda.[14] In
practice, each particular area of local law has distinct rules about when
referenda or initiatives are required, how the process must be carried
out, and what percentages are necessary for approval or disapproval of a
question. This vexing arrangement results from a historical anomaly of
Illinois' statutes controlling local government: The Illinois Municipal
Code,[15] originally called the Cities and Villages Act, was originally limited in application to only its eponymous cities and villages, leading to
myriad individual statutes, each specific particular procedures for particular municipalities of other sorts (park districts, school districts, etc.).[16]
Today, Illinois' statutes have distinct portions covering local government,
counties, townships, municipalities, and special districts (park, mass
transit, school, etc.).[17]

The scattered nature of statutes governing these matters is bad news for researchers. The good news is that the Illinois Municipal Code requires that each incorporated municipality must publish all its ordinances as books or pamphlets, or publish individual ordinances at least once within 30 days of passage.[18] Since all local binding referenda or initiatives that pass ultimately become ordinances, they can therefore be located, as published, like any other ordinance. Determining whether a particular ordinance originated as a referendum or initiative requires knowledge of, or consultation of, the statutes to see what particular local actions require such measures. Remember that when binding local referenda and initiatives occur, it is almost always because they are statutorily required, so knowledge of the subject at hand (annexation of territory to an airport authority's jurisdiction, etc.) can usually lead a researcher relatively painlessly to the relevant statute. Researchers with a general interest in such measures and no specific topic in mind must take the somewhat more onerous, but not much more difficult, route of perusing the index to an annotated copy of Illinois statutes under the term "initiative and referendum."

Discovering the details behind a measure can be more taxing. Illinois' Open Meetings Act,[19] Local Records Act,[20] and the Illinois Freedom of Information Act[21] make the minutes of board meetings and other proceedings of local government quite accessible to anyone willing to file the proper paperwork. Such records may well illuminate the reasons a local government acted in a way that led to a backdoor referendum (the common scenario) or any controversy that led to an initiative (the far less likely scenario). Regardless of whether they are back door referenda or true initiatives, before such measures are put on the ballot, local actions statutorily requiring passage by the electorate must be certified for the ballot by election officials and county clerks.[22] Therefore, the relevant Clerk of the Court or Election Board may have a record of such measures, even where they were not approved and did not become ordinances.

BIBLIOGRAPHY & USEFUL CONTACTS

In one sense, Illinois has no meaningful statewide initiative or referendum process. However, its strong home rule system means that local referenda (and, rarely, initiatives) are often statutorily mandated when they do occur, so the statutory code itself is key to researching such measures. The following resources will augment the preceding brief introduction to the basics for interested researchers.

State of Illinois Local Election Officials Handbook for the 2007 Consolidated Elections 33-36 (Illinois State Board of Elections 2007).
  Explains process to be followed during actual local electoral procedures involving initiatives and referenda.

Bernita J. Davies & Francis J. Rooney, *Research in Illinois Law* (Oceana Publications 1954).
  Although older, this concise book remains valuable for its explanation of entities like the Illinois Legislative Reference Bureau and the Illinois Legislative Council, and its lists of their reports and bulletins. While necessarily incomplete, these lists remain useful as starting points, especially for historical research.

Laurel Wendt, *Illinois Legal Research Guide* (2d ed., William S. Hein & Co. 2006).
  Includes explanations of initiatives to amend the constitution and a good explanation of the legislative process in Illinois, including a concise overview of its sometimes confusing home rule system.

Mathias W. Delort & Barbara B. Goodman, *Referenda*, in *Election Law* ch. 15, 15S-1 to 15S-5, 15-1 to 15-23 (Mathias W. Delort ed., Illinois Institute for Continuing Legal Education 2002 & Supp. 2005).
  An excellent overview of both initiatives and referenda in Illinois, despite the title (recall that Illinois employs some unusual terminology!).

Kurt P. Froelich, *Home Rule and Intergovernmental Cooperation and Conflict* in *Municipal Law and Practice in Illinois* vol. 3, ch. 29, 29S-1 to 29S-13, 29-1 to 29-104 (Stewart H. Diamond ed., Illinois Institute for Continuing Legal Education 2000 & Supp. 2003).
  A good introduction to Illinois' home rule system for local governments, important because referenda are so intrinsic to it.

Illinois State Bar Association Local Government Law Section Council, *County Government Law: A Reference Guide* (Taxpayers' Federation of Illinois 2000).
  Good for keeping abreast of local law in Illinois, since most referenda and initiatives occur at the local level. Published annually.

Illinois Legislative Council
c/o Illinois State Archives
Margaret Cross Norton Building
Capitol Complex
Springfield, IL 62756
Telephone: 217-782-4682
Fax: 217-524-3930
http://lifegoeson.com/departments/archives/archives.html

The legislature's fact-finding agency. Many of its incredibly comprehensive reports, available from the state's archives, may prove useful for researching the details behind a specific initiative or referendum. (The council itself actually consists of legislators, but it employs professional researchers.)

Illinois Legislative Reference Bureau
112 State House
Springfield, IL 62706
Telephone: 217-782-6625
http://www.ilga.gov/commission/lrb_home.html

Charged with publishing statutes and aiding legislators with drafting and revising them.

Taxpayers' Federation of Illinois
430 E. Vine Street, Suite A
Springfield, Illinois 62703
Telephone: 217-522-6818
Fax: 217-522-6823
www.taxpayfedil.org

NOTES

1. 10 Ill. Comp. Stat. 5/28-1 to 28-13 (2006).
2. 30 Ill. Comp. Stat. 350/3 (2006).
3. 10 Ill. Comp. Stat. 5/28-2 (2006).
4. *Id.*
5. Ill. Const. art. XIV, § 3.
6. 5 Ill. Comp. Stat. 20/2 (2006).
7. 1901 Ill. Laws 198.
8. *Id.*
9. 10 Ill. Comp. Stat. 5/28-6 (2006).
10. 10 Ill. Comp. Stat. 5/28-1, 28-6.

11. 60 Ill. Comp. Stat. 1/80-80, 55 Ill. Comp. Stat. 5/5-1005.5, 65 Ill. Comp. Stat. 5/3.1-40-60, 70 Ill. Comp. Stat. 1205/8-30.

12. M. Dane Waters, *Initiative and Referendum Almanac: A Comprehensive Guide to the Initiative and Referendum Process*, 190 (Carolina Academic Press 2003).

13. *Id.*

14. 30 Ill. Comp. Stat. 350/5 (2006).

15. 65 Ill. Comp. Stat. 5/1-1 et seq. (2006).

16. 1961 Ill. Laws 576-1369, George M. Platt, *The Illinois Municipal Code, in West's Smith-Hurd Illinois Compiled Statutes Annotated* ch. 65, pp. 375-386 (West 2006).

17. 50 Ill. Comp. Stat. 5/1 et seq. (2006), 55 Ill. Comp. Stat. 5/1 et seq. (2006), 60 Ill. Comp. Stat. 1/1-1 et seq. (2006), 65 Ill. Comp. Stat. 5/1-1-1 et. seq. (2006), 70 Ill. Comp. Stat. 5/1 et seq. (2006).

18. 65 Ill. Comp. Stat. 5/1-2-4 (2006).

19. 5 Ill. Comp. Stat. 120/1 et seq. (2006).

20. 50 Ill. Comp. Stat. 205/15 (2006).

21. 5 Ill. Comp. Stat. 140/1 et seq. (2006), 5 Ill. Comp. Stat. 160/4 (2006).

22. 65 Ill. Comp. Stat. 5/1-1-8 (2006).

Researching Initiatives and Referenda: A Guide for Maine

Christine I. Hepler

INTRODUCTION

For over a century, Americans have used the initiative and referendum processes to address issues at all levels of government. In the November 2006 elections a total of 204 ballot propositions went before voters in 37 states.[1] In Maine, there were two initiatives, including one to amend the Maine Constitution to clarify the deadline by which a signature on a petition for an initiative or a People's Veto referendum is valid.[2]

The initiative and referendum processes have their origins in the belief of government of, by, and for the people. The citizens of New England have a long history of participatory government, and in the colonial times it often took the form of citizens placing proposed ordinances on the agenda of annual town meetings.[3] The initiative and referendum movement became more formal after the Revolutionary War when some of the state constitutional conventions suggested voter ratification of the state constitutions.[4]

The initiative and referendum processes we are familiar with today, however, were formed with the Populist/Progressive movement of the 1890s and 1900s. This movement resulted from general dissatisfaction with government and its inability to effectively address the problems of that period.[5] Dissatisfied citizens needed a vehicle by which they could get their reforms approved while avoiding the state legislatures that were blocking their proposals.[6] They sought reform through using initiatives and referenda.

This paper will discuss the history of the initiative and referendum processes in Maine, including the steps needed to get an initiative or referendum on the state ballot. Finally, it will conclude with a selected annotated bibliography of Maine resources for more information on this topic.

EARLY HISTORY OF THE INITIATIVE AND REFERENDUM PROCESSES IN MAINE

The nineteenth century was marked by a general dissatisfaction with representative government. As a result, some states began to experiment with the initiative and referendum processes in hopes of remedying governmental abuses.[7] Maine was no exception. The primary reason the citizens of Maine were dissatisfied with the government was the poor economic status of the state. Many felt that this was the result of low tax rates on timberlands and railroads.[8] As a result, the citizens of

Maine began to pay attention to what was happening in certain Western States that had adopted some form of direct democracy and were greatly influenced by the experiences of those in Oregon and Oklahoma.[9]

An early champion of the initiative and referendum processes in Maine was Roland T. Patten, a Republican from Skowhegan. He first pushed for his party to adopt the initiative and referendum processes in 1902. Unable to persuade his own party, Patten left the Republicans, became the leader of Maine's Socialist Party, and lobbied all four parties–Republican, Democratic, Socialist and Prohibitionist–to support the initiative and referendum processes.[10]

In 1903, Democratic State Representative Cyrus W. Davis of Waterville introduced the first statewide initiative and referendum bill to the state legislature.[11] No action was taken on this measure, except for it to be referred to the next legislative session.[12] In the meantime, Patten started the Initiative and Referendum League of Maine, and he allied his new organization with the state Grange and the Federation of Labor. These efforts resulted in growing support for the initiative and referendum processes through all political parties in Maine.[13] In fact, in 1905 there was enough support for this movement that a resolve providing for initiatives and referenda made it to the final stages of the legislative processes before being defeated.[14]

In 1906, Maine's four political parties endorsed the initiative and referendum processes and Cyrus Davis made it a central issue in his Democratic gubernatorial campaign. Although Davis lost this election for governor, there was growing support for the initiative and referendum processes. Indeed, an increasing number of those elected to the State legislature supported the Initiative and Referendum League.

In 1907, popular pressure was so substantial that a resolve was enacted amending the Maine Constitution providing for direct democracy.[15] This was done despite considerable resistance by the Speaker of the House, the President of the Senate, and the Judiciary Committee. The measure was approved by a popular vote of more than two to one, with every county in the state voting in the affirmative.[16] This amendment passed despite opposition from many constituencies, including banks, timberland owners, and railroads. It was not the law the League wanted because it did not allow for amending the state Constitution, but it was a significant start.[17] This amendment added seven new sections to the Maine Constitution, and became effective on January 6, 1909,[18] making Maine the first Eastern State to adopt statewide initiative and referendum legislation.

RECENT USE OF INITIATIVES IN MAINE

Only seven initiatives were on the ballot during the first sixty years of
the initiative process, and there were none during the 1950s and 1960s.[19]
It was not until 1972, when the Maine voters approved an initiative to
change a ballot form to eliminate party columns, did the citizens of Maine
re-discover the power of the initiative process. In the 1970s and 1980s,
Mainers used the initiative process to deal with energy and environmental issues.[20] The two biggest referendum issues during this time were the
approval of the 1976 initiative to enact a beverage container deposit bill
(commonly referred to as the Bottle Bill)[21] and the defeat in 1980 and
1982 of initiatives to ban nuclear power.[22] More recently, in the early
1990s state lawmakers proposed changes to the initiative process after
the passage of a term limits initiative.[23]

A total of fifty-five statewide initiatives have been presented to Maine
voters since its inception. The Maine State Law and Legislative Reference Library in Augusta has compiled several charts summarizing votes
on initiated bills, People's Vetoes, and referenda. They include the year
the proposal was made, the bill number, title of the legislation, legislative action on the bill, the form of the ballot question, date of the vote, vote
total, citation to the enacted law, and relevant comments.[24]

BASICS OF MAINE'S INITIATIVE
AND REFERENDUM PROCESSES

The Initiative Process

In state and local politics, the word initiative means "a new law or
resolution proposed and placed on the ballot by citizen petition, and
enacted directly by popular vote."[25] This process is set out in the Maine
Constitution, Article IV, Part Third, §§ 16-22. Maine citizens may propose any bill, resolve or resolution, including bills to amend or repeal
emergency legislation. However, one cannot use the initiative process
to amend the Maine Constitution.[26] Initiative proposals must be made to
the Legislature by means of a petition, addressed to the Legislature or
any separate branch of the Legislature and filed with the Secretary of
State on or before the fiftieth day after the start of the first regular Legislative session or on or before the twenty-fifth day after the date of the
start of the second regular session.[27]

The Maine Constitution further provides that the petition must contain the signatures of not less than ten percent of the total votes cast in the last gubernatorial election preceding the filing of such petition and that each signature must be dated and cannot be older than one year from the written date on the petition.[28] The measure must then be submitted to the electors with any amended form, substitute, or recommendations from the Legislature, and in a way that the people can choose between the competing measures or reject both.[29]

When there are competing bills and neither receives a majority, the bill that receives more than one-third of the total votes given may be submitted by itself at the next statewide election to be held not less than sixty days after the first vote.[30] If an initiated measure is enacted by the Legislature without change, it shall not go to a referendum vote unless that vote is the result of a People's Veto and in accordance with the procedures set out in that section of the Maine Constitution.[31] The Legislature may order a special election on any measure that is subject to a vote of the people.[32]

To have an initiative placed on the ballot, a voter must first submit a written application to the Secretary of State on a form designed by that department.[33] The completed application must contain the names, addresses and signatures of five Maine registered voters, in addition to the applicant, who are designated to receive any notices related to the processing of the application.[34] The voter submitting the application must sign it in the presence of the Secretary of State, the Secretary of State's designee, or a notary public.[35] The application must contain the full text of the proposed law.[36]

The Secretary of State must review the application and determine the form of the petition to be submitted to the voters. The date the approved petition is provided to the applicant is the date of issuance for purposes of determining the validity of the signatures on the petition.[37] As previously mentioned, the voters in the November 2006 election approved an amendment to the Maine Constitution that is intended to clarify the deadline by which a signature on a petition is valid. The petition needs to be filed with the Secretary of State no later than eighteen months after the date the petition was furnished or approved by the Secretary of State. For a signature to be valid it cannot be older than one year at the time the petition is filed with the Secretary of State. This one-year requirement was in the Maine Constitution. This amendment clarifies that the one-year period runs from the date the petition is filed with the Secretary of State.[38] This amendment passed by a vote of 270,922 to 229,749.[39]

The Secretary of State must review the application within ten business days and either reject it, accept it as submitted, or accept it and provide a revised draft of the proposal to the applicant.[40] The Secretary of State can reject an application for only two reasons: (1) if it does not conform to the form required by the Secretary of State or (2) if it does not conform to the drafting requirements laid out in the Maine Revised Statutes.[41] If the Secretary of State rejects an application, he must provide a written statement of the reasons the application was rejected.[42]

If the applicant chooses to revise a proposal, he must submit each revision to the Secretary of State according to the rules previously stated and the Secretary of State must review it accordingly.[43] In addition, the Secretary of State must provide a revised draft or written response suggesting how the proposed law may be modified to conform to the statutory requirements.[44] Written consent from the applicant must be provided to the Secretary of State before the ballot question is drafted.[45]

After the Secretary of State has provided the ballot question to the applicant, the Elections Division will provide an approved petition form to be circulated by the petitioners. The proponents must print or duplicate additional petition forms as needed, in the exact format provided by the Secretary of State.[46] According to the Secretary of State's Web site, the petition form must be printed on paper no larger than 11 × 17 inches. The ballot question and title must be conspicuously placed on the face of the petition, and it must include the text of the legislation, instructions for petitioners, common reasons signatures are rejected, the circulator's verification, and the certification of the Registrar.[47]

The date the approved form of the petition is provided to the applicant is the date of issuance. The petition may be circulated for one year from the date of issuance. Any registered Maine voter may circulate petitions.[48] In addition, the ballot question must be displayed on the face of the petition and a concise summary of the proposed law drafted by the Maine Revisor of Statutes must be attached to the petition.[49]

Once the signatures are collected, they must be submitted to the appropriate city, town, or municipal officials for counting and verification, ten days before the petition is due by the Secretary of State. These officials must return the petition to the proponents five days before they are due to the Secretary of State.[50]

The People's Veto Referendum Process

In Maine, there are two mechanisms that provide for the people to vote on whether a particular piece of legislation should take effect: a People's Veto and a referendum. A People's Veto "is the procedure established in the Maine Constitution where the people can petition for a REFERENDUM on the question of whether legislation passed by the Legislature but not yet in effect should take effect."[51] In Maine, a referendum is defined as a "popular vote on proposals that may be initiated by the people or by the Legislature. Referenda may be binding or advisory, statewide or restricted to a lower level of government."[52] By definition, a referendum can be one initiated by the people, also known as a People's Veto, or by the Legislature. When initiated by the Legislature, there is a requirement in the legislation that it go to a vote of the people before it is enacted. This paper will focus on the procedures of the People's Veto and will use the terms referendum and People's Veto to refer to only the People's Veto and not to a legislative referendum.

The process for the People's Veto Referendum are contained in Article IV, Part Third, §§ 17, 19, 20, and 22 of the Maine Constitution and Title 21-A, §§ 901 et seq. regarding ballots. Upon written petition addressed to the Governor, any act, bill, resolve, or resolution passed by the Legislature, can be referred to the voters for approval before it will take effect.[53] Any legislation specified in a petition for a referendum shall be suspended when the petition is filed. If the petition is invalid, the legislation will take effect the day after it was determined that the petition was invalid.[54] As soon as this suspension takes place, the Governor is required to notify the public that a vote on the referendum is to take place at the next statewide or general election, the date of which cannot be less than sixty days after the petition is filed. If the Governor fails to provide this notice, the Secretary of State is authorized to do so.[55]

To initiate this process, a voter must submit a written application to the Secretary of State.[56] The Secretary of State determines the form of this application.[57] Unlike with an application for a direct initiative where the state specifically requires the full text of the initiative to be included in the application, the statute says nothing about whether the application must contain the full text of the referendum.[58] However, in the procedures set forth on the Secretary of State's Web site for a referendum, it states that "**(t)he application must contain either the full text of or a reference to the public law to be vetoed.**"[59] Furthermore, the completed application must contain the names, addresses and signatures of five Maine registered voters, in addition to the applicant, who are designated to receive any notices related to the processing of the application.[60] The voter submitting the application must sign it in the presence of the presence of the Secretary of State, the Secretary of State's designee or a notary public.[61] An application for a referendum petition must be filed with the Secretary of State within ten business days after adjournment of the legislative session at which the act in question was passed.[62] The Secretary of State has ten days to review the application and either reject it or accept it and provide the ballot question.[63]

Once the Secretary of State accepts the application and provides the applicant with the ballot question, the Department of Elections will provide the applicant with an approved petition form to be circulated.[64] For a referendum to be put on the ballot, the proponents of the referendum must collect signatures equaling ten percent of the total votes cast in the last gubernatorial election, the same requirement as with the initiative process. The deadline, however, is different. The petition for a referendum must be filed within ninety days after adjournment of the legislative session at which the Act was passed.[65] Once the signatures have been collected, the petitions need to be submitted to the proper city, town, or municipal official for verification. These officials must return the petitions within two days.[66]

RESEARCH TOOLS

Almanacs and Encyclopedias

Waters, M. Dane, *Initiative and Referendum Almanac* (Carolina Academic Press, 2003).

This comprehensive resource includes a detailed history of the initiative and referendum processes in the United States, as well as a state-by-state comparison of statewide initiative processes, and the use of the initiative and referendum in American cities. It was written by Dane Waters, the founder of the Initiative and Referendum Institute at the University of Southern California. This resource also includes a state-by-state description of the initiative and referendum processes for each state, including Maine. In the Maine section, there is (1) a brief summary of the history of the initiative and referendum processes in Maine; (2) the governing Constitutional provisions and statutes; and (3) a step-by-step description of how to complete the initiative and referendum processes in Maine. In addition, there are charts of the usage of the statewide initiative in Maine and a detailed chart summarizing the votes of all statewide initiatives from 1911-2000. This is an excellent resource for information about the use of initiatives and referenda in the United States as well as for the processes in the State of Maine.

American Jurisprudence and *Corpus Juris Secundum.*
Maine does not have its own state legal encyclopedia. As such, a researcher must rely on *American Jurisprudence* and *Corpus Juris Secundum* for background information on the initiative and referendum processes. Although national in scope, these resources are helpful as references to applicable key numbers from the West Key Number Digest system, which then can be used in the *Maine Key Number Digest.* Am. Jur. and C.J.S. also provide references to applicable A.L.R. sections, the A.L.R. Index, Am. Jur. Legal forms, and Maine cases on point.

Applicable Sections from American Jurisprudence include:

*   Adoption and Amendment of Constitutions §§ 10-39,
*   Elections § 10,
*   Initiative and Referendum §§ 1-53,
*   State and Local Taxation § 46, and
*   Zoning & Planning §§ 53 and 55.

Applicable Sections from Corpus Juris Secundum include:

*   Constitutional Law § 261,
*   Counties § 147,
*   Municipal Corporations § 1005, and
*   Statutes §§ 108-144.

Annotated Code

The statutes governing the Maine initiative and referendum processes are found in West's *Maine Revised Statutes Annotated.* In addition to the text of the statutes, the *Maine Revised Statutes Annotated* contains notes of decisions (cases that show how the statute has been interpreted by the courts), cross references to other applicable statutes, references to the West Key Numbers for this area of law, references to other secondary sources on point, such as *Corpus Juris Secundum* and law review articles, and references to legislative history material.

The Maine Revised Statutes are available online at http://janus. state.me.us/legis/statutes/. The online statutes are not annotated, but they do provide references to legislative history material. The Maine Constitution is available online at http://janus.state.me.us/legis/const/, but it is not annotated.

Digests

The two digests indexing Maine cases are the *Maine Key Number Digest* and the *Atlantic Digest*, both published by West. They provide a subject arrangement index to published Maine cases. The terms "initiative" and "referendum" are indexed separately in the Descriptive Word Index for each digest. The most extensive treatment of initiative and referendum are as sub-topics under the main topic "Statutes," key numbers 301-327 for initiatives and key numbers 341-367 for referenda.

Periodicals and Periodical Literature

Maine newspapers are a helpful historical resource for researching a specific initiative or referendum. There are two electronic databases that index Maine newspapers.

First, Maine Newsstand provides access to full-text articles from Maine's five major newspapers: the *Bangor Daily News*, the *Kennebec Journal*, the *Morning Sentinel*, the *Portland Press Herald* and the *Lewiston Sun Journal*. It is available through Marvel, Maine's Virtual Library[67] and through Mariner.[68] Maine Newsstand only contains articles back to the early 1990s.

Second, the Maine News Index consists of an index of Maine newspapers back to 1945, and it is maintained by the library staff at the Portland Public Library.[69] Unlike the Maine Newsstand which contains full-text articles, this database only provides abstracts of the articles.

SELECTED LEGISLATIVE HISTORY MATERIAL

Legislative Reports

A search of the URSUS catalog provides citations to several reports from the Maine Legislature regarding the initiative and referendum processes in Maine as well as several reports on initiatives and referenda voted on by Maine citizens.

Compiled Legislative History

The library staff at the Maine State Law and Legislative Reference Library in Augusta has compiled three legislative histories regarding the initiative and referendum processes. One copy of these legislative histories is for use in the library. There are additional copies which may be borrowed by any Maine resident or by nonresidents through Interlibrary Loan.[70] They are:

- *Citizen Initiated Legislation* (Updated 12/2006)
- *Maine's Constitutional Provisions for the Citizen Initiative and People's Veto*
- *Maine's Statutory Provisions for the Citizen Initiative and People's Veto*

MAINE INTERNET RESOURCES

Maine Secretary of State Bureau of Corporations, Elections and Commissions, at http://www.maine.gov/sos/cec/elec/.
This is the primary internet resource for information on Maine elections, including initiatives and referenda. The Elections Division supervises and administers all elections of federal, state, and county offices and referenda, and in that capacity advises election officials from municipalities, candidates, and the general public regarding election laws and procedures. In addition, the Elections Division prepares, proofreads, and distributes ballots and elections materials; tabulates official elections results; supervises recounts in contested races; and oversees the application of state laws pertaining to candidate and citizen initiative petitions.

From the index page, a researcher can access information regarding upcoming elections, voter registration, and election results. The Election Results page provides access to results back to 1992. This includes not only results from the general elections but also results from initiative votes. Most importantly, the link for the Citizen's Initiatives and People's Vetoes provides detailed information on the process needed to get an initiative on the ballot, initiative deadlines, a list of ballot questions, and a list of proponents of the initiatives.

Maine State Law and Legislative Reference Library listing of votes on People's Vetoes, at http://www.maine.gov/legis/lawlib/peoplesveto.htm.
This is a comprehensive list of all People's Vetoes put before Maine citizens since the inception of the process compiled by the Reference Staff at the Maine State Law and Legislative Reference Library. The information compiled includes the year the suspended legislation

was enacted, title of the legislation, disposition of the legislation, the ballot question, date of the vote, and vote totals for both yes and no votes.

Maine State Law and Legislative Reference Library listing of votes on Initiated Bills, at http://www.maine.gov/legis/lawlib/inivot.htm.
This is a comprehensive list of all initiatives put before Maine citizens since the inception of the process compiled by the Reference Staff at the Maine State Law and Legislative Reference Library. The information compiled includes the year the initiative was proposed, the bill number, title of the legislation, the ballot question, date of the vote, vote totals, citation to the chartered law, and comments.

Maine State Law and Legislative Reference Library listing of votes on Referenda, at http://www.maine.gov/legis/lawlib/refvot.htm.
This is a comprehensive list of all the referenda put before Maine citizens since the inception of the process compiled by the Reference Staff at the Maine State Law and Legislative Reference Library. The information compiled includes the year the bill was enacted, the bill number, title of the legislation, legislative action, citation of the enacted law, form of the ballot question, date of the vote, and vote totals.

SELECT ANNOTATED MAINE BIBLIOGRAPHY

Edward E. Chase, *A History of the Operation of the Initiative and Referendum in Maine from 1907-1951* (unpublished ms., 1952) (copy available at the Maine State Law and Legislative Reference Library).
This paper briefly lays out the history of the initiative and referendum processes in Maine from 1907-1951. The author's stated purpose is to review the use of initiatives and referenda in Maine and provides conclusions based on that use.[71] It starts with a section on the adoption of the processes in the state, and then provides detailed information on the first uses of the referendum in the state, including a discussion of a proposal to divide the town of York, Maine, an act to set a uniform standard for the alcohol level of beer, and an act to restore the Portland Bridge. This is followed by a discussion about the Direct Primary bill, the first use of the initiative in Maine, as well as by a discussion of subsequent uses of both the initiative and referendum processes. The author concludes with several broad

generalizations.[72] This paper is unpublished, but it is available at the Maine State Law and Legislative Reference Library in Augusta.

Kenneth Wade Fredette, *The Initiative and Referendum Process: The Maine Experience* (unpublished J. D. Independent Writing Project, U. of Maine School of Law, 1993) (copy available at the Donald L. Garbrecht Law Library, U. of Maine School of Law).
This student paper provides a history and description of the initiative and referendum processes in Maine and a discussion of the issues related to both. In addition, the author argues for citizen-initiated constitutional amendments. It contains a detailed discussion of the resolution proposed during the First Regular Session of the 116th Maine Legislature calling for an amendment to the Maine Constitution, allowing for citizens to initiate amendments to the Constitution. The paper suggests that this proposal would have been supported if additional safeguards were put in place.

Lawrence Lee Pellitier, *The Initiative and Referendum in Maine* (Bowdoin College, 1951).
This book provides a detailed history of the early uses of initiative and referenda in Maine. It starts with a detailed description of the wrangling needed to pass the 1907 Constitutional Amendment allowing for initiatives and referenda. It continues with a section on those opposing and supporting these processes. There are separate sections describing the steps needed to get an initiative or referendum on the ballot, though these steps are now outdated. This article also provides valuable information on the early usage of initiatives and referenda in Maine. Finally, there are three appendices that provide information on measures submitted to the voters from 1910-1951, votes on initiated statutes, referenda and Constitutional Amendments from the same time period, and popular vote totals on measures presented at general and special elections.

Marshall J. Tinkle, *The Maine State Constitution: A Reference Guide* (Greenwood Press, 1992).
As stated in the title, this is a reference guide for the Maine Constitution. It starts with the history of the Maine Constitution and continues with a separate discussion of each section of the Constitution. The discussion of Article IV, Part Third of the Maine Constitution begins on page seventy-four.[73] The sections pertaining to the initiative and referendum processes begin on page eighty-seven. The author provides

the text of the Constitution as they existed at the time of publication and provides comments and citations to cases that interpret these sections. It should be noted that this book was written in 1992 and has not been updated. Accordingly, some of the material is out of date.

NOTES

1. *Fall Ballot Measures,* 2006 Ballotwatch, 1 (Nov. 1, 2006), http://www. iandrinstitute.org/BW%202006-3%20(November%20update).pdf.

2. Me. L. D. 2033, 122nd Leg., 2nd Sess. (Feb. 28, 2006) (hereinafter referred to as LD 2033).

3. David D. Schmidt, *Citizen Lawmakers: The Ballot Initiative Revolution,* 4 (Temple University Press, 1989).

4. *Id.*

5. M. Dane Waters, *Initiative and Referendum Almanac,* 3 (Carolina Academic Press, 2003).

6. *Id.*

7. Lawrence Lee Pellitier, *The Initiative and Referendum In Maine,* 7 (Bowdoin College, 1951).

8. J. William Black, *Maine's Experience With The Initiative and Referendum,* 43 The Annals 161-163 (1912).

9. *Id.* at 161.

10. *Id.* at 164.

11. *Id.* at 163-164.

12. Pellitier, *supra* n. 6 at 8.

13. Waters, *supra* n. 5 at 205.

14. Pellitier, *supra* n. 6 at 8.

15. *Id.* at 8-9.

16. *Id.* at 9.

17. Waters, *supra.* n. 5 at 205.

18. Me. Const. art. IV, pt. 3, §§ 16-22. A comprehensive legislative history of this law, entitled *Maine's Constitutional Provisions for the Citizen Initiative and People's Veto* is available at the Maine State Law and Legislative Reference Library in Augusta. The library staff has also compiled a legislative history for the statutory provisions for the initiative and referendum processes, entitled *Maine's Statutory Provisions for the Citizen Initiative and People's Veto.*

19. Waters, *supra* n. 5, at 205.

20. *Id.*

21. This was an initiative to allow deposits on beverage containers to encourage recycling. Compiled legislative histories of the Maine Bottle Bill and the Maine Bottle Bill Update are available at the Maine State Law and Legislative Reference Library in Augusta.

22. Waters, *supra* n. 5, at 205.

23. *Id.* at 206.

24. There are three separate pages on the Maine State Law and Legislative Reference Library's Web site that provide voter information on initiatives, People's Vetoes and referenda. They are as follows: *People's Vetoes 1909*-online at http://www.

state.me.us/legis/lawlib/peoplesveto.htm; *Votes on Initiated Bills 1910-*, online at http://www.state.me.us/legis/lawlib/inivot.htm; and *Votes on Referenda on Acts of the Maine Legislature 1910-*, available online at http://www.state.me.us/legis/lawlib/refvot.htm.

25. Schmidt, *supra* n. 3, at 3.

26. Me. Const. art. IV, pt. 3, § 18(1).

27. *Id.*

28. Me. Const. art. IV, pt. 3, § 18(2).

29. *Id.*

30. *Id.*

31. *Id.*

32. *Id.*

33. 21-A Me. Rev. Stat. Ann. Sec. 901 (pamph. 2006). A printable version of this application is available on the Secretary of State's website at http://www.maine.gov/sos/cec/elec/initapp.pdf.

34. Me. Const. art. IV, pt. 3 § 18.

35. *Id.*

36. 21-A Me. Rev. Stat. Ann. § 901 (pamph. 2006).

37. *Id.*

38. *See* Me. Dept. of Sec. of State, *Maine Citizen's Guide to the Referendum Elections* for an explanation of this initiative, online at http://www.maine.gov/sos/cec/elec/2006/intent06.html.

39. Me. Dept. of Sec. of State, *General Election Tabulations: Referendum Questions*, online at http://www.maine.gov/sos/cec/elec/2006g/ref06.html.

40. 21-A Me. Rev. Stat. Ann. § 901 (3-A) (pamph. 2006).

41. *See* 21-A Me. Rev. Stat. Ann. § 901(3-A)(B) (pamph. 2006). The drafting conventions include but are not limited to: (1) correct allocation to the statutes and correct integration with existing statutes; (2) bill titles and statute section headnotes that objectively reflect the content of the bill, section or sections to which they apply; (3) conformity to the statutory numbering system; and (4) ensuring that bills enacting statutes do not contain provisions that describe intent or make testimonial statements without creating a legal requirement or duty.

42. 21-A Me. Rev. Stat. Ann. § 901 (6) (pamph. 2006).

43. Me. Rev. Stat. Ann. § 901 (3-A) (pamph. 2006).

44. *Id.*

45. *Id.*

46. 21-A Me. Rev. Stat. Ann. § 901 (3-B) (pamph. 2006).

47. Me. Sec. of State, *Citizen Initiative Application Packet*, ¶ 6 available online at http://www.maine.gov/sos/cec/elec/initpak.htm.

48. *Id.*

49. 21-A Me. Rev. Stat. Ann. §§ 901(4) & (5) (pamph. 2006). *See also* Me. Const. art. IV, pt. 3 § 20.

50. Me. Const. art. IV, pt. 3 § 20.

51. Me. Office of Policy and Legal Analysis, *Legislators' Handbook,* 123 (2004), available online at http://www.state.me.us/legis/opla/leghand04.pdf. (Emphasis in the original).

52. *Id.* at 125.

53. Me. Const. art. IV, pt. 3, § 17.

54. Me. Const. art. IV pt. 3 § 17(2).

55. Me. Const. art. IV pt. 3 § 17(3).

56. 21-A Me. Rev. Stat. Ann. § 901 (pamph. 2006).

57. A printable version of the application and the requirements of the applicant can be found on the online at http://www.maine.gov/sos/cec/elec/peopapp.pdf.

58. 21-A Me. Rev. Stat. Ann. § 901 (pamph. 2006).

59. Me. Dept. of Sec. of State, *People Veto's Application Packet online at* http://www.maine.gov/sos/cec/elec/peoppak.htm (Emphasis in the original.).

60. *Id.*

61. 21-A Me. Rev. Stat. Ann. § 901 (pamph. 2006).

62. 21-A Me. Rev. Stat. Ann. § 901(1) (pamph. 2006).

63. 21-A Me. Rev. Stat. Ann. §901 (3-A) (pamph. 2006) does not mention the referendum application specifically when it requires the Secretary of State to review the applications for a direct initiative within ten days of their receipt. However, the Secretary of State's Web site states that the review of a referendum application be completed within ten days. Available online at http://www.maine.gov/sos/cec/elec/peoppak.htm.

64. 21-A Me. Rev. Stat. Ann. § 906 (pamph. 2006) provides the requirements for the form of the ballot.

65. Me. Const. art. IV pt. 3, § 17(1).

66. Me. Const. art. IV, pt. 3, § 20.

67. Marvel can be found online at http://libraries.maine.edu/mainedatabases/. The researcher must register to use the Marvel databases and these databases are only available within the state of Maine. See http://libraries.maine.edu/mainedatabases/gettingstarted.htm for help getting started with Marvel.

68. Mariner is the collection of databases available to those who have cards from URSUS member libraries. URSUS is the shared catalog of the University of Maine System Libraries, the Maine State Law and Legislative Reference Library and the Maine State Library. Mariner is available online at http://libraries.maine.edu/mariner/. From here the researcher must click "Indexes and Databases" and then click "Featured Databases."

69. The Maine News Index can be found online at http://mni.portlandlibrary.com/ics-wpd/mniquery.htm.

70. The library staff has also compiled several legislative histories on citizen initiated bills. You can see a complete list of all of the compiled legislative histories available at the Maine State Law and Legislative Reference Library online at http://www.maine.gov/legis/lawlib/legishy.htm.

71. Edward E. Chase, *A History of the Operation of the Initiative and Referendum in Maine From 1907-1951, (unpublished ms., 1952)* p. 2 (copy available at the Maine State Law and Legislative Reference Library).

72. *Id.* at pp. 38-40.

73. I am providing page numbers rather than chapters because the author does not break this text up into chapters.

Democracy's Harvest: Resources for Massachusetts Voters' Initiatives and Referendums

Spencer E. Clough

Democratic nations care but little for what has been, but they are haunted by visions of what will be; in this direction their unbounded imagination grows and dilates beyond all measure . . .

Alexis de Tocqueville,
Democracy in America, vol. 2, sec. 1, ch. 17 (1840).

And thou shalt not glean thy vineyard, neither shalt thou gather every grape of thy vineyard, thou shalt leave them for the poor and stranger.

Exodus 19:10

I shall enter on no encomium upon Massachusetts: she needs none. There she is. Behold her and judge for yourselves.

Daniel Webster,
Second Speech on Foote's Resolution, January 26, 1830.

INTRODUCTION

On a crisp, clear October morning, any Bay Stater[1] reaching into her or his mailbox found, along with the usual circulars, bills, and L. L. Bean's Holiday catalogs, a mailing from the Secretary of the Commonwealth regarding the 2006 election.[2] While the main focus for the electorate has been on a contentious and historic gubernatorial race,[3] other issues confront this voter as the result of the time, energy and financial resources of several different interest groups. Whether the recipient of the Secretary's brochure takes the time to read it, or that brochure follows the same fate as much of the rest of the daily mail, this could be the earliest connection for that voter with what is now recognized as a vital democratic institution in this state, the initiative and referendum, also known colloquially as a "ballot question." The Secretary has just delivered to him or her, more than a reminder about the rights and procedures for electing other governmental officials as the bulk of this brochure describes in detail the current ballot questions created largely outside of

the legislative processes and presented to the citizenry of the commonwealth for approval as new, directly made law.

Ballot questions for the past ninety years, have changed the legal
landscape of Massachusetts on an array of issues, frequently having an
impact on the social guidelines that reflect both the changing beliefs,
thoughts and mores of the Commonwealth, as well as shaping State
government itself. In 2006, the three questions offered reflect just these
desired legal effects. They include a proposal to allow wine sales in grocery stores, another on multiple ballot listings for electoral candidates,
and a final question on collective bargaining rights for state-subsidized
child care workers.[4] So too, do the questions missing from this year's
ballot reflect the shifting concerns of the State: a ban on greyhound
racing,[5] a proposed universal healthcare system,[6] and a constitutional
amendment to ban same-sex marriages.[7] Even the gubernatorial candidates look to fuel their political campaigns by debating the meaning of a
prior ballot question that concerned reducing the state's individual
income tax.[8]

Will the child care worker, the nominee, the vintner, and the voter,
find reasons to raise a glass in toast to this year's new crop of statutes?
What will become of these and other ballot questions over time as they
are either implemented or they are forgotten? What situations give rise
to the need for these or other proposals? Who authors them, pays for their
consideration, and works to get them on the ballot? These questions represent a basic level of curiosity about Massachusetts' initiatives and referendums; other more subtle or sophisticated inquiries may be entertained
by later researchers. However, these questions serve as a way to focus
this work on a sampling of the documents and electronic resources
available to legal and historical researchers who need more information
on these laws. It is hoped that this will be a useful guide to researchers
since, as these laws are passed directly by the people of the Commonwealth of Massachusetts, and as their documentation is not otherwise
found among the usual legislative history sources, these resources
might otherwise be obscure or difficult to locate.

GLOSSARY

As alluded to by the use of the terms "Bay Stater" and "ballot question" in the introduction above, some of the terminology used here is
unique to Massachusetts or has a special significance to this aspect of

statutory research and requires some definition for use by researchers otherwise unfamiliar with this subject or territory.

Article XLVIII: is the legal, constitutional authority for publicly created initiative petitions, referendums and constitutional amendments;[9] a reform study in 1975 by the General Court described this amendment as: "the longest and most complicated article in the Massachusetts Constitution."[10]

Attorney General: the chief legal officer for the state; her role in initiatives and referendums is to certify that the proposed law or amendment is legal and constitutional, and then must draft a summarized version of it for the public.[11]

Ballot Question Committee: a public interest group formed specifically to move their initiative or referendum through the process to final law,[12] e.g., Grocery Stores and Consumers for Fair Competition, which promoted wine sales in supermarkets and grocery stores in the 2006 election.[13]

Commonwealth: this is largely a cosmetic distinction, Massachusetts would be known as a state except that the John Adams labeled it a Commonwealth when he wrote the Massachusetts Constitution of 1780;[14] both "state" and "commonwealth" will be used here interchangeably, but Commonwealth is the preferred official designation, though it contains no special privileges and powers.[15]

Constitutional Amendment: private citizens in Massachusetts may propose their own amendment to the constitution.[16] During the 2006 election some groups had hoped to promote an amendment to prohibit same-sex marriage; that move defeated when the General Court recessed until after the election without taking action on the amendment.[17]

Constitutional Convention of 1917: originated the initiative and referendum process and first used it to add Article XLVIII to the constitution.[18]

General Court of Massachusetts: this is the State legislature;[19] the name continues from its colonial predecessor when it was both a court of general jurisdiction and a legislature. There was debate during the Constitutional Convention of 1917 to change the name to "the Legislature" but tradition won out.[20]

Initiative Petitions: are created for an entirely new statutory proposal or to repeal or amend a section of another statute as opposed repealing a statute in its entirety.[21]

Proposition 2 1/2: statewide this is the most famous of the initiative petitions; it was a "tax revolt" measure authored and promoted by "Citizens for Limited Taxation."[22] Enacted in 1980, this law holds annual property tax increases by municipalities at 2.5 of the full, fair value of all property in the community.[23]

Public Policy Questions: allows voters to send non-binding instructions to their state senator or representatives.[24] By example, the 7th Norfolk District voters during the 2006 election were offered a question on instructing their representative as to the medical use of marijuana.[25]

Referendum Petition: is used when the petitioner wants to repeal an entire law not just a section of it as the repeal of a section would be dealt with in an initiative petition.[26] The legislature views this as "the people's power to *refer* legislation recently enacted by the General Court to the voters for their approval."[27]

Secretary of the Commonwealth: is the chief information officer for the Commonwealth; this office also oversees the Elections Division, with responsibility for printing petitions, ballots, and distributing ballot question information to the electorate, and also operates the State Archives.[28]

Supreme Judicial Court: is the court of final resort for the Commonwealth; the court has the authority to challenge the Attorney General's certification on the legality of initiative and referendum proposals, ensuring that the Attorney General's decisions are made by applying the standards in Article XLVIII, and not as a matter of policy.[29]

HISTORY

The kernels for initiatives and referendums were planted early; Massachusetts, with some puffery, claims to be the first state[30] to use a public referendum as the proposed first Massachusetts constitution was offered to and then rejected by voters in 1778.[31] Those early seeds lay dormant for a long time, until the fourth constitutional convention of

1917, when labor unions and Progressives joined to push for greater control over the legislature in partial response to an opinion of the Supreme Judicial Court from twenty years earlier, *In re Municipal Suffrage to Women*.[32] The ensuing constitutional debates cover thousands pages of text involving issues which still seem familiar today.[33] The questions disputed then included the desirability of social welfare legislation, the role of lobbyists in a representative government, the effectiveness of the legislature, the intent of the framers of the constitution, the interests of the wealthy few versus the majority, and the power of corporations versus individuals.[34] As a subtext, the convention took place during an era when the Protestant status quo was increasingly threatened by the expanding immigrant and Roman Catholic populations.[35] Ultimately the convention voted 163 to 125 to deliver the amendment for initiatives and referendums to the electorate for ratification. The voters were less impressed with the amendment than the representatives to the convention as the ratification slipped into law by a slim majority of 8,543 ballots, or merely 2.5% of the 332,749 votes cast on the issue.[36] A further 96,698 voters casting votes in that election did not vote either yes or no; and when the returns are broken down by county, only two, Suffolk, containing Boston, and Plymouth actually passed this amendment.[37] Thus, indicating that there was a major difference between the urban and rural voters over initiatives and referendums, and regional differences between eastern interests and western, as well as pitting the North Shore versus South Shore.

Subsequent initiative and referendum petitions filed with the Secretary of the Commonwealth, both voted on or not, provide testimony to the ingenuity for legal innovation, as well as to the social concerns of the Bay State over time. A sampling of these includes "Sport and Games on the Lord's Day" in 1928, "Restricting low level radioactive waste disposal in nuclear power plant construction" in 1982, and the "Opening of retail stores on Sunday mornings and certain holidays" in 1994.[38] A search through these petitions reveals a history of the Commonwealth's society in flux throughout the 20th century, particularly as it shed the assumptions, protocols, and conventions of its earlier Puritanical and patriarchal forefathers.

While these aspects of social life and the law are significant, the yield from these initiative and referendum petitions filed tells a significant political story of its own. One study found that of 47 proposed constitutional amendments filed between 1933 and 2000 only two were successful in negotiating the entire procedure to a place on the ballot;[39] one more appeared after the study.[40] Of these proposed constitutional amendments only two have been passed by the voters into law. There have been 18 referendum questions, to repeal a law entirely, on the ballot with a positive vote on ten of these. Of initiative petitions, 51 have been sent to the voters, and 24 have been adopted by them.[41] Such activity indicates that voters of the Commonwealth are adaptable but not easily swayed by just any legal novelty or innovation that is tossed in their direction.

Petition filings also chart an aspect of the life cycle of Massachusetts' political activism. Filings with the Secretary of the Commonwealth for both constitutional amendment initiatives and other initiative petitions between 1919 and 2002 totaled 301, indicating that only about 17% reach the ballot, and a mere 8% become law. Bay Staters have only sought to overturn existing legislation through referendums on 48 occasions in the same time period, though with 10 having been passed by the electorate, their success rate is a respectable 20%. In the decades through the 1940s and during the 1960s there were usually about twenty to thirty petitions filed every ten years, although the 1950s were unusually quiet period for political activists with only three petitions filed during that decade. Since the 1970s however, the numbers of petitions filed have exploded: 1970s = 62, 1980s = 72, 1990s = 89. During the first couple of years of this century, 2000 to 2002, sixteen petitions were filed.[42]

Spending on initiatives and referendums has also been explosive proving that such activism does not come easily or cheaply. Statewide ballot spending reached $10 million in 1998 and $15 million in the 2000 election.[43] Grocery stores seeking to put wine on their shelves and those seeking to prevent wine sales had reached nearly $8 million one month prior to the 2006 election, thereby nearly reaching the $9 million record for spending on a single ballot question set in 1988.[44]

As a tool for Massachusetts voters the initiatives and referendums process grants them some governance over the legislature and provides an avenue to statutory and constitutional change on topics the General Court is unwilling or unable to bring itself to consider. Though, being New Englanders, our voters combine a mixture of conservatism and a love of tradition with their concern for social issues and a tolerance for eccentricity. These characteristics are fully apparent in this manner of law making.

PROCEDURE

The rigorous procedure for initiatives and referendums takes no less than sixteen months from the start to the final tally, more if the initiative concerns a constitutional amendment. Activists usually officially begin their work in an odd-numbered year as ballot questions may only be presented to the electorate in even-numbered years. As may be seen below, the ballot question process is challenging, with two rounds of signature-gathering, and a great deal of scrutiny by officers of the Commonwealth. It is a process that could only attract the most dedicated or motivated, as well as financially well-supported, activists.

Year One: An Odd Numbered Year

1. August: by the first Wednesday, the newly proposed law, accompanied by ten valid registered voters' signatures, must be submitted to the Attorney General.
2. September: by the first Wednesday, a determination that the proposal meets constitutional requirements and a summary of the law is made by the Attorney General.
3. The proposal is then filed by the petitioners with the Secretary of the Commonwealth who prints petition form blanks within fourteen days of receipt of the filing.
4. Late November: Petitioners must gather certified voter signatures equal to 3% of the voters in the last gubernatorial election, of which no more than one fourth can be from any single county, to be filed with the respective local election officials for certification of the voters' registration.
5. December: by the first Wednesday, the voters' signatures gathered in November are then filed with the Secretary of the Commonwealth.

Year Two: An Even Numbered Year

6. January: the Secretary of the Commonwealth sends the ballot question to the House clerk by the first meeting of the General Court for the year. The General Court sends the proposal to committee for consideration after which the legislature may approve, disapprove, formulate a substitute proposal, or take no action. If approved by the legislature and then signed by the Governor an initiative becomes law at this point without being sent to the electorate.
7. May: Legislative activity on the proposal must conclude by the first Wednesday.
8. July: Early in the month, petitioners must gather another .5% of the signatures of the registered voters from the past state election for filing with the Secretary of the Commonwealth.

9. October: The Secretary of the Commonwealth sends information regarding the ballot questions to registered voters.
10. November: the proposal appears as a ballot question on the election ballot.
11. Passage requires that 30% of voters must vote on the question and a majority of those voters must pass favorably on it.
12. December: unless the ballot question specifically stated that it shall become effective immediately, the law becomes effective 30 days after either the election or certification of the election by the Governor's Council.[45]

Constitutional amendments follow a similar path, but carry an additional legislative requirement of passage by 25% of both houses of the General Court in two successive legislative sessions. This later step adds another two years to this process.[46]

Resources on the Procedure Include

State Ballot Question Petitions, Secretary of the Commonwealth, Elections Division, 2005, at www.sec.state.ma.us/ele.
This is an official state source from the Secretary of the Commonwealth's subdivision, with detailed descriptions of the transactions for each type of ballot question, and includes the specific dates and voter requirements for a ballot question.

The Initiative Petition Process, 2005-2006, from the office of the Massachusetts Attorney General, at http://www.ago.state.ma.us/sp.cfm?pageid=1246.
Another official source that is worth using in conjunction with the Secretary of the Commonwealth's publication. The Attorney General's material is more synthetic in its organization and gives more detail about her role in the process.

Legislative Procedure in the General Court of Massachusetts, 2003.
Prepared jointly by the Clerks of the House and the Senate, this work outlines the basics of the procedure with more detail given to the legislative actions in §§ 13.1 and 13.2; this print source is not generally distributed beyond the members of the legislature and their staff, but may be found at the State Library.

Issue: Ballot Questions, at http://www.issuesource.org/issue.cfm? ID=135&Mode=Background.
An unofficial source from the policy group MassINC, this publication provides a broad overview of the process with points about current ballot questions.

LEGAL AUTHORITY: THE CONSTITUTION, STATUTES, REGULATIONS, A PENDING BILL, AND THE RECORDS RETENTION SCHEDULE

Several sources provide the legal authority for the activities that surround the initiative and referendum process, its administration and subsequent treatment. Here are several fundamental documents of which a researcher concerned with ballot questions needs to be aware.

Article XLVIII: Created by the 1917 Constitutional Convention, this is the authority in the Massachusetts Constitution giving the citizenry the power to submit laws and constitutional amendments to the electorate. The bulk of this amendment deals with the procedure but also limits the subject matter of such proposals in section 2 by excluding laws about religion, judges, judicial decisions or the operation of a specific municipality; it has also been further amended by Articles LXVII, LXXIV, LXXXI and CVIII. An official version of the Massachusetts Constitution is found in volume 1 of the *Massachusetts General Laws 2004*, which is republished every two years. Unofficial versions may be found in the *Massachusetts General Laws Annotated* (MGLA), by Thomson/West, or the *Annotated Laws of Massachusetts* (ALM), by Lexis Publishing, or online at www.mass.gov/legis/const.htm.

Mass. Gen. Laws ch. 53 §22A: This statute addresses petition signatures, voter certification, and the publication of petition forms by the Secretary of the Commonwealth. Versions of this statute may be found in the same sources as the constitutional amendment above.

Mass. Gen. Laws ch. 55 §6B: Defines the purpose of a ballot question committee including restricting its financial activities solely to that of the question for which it was formed and restricting any involvement with the campaigns of a candidate.

Further statutory sections may be found by consulting the indexes to either of the unofficial statutory sources. Under the subject heading "Initiative and Referendum" in the Mass. Gen. Laws Ann. there are two columns of references to codified statutes in other chapters of the *General Laws*.

Senate Bill 2251 "An act providing further public information and strengthening petition anti-fraud safeguards for initiative and referendum questions" Mass. S.2251, 184th General Court, 1st Session (2005): Currently pending in the House of Representatives Committee on Ways and Means, this a redraft of an earlier bill, sponsored by Senator Edward J. Augustus, Jr., and is a proposed antidote to "bait and switch" tactics used by some ballot question groups to obtain signatures from voters; it is alleged that some groups represent themselves as collecting for a more popular issue when in fact they are collecting signatures for another that was more controversial; the bill also attempts to limit the method of reimbursement for professional signature collectors.[47] No action has been taken on this legislation since November 7, 2005.[48]

950 CMR sec. 48 et. seq.: The Secretary of the Commonwealth has promulgated regulations, under Mass. Gen. Laws c.53, §7 that address issues of "accuracy, uniformity and security from forgery and fraud" in the gathering of signatures; these regulations are published in the Code of Massachusetts Regulations at Chapter 950, §§ 48.01 to 48.08, and deal largely with the format of the petition forms, the signatures, and finally defining the point at which the ballot questions actually become a public record.

Massachusetts Statewide Records Retention Schedule 06-06: Subtitled "A publication of the Records Conservation Board produced in conjunction with the Massachusetts Archives and the Supervisor of Public Records Office," this body of standards sets out the retention and disposal scheme for records from many state agencies including the Secretary of the Commonwealth and the Attorney General's office. The files used by these two offices during the initiative and referendum process are also covered in these schedules. Copies of this document are available in print at the Supervisor of Public Records Office, the State Archives, or the State Library.

THE SECRETARY OF THE COMMONWEALTH

As noted in sections above, the Secretary of the Commonwealth is the state officer most substantially involved in the entire initiative and referendum process. This office serves as a center for public information within the state, and also oversees all elections. These functions fall under the jurisdiction of different subdivisions within the Secretary's authority, each with its own separate sphere of responsibility, as well as separate offices in different sections of Boston. The main administrative office for the Secretary is on the third floor of the State House on Beacon Street in Boston, with online access provided at www.sec.state.ma.us/.

Elections Division: This subdivision of the Secretary's office administers all aspects of elections including voter registration, voting equipment, primaries, electoral districts and ballot questions. The main elections office is located at the main location for many state agencies, One Ashburton Place, room 1705, in Boston, near the State House, or it can be located online at www.sec.state.ma.us/ele. Online resources include *How to Place a Public Policy Question on the 2006 State Election Ballot, How to Request a Recount,* and *A Guide to State Ballot Questions.* This later publication is a valuable 19 page guide to the entire process. An electronic version of *The Official Massachusetts Information for Voters 2006*, the brochure sent to all voters, can also be found online at www.sec.state.ma.us/ele/elepdf/IFV_2006.pdf. The Elections Division holds petition files for the most recent ballot questions at their office until they are sent later, usually within a few years, to the State Archives.

State Archives: Organizes and preserves the official records of Massachusetts government including the Secretary's records, legislative materials and the records from the Governor's office and executive agencies. Among these are the initiative and referendum petitions and records from the Secretary's office from 1919 to 2002, as well as records from the Attorney General's office from 1919 to 1953. The archives are located on Morrissey Boulevard at Colombia Point in Dorchester, south of Boston, between the campus of the University of Massachusetts at Boston, and the John F. Kennedy Library and Museum. The archive requires all visitors to register in order to use materials in the reading room or from the vault. Online they may be located at www.sec.state.ma.us/arc/arcidx.htm, though as of this writing they have not loaded any materials related to ballot questions on this site, so the documents held by this agency need to be viewed in person.

THE ATTORNEY GENERAL

Information available from the Attorney General's office, especially online, overlaps somewhat with that from the Elections Division of the Secretary of the Commonwealth's office. However, there are some differences and for anyone interested in proposing a ballot question it would be worth looking at the information and materials from both offices together. The Attorney General's main office is located in One Ashburton Place, near the State House, in Boston. Online information may be found at www.ago.state.ma.us/. The Attorney General's description of the process is available at www.ago.state.ma.us./sp.cfm?pageid=1246, and offers further information from Assistant Attorney General Peter Sacks at peter.sacks@ago.state.ma.us. Currently filed petitions are also listed at www.ago.state.ma.us/sp.cfm?pageid=2144, this provides links to the text of the ballot questions and contact information for the sponsors. Three recent Attorney General's opinions regarding initiatives and referendums may also be found online by searching from the main page under "ballot questions" or from www.ago.state.ma.us/sp.cfm?pageid=1019.

Attorney General opinions may also be found online in Lexis' Mass AG database; searching under the term "ballot question" produces slightly less than a dozen decisions from between 1980 and 2001; alternatively they may also be found in hard copy at the State Library, the State Archives, or through the Attorney General's office. Initiative petition files for the period from 1919 to 1953 are kept at the State Archives; however, petition files from that period to the present are kept at the Attorney General's office or stored offsite and may require a "Freedom of Information Act" petition to gain access to them.

THE OFFICE OF CAMPAIGN AND POLITICAL FINANCE

Established in 1973 under the Campaign Finance Law,[49] the Office of Campaign and Political Finance is an independent agency charged with supervising compliance with this law located in Room 411, One Ashburton Place, on Beacon Hill in Boston, or online at www.mass.gov/ocpf.[50] For ballot question committees this means reporting on all financial matters related to their promotion of any initiatives and referendums. Online the OCPF provides *Statewide Ballot Question Committees: a Listing of Committees and CPF ID Numbers, June 2006* at www.mass.gov/ocpf/comm/bq0606.pdf; this lists all currently operating committees with their address and treasurer, e.g., 95331, Wine Merchants and

Concerned Citizens for S.A.F.E.T.Y. (Stopping Alcohol's Further Extension To Youth), One Beacon Street, Suite 1320, Boston, MA, 02108, Richard Goldstein. Campaign finance reporting forms for ballot question committees are available at www.mass.gov/ocpf/forms/102bq.pdf; and a guide for the rules governing these committees is found at www.mass.gov/ocpg/guides/statebq1203.pdf.

THE GENERAL COURT

As the legislature reviews initiative and referendum proposals before they are presented to the electorate, and is substantially involved in the constitutional amendment process, some materials concerning these proposals will make an appearance in official legislative sources. Missing from these materials are the written committee reports required by law but uncollected in a central place, though they may be available through the reviewing committee. Those existent legislative documents are found at the State Archives or, more proximate to the legislature, in the State Library at the State House on Beacon Street in Boston.

The State Library: is found in room 341 on the third floor of the State House, next to the Secretary of the Commonwealth's office; here researchers will find copies of the official session laws contained in the *Massachusetts Acts and Resolves,* bills, and from the Legislative Reference Council, reports contained in the *House and Senate Documents,* records of the legislative activity in the *House and Senate Journals,* as well as *The Debates in the Massachusetts Constitutional Convention, 1917-1918.* With the growth of initiative and referendum activity in the 1970s a movement to revise the procedure produced an exhaustive 179 page report by the now defunct Legislative Research Council that appears in the *House Documents, 1975,* as House Bill 5435, titled "Revising Statewide Initiative and Referendum provisions of the Massachusetts Constitution." The object of the report was to "identify any problem areas attributable to vagueness or contradictory requirements. . .;[51] the report also examines two prior reform efforts in 1932 and in 1967.[52] At times the General Court has also submitted questions regarding a ballot question to the Supreme Judicial Court for certification of the law's constitutionality; an example of the justices' opinion on a policy question regarding the repeal of Prohibition, may be found in the *House Documents, 1928,* at HB 1101.

COURT DECISIONS

With as many state officers holding some oversight powers over, or an interest in the outcome of, some part of the initiative and referendum process it is no small wonder that many conflicts have required adjudication by the Massachusetts Supreme Judicial Court. Below are a few cases that illustrate the conflicts that arise and how they may be used by interested parties to maneuver. While searching for these cases may be easily done by reference to annotated versions of the constitutional amendments or statutes on which their authority rests, the digest system does provide an alternative method of searching for these cases. It is also possible to perform term searches online using phrases like: "initiative petition," "referendum petition," "initiative amendment," "article 48," or "ballot question."

Schulman v. AG, 447 Mass. 189 (2006).
The plaintiff sought to block the proposed constitutional amendment banning same-sex marriages by challenging the Attorney General's certification as the amendment would be in conflict with a prior judicial decision; the Court ruled against the plaintiff by finding the Attorney General's certification was within his purview under Article XLVIII.

Opinion of the Justices to the Acting Governor, 438 Mass. 1201 (2002).
The justices answered the Governor's question as to whether the legislature's adjournment by roll call vote constituted a "final action" upon a constitutional amendment such that she would not have the authority to compel the legislature to reconvene to consider the amendment; the Court responded that as no vote was taken on the amendment, and that the legislature had only voted to adjourn, it was not possible to find that a final action had occurred. The justices then declined to answer a related question about the governor's power as having been answered in a prior case.

Opinion of the Justices to the House of Representatives, 422 Mass. 1212 (1996).
The House asked the Court to rule on the constitutionality of an initiative that attempted to cut legislative salaries and expenses in half while effectively reducing the legislative work to six months per year; finding several constitutional deficiencies with the proposal the

court rejected it in part for being in conflict with another two year old
law on term limits that had been passed by a state-wide ballot
question.

Limits v. President of the Senate, 414 Mass 31 (Mass 1992).
Plaintiffs sought to use the court to compel the legislature to come to
a final vote on a constitutional amendment requiring term limits; the
court found that Article XLVIII specified the Governor was the state
officer with the power to compel such a final action.

In re Municipal Suffrage to Women, 160 Mass. 586 (1894).
Leading the Way, credits this case with inspiring the drive to create
initiative and referendums in the Commonwealth; the case is interesting reading for the majority's argument in favor of a representative
government with delegated powers to the legislature superior to that
of the people; at times the majority opinion is just unabashedly snob-
bish.[53] Another reason to read the case is for Oliver Wendell Holmes,
Jr's dissent.

Massachusetts Digest 2d: If a researcher uses the West digest system
in print or online, the topic for finding cases about initiatives in "Statutes," and the key number range is 301 to 327, e.g., "Initial certification
by Attorney General," Statutes key 304. Referendums are covered by
the topic statutes under the key numbers 341 to 367, e.g., "Certification
of sufficiency of petition," Statutes key 355.

ESSENTIAL REFERENCE TOOLS

New Englanders throughout the years have relied upon a publication
from our New Hampshire neighbors for "useful information for people
in all walks of life," *The Farmer's Almanac.*[54] In a more sophisticated
format, similar kinds of general political forecasts, suggestions, common sense, and information are available for novices and veterans alike
here in the Bay State. These are several sources that are essential guides
for anyone working in the field of Massachusetts politics.

The Massachusetts Political Almanac, edited by Kenneth G. Morton
and Paplinka Paradise, from the Center for Leadership Studies, is an important guide to the entire apparatus of Bay State government; how the

branches are related and operate together; who is who and where they sit; "if you can't tell the players without a scorecard," this is the score-card to have when playing on Beacon Hill; purchase of a copy provides the owner with a password for online access at www.masspa.com.

Lobbying on a Shoe String, by Judith Meredith, from the Massachu-setts Law Reform Institute, is a wonderful primer on the Massachusetts legislature written for grassroots political activists from an insider's view point; while it is not directly on point for initiatives and referendums, it informs readers about the workings of the General Court that are essen-tial to understand before proceeding with a ballot question issue.

The Handbook of Massachusetts Legal Research, edited by Mary Ann Neary and produced by Massachusetts Continuing Leading Education, (MCLE), is available online from Lexis or in print from the publisher; although it does not deal at length with initiatives and referendums this source is the most complete single guide available for conducting research on any legal topic in Massachusetts.

Leading the Way, edited by Cornelius Dalton, unfortunately, this his-tory of the General Court ends in 1980, has not been updated and is out of print since 1984; however, it is still the best narrative history on the legislature, considering both the political and social context of this body; this work includes an entire chapter devoted to the Constitutional Convention of 1917.[55]

JOURNAL ARTICLES AND NEWS ARTICLES

It is no surprise that the Massachusetts initiative and referendum pro-cess as a local political issue has attracted little attention in law reviews. The topic has been more thoroughly explored in other sources that are full of practical information, including one medical journal article! Most common of all articles are the myriad of editorials and news sto-ries that have tracked this issue over time. Researchers would be ad-vised to spend time using related key terms to search periodical indexes and newspapers for more information on specific issues.

Robert G. Stewart, *The Law of Initiative Referendum in Massachusetts*, 12 New Eng. L. Rev. 455 (1977).
    While this is a dated work, it is one of the few to look at the entire ini-tiative and referendum process from a legal standpoint and realize

that growing numbers of activists would use this law in the future; at the time, the author was able to state that: "(Article XLVIII's) use has been modest." The situation has changed.

Kenneth Bresler, *Rediscovering the Right to Instruct Legislators,* 26 New Eng. L. Rev. 355 (1991).
This author believed that the right to instruct legislators, contained in the public policy questions, was another power underutilized by voters; part of the article examines the similarities and differences between this power and initiatives and referendums.

John McDonough, *Taking the Laws into Their Own Hands,* 7 Cmmw. 52-62 (MassINC, Fall 2002).
This piece analyzes the problems of initiatives and referendums, including the actions of the state legislature, growing numbers of petitions, and "booby traps"; this author also lays out five arguments against the process and then three for it; where one of the earlier authors, Robert Stewart, saw growing activism in the future, this author stands at the other end of a time period and foresees diminishing activism observing: "It's possible the initiative surge since 1976 is a spent force." This is a void into which he sees corporate interests as rapidly entering.[56]

William E. Dorman, *Questions as to the Meaning of the Amendments,* 4 Mass. L. Q. 142 (1918-19).
These were likely the first legal writings on ballot questions and were meant as instructions to the bar.[57] This article poses and answers twelve questions about biannual elections, the role of the Attorney General, and the timing of parts of the procedure.

Blake Cady, M.D., *History of Successful Ballot Initiatives-Massachusetts,* 83 Cancer 2685 (1998).
The author presents a review of the activities that led to acceptance of a $.25 increase in the excise tax on cigarettes by way of a ballot question. This is interesting and useful as it recounts what is needed for a successful grass-roots campaign, and is written from the viewpoint of someone standing outside the legal or political mainstream. It serves as an example of the way in which initiatives were intended to be used as they were developed by the Progressives as a vehicle for social change.

Barbara Anderson, *Celebrating Prop 2 1/2,* Bos. Globe A23 (Nov. 4, 2005).
A recounting of the history and achievements of the most successful ballot question by the head of Citizens for Limited Taxation, the author of this initiative. This, too, is an example of the potential power for change for which initiatives may be used.

CONCLUSION: SWEET SUCCESS OR SOUR GRAPES?

Election Day was an unusually warm and beautiful November day for our voter to make her or his way to the polls. By week's end, if he or she had not already done so, that copy of *The Official Massachusetts Information for Voters* became useless and then was tossed out with the newspapers for recycling, or became the subject of some form of political archaeology.[58]

As life settled into the routine preparations for the Thanksgiving holiday, the Commonwealth had changed historically, and yet had also stayed the same. Massachusetts had overwhelmingly elected its first African-American Governor, Deval Patrick. However, the vintner had nothing to cheer about as the ballot question to put wine in supermarkets failed; child care workers also lost their bid for union representation; and political candidates would still only be listed once on ballots. All of this year's ballot questions were defeated.[59] While the voter may be the only one with a reason to raise her or his glass in celebration it will still only be with a libation purchased from what is known colloquially as a "packie."[60] The cost of the campaign was historic: both sides of the wine sales question spent a record breaking $13 million total.[61] Keeping with the eccentricities of the Commonwealth, voters in those districts with a policy question about the decriminalization of marijuana voted to send such instructions to their state representatives.[62]

Since the ballot questions considered were finally tallied and accepted, the continuing political fall-out has been over the unresolved constitutional amendment to ban same-sex marriages. Two days after the election the General Court convened in a joint session voted by a simple majority to recess without considering the amendment. A vote by the legislature to openly oppose the amendment would have required better than a three-fourths majority; a vote to submit the amendment to the voters would only have required better than 25% of the members.

The General Court's actions though have failed to quell the political maelstrom.[63]

Ultimately, after nearly ninety years of ballot questions, the story is that this story continues to develop. In *The Boston Sunday Globe*, one month after the election, our voter read this observation on the topic: "And if the Legislature–and perhaps the governor–have no confidence in Article 48's rules, wouldn't it at least make sense to try to change them?"[64] For legal researchers this question is ripe with implications for the future.

NOTES

1. Mass. Gen. Laws. ch. 2 § 35 (2004); "Bay Staters shall be the official designation of citizens of the commmonwealth."

2. This author received his brochure in the mail from the Secretary of the Commonwealth on October 6, 2006.

3. *Seven Weeks to History*, Boston Globe editorial, A12, September 20, 2006. "One thing is certain: Voters will make history in November by electing either the first woman or first black governor of Massachusetts."

4. The Office of the Secretary of the Commonwealth, *The Official Massachusetts Information for Voters: the 2006 Ballot Questions*, (2006).

5. Ari Bloomekatz, *SJC Rules That Initiative to Ban Dog Racing Illegal*, Boston Globe, B8, (July 14, 2006).

6. Jeffrey Krasner, *Group to Back Healthcare Law's Implementation*, Boston Globe, D3, (July 6, 2006).

7. Andrea Estes and Russell Nichols, *Lawmakers Delay Vote on Gay Marriage Measure*, Boston Globe, A1, (July 13, 2006).

8. Scot Lehigh, *Campaign Fun With Tax Cuts*, Boston Globe, A19, (May 5, 2006). "Fifty-six percent of the voters did say yes to the tax cut six years ago."

9. Mass. Const. amend. XLVIII, §1 et seq.

10. Mass. H. 5435, 169th General Court, 1st Session, 21 (1975), *Revising Statewide Initiative and Referendum Provisions of the Massachusetts Constitution.*

11. Mass. Gen. Law ch. 12 §1 et seq.; Mass. Gen. Law ch. 54 §53.

12. Mass. Gen. Law ch. 55 §6.

13. *Supra, The Official Massachusetts Information for Voters: the Ballot Questions*, at 5.

14. David McCullough, *John Adams*, 221 (Touchstone, 2002). "It was titled 'A Constitution or Form of Government for the Commonwealth of Massachusetts,' Adams having chosen the word 'commonwealth' rather than 'state,' as had Virginia, a decision that he made on his own and that no one was to question."

15. Mass. Const., Part the Second, *The Frame of Government*, Title of the body politic. "The people . . . agree with each other, to form themselves into a free, sovereign, and independent body politic, or state by the name of 'The Commonwealth of Massachusetts'."

16. Mass. Const. art. XLVIII, ch. I.

17. *Supra, Campaign Fun with Tax Cuts*, n. vii.

18. *The Debates of the Massachusetts Constitutional Convention of 1917* (Wright and Potter Printing Company, State Printers 1918) vols. I-IV.

19. Mass. Const. Part 2, Chapter 1, §1, Article 1 "The legislative body shall assemble every year . . . and shall be stiled [sic], The General Court of Massachusetts."

20. Cornelius Dalton, editor, *Leading the Way: a History of the Massachusetts General Court 1629-1980.* 222 (Office of the Massachusetts Secretary of State, 1984). "Former Senator Henry Parkman of Boston opposed the Pillsbury proposal. Parkman said that he was 'old fashioned enough to hope that the words 'General Court' may be retained."

21. Mass. Const. art. XLVIII, ch. IV.

22. Barbara Anderson, *Celebrating Prop 2 1/2* , A23 Boston Globe, Nov 4, 2005.

23. Mass. Gen. Law ch. 51 §22 c.

24. Mass. Gen. Law ch. 53 §19.

25. Fred Hanson, *Medical Marijuana-Timilty: No Stance Yet on Pot Question,* Patriot Ledger, 9 (Oct. 24, 2006).

26. Mass. Const. Article XLVIII, The Referendum, ch. III.

27. Patrick Scanlon and Steven T. James, *Legislative Procedure in the General Court of Massachusetts,* 52 (Senate Clerk and Clerk for the House of Representatives, 2003). This booklet is held in the collection of the State Library.

28. Mass. Gen. Law ch. 9, §§ 1-20A.

29. Mass. Gen. Law ch. 211 §§ 1-28.

30. Massachusetts possesses an elder sibling's strong psychological need to be first in many areas, for evidence of this see: *Famous Firsts in Massachusetts,* from the Secretary of the Commonwealth's Citizen Information Service at http://www.sec.state.ma.us/cis/cismaf/mf4.htm.

31. *$Laws for Sale$: A Study of Money in the 1994 Ballot Questions,* 3 (Money and Politics Project, Commonwealth Coalition).

32. *In re Municipal Suffrage of Women,* 160 Mass. 586, 587 (Mass. 1894). In this advisory opinion the Supreme Judicial Court stated: "By the constitution of Massachusetts, as originally adopted, not only were the powers of the representatives of the people limited, but the powers of the people themselves were limited."

33. *Supra, Debates of the Constitutional Convention of 1917*; Vol. II is devoted to the initiative and referendum debates alone.

34. *Supra, Leading the Way,* at 211-215.

35. *Id.*, at 215. Quoting Raymond L. Bridgman on another issue before the convention: "Though the official record cannot show the truth, yet the real cause of the collision over the Anti-aid Amendment was the antagonism of Catholic and Protestant."

36. *Id.*

37. Executive Department, Council Chamber, *The Official Returns of the Votes and Blanks Cast Upon the Nineteen Constitutional Amendments Submitted by the Constitutional Convention and Adopted at the State Election, November 5, 1918.* 4 Mass. L. Q. 120 (1918-1919).

38. Mass. Elections Division, index to initiatives and referendums on file at the State Archives.

39. Robert G. Miller, *Legislative History of Petitions for Initiative Petition Amendments to the Massachusetts Constitution, 1933 to 1992,* 3 (1993). This unpublished study is in the collection of the State Library for Massachusetts.

40. John McDonough, *Taking the Laws into Their Own Hands,* 7 Cmmw. 52-62, (MassINC, Fall 2002).

41. *An Overview of Massachusetts Statewide Ballot Measures: 1919-2004* (Office of the Secretary of State) http://www.sec.state.ma.us/ele/elebalm/balmpdf/balmtype.pdf.

42. Mass. Elections Division, initiative and referendum petitions 1919 to 2002, on file at the State Archives.

43. Mass. Office of Campaign and Political Finance, *Statewide Ballot Question Spending Reaches Almost $10 Million*, Press Release (Dec. 22, 1998) www.mass.gov/ocpf/pr_bqsp.pdf; and *Statewide Ballot Question Spending Exceeds $15Million*, Press Release (Dec. 20, 2000).

44. Andrew Ryan, *Wine Sale Question Nearing Record on Campaign Spending,* Boston Globe D4 (October 12, 2006).

45. Mass. Secretary of the Commonwealth, *State Ballot Question Petitions,* http://www.sec.state.ma.us/ele/elepdf/state_ballot_question_petitions.pdf (April 2005); and Mass. Atty. Gen., *The Initiative Process, 2005-2006: An Overview for Interested Members of the Public,* http://www.ago.state.ma.us/sp.cfm?pageid=1246 (2006).

46. *Supra, The Initiative Process, 2005-2006.*

47. Email from Marissa Goldberg of Senator Edward Augustus' office to the author, (October 27, 2006, 11:31 a.m. EDT) (copy on file with the author): "As a Fox News Undercover report recently revealed, I strongly believe that unscrupulous, out-of-state paid signature gathering firms have hijacked the Commonwealth's initiative petition process. I am deeply concerned that paid signature-gatherers are using unscrupulous tactics–including "bait and switch" fraud–to deceive voters and use any means necessary to acquire the signatures they need to push their narrow agenda on Massachusetts citizens." Senator Augustus is the Senate chair of the Joint Committee on Election Law.

48. The status of this bill was found at http://www.mass.gov/legis/184history/s02251.htm. This bill will likely die in committee if it is not enacted before the end of the session January 2, 2007.

49. Mass.Gen. Laws ch. 55 §1.

50. Kenneth G. Morton and Papalinka Paradise, editors, *Massachusetts Political Almanac, 2005 edition* 554 (Center for Leadership Studies 2005).

51. *Supra*, Mass. H. 5435 at 2.

52. *Id.* at 22.

53. *In re Municipal Suffrage to Women*, 160 Mass. 586, at 587; "But the model adopted was in other respects the English form of government. While a purely democratic form of government existed in the towns of New England, few if any persons seem to have been in favor of such a form of government for the state." Also, at 589, "Apparently, it was thought that the persons selected for the executive, legislative, and judicial offices, . . . , would be men of good character and intelligence, of some experience in affairs, and of some independence of judgment, and would have a better opportunity of obtaining information, taking part in discussion, and carefully considering conflicting opinions, than the people themselves; . . . ."

54. *The Farmer's Almanac,* Yankee Publishing Inc., Dublin, N.H.

55. *Supra, Leading the Way,* chapter 48, "Constitutional Reform," at 211.

56. *Supra, Taking the Laws into Their own Hands,* at 62, McDonough's closing anticipates the conclusions of the Sunday Globe article four years later cited in this article's final paragraph. However, McDonough is more favorably disposed to keeping intiatives and referendums in their current form: "It's hard to see how we could make the Massachusetts ballot-initiative process better. But it's easy to see how we could make it worse."

57. F.W.G. *The Significance of the Returns,* 4 Massachusetts Law Quarterly 140 (1918-1919). "The people of Massachusetts have got the I. and R. and they have got to learn to live under it and make it work as wisely as they can. In order to do this, it is necessary for most of them to learn more about the structure of their government and how it works than they know today. This is true of all of us at the bar as well as the rest of the community."

58. Your author picked a spare copy out of the recyclable bin at the town's transfer station, (the town dump), that Saturday.

59. Bruce Mohl, *Law Allowing Wine in State Food Stores is Rejected,* Boston Globe, November 8, 2006; Lane Lambert, *Question 2: Multiple Listing of Candidates is Soundly Rejected,* Patriot Ledger, November 8, 2006; Lane Lambert, *Question 3: Effort to Allow Child Care Union Comes Closest,* Patriot Ledger, November 8, 2006.

60. In Massachusetts liquor is sold at a retail store known as a package store, or more familiarly called a "packie."

61. Mass. Office of Campaign and Political Finance, *$15.3 Million Spent on Statewide Ballot Questions in 2006* Press Release (December 14, 2006) www.mass.gov/ocpf/bq2006.pdf.

62. Tamara Rice, *Nonbinding Question: Decriminalizing Marijuana Favored,* Patriot Ledger, November 9, 2006. "Voters would rather have a little dope in their pockets than wine in the supermarkets."

63. Andrea Estes and Scott Helman, *Legislature Again Blocks Same-Sex Marriage Ban: Lawmakers Recess without Voting on Constitutional Amendment,* Boston Globe, A1, November 10, 2006. "Shortly after the vote, (Governor) Romney called a press conference and blasted the 109 lawmakers who voted to recess, saying, 'we have witnessed the triumph of arrogance over democracy'."

64. Dave Denison, *Coming to Grips with the Grass Roots,* Boston Sunday Globe, K4, December 10, 2006.

Initiatives and Referenda in Michigan: A Research Guide

Tammy R. Pettinato

INTRODUCTION

Initiatives and referenda are a key part of the democratic process in Michigan. In the 2006 election alone, there were four initiatives and one referendum on the ballot; three of which received the necessary majority to become a part of the Michigan Constitution.[1] Yet researching the I&R process is not a simple task, and little has been written to ease this burden. The purpose of this article is to address this gap in the literature, and to provide a starting point for those interested in researching I&R in Michigan. Below, I give an overview of the history of I&R in Michigan, a general outline of how the process works, and a selected list of resources, both primary and secondary, that provide valuable information for researchers seeking to explore this important part of Michigan's legislative system.

HISTORY

The history of direct government in Michigan can be traced as far back as the state's first constitution, written in 1835, which required majority electoral approval for the calling of a constitutional convention and the passing of a constitutional amendment.[2] However, the first provision for initiatives and referenda did not appear until 1908 when an indirect constitutional initiative was adopted by a mere three votes following several years of popular agitation.[3] The debate over the reform was highly contentious, pitting urban dwellers of both major political parties, who argued that initiatives and referenda make government more democratic, against mostly Republican rural voters who feared that a contemporary flood of migration to the cities would leave them outnumbered, thus causing their concerns to be overshadowed by a dominant majority with excessive control in law-making.[4] The result was an amendment that, in part because of a 20% petition requirement and the reservation of veto rights to the legislature, soon raised the ire of reformers who pushed for a less restrictive version.[5]

They got it in 1913 when a new initiative and referendum amendment was passed easing petition requirements and providing for more direct voter input.[6] Since then, Michigan's I&R process has gone through few significant changes, with the exception of a 1941 constitutional amendment giving state election officials the power to regulate the petitioning process and insure that signatures were legitimate.[7] Note, however, that the 1963 constitution did contain revisions, and it is this constitution that should be consulted for current research.[8]

BASICS OF MICHIGAN I&R PROCESS

Michigan's constitution provides for indirect statutory initiatives,[9] popular referenda,[10] and direct constitutional initiatives.[11] Procedures for filing initiatives and referenda are outlined both by the constitution, and, in more detail, by statute. Both the statutory initiative and the referendum have important subject limits. The statutory initiative may only be used to propose laws that the legislature itself could constitutionally enact.[12] Thus, it often falls to the courts to determine the appropriate material for this measure.[13] The referendum may not be used on appropriations acts or "to meet deficiencies in state funds."[14]

Petitions must be sponsored by a person qualified to vote in Michigan.[15] They must be formatted in accordance with detailed statutory requirements, and the Secretary of State has authority to issue additional requirements as to form.[16] Staff at the Michigan Department of State's Bureau of Elections will consult with interested parties as to proper format and submit the petition form to the Board of State Canvassers for approval.[17] Note that this pre-approval is *not* required; however, it is recommended by the Secretary of State to avoid having a petition thrown out due to formatting defects.[18] Furthermore, the Board will not review the substance of the initiative or referendum, and the Secretary of State recommends that sponsors obtain legal counsel in drafting the language of the petition.[19]

The requirements for obtaining signatures and filing forms varies depending on the type of initiative or referendum in question. For an initiative to amend the constitution, the petition must be signed by registered electors comprising at least 10% of the total vote in the last gubernatorial election.[20] The petition must be filed with the Bureau of Elections "at least 120 days before the election at which the proposed amendment is to be voted upon."[21] For initiatives on legislation, the petition and filing requirements are 8% and 160 days respectively, and for referenda 5% and 90 days, respectively.[22] After receipt, the Board of State Canvassers will verify that the petition contains the required number of signatures and that the signers are registered voters.[23] The process after a petition has been accepted also varies depending on the type of initiative or referendum in question. Initiatives to amend the constitution are submitted directly to the populace at the next general election that occurs at least 120 days after filing.[24] To be adopted, a proposed amendment must garner a majority of votes, and if it does, it will take effect after 45 days.[25] Referenda are also submitted directly to the populace, and the law that is addressed will not be effective until approved by a majority of voters.[26]

As to legislative initiatives, the legislature has 40 session days to approve or reject the proposal.[27] If the proposed law is not enacted, it goes to the people for vote in the next general election.[28] The legislature may also propose a competing version, and both will be put on the ballot.[29] Once again, a majority vote is required for passage.[30]

After voter approval, a legislative initiative or referenda "takes effect 10 days after the official declaration of the vote."[31] An adopted initiative may not be either vetoed by the Governor or amended or repealed by the legislature unless by a three-fourths vote in both houses.[32] Adopted referenda, on the other hand, may be amended by the legislature.[33]

RESEARCHING I&R IN MICHIGAN

As in other states, researching I&R in Michigan can be a cumbersome process. Researchers will likely find themselves consulting a number of different resources and will have to adjust their approach depending on the type of I&R research they are conducting, the date of a specific proposal, whether or not it was enacted into law, and other considerations. I have outlined some resources below that will be helpful in beginning a research project on I&R in Michigan. I have divided the list between state publications and secondary resources, and further subdivided each of these categories into print and Web resources. However, it should be noted that these resources are only a starting place and each individual research project may take the searcher in new, and possibly unforeseen, directions.

I. State Publications

A. Print Resources

The Michigan Manual. Legislative Service Bureau. Lansing: State of Michigan. 2006.

The Michigan Manual is a biennial state publication containing information on various aspects of government in the state, including elections. The 2005-2006 edition contains a brief overview of the I&R process, separate tables showing all initiatives, referenda, and constitutional amendments (with those proposed by petition identified in a "method of proposal column") from 1964-2005, and a table breaking down the vote for each ballot measure by county. I&R that were ultimately enacted are also cross-referenced with the Michigan Compiled Laws, the official legislative code of the state. The Michigan Manual is also available online back to 1999-2000 at the Michigan Legislature's Web page, at http://www.legislature.mi.gov (see below).

Public and Local Acts of the Legislature of the State of Michigan. Legislative Service Bureau. Lansing: State of Michigan.
The *Public and Local Acts of the Legislature of the State of Michigan* are annual official state publications covering enacted legislation and other selected documents from a given session of the Michigan Congress. They have been published under this title since the 1915 session, and older copies are available under the title *Laws of Michigan*. These volumes include the full text of initiatives, referenda, and constitutional amendments that were passed during a given session, where applicable. Especially valuable for I&R researchers is that beginning in the 1972 volume, years in which an initiated law were enacted have the heading "Initiated Law" in the table of contents. Constitutional Amendments are under a separate heading, but "compiler's notes" identify them as being initiated by the electorate. Those researching I&R prior to 1972 will need to know the year and subject matter of a given act in order to use the subject index provided in each volume. These volumes are also available online back to 1998 via the Michigan Legislature's Web site, at http://www.legislature.mi.gov (see below).

Journal of the Senate of the State of Michigan. Lansing: State of Michigan.
Published since 1871, the *Journal of the Senate of the State of Michigan* is an official state publication covering the daily activities of the Michigan Senate. These are useful for obtaining the full text of legislative initiative petitions, including those that were not ultimately enacted. In years in which a petition was initiated, the heading "initiative petition" appears in the general index. This information is also included in the official journal of the House of Representatives, both of which are included back to 2003 on the Michigan legislature Web site http://www.legislature.mi.gov (see below), but using the index in the *Senate Journal* is slightly easier. Note that initiatives to enact a constitutional amendment are not covered.

Michigan Compiled Laws Annotated. St. Paul: West Pub. Co. 2003; Michigan Compiled Laws Service. Charlottesville, VA: LexisNexis. 2001.

The *Michigan Compiled Laws Annotated* is a Thomson West publication, which includes both Michigan Statutes and the Michigan Constitution. Historical Notes, Cross References, Law Review and Journal Commentaries, Library References, and Notes of Court Decisions are provided. Although the heading "Initiative and Referendum" is included in the General Index, statutes or amendments that were adopted through the I&R process are not identified here. Instead this information is in the "Historical Notes" for given laws and amendments. The *Michigan Compiled Laws Service* has similar information using slightly different headings, although the topic "Initiative and Referendum" is not included in the general index.

B. Web Resources

Michigan Secretary of State, *at* http://www.michigan.gov/sos.

Under the heading "Elections in Michigan," the Michigan Secretary of State's Web site contains the complete text of current statewide ballot proposals, including the date of proposal and the date the proposal was accepted by the Board of State Canvassers. The Web site also publishes three tables including all constitutional amendments, initiatives and referenda since 1963. Each table includes the subject, the date of the election, the letter or number of the proposal, the result of the vote, and the total vote count for and against. The constitutional amendments and referenda tables also include a section on the method of proposal. However, these tables do not include the full text of the ballot proposals. The Secretary of State's Web site also publishes an extensive guide to proposing an initiative or referenda including current signature requirements and filing deadlines.

Michigan State Legislature, *at* http://www.legislature.mi.gov.

The Michigan State Legislature's Web site has an "Initiatives" heading that contains materials from the House and Senate journals regarding legislative initiatives. Currently, it only goes back to 2006.

II. Secondary Sources

A. Print Resources

Grossman, Barbara F., "The Initiative and Referendum Process: The Michigan Experience." *Wayne Law Review* **28 (1981-1982): 77-136.**
Barbara Grossman's article contains a comprehensive overview of the I&R process in Michigan. Included are discussions of the appropriate subject matter for the I&R process, procedural requirements, federal constitutional issues, legislative implementation of state constitutional requirements, and the administrative process of verifying signatures and certifying petitions. There is also extensive discussion of court cases that have interpreted the constitutional and statutory requirements involved in each of these areas as well as some discussion of the rationale behind various requirements.

Daniel S. McHargue, *Direct Government in Michigan: Initiative, Referendum, Recall, Amendment, and Revision in the Michigan Constitution* **(Lansing: State of Michigan, 1961).**
Daniel McHargue's study of direct government in Michigan contains a wealth of valuable information on the history of I&R in Michigan as well as the central concerns surrounding its continued use. It also contains tables of all initiatives and referenda proposed in Michigan from 1914 to 1961, including a brief description, the vote count, and whether or not initiative or referenda was enacted. Especially interesting for historical research are relevant excerpts from the 1908 constitution as it was revised in 1913, which show the extensive procedural requirements originally contained in the I&R provisions that were removed in the 1963 constitution and left to statute. McHargue also analyzes the I&R process in other states and makes recommendations as to its continued use in Michigan.

Michigan Law and Practice Encyclopedia. **2nd ed. Newark, NJ: Mathew Bender & Company, Inc. 2003.**
The *Michigan Law and Practice Encyclopedia* includes general information on I&R in Michigan as well as very basic historical information on its development, with citations to other sources. The relevant heading and section numbers are Statutes §§141-145. However, individual laws and amendments that were adopted by the I&R process

are not explicitly identified either in the index or in their individual entries.

Campbell, Henry M., "The Initiative and Referendum." Michigan Law Review 10 (1911-1912): 427-436.
Henry Campbell's article was published during the height of the debates surrounding whether to revise the 1908 Michigan constitution to ease the I&R requirements. The article offers an interesting historical perspective on the concerns of the opposition. Campbell argued that I&R could ultimately lead to chaos in the legislative process by giving too much power to the temporary whims of majorities and worried about the quality of the laws that would be introduced by people lacking the qualifications of elected legislators.

B. Web Resources

Citizen's Research Council of Michigan, *at* http://www.crcmich.org/.
The Citizen's Research Council of Michigan is an independent, nonpartisan, non-profit research organization founded in 1916 "to bring about sound governmental policy through factual research." The Council publishes reports (longer, in-depth analysis), memorandums (short reports or summaries of longer reports), and notes (quick reference guides on public policy issues), most of which it provides free of charge. These include analyses of initiatives and referenda, although these are not catalogued separately from other research papers. Abstracts of these documents are searchable by subject or year, going back to 1916. Some documents are available online, and those that are not may be obtained by emailing the Web site. This site also includes extensive analysis of all ballot issues from the most recent election including ballot language and the text of the proposed amendment or initiative.

The Inter-University Consortium for Political and Social Research, *at* http://www.icpsr.umich.edu/.
The Inter-University Consortium for Political and Social Research is a member-based organization housed in the University of Michigan's Institute for Social Research that collects a vast quantity of social science research which is made available to all member colleges and universities via subscription. It includes a collection of referenda and primary election materials for each state, and the Michigan portion

has data from 1968 to 1990. Here, the researcher can find the text of proposed measures, which election they were on the ballot, and the outcome, including voter tallies, of the vote.

Initiative and Referendum Institute, *at* https://www.iandrinsitute.org. The Michigan section of the Initiative and Referendum Institute's Web site contains a valuable collection of information on the I&R process in Michigan. Included is an overview of the history of I&R in the state, information on the types of I&R offered, and a summary of the process for getting a measure on the ballot. Perhaps most valuable to the researcher is a table listing all of the statewide initiatives from 1914-2000, which includes the year of the proposal, the measure number where applicable, the type of initiative proposed (constitutional or legislative), the subject matter, a description of the initiative, and whether it passed or failed.

Michigan Public Radio, *at* http://www.michiganradio.org. Michigan Public Radio offers a searchable database of broadcasts, some of which address initiatives and referenda. Note, however, that you must have the name of the initiative or referenda in question in order to be able to find an appropriate broadcast.

The Michigan Daily, *at* http://www.michigandaily.com. *The Michigan Daily* is the main student newspaper at the University of Michigan. Student journalists often write articles and opinion pieces on state government, including proposed initiatives and referenda. The online archives are searchable from 2000 to the present.

NOTES

1. Michigan Department of State Web site, http://www.michigan.gov/sos. The three initiatives that passed all proposed constitutional amendments. The fourth initiative, which didn't pass, was a legislative initiative.
2. Daniel S. McHargue, *Direct Government in Michigan: Initiative, Referendum, Recall, Amendment, and Revision in the Michigan Constitution* (Lansing: State of Michigan, 1961), 17.
3. McHargue, *Direct Government in Michigan*, 22.
4. McHargue, *Direct Government in Michigan*, 22.
5. McHargue, *Direct Government in Michigan*, 19.
6. McHargue, *Direct Government in Michigan*, 19.
7. McHargue, *Direct Government in Michigan*, 23.

8. *Michigan Law and Practice Encyclopedia.* 2nd ed. Newark, NJ: Mathew Bender & Company, Inc. 2003. 527-529.

9. Mich. Const. art II, § 9.

10. Mich. Const. art II, § 9.

11. Mich. Const. art XII, § 2.

12. Mich. Const. art II, § 9.

13. Barbara F. Grossman, "The Initiative and Referendum Process: The Michigan Experience." 28 Wayne L. Rev. 77 (1981-1982).

14. Mich. Const. art II, § 9.

15. Mich. Comp. L. Ann. § 168.544c (West 2003).

16. Mich. Comp. L. Ann. §§ 168.482, 168.544c, 168.544d (West 2003).

17. Mich. Dept. of State. 2006. Bureau of Elections. *Initiative and Referendum Petitions,* http://www.michigan.gov/sos.

18. Mich. Dept. of State. 2006. Bureau of Elections. *Initiative and Referendum Petitions*, http://www.michigan.gov/sos.

19. Mich. Dept. of State. 2006. Bureau of Elections. *Initiative and Referendum Petitions*, http://www.michigan.gov/sos.

20. Mich. Const. art XII, § 2.

21. Mich. Const. art XII, § 2.

22. Mich. Const. art II, § 9; Mich. Comp. L. Ann. § 168.471 (West 2003).

23. Mich. Comp. L. Ann. § 168.476 (West 2003).

24. Mich. Const. art XII, § 2.

25. Mich. Const. art XII, § 2.

26. Mich. Const. art II, § 9.

27. Mich. Const. art II, § 9.

28. Mich. Const. art II, § 9.

29. Mich. Const. art II, § 9.

30. Mich. Const. art II, § 9.

31. Mich. Const. art II, § 9.

32. Mich. Const. art II, § 9.

33. Mich. Const. art II, § 9.

Researching Initiatives and Referendums: A Guide for Mississippi

Stacey A. Lane

history, legislature, legislative branch, judicial branch, executive branch, local government, county clerk, clerk of the court, constitutional amendment, term limits

HISTORICAL BACKGROUND OF I&R IN MISSISSIPPI

Mississippi is unique among all the other states in several ways when it comes to the initiatives and referendum process. Mississippi is the only state to have first gained the initiatives and referendum process and then lost it through a legal technicality.[1] When political pressure mounted on the Mississippi legislature in the late 1980s and early 90s, the Hospitality State was the last state in the Union to adopt an initiatives and referendum process for its citizens.[2]

The Mississippi Legislature, in 1914, adopted the first initiative and referendum procedure.[3] A detailed and extensive history of the original 1914 initiative and referendum process and its eventual failure at the hands of Mississippi Supreme Court is available in *State ex rel. Moore v. Molpus*, 578 So.2d 624 (Miss. 1991). The initial version of the initiatives and referendum grant of power was extensive, straightforward and relatively easy for a citizen to meet its requirements. An initiative petition, either for statutory or constitutional amendments, called for the signatures of 7,500 qualified voters to be placed on the ballot for the entire state.[4]

> A Referendum petition would have required only 6,000 signatures and would have had to be filed within ninety days after the adjournment of the legislative session during which the questioned measure has been passed.[5]

Furthermore, the statute held that the Governor could not veto an initiative or referendum approved in this fashion. If a measure were to be subsequently repealed or amended, it could only be changed by a vote of three-fourths of the members of each house of the legislature.[6] Unfortunately, this straightforward and powerful grant of direct democracy did not last long in Mississippi.

Howie v. Brantley, 74 So. 662 (Miss. 1917) saw the constitutional challenge of the validity of the initiatives and referendum amendment.[7] In 1917, through *Howie* the Mississippi Supreme Court upheld the initiatives and referendum amendment.[8] Five years later a number of citizens filed an initiative petition seeking to reduce the $40,000 annual salary of the State Revenue Agent, Stokes V. Robertson.[9]

Understandably motivated that his pay not be cut, Revenue Agent Stokes V. Robertson pulled out all the stops. He argued that the petition attacking his salary must fail because the I & R Amendment had been submitted to the voters in a form that offended Section 273's mandate that such amendments shall 'be submitted in such manner and form that the people may vote for or against each amendment separately. . .'[10]

The case found its way back to the Mississippi Supreme Court. Going against s*tare decisis* and their decision from five years earlier, the Court reversed itself and held the initiatives and referendum amendment void on the grounds it was "in law more than one amendment."[11] The amendment was deemed to be "contrary to Section 273, had been submitted in a form which combined in one measure the disparate subjects of legislative enactments and constitutional amendments."[12]

While officially defeated by Mississippi's highest court, the debate over Mississippi's initiatives and referendum would continue until the 1990s. In the 1991 *Moore v. Molpus* case, the State Attorney General and two representatives of the Mississippi legislature attempted to have the Mississippi Supreme Court revisit and overturn the *Power* decision.[13] The plaintiff's hoped to repeal the state's constitutional ban on all lotteries. The Court refused.[14] Again, the initiative and referendum process experienced defeat in Mississippi. The issue would remain alive in the legislature and in popular support until the successful passage of Senate Concurrent Resolution No. 616 during the 1992 regular session.[15]

The initiative and referendum revival had been a widely discussed campaign issue in the early 1990s.[16] After passing in the ballot with over 70% approval by voters in 1992 fall elections, the initiative and referendum process was again available to the citizens of Mississippi.[17] The legislation was largely recognized as a progressive government reform.[18] In the 1993 Legislative Session, the Mississippi House and Senate passed enabling legislation for the initiative and referendum process as called for by the newly amended constitution.[19] The new laws applicable for the initiative and referendum process would be available under Miss. Code Ann. § 23-17-1. The new constitutional amendment read in part: "The Legislature may enact laws to carry out the provisions of this section, but shall in no way restrict or impair the provisions of this section or the powers herein reserved to the people."[20]

THE I&R PROCESS IN MISSISSIPPI

The John C. Stennis Institute of Government at Mississippi State University published another edition of a handbook about the initiative and referendum process entitled *Mississippi's Initiative and Referendum: A Primer.*[21] In this primer the author observed that the Mississippi initiative and referendum procedure is a difficult process.[22] First, it requires the second highest signature threshold in the country.[23] Second, the "geographic distribution requirement of those signatures is far more difficult to meet than any other state."[24] Third, it has a "super-majority" voting requirement unlike any other state.[25] Fourth, certain topics of law are off limits. For instance, the Bill of Rights of the Mississippi Constitution, the Mississippi Public Employees' Retirement System, right to work laws, and the initiative process itself, cannot be changed with the initiative or referendum process.[26]

Between the constitutional amendment and the legislative enactment that prescribe the details of the initiative process there are at least nineteen separate steps that must be observed before an initiative can make it to the referendum stage in Mississippi.[27] The Mississippi Secretary of State has prepared a document for citizens to help educate them on the complicated initiatives and referendum process.[28]

To start the process, a sponsor must draft a proposed initiative. Once drafted, the sponsor must file with the Mississippi Secretary of State a typed copy of the proposed initiative. With the proposed initiative, an affidavit claiming that the sponsor is a registered voter in Mississippi must be included. The Secretary of State will then forward a copy of the potential initiative and its text to the "Revisor of the Statutes," an attorney in the Attorney General's office.[29] Within ten working days of receipt of the text, the Revisor makes all advisory recommendations to the sponsor regarding the initiative language. The Revisor of the Statutes also issues a Certificate of Review to the sponsor that the initiative has been reviewed. The sponsor is free to accept or ignore any of the recommendations or revisions from the Revisor of the Statutes.[30]

Within fifteen working days, as called for by statute, the Secretary of State will notify the sponsor that the Secretary of State has submitted the initiative to the Revisor of the Statutes. The sponsor must then submit both the initiative measure, including revisions if necessary, and the Certificate of Review to the Secretary of State. The Secretary of State assigns the proposal a serial number, and then forwards a copy of the initiative text to the Attorney General.[31]

Within the next seven days of receiving the initiative from the Secretary of State, the Attorney General will draft the title of the proposal that will appear on the ballot and a summary of the proposed initiative. The ballot title will not exceed twenty words and the ballot summary will not be longer than seventy-five words.[32] The Attorney General files both the title and summary with the Secretary of State, who will then notify the sponsor by certified mail of the exact language in the ballot title and summary.

Within ten days of the title and summary being filed by the Attorney General, the Secretary of State will publish "such title and summary in a newspaper or newspapers of general circulation throughout the State of Mississippi."[33]

> If any person is dissatisfied with the ballot title or summary formulated by the Attorney General, he or she may, within five (5) days from the publications of the ballot title and summary by the office of the Secretary of State, appeal to the circuit court of the First Judicial District of Hinds County by petition setting forth the measure, the title or summary formulated by the Attorney General, and his or her objections to the ballot title or summary and requesting amendment of the title or summary by the court.[34]

The ruling of the Hinds County court will be final. There is no right of appeal once a decision has been rendered.

Once the ballot title and ballot summary have been finalized, the sponsor may begin collecting signatures. Under Mississippi law, signatures can only be collected on paper of "good writing quality and not less than eight and one-half (8-1/2) inches in width and not less than fourteen (14) inches in length."[35] Each petition, in order to be qualified, will have the full text of the initiative on it with language that has been approved by the Secretary of State.[36] A sample petition and its requirement can be found in Miss. Code Ann. §23-17-19.

Finally, the initiative text must include a cost analysis that will list the amount and source(s) of revenue needed to implement the initiative. If the initiative requires a cut in state revenue or a reallocation from current programs, the initiative text must state the program(s) where funding will be cut or eliminated in order to properly implement the initiative.[37] Additionally, if the voters reject an initiative proposal, no similar proposal can be submitted to the people for two years after the date of election at which it was rejected.[38]

So far in the initiative process, a sponsor has dealt with the executive and possibly judicial branches of Mississippi State government. Yet another difficult hurdle to overcome in the Mississippi initiative process concerns signatures. The requirement in Miss. Code Ann. §23-17-17(2) that only qualified Mississippi electors may circulate petitions or obtain signatures for them, was found unconstitutional in *Term Limits Leadership Council, Inc. v. Clark*, 984 F. Supp. 470 (S.D. Miss. 1997). Nevertheless, there is still a distribution requirement for signatures written into statute. Twenty percent of signatures must come from each of the five congressional districts. If less than twenty percent of the certified signatures are submitted from any of the five congressional districts, the entire petition will be invalid.[39] Under statutory authority, the collection of signatures must take place over no more than twelve months.[40] The Mississippi Constitution outlines the number of signatures necessary.[41] The number of signatures needed is based on the gubernatorial vote in the prior statewide general election. A sponsor must obtain a minimum of twelve percent of the total number of votes cast for all candidates for governor in the last election.[42]

If the sponsor collects the required amount of signatures but fails to get the minimum number of signatures as broken down by congressional district, the petition will still be invalid.[43] For example, to put these numbers into perspective for the 2007 election cycle: If an initiative were to survive to the 2007 election cycle in Mississippi and make the ballot, a minimum of 91,673 certified signatures must be gathered; with at least 18,355 certified signatures from each of the five congressional districts.[44] The number of signatures required represents 12% of the total number of votes cast for governor in the last gubernatorial general election.[45] All signatures on the petitions must be certified by county circuit clerks as those of registered Mississippi voters.[46] Signatures are due for certification at least ninety days prior to the convening of the legislature to which it will be submitted.[47] A petition filed after the ninetieth day cannot be submitted until the next legislative session. Each of the county circuit clerks in Mississippi are responsible for verification of each and every signature collected within their districts. All collected signatures, in order to determine their validity, must be given to the clerks within each of the districts where the signatures were collected.[48]

Once the circuit clerks certify the specific number of legitimate signatures, the clerks must then return the petitions to the Secretary of State.[49] This process must be completed ninety days before the beginning of the upcoming legislative session.[50] In addition to the petition's signatures, the petitioner must pay the statutorily defined filing fee of

$500 to the Secretary of State.[51] According to Miss. Code Ann. §23-17-23, the Secretary of State is required by law to refuse the petition if: the filing fee is not paid, the petition is not on the correct form, there are not enough signatures or the signatures are in some way invalid, either at the statewide or at the congressional district level, and/or if the time for filing has expired. If one or more of these conditions occurs, the Secretary of State must mark the petition as "submitted" on the date received and hold it in case of appeal.[52]

Appeals for rejected petitions must be filed within ten days of the refusal by the Secretary of State to file the petition.[53] The Mississippi Supreme Court has jurisdiction. The petitioner "may apply to the Supreme Court for an order requiring the Secretary of State to bring the petition before the court and for a writ of mandamus to compel him to file it."[54]

If there is no appeal or if the Mississippi Supreme Court finds for the Secretary of State, by upholding the decision not to file the petition, then the petition will be destroyed and the process either ends or will start over again in the next petitioning cycle.[55] At this point the petitioner has involved the executive, judicial, and local county governments in the initiative process. Should the Secretary of State be required to accept and file the petition, the next step is to go to the third branch of state government, the legislature.

The Secretary of State is required to file a complete text and accompanying petitions of each qualified initiative measure with the Clerk of the House and the Secretary of the Senate on the first day of the regular legislative session.[56] The chief legislative budget officer will be directed to compile a fiscal analysis of the initiative and submit it to both chambers of the legislature.[57]

The legislature can take four different routes when presented with an initiative.[58] First, they can do nothing. Second, the legislature can adopt it by a majority vote in both the House and the Senate. Third, they can amend it through a majority vote of both chambers. Finally, they have the option of rejecting it and offering an alternative to the petition.

If the legislature ignores the measure, and does not act within four months, the measure goes directly to the ballot for a popular vote in the next statewide general election.[59] If the legislature chooses to adopt the measure, it will also go automatically to the next general election.[60] If the legislature amends the initiative measure in any way, the amended version will be given a modified serial number. The new serial number will be the same as the prior serial number but followed by an "A." The amended measure will also receive a new ballot title, a modified summary, and a new fiscal analysis by the chief budget officer.[61] In this particular case, both the original and the amended measures are eligible for the ballot as separate measures and are voted on separately.[62] "If conflicting initiatives or legislature alternatives are approved at the same election, the initiative or legislative alternative receiving the highest number of affirmative votes shall prevail."[63] Miss. Code Ann. §23-17-35 provides an example of an alternative initiative measure and illustrates what a voter would see on the ballot.

Finally, if the legislature decides to reject the petition and offer a completely different alternative, both pieces are placed on the ballot, but are tied together.[64] Like the amended versions of a measure, the alternative measure presented by the legislature will include a new serial number followed by an "A," a new summary, and have a new title and a new financial analysis accompanying it.[65] When the legislature offers an alternative measure, a voter is able to cast two separate votes when normally only one would take place. Voters would have to decide if they favor one of the two measures or if they reject both versions. Similarly, Miss. Code Ann. §23-17-37 provides a sample form for a rejected measure with a legislative alternative choice for voters.

Both the Mississippi Code and the Constitution contain similar provisions requiring that no more than five initiative measures will be presented to voters on a single ballot.[66] Petitions meeting all the requirements of the initiative process will be accepted on a first come, first serve basis for placement on the ballot.

When the Secretary of State makes the final decision as to which measures will be on the ballot, the Secretary of State is required to begin voter education.[67] The Secretary of State is required to produce an educational pamphlet containing all of the initiative measures and legislative alternatives.[68] The pamphlet will include ballot titles and summaries, arguments or explanations for and against each measure or alternatives limited to a maximum of three hundred (300) words, and a fiscal analysis of each prepared by the chief legislative budget officer."[69] Finally, the Secretary of State is required to hold at least one public hearing in each congressional district on each measure to be placed on the ballot and give public notice of the meeting at least thirty days before it is held.[70]

For an initiative measure to pass, including measures amended by the legislature, a majority vote greater than 50% is required. In addition, a majority vote in favor representing at least 40% of the total votes cast in the election is required.[71]

Yet this "super-majority" requirement is not the only statistical obstacle an initiative must face. Even if a measure garners the needed majority vote representing 40% of the all the votes cast, it could still face a defeat.[72]

If a second measure receives a higher majority vote in favor of it, while meeting the 40% requirement, the measure receiving the lower majority vote will fail.[73]

If the initiative passes in the referendum according to the tabulations above, it will take effect within thirty days of the election unless otherwise provided for in the text of the proposal.[74] If the measure is "rejected by a majority of the qualified electors voting thereon," the same or substantially same measure cannot be resubmitted for vote for two years.[75]

WHERE TO LOCATE DOCUMENTS RELATED TO MISSISSIPPI I&R RESEARCH

Mississippi Secretary of State, at http://www.sos.state.ms.us/.

As previously described, the primary sources that support the majority of this article include the General Laws of the State of Mississippi, 1992, Chapter 715, General Laws of the State of Mississippi, 1993, Chapter 514, section 273 of the Mississippi Constitution and the Mississippi Code Annotated §§23-17-1 through 23-17-61. In addition to the statutory and constitutional provisions that have been cited numerous times above, the Secretary of State offers information on the various initiatives that have been submitted.[76] The Secretary of State offers Web site visitors a brief overview of the initiative and referendum process in Mississippi as well as other press releases from the office.[77]

A number of initiative proposals have been filed with the Secretary of State and attempted to navigate through this complex and frustrating process.[78] The title and summaries of the initial initiatives, since the reauthorization of the initiatives process in 1992, are listed on the Secretary of State's Web site.[79] One initiative, commonly referred to as the "term limits initiative," has surmounted every hurdle up to placement on the ballot twice and failed both times.[80] Others have gotten stalled at different points along the way. Both initiative measures No. 13 and No. 20, which concerned lotteries, gaming and gambling, were ruled unconstitutional by Hinds County Circuit Court in 1998 and 1999 respectively.[81] At the time of this writing, one initiative, "Ultimate Human Life Amendment," is currently active and could possibly end up on the ballet in 2007.[82] A researcher looking for primary sources should start an inquest by contacting the Mississippi Secretary of State, Elections Division at 401 Mississippi St. Jackson, MS, 39201, P.O. Box 136, Jackson, MS 39205, Phone: (601) 359-6359, FAX (601) 359-5019.

While many primary source materials including the proposed initiatives, their current status, the sponsor contact information and other details are hosted on the Mississippi Secretary of State's Web site, more information could be accessed by contacting the state agency. Documents that might be useful to a researcher and available from the agency include the education pamphlets prepared by the Secretary of State and distributed to voters, the current signature requirements for preparing a petition based on the last gubernatorial general election, and voter statistics from prior elections. The Secretary of State has generally placed announcements pertaining to the initiative and referendum process in the *Clarion-Ledger*, a newspaper of general circulation within Mississippi. Publications such as notice of hearings, the text of initiatives and other requirements outlined in the statutes have generally been published in this newspaper.

The Initiative and Referendum Institute, at http://www.iandrinstitute. org/Mississippi.htm.

The Initiative & Referendum Institute, located at the University of Southern California, offers a wide range of resources across all states that have some form of initiative and referendum process. Its Web site in particular is useful for research concerning the initiative and referendum process in Mississippi.[83] On this Web site researchers can expect to find general background and historical information on the Mississippi initiative and referendum process, several secondary articles written about the process, information about current initiatives, information about past initiatives such as the term limits initiatives discussed above, and the basic steps in order to undertake an initiative campaign.

The John C. Stennis Institute of Government at Mississippi State University, at http://www.msgovt.org/policy.html.

> If the legislature needs a definitive study on the effects of a change in state law, a municipal government desires a salary survey, or an association of government officials requests training on the latest legal issues, the Institute responds with its wide variety of resources.[84]

The Stennis Institute of Government offers one of the more complete descriptions and studies of the Mississippi initiative and referendum process in its publication *Mississippi's Initiative and Referendum: A*

Primer and is cited several times in this article.[85] This particular Institute focuses on research and study of public policy issues ranging from the initiative process, to constitutional issues in Mississippi law to policies directed at natural disasters and the effects of Hurricane Katrina and would likely provide solid secondary resources for would-be researchers. Many of these studies are located on its Web site.[86]

CONCLUSION

Mississippi is unique among the states that offer an initiative and referendum process to its citizens. First, Mississippi is the only state to have first adopted an initiative and referendum and then lost it on a legal technicality. Second, Mississippi is the last state in the United States to implement an initiative and referendum. The citizens of Mississippi have only had access to the initiative process since 1992. Currently, there are over nineteen different, complex steps needed in order to see an initiative on the ballot. The main hurdles to overcome when utilizing the initiative process in Mississippi include:

1. The second highest signature threshold in the country.
2. The "geographic distribution requirement for the signatures.
3. A "super-majority" voting requirement unlike any other state.

Due to this difficult and demanding process only two initiatives have made it to the ballot. Both have failed at the ballot.

ANNOTATED BIBLIOGRAPHY

Primary Sources

General Laws of the State of Mississippi, 1992, Chapter 715
This chapter outlines the initial amendment and introduction of the initiative and referendum process to the Mississippi Constitution.

General Laws of the State of Mississippi, 1993, Chapter 514
This chapter provides the basis of the enabling legislation for the initiative and referendum process, which eventually became Mississippi Code Annotated §§23-17-1 through 23-17-61.

Mississippi Constitution, 1870, Article 15, Section 273
The portion of the Mississippi Constitution that contains the amendment to include initiative and referendum process as well as prescribes steps necessary in order to have an initiative placed on the ballot.

Mississippi Code Annotated §§23-17-1 through 23-17-61.
This section of the Mississippi Code contains the statutory authority authorizing the initiative and referendum process in Mississippi.

Mississippi Official and Statistical Register 1996-2002. Jackson, MS: Mississippi Secretary of State.
Statistics produced every four years that detail voter activities. This volume is important in the initiative and referendum process since the number of signatures needed for a petition will depend on the number of voters within the prior gubernatorial election.

Mississippi Official and Statistical Register 2002-2006. Jackson, MS: Mississippi Secretary of State.
Statistics produced every four years that detail voter activities. This volume is important in the initiative and referendum process since the number of signatures needed for a petition will depend on the number of voters within the prior gubernatorial election. These statistics would be needed to determine the number of signatures required for initiatives placed on the 2007 ballots.

Secondary Sources

John C. Stennis Institute of Government, *Mississippi's Initiative and Referendum: A Primer* 3 (Mississippi State University 1995), available at http://iandrinstitute.org/Studies.htm.
This article provides the most detailed and in-depth information regarding the initiative and referendum process in Mississippi. The Stennis Institute of Government provided an updated version of this article in 1995 which detailed the history of the initiative in Mississippi as well as outlined the numerous and complicated steps that a sponsor must follow in order to place a measure on the ballot. The article includes a chart in order to clarify the confusing process a citizen would need to take in order to initiate an initiative campaign.

Mark Garriga, *Initiative and Referendum in Mississippi: Dead Again?* 2 (Initiative and Referendum Institute 2004), available at http://iandrinstitute.org/Studies.htm.

Similar to the Stennis Institute article, Garriga's article offers another informative work explaining and clarifying the complicated initiative process in order to place an initiative on the Mississippi ballot. This article looked primarily at new legislation aim at curtailing the initiative process in Mississippi.

Mississippi Law Research Institute, *Report of Law Research on Initiative and Referendum Legislation S.C.R. 515* (The University of Mississippi Law Center, University of Mississippi 1978).
This older government publication details the history of the initiative movement in Mississippi starting in 1914 and follows the push for a new initiative process until 1978. This work provides a solid history of the original initiative process that Mississippi lost in 1922.

M. Dane Waters, *Initiative and Referendum Almanac* (Carolina Academic Press 2003).
While not specific to Mississippi, this work offers a detailed chapter on the initiative process in Mississippi, in addition to all other states who provide some form of initiative process. The Mississippi chapter provides the entire Article and Section of the Constitution that details the Mississippi initiative process, the full text of statutes concerning the initiative process and easy to read charts detailing the two measures that have been placed on the ballot, as well as a brief overview of the initiative process.

John W. Winkle III, *The Mississippi State Constitution: A Reference Guide* (Greenwood Press 1993).
This work details the Mississippi State Constitution and devotes a chapter that walks a reader step by step through Section 273, the section pertaining to the amendment procedure and the initiative process.

Zimmerman, Joseph F., *The Initiative: Citizen Law-Making.* (Praeger Publishers 1999).
While not specific to Mississippi, this work offers various comparisons of the initiative process across states, including Mississippi.

NOTES

1. M. Dane Waters, *Initiative and Referendum Almanac* 242 (Carolina Academic Press 2003).
2. *Id.*

Stacey A. Lane

3. 1914 Gen. Laws Miss. 520 (House Concurrent Resolution No. 24).
4. *State ex rel. Moore v. Molpus*, 578 So. 2d 624, 627 (Miss. 1991).
5. *Id.* at 627-628.
6. *Id.* at 628.
7. *Id.* at 629.
8. *Id.*
9. *Id.*
10. *Id.* Note: Section 273 within this paragraph refers to Miss. Const. art. XV, § 273.
11. *Id.* at 630.
12. *Power v. Robertson*, 93 So. 769, 777 (Miss. 1922).
13. *Moore*, 578 So. 2d at 627.
14. *Id.* at 644.
15. Waters, *supra* n. 1, at 242.
16. *Id.*
17. *Id.*
18. *Id.*
19. John C. Stennis Institute of Government, *Mississippi's Initiative and Referendum: A Primer* 3 (Mississippi State University 1995), available at http://www.iandrinstitute. org/New%20IRI%20Website%20Info/I&R%20Research%20and%20History/I&R% 20Studies/Stennis%20Institute%20-%20Mississippi's%20Initiative%20 and%20 Referendum%20A%20Primer%20IRI.pdf.
20. Miss. Const. art. XV, §273(13).
21. Stennis Institute of Government, *supra* n. 19.
22. *Id.* at 4.
23. *Id.* at 2.
24. *Id.*
25. *Id.*
26. Mark Garriga, *Initiative and Referendum in Mississippi: Dead Again?* 2 (Initiative and Referendum Institute 2004), available at http://www.iandrinstitute.org/ New%20IRI%20Website%20Info/I&R%20Research%20and%20History/I&R%20 Studies/ Garriga%20-%20Initiative%20and%20Referendum%20in%20Mississippi%20IRI. pdf. *See also* Miss. Const. art. XV, § 273(5)a-d.
27. Stennis Institute of Government, *supra* n. 19 at 2.
28. This document is available at the Secretary of State's homepage at http:// www.sos.state.ms.us/elections/initiatives/ as well as Initiative & Referendum Institute homepage at http://www.iandrinstitute.org/Mississippi.htm and is based on information compiled from M. Dane Waters works, *see* Waters, *supra* n. 1, at 249-250.
29. Miss. Const. art. XV, §273(4) and Miss. Code Ann. §23-17-1(3) (1972).
30. Miss. Code Ann. §23-17-5 (1972).
31. *Id.*
32. Miss. Code Ann. §23-17-9 (1972).
33. Miss. Code Ann. §23-17-11 (1972).
34. Miss. Code Ann. §23-17-13 (1972).
35. Miss. Code Ann. §23-17-17 (1) (1972).
36. Miss. Code Ann. §23-17-17 (2) (1972).
37. Miss. Const. art. XV, §273(4) and Miss. Code Ann. §23-17-1(3) (1972).
38. Miss. Const. art. XV, §273(11).
39. Miss. Const. art. XV, §273(3).
40. Miss. Code Ann. §23-17-3 (1972) & Miss. Code Ann. §23-17-23 (1972).

41. Miss. Const. art. XV, §273(3).
42. *Id.*
43. *Id.*
44. Mississippi Secretary of State, *Initiative Measure No. 23,* available at *http:// www.sos.state.ms.us/elections/Initiatives/initiative0023.asp.*
45. *Id.*
46. Miss. Code Ann. §23-17-21 (1972).
47. Miss. Code Ann. §23-17-3 (1972).
48. Miss. Code Ann. §23-17-21 (1972).
49. *Id.*
50. Miss. Code Ann. §23-17-3 (1972).
51. Miss. Code Ann. §23-17-23 (1972).
52. Miss. Code Ann. §23-17-23(e) (1972).
53. Miss. Code Ann. §23-17-25 (1972).
54. *Id.*
55. Miss. Code Ann. §23-17-27 (1972).
56. Miss. Const. art. XV, §273(6).
57. *Id.*
58. Miss. Code Ann. §23-17-29 (1972).
59. *Id.*
60. *Id.*
61. *Id.*
62. *Id.*
63. *Id.*
64. Miss. Code Ann. §23-17-31 (1972).
65. Miss. Code Ann. §23-17-33 (1972).
66. Miss. Code Ann. §23-17-39 (1972) & Miss. Const. art. XV, §273(9).
67. Miss. Code Ann. §23-17-45 (1972).
68. *Id.*
69. *Id.*
70. Miss. Code Ann. §23-17-45(2) (1972).
71. Miss. Code Ann. §23-17-37 (1972).
72. Miss. Const. art. XV, §273(8).
73. *Id.*
74. Miss. Const. art. XV, §273(10) & Miss. Code Ann. § 23-17-41 (1972).
75. Miss. Const. art. XV, §273(11) & Miss. Code Ann. § 23-17-43 (1972).
76. Mississippi Secretary of State, *Initiatives* at *http://www.sos.state.ms.us/elections/ Initiatives/index.asp.* Note: to navigate through the various proposed initiatives use the menu on the left hand side of the page.
77. Mississippi Secretary of State, *The Initiative Process in Mississippi: An Overview–Two citizen measures at different stages in process* at http://www.sos.state.ms. us/ed_pubs/PressReleases/Articles.asp?prno=1909&search=>.
78. Mississippi Secretary of State, *supra* n. 74.
79. *Id.*
80. Waters, *supra* n. 1, at 243.
81. Mississippi Secretary of State, *Initiative Measure No.13 & Initiative Measures No. 20* at http://www.sos.state.ms.us/elections/Initiatives/initiative0013.asp and http:// www.sos.state.ms.us/elections/Initiatives/initiative0020.asp.
82. Mississippi Secretary of State, *supra* n. 44.

83. Initiative & Referendum Institute, Mississippi, available at http://www.
iandrinstitute.org/Mississippi.htm.

84. John C. Stennis Institute of Government, *John C. Stennis Institute of Govern-ment Website*, available at http://www.msgovt.org/.

85. Stennis Institute of Government, *supra* n. 19.

86. John C. Stennis Institute of Government, *Policy and Research Publications*,
available at http://www.msgovt.org/policy.html.

Researching Initiatives and Referenda: A Guide for Missouri

Margaret McDermott

INTRODUCTION

At times during the 2006 election initiatives and referenda petitions overshadowed the election of both federal and state officials. In Missouri, Constitutional Amendment 2 dealing with stem cell research received national attention with well-known personalities speaking for and against the ballot initiative. A researcher will understandably ask what the drafters of the initiative, the Missouri Coalition for Life Saving Cures, intended by the measure which passed by a narrow 45,533 vote margin.[1] He will want to know in addition to the "official ballot title," the "fair ballot language," and the actual text, what other documents are available.

The legal researcher who has become accustomed to the numerous documents generated along the legislative process at both the federal and state level may expect such a paper trail in the state I&R process. To further complicate matters, Missouri permits people in third class cities with a commission form of government to draft petitions for initiatives or referenda on local ordinances.[2]

This guide is intended to assist researchers in obtaining a basic under-standing of the history and general principles of the I&R process. The discussion of the basics of the process in Missouri will provide the reader with citations to the relevant statutes and regulations as well as articles of the Missouri Constitution. The bibliographies for Internet and paper resources at the end of the article will provide the user with cita-tions to secondary sources which discuss how the I&R process has been used in Missouri, and how ballot initiatives have later been interpreted by the courts.

INITIATIVES

Frequently among voters there is confusion between initiatives and referenda. Initiatives may be defined as instances when the citizens of a state collect signatures on a petition in order to place advisory questions, statutes, or constitutional amendments on a ballot for the voters to adopt or reject.[3] To add to the confusion there are "direct initiative amend-ments" and "indirect initiative amendments." "Direct initiatives amend-ments" arise when a constitutional amendment is proposed by the people and placed directly on the ballot.[4] "Indirect initiative amend-ments" are when an amendment is proposed by the people, but must first be submitted to the state legislature before being placed on the ballot for consideration.[5]

In addition to initiative amendments some states provide for statutory initiatives. As with initiative amendments there are both "direct initiative statutes" and "indirect initiative statutes." A "direct initiative statute" is when a statute proposed by the people is placed directly on the ballot for approval or rejection.[6] An "indirect initiative statute" is when a statute proposed by the people must first be submitted to the state legislature before being placed on the ballot for approval or rejection.[7] Missouri law provides for direct initiatives in the case of both constitutional amendments and statutes.[8]

REFERENDA

In addition to the initiative process, many states provide for referenda in which laws and amendments proposed by the state legislature may be placed before the voters for approval or rejection. This is referred to in general terms as the "referendum process." Referenda may be further divided into two categories, the "popular referendum" and the "legislative referendum."[9] The "popular referendum," available in 24 states, is when people have the power to collect signatures on a petition allowing for legislation enacted by the state legislature to be referred to the voters for acceptance or rejection. The Missouri Constitution provides for "popular referenda."[10] The "legislative referendum," available in some form in all states, is when state legislators, elected officials, state agencies or departments submit to the voters constitutional amendments or statutes for approval or rejection.[11]

BRIEF HISTORY OF INITIATIVES
AND REFERENDA IN MISSOURI

The initiative and referenda process in Missouri was adopted as Article III, section 57 of the state constitution in November, 1908.[12] Traced by many historians such as Steven Piott to a belief among the citizens that popular control of government had been lost to special interests, the I&R movement was primarily the work of the Direct Legislation League of Missouri headed by St. Louis attorney Silas L. Moser.[13] In 1900 the first I&R bill was introduced in the House of the Missouri legislature and defeated in that chamber by a single vote. Four years later I&R legislation was approved by both houses of the state legislature, but rejected by a 53,000 vote margin.[14] In 1907 the Direct Legislation League of Missouri successfully lobbied the legislature and another I&R amendment was passed. This time the League coordinated a statewide campaign to better inform Missouri voters.[15] After a year of speeches and pamphlets, this effort was successful and in 1908 voters approved the first I&R process by 35,868 votes.[16]

BASICS OF MISSOURI'S INITIATIVE AND REFERENDA PROCESS

Missouri's initiative and referendum laws are typical of many states. The process includes both constitutional initiatives and referenda[17] and statutory initiatives and referenda.[18]

In order to place a statutory initiative on the ballot 5% of the eligible voters in each of the two-thirds of the congressional districts must sign the petition, which must be submitted four months prior to the election.[19] Constitutional initiatives, however, require 8% of the eligible voters in each of the two-thirds of the congressional districts.[20] The number of eligible voters is determined by the total vote for governor at the general election preceding the filing of the petition.[21] Initiatives are limited by statute to one subject.[22] The petition is submitted to the Secretary of State who determines compliance and verifies the signatures.[23] The Office of the Secretary of State is also required to submit to the Attorney General a "Fair Ballot Language" statement which explains what a vote for or a vote against the measure represents. The statement is also required to include a statement as to whether the initiative will have any impact on taxes.[24]

The referendum procedure is similar. Voters may order a vote on legislation when 5% of the eligible voters in each of two-thirds of the congressional districts request a vote within ninety days after the adjournment of the General Assembly that passed the bill.[25] Proposed statutes and constitutional amendments may also be submitted to the voters by a majority vote in both houses.[26]

LOCATING RELEVANT DOCUMENTS DEALING WITH MISSOURI INITIATIVES AND REFERENDA

Those attempting to locate documents generated in the initiative and referendum process will discover that secondary materials will be their most valuable resource. Newspapers and legal publications such as local bar journals and magazines may assist the researcher in documenting the entire process. Another valuable source will be organizations, such as the League of Women Voters, who monitor these state initiatives. The Web sites of the organizations supporting and opposing the initiative will also be helpful. For example, in the case of Missouri's controversial Constitutional Amendment 2, dealing with stem cell research, the Web sites of "Missourians for Lifesaving Cures" and "Missourians Against Human Cloning" will provide a wealth of documents and citations to additional sources. The question for the researcher to consider is will the information and documents remain available at this site after the election.

The information provided to the Secretary of State includes the name of the organization who submitted the petition and contact information for individuals involved in sponsoring and lobbying for the petition. This provides the researcher with valuable information and possible leads. As with initiatives, ballot measures referred to voters by the General Assembly may include an official summary statement and a fiscal note summary.[27] If the general assembly fails to provide a summary statement, one will be provided by the Secretary of State.[28] Fiscal notes and a fiscal note summary will be provided by the State Auditor if one is not provided by the General Assembly.[29]

RESEARCH TOOLS

M. Dane Waters, *Initiative and Referendum Almanac,* Durham, N.C.: Carolina Academic Press, 2003.
  This work is an extremely important and comprehensive guide to the initiative and referendum process. It includes discussions of the history of I&R, as well as numerous essays covering major reforms which may be attributed to the process. Of particular value is the state-by-state compilation of relevant laws and a checklist of steps required to utilize the process. This is a companion volume to *The Battle Over Citizen Lawmaking* edited by M. Dane Waters in 2001. That volume contains essays which discuss I&R regulations and the issues involved in their implementation.

Missouri Local Government Law, Jefferson City, MO: Missouri Bar, 2002.
  This desk book published by the Missouri Bar is a classic tool covering various aspects of local government law. Chapter Four includes a

discussion labeled "Initiative and Referendum." The section discusses general procedures for initiatives and referenda requested at the municipal level and sets out the various exceptions which exclude certain subjects from the process. Most importantly it provides citations to Missouri cases dealing with issues involving the exceptions which have been carved out by municipalities.

Missouri Time Limitations, Jefferson City, MO: Missouri Bar, 2006.
This Missouri Bar volume includes a helpful chart with all the important actions required in the I&R process. Along with each action it provides a citation to the appropriate statute, the time limit, and a statement about the point from which the time limit is computed. The section also includes comments by attorneys and citations to court decisions which have interpreted these time limitations.

Annotated Codes

Vernon's Annotated Missouri Statutes contains not only the relevant state statutes and state constitutional provisions, but also provides historical notes, cross references, citations to secondary sources, relevant West Topics and key numbers, and citations to court decisions. The general index to the set uses "Initiative and Referendum" to bring together statutes and constitutional provisions.

The *Missouri Code of State Regulations* contains the regulations from the Missouri Secretary of State regarding the Signature Verification Procedures for Initiatives and Referenda[30] and Processing Procedures for Initiatives and Referenda.[31]

Digests and Encyclopedias

West's Missouri Digest 2d published by Thomson/West organizes Missouri case law into 414 topics. The Descriptive Word volumes and the Key Word volumes use both "Initiative" and "Referendum" to refer users to Missouri cases. The most relevant topics are *States*–Key Number 12, 13, 73; *Statutes*–Key Numbers 301-327 and 341-367; *Elections*–Key Numbers 24, 33(5), 175, 184, 189, 317; and *Constitutional Law*–9, 9(1), 9(2), 9(3), 9(5).

Missouri Practice, also published by Thomson/West, is the set most comparable to a state legal encyclopedia for Missouri. It contains a discussion of the I&R process with numerous citations to the Missouri

Constitution, statutes, case law, and secondary sources.[32] The *Statutory Forms* volume of the set provides the forms required for the process.[33]

Newspaper and Periodical Indexes

Academic Search Premier is a multidisciplinary database providing indexing and abstracts to a variety of peer-reviewed scholarly journals. Approximately half of the peer-reviewed articles are available in full-text. A researcher will find citations to major political science journals which provided background and current information on the I & R process. The online thesaurus suggests the subject term "referendum" and broader terms such as "direct democracy."

America: History and Life is an index to scholarly literature on the history of the United States. It covers both articles and dissertations which will not be located elsewhere. This bibliographic index uses the subject terms "initiatives," "referendum," and "elections (state)."

Index to Legal Periodicals and **LegalTrac** will provide citations to legal periodical literature. *ILP* indexes law reviews and books under the subject "Initiative and Referendum" and the broader subject "Direct Democracy." *LegalTrac* uses the subject "Referendum" with various subheadings such as "cases," "laws," "management" or "litigation." *LegalTrac* indexes not only journals but numerous legal newspapers. Both publications index the *Journal of the Missouri Bar* beginning in 1980.

America's Newspapers available from NewsBank, Inc. contain articles from newspapers such as the *St. Louis Post-Dispatch* (1988-present), *The Kansas City Star* (1991-present), and the *Springfield News-Leader* (1999-present). A search of the *St. Louis Post-Dispatch* for example retrieves several articles discussing and debating the wording of the recent stem cell initiative appearing on the Missouri ballot in the 2006 election.

PAIS International indexes and abstracts books, journal articles, dissertations, conference proceedings, reports, and government documents. The subject areas covered include political and social issues, public administration, law, and political science. *PAIS* uses the descriptor "Referendum–United States." For specific states you may also include the name of the state. When doing research on a particular initiative or referendum using other descriptors such as "stem cell research-public opinion" will produce the best results.

INTERNET RESOURCES

The Web sites of organizations, state governments, and newspapers will be helpful for those doing research on current state initiatives and referenda. Many times the most relevant dialog on initiatives will be found in local newspapers and the sites of non-profit organizations such as the League of Women Voters. As with most materials on the Web, one needs to assess the authority and reliability of the materials. This bibliography is not intended to be exhaustive, but only as a starting point for research. Most of these sites provide links to numerous additional electronic resources.

General Resources

Council of State Governments, *at* http://www.csg.org/.
The CSG is probably best known for publications such as the *The Book of the States* which provides tables of "State Initiatives and Referendums" with basic information such as subject, the type of ballot initiative (initiative, legislative referendum, popular referendum) and whether the measure passed. There are also other CSG publications such as *Spectrum: The Journal of State Government* and *Stateline Midwest* which discuss the results of initiatives and referendums up for consideration in various states. This site also provides links to other resources which monitor state I&R activities.

Initiative and Referendum Institute at the University of Southern California, *at* http://www.iandrinstitute.org.
This Institute at the University of Southern California provides a wealth of information regarding the I&R process in each state. The I&R Institute gives a brief history of the process in each state as well as an overview of the current process for the state. In addition they provide numerous reports on the I&R process, access to their newsletter "Ballotwatch," and a state-by-state survey of the voting results of propositions most recently found on the ballots in all fifty states.

National Conference of State Legislatures, at http://www.ncsl.org.
This site provides current information and surveys on state initiatives and referenda. You will find a state-by-state review of initiatives voted on during each election, as well as general reports on the I&R process. A "ballot measure database" is available which permits you to search by state, topic area, measure type, and year. There also is a "State Legislature" Internet database containing information taken from the home pages and Web sites of the fifty state legislatures, and the District of Columbia and the Territories.

Missouri Resources

League of Women Voters of Missouri, *at* http://www.lwvmissouri. org/aboutus.php and **League of Women Voters of St. Louis,** *at* http:// www.lwvstl.org/.
Both the League of Women Voters of Missouri and the League of Women Voters of St. Louis sites provide voter information and are the places you are likely to first find information on the propositions up for consideration. Information on other election resources such as the *Missouri Voters' Handbook* will be helpful in understanding the I&R process.

Make Your Voice Heard: Missouri's Initiative Petition Process and the Fair Ballot Access Act. Prepared by the Missouri Secretary of State, *at* http://www.sos.gov/elections/pubs/makeyourvoiceheard/myyhintro.asp.
This publication of the Missouri Secretary of State's office contains relevant sections of the *Missouri Constitution,* the *Revised Statutes of Missouri,* and the *Missouri Code of State Regulations.* It also contains charts with the number of votes cast in the last gubernatorial election and the number of signatures required for statutory change (5%) and for constitutional change (8%). Filing instructions and forms are included as well as the registration form required for the initiative or referendum petition circulators.

2006 Initiative Petitions Approved for Circulation in Missouri prepared by the Missouri Secretary of State, *at* http://www.sos.mo.gov/elections/ 2006petitions/06init_pet.asp#200608.
The Missouri Secretary of State provides the full-text of all initiative petitions which have been approved for circulation for the most recent election. The information provided includes the organization who

submitted the petition, contact information, the "official ballot title" as certified by the Secretary of State, a fiscal impact statement for state and local governments, and a link to the full-text of the initiative. Initiative petitions going back to 2002 may be found *at* http://www. sos.missouri.gov/elections/initiativesQuestions.asp.

Missouri Secretary of State. *Official Manual of the State of Missouri, at* http://www.sos.mo.gov/BlueBook/20052006/default.aspx?Node=20& sNode=360&Exp=Y#360.
The *Official Manual* contains a chapter on "Missouri Elections." This chapter includes voting results arranged by county for each ballot initiative, as well as the official ballot language for each initiative.

Reeves, Eugene E., *Preparing an Election Petition in Missouri.* University of Missouri Law Extension Center, *at* http://muextension.missouri. edu/explore/commdm/dm5361.htm.
This electronic publication prepared by the Director of the Law Extension Center at the University of Missouri covers all the mechanics of preparing a petition. It includes everything from the wording requirements for the petition, requirements for obtaining signatures, and the publication and filing requirements. Sample forms are included for a petition to amend the Constitution of Missouri, a petition for an initiative, and a petition for a referendum.

University of Missouri, Western Historical Manuscript Collection, Columbia, Missouri. (Description of the Collection available *at* http:// www.umsystem.edu/whmc/).
For those doing research on early petitions and the figures involved in developing the I&R process in Missouri, the collection at the State Historical Society of Missouri will be helpful. The papers of influential individuals such as N. D. Houghton will be useful in doing historical research.

SELECTED BIBLIOGRAPHY

Comment, *The Future of Initiative and Referendum in Missouri*, 48 Mo. L. Rev. 991 (Fall 1983).
This Comment provides a general introduction to the initiative and referendum process and then contains a step-by-step discussion of

the process in Missouri. The citations to primary and secondary sources will be valuable to anyone doing extensive research.

Comment, *The Initiative Process in Missouri: A Call For Statutory Change*, 51 Mo. L. Rev. 215 (Winter 1986).
This Comment is still frequently being cited in current discussions of Missouri's I&R process. It provides an excellent outline of the statutory scheme which will be helpful for those unfamiliar with the process. It covers provisions on who may sign an initiative petition and who may circulate a petition, procedures for filing petitions, and the proper channels for judicial review.

Comment, *Missouri's Silenced Citizen Legislators: How the Initiative is Denied to Citizens in Fourth-Class Missouri Municipalities*, 41 St. Louis U. L.J. 1081 (Spring 1997).
This Comment provides arguments for and against the initiative process and an excellent survey of the process in various states. It then proceeds to discuss use of the initiative process in third-class cities and explains how it is denied to fourth-class cities in Missouri. Valuable citations to Missouri statutes, the Missouri Constitution and case law are provided for additional research.

Karsch, Robert F., *The Government of Missouri.* Columbia, Missouri: Lucas Brothers Publishers, 12th ed., 1974.
Although dated, the chapter on "Initiative and Referendum" will provide valuable background material. The bibliography at the end of the chapter will also be helpful in providing citations to additional sources.

Lauer, T. E., *Municipal Law in Missouri*, 28 Mo. L. Rev. 555 (Fall 1963).
This article is an excellent overview of Missouri case law involving both the initiative and referendum procedure in municipal legislation. It provides numerous citations to case law in which the use of initiatives at the municipal level has been challenged.

Neely, Alfred S., *"Public Controls and Influences" Missouri Practice: Administrative Practice and Procedure* 20 (2001): § 4.07.
Volume 20 of *Missouri Practice* which deals with administrative practice and procedure contains a valuable discussion of both the initiative

and referendum process in Missouri. It also provides current citations to cases, statutes, the Missouri Constitution, and secondary sources.

Piott, Steven L., *Giving Voters a Voice: The Origins of the Initiative and Referendum in America.* Columbia, Mo., University of Missouri Press, 2003.
This is an historical study of the origins of the initiative and referendum process in sixteen states including Missouri. In an expansion of his 1994 article in *Gateway Heritage,* the author provides an excellent account of the dynamics and political compromises which took place in each state. An extensive bibliography is provided for further research.

Piott, Steven L., *Giving Voters a Voice: The Struggle for Initiative and Referendum in Missouri*, 14 Gateway Heritage 20 (Spring 1994).
This article is written by an historian who has done extensive research on the history of the I&R process in Missouri. He provides citations to primary sources such as the *Direct Legislation Record* and the *Official Manual of the State of Missouri,* as well as secondary sources such as local newspaper articles. For anyone wishing to research the history of I&R in Missouri this will prove invaluable.

Pletz, John S., *Election Contests in Missouri*, 46 J. Mo. B. 259 (June 1990).
This article is an excellent discussion of issues such as the pre-election procedures for challenging ballot titles and the overall sufficiency of the initiative petition.

Schacter, Jane S., *The Pursuit of Popular Intent: Interpretive Dilemmas in Direct Democracy*, 105 Yale L.J. 107 (October 1995).
This article discusses the "interpretative methodology used by courts in construing statutory law enacted through the initiative process." Professor Schacter examines a collection of fifty-three decisions by the highest courts in states permitting voters to consider initiatives. This set includes eleven states including Missouri. While only one case the author considers is from Missouri, it is an interesting look at how courts have gone about determining popular intent.

Schmidt, David D., *Citizen Lawmaker: The Ballot Initiative Revolution.* Philadelphia, PA: Temple University Press, 1989.
This work provides a state-by-state brief history of the initiative process. The author also includes initiative and referendum election results

(1987-1988); statewide initiatives passed (1970-1986) and a guide to the rights and requirements for each state.

Van Eaton, Anson Eugene, *The Initiative and Referendum in Missouri. Columbia, Mo.: University of Missouri–Columbia, 1954 (Ph.D. Dissertation).*
This dissertation covers the history of the initiative and referendum process in Missouri from 1908 through 1953. The author also includes an analysis of how direct proposals have been publicized during that time period. Among the direct initiatives of note is a constitutional amendment adopted in 1920 mandating every twenty years a ballot proposal to the voters asking if there should be a constitutional convention. As a result Missouri has had two constitutional conventions and adopted its current Constitution.

Zimmerman, Joseph F., *The Referendum: The People Decide Public Policy.* Westport, Conn.: Praeger, 2001.
An excellent overview of the legal foundations of "The Referendum," accompanied by a discussion of how courts have dealt with such questions as petitioner signers' privacy, and procedural and single subject requirements. It also includes tables providing state information on such things as requirements for circulating petitions, elections where initiatives can be voted on, and whether an approved initiative can be amended, vetoed, or repealed. An extensive bibliography includes monographs, government documents, journal and newspaper articles, and unpublished materials such as hearings, proceedings and dissertations.

NOTES

1. Updates on Results were incomplete in Wednesday's Edition, *St. Louis Post-Dispatch* (November 10, 2006) at C8.
2. Mo. Rev. Stat. § 78.200 (2000).
3. M. Dane Waters, *The Initiative and Referendum Almanac* (2003) at 11.
4. *Id.*
5. *Id.*
6. *Id.*
7. *Id.*
8. *Id.* at 12.
9. *Id.* at 11.
10. Mo. Const. art. III, § 49.
11. M. Dane Waters, *The Initiative and Referendum Almanac* (2003) at 11.

12. David D. Schmidt, *Citizen Lawmakers: The Ballot Initiative Revolution* (1989) at 246.

13. Steven Piott, *Giving Voters a Voice: The Struggle for Initiative and Referendum in Missouri,* 14 Gateway Heritage 20 (1994).

14. David D. Schmidt, *Citizen Lawmakers: The Ballot Initiative Revolution* (1989) at 246.

15. *Id.* at 247.

16. *Id.*

17. Mo. Const. art III, § 49; Mo. Const. art III, § 52(a).

18. Mo. Const. art. III, § 49.

19. Mo. Const. art. III, § 50.

20. *Id.* For a general discussion *see* Comment, *The Future of Initiatives and Referendum in Missouri,* 48 Mo. L. Rev. 991 (1983).

21. Mo. Const. art III, § 53.

22. Mo. Const. art. III, § 50.

23. Mo. Rev. Stat. § 116.120 (2000).

24. Mo. Rev. Stat. §116.025 (2000).

25. Mo. Const. art. III, § 52(a).

26. *Id.*

27. Mo. Rev. Stat. § 116.155 (2000).

28. Mo. Rev. Stat. § 116.160 (2000).

29. Mo. Rev. Stat. § 116.170 (2000).

30. Mo. Code Regs. Ann. tit. 15, § 30-15.010 (2000).

31. Mo. Code Regs. Ann. tit. 15, § 30-15.020 (2000).

32. Alfred S. Neely, *Public Controls and Influences*, 20 Mo. Practice: Admin. Prac. & Proc. § 4.07.

33. James Burlison, *Elections*, 11 Mo. Practice: Statutory Forms § 116.030.

Researching Initiatives and Referendums: A Guide for Big Sky Country– Montana

Lisa Mecklenberg Jackson

INTRODUCTION

Initiatives and referendums are "hot" these days–both at a national level and in Montana. A total of 205 propositions in 37 states were decided in November 2006, up from 162 in 2004. Those states with the most propositions include Arizona (19), Colorado (14), California (13), South Dakota (11), Oregon (10), and Nevada (10). Louisiana had 21 measures for the year (13 in September and 8 in November).[1] Montana, though sparse in population, held its own in this arena with six propositions on the ballot in November, 2006, but only three were actually counted. In late October, the Montana Supreme Court upheld a lower court ruling that CI-97 (TABOR), CI-98 (judicial recall), and I-154 (eminent domain/regulatory takings) were invalid because of fraudulent signature collection.[2] Those three measures appeared on the ballot, but votes were not counted. The measures that did appear on the ballot were C-43 (changes name of state auditor to insurance commissioner), I-151 (raises minimum wage and indexes it to inflation), and I-153 (prohibits lobbying by government officials for two years after leaving office).[3] These measures will be discussed in more detail below.

WHAT TYPES OF BALLOT ISSUES ARE THERE IN MONTANA?

Initiative. An initiative is a proposal by petition to enact a new law by a vote of the people on any matter except the appropriation of money, or local or special laws. If the petitions are signed by the required number of electors, the proposed initiative must be submitted to the qualified electors.

Referendum. A referendum is a proposal by which the people, by their majority vote, can approve or reject a previously enacted statute, except an appropriation of money. A referendum may be originated by the legislature itself or by the people.
By the legislature. At the time a piece of legislation is considered, the legislature may, in its discretion, decide to have its action ratified by a vote of the people.

By the people. After the legislature enacts a statute, the people may petition to refer such statute to a vote of the people. This is referred to as an initiative referendum. If the petitions are signed by the required number of electors, the proposed referendum must be submitted to the qualified electors.

If petitioners wish to render an enacted statute inoperative pending a vote, a referendum petition containing a greater number of signatures is required. If suspended, the act becomes operative only after such time it is approved at an election.

Referendum petitions must be filed with the Montana Secretary of State no later than six months after the adjournment of the legislature that passed the act.

Constitutional Amendment. A constitutional amendment is a proposal originated by either the legislature or the people to change the constitution.[4]

By the legislature. Amendments may be proposed by any member of the legislature. They must be adopted by an affirmative vote of two-thirds of all the members in order to be submitted to the qualified electors.

By the people. Amendments may be proposed by initiative. If the petitions are signed by the required number of electors, the proposed amendment must be submitted to the qualified electors.

Constitutional Convention. A question on whether to hold an unlimited constitutional convention to revise, alter, or amend the constitution may be originated by either the legislature or the people.

By the legislature. The legislature, by an affirmative vote of two-thirds of all the members, may at any time submit to the qualified electors the question of whether there will be a constitutional convention.

By the people. The people may, by petition, direct the Secretary of State to submit to the qualified electors the question of whether there will be a constitutional convention. If the petitions are signed by the required number of electors, the proposed convention call must be submitted to the qualified electors.

Effective Dates

Initiative. Unless the petition states otherwise, a statutory initiative approved by the people is effective on October 1 following approval. If the measure delegates rulemaking authority, it cannot be effective sooner than October 1 following approval.

Constitutional Amendment. Unless the legislature or the amendment provides otherwise, a constitutional amendment proposed by the legislature or by initiative and approved by the people is effective on July 1 following approval.

Referendum. Unless the legislature specifically provides an effective date in an issue put before the people, or unless suspended by law, an act referred to the people is in effect as the law provides until it is approved or rejected at the election.

HISTORY OF INITIATIVE AND REFERENDUM IN MONTANA

The adoption of Article V, Section 1, on November 6, 1906 initiated the process of initiative and referendum in Montana. Future initiative and referendum measures included such diverse topics as a bond issue for an insane asylum in 1911, establishing an athletic commission in 1914, a bond issue for a twine factory at the state prison in 1916, requiring certificates of good health before issuance of marriage licenses in 1936, an attempt to legalize gambling in 1964, requiring legislative approval of any nuclear facility licensed under the Montana Major Facility Siting Act in 1976, requiring public disclosure of money spent to influence the actions of public officials in 1980, requiring refundable deposits on all beverage containers sold in Montana in 1988, an anti-intimidation act in 1996, game farm reform in 2000, and the Montana Medical Marijuana Act in 2004.[5]

In March, 2005, the Hon. Donald W. Molloy, Chief Judge of the United States District Court in Missoula, issued a ruling regarding amendments to the Montana Constitution on the geographical signature requirements for ballot issues.[6] According to the ruling, the amendments, which were passed by the voters in November 2002, violated the equal protection clause of the U.S. Constitution. The amendments in question, CI-37 and CI-38, required signature gatherers to gather a certain percentage of signatures by county, instead of by legislative district. Following the district court decision, the Montana Attorney General has determined that signatures must again be gathered by legislative district instead of by county.[7]

CURRENT STATE OF AFFAIRS

There is currently legislation, Senate Bill 96, before the Montana Legislature that would significantly revamp the way ballot measures are conducted in the state.[8] SB96 addresses nearly every step of the ballot measure process, from the submission of the text of a proposed measure, to the gathering of signatures, to the process used to challenge statements. Here are a few highlights:

- Signature gatherers would have to be Montana residents, and payment per signature would be prohibited.
- Signature gatherers would no longer be able to swear they "assisted" in gathering signatures and would instead have to swear they "gathered" signatures.
- Ballots would have to have notice of conflicting ballot measures and "Abbreviated" ballots would be eliminated. There is a 100-word statement explaining the purpose of each ballot measure.

The proposed changes would also state that the ballot process begin and end in the Secretary of State's office. Under existing law, the text of a ballot measure must be submitted to the Montana Legislative Services Division. Under SB 96, the text would go to Legislative Services only after it was submitted to the Secretary of State's office.

Another important provision would give the Montana Supreme Court original jurisdiction to hear challenges to the 100-word statement or determination of legal sufficiency. In recent years, challenges were taken up in Montana's district courts, then quickly appealed to the Montana Supreme Court. With these changes, it is possible challenges can be heard and resolved long before voters go to the polls. In the event a court revises the ballot statement, signatures gathered on petitions prior to the review would be void, and a court would be required to make a final determination no later than the deadline to certify the measure for the ballot.

KEY STEPS IN THE MONTANA BALLOT ISSUE PROCESS

Getting Started . . .

1. An individual or group submits a proposed ballot issue to Montana Legislative Services for its review.

2. Legislative Services reviews the proposal and makes recommendations to the issue's sponsor. The sponsor responds in writing, accepting, modifying, or rejecting the suggested recommendations.
3. The sponsor submits the proposed ballot issue in petition form to the Montana Secretary of State.
4. The Secretary of State forwards a copy of the proposal to the Montana Attorney General and both agencies review the proposed ballot issue for form.
5. The Attorney General reviews the proposal; writes the explanatory statement and "for" and "against" statements; seeks a fiscal note, if necessary, from the Office of Budget and Program Planning, and forwards approval or rejection of the issue, statements, and a fiscal statement to the Secretary of State.
6. The Secretary of State reviews the Attorney General's material, works with the sponsor as needed on the petition format, and notifies the sponsor of either the approval or rejection of the petition, or the conditional approval if there are only technical defects that must be corrected prior to final approval.
7. The sponsor makes corrections and changes, if required, to the petition and submits another copy to the Secretary of State for review.
8a. Once all changes and corrections have been made, approval of the petition form is given, and petition signatures may be gathered.
8b. Within 30 days of approval of the petition form, the Attorney General shall forward to the Secretary of State the determination regarding the petition's legal sufficiency, if the Attorney General has not already done.

Collecting Signatures . . .

9. Petitions with signatures are submitted to county election administrators in each county where signatures are gathered to be verified. The election administrators forward the numbers of verified signatures along with the original petitions to the Secretary of State.
10. The Secretary of State tallies the number of signatures gathered and if enough signatures are gathered in a sufficient number of legislative districts, the issue is qualified to go on the ballot.

Making the Arguments . . .

11. Sponsors of qualified ballot issues form a committee to prepare arguments in support of the issue, and certain elected officials choose committee members to prepare arguments against the issue (see Appointment of Pro and Con Committees below). Rebuttals of these arguments are also written by the opposing committees. These arguments, along with the text and form of the ballot issue, are printed in a voter information pamphlet (see Appendix B) that is sent to all Montana households with an active registered voter.

After the Election . . .

12. If a ballot issue is adopted by the vote of the people, it becomes a part of the constitution or state law.

The number of signatures required on ballot petitions is based on a percentage of the total number of votes cast for Governor in the last general election. Effective March 2005, the signature gathering requirements for statutory and constitutional initiatives have changed, as reflected below.

To qualify a **statutory initiative**, at least 5% of the votes cast for Governor are needed in each of at least 1/3 (34) of the legislative representative districts. To qualify a **constitutional initiative**, at least 10% of the votes cast for Governor are needed in each of at least 2/5 (40) of the legislative representative districts.

To qualify an **initiative referendum**, at least 5% of the votes cast for Governor are needed in each of at least 1/3 (34) of the legislative representative districts. If at least 15% is gathered in each of at least a majority (51) of the districts for a referendum, the statute is suspended pending the result of the vote.

To qualify a **call for a constitutional convention**, at least 10% of the votes cast for Governor is needed in each of at least 2/5 (40) of the legislative representative districts.

APPOINTMENT OF PRO AND CON COMMITTEES

Once a petition has qualified to appear on the Montana ballot, committees are formed to write arguments for and against the issue. These arguments appear in an information pamphlet that is distributed before each election to all households with active registered voters. The size of the committees and who appoints them depends on the type of petition.

Initiative petitions (constitutional initiatives and statutory initiatives). A three-member committee supporting the issue is appointed by the sponsor who submitted the petition. A five-member committee opposing the issue is appointed by the Governor, Attorney General, President of the Senate and Speaker of the House of Representatives. The four appointed persons appoint the fifth member.

Referenda from the legislature. A three-member committee supporting the issue is composed of one senator known to favor the measure appointed by the President of the Senate, one representative known to favor the measure appointed by the Speaker of the House of Representatives and one individual (who need not be a legislator) appointed by the first two members. A three-member committee opposing the issue is appointed in the same manner as the committee supporting the issue (but, if possible, members should be known to have opposed the issue).

Referenda from the people. A three-member committee in favor of repealing the bill that was referred by the petition sponsor is appointed by the petition sponsor, and a three-member committee against repealing the bill that was referred by the petition sponsor is composed of one senator appointed by the President of the Senate, one representative appointed by the Speaker of the House of Representatives and one individual (who need not be a legislator) appointed by the first two members.

The argument, consisting of written material, must be filed with the Secretary of State no later than 105 days before the election at which the issue will be voted upon by the people. Copies of these arguments are provided to the opposing committee, which may prepare a rebuttal argument. The written material must be filed with the Secretary of State no later than 10 days after the deadline for filing the original arguments. These materials are compiled into a voter information pamphlet which is sent to all Montana households with active registered voters. These voter information pamphlets are extremely useful in researching initiatives and referenda in Montana and are available at the Montana Secretary of State's Office and the Montana Legislative Library.[9]

LOCATING DOCUMENTS

Any questions a researcher may have regarding referendum and initiatives in Montana can essentially be answered through the use of three state offices: The Secretary of State's Elections Bureau office, the Montana

Legislative Library, and the Montana Historical Society. The Secretary of State's office is the official depository of initiative and referendum documents for the state, the Legislative Library contains all of the correspondence related to drafting of the initiative and referendum measures, and the Montana Historical Society contains the older records from both the elections bureau and the library.

NOTES

1. *Fall Ballot Measures 2006*, Ballotwatch, Initiative and Referendum Institute, 2006 No. 3.

2. *Not In Montana: Citizens Against CI-97 v. State*, 334 Mont. 265, 147 P.3d 174, 2000 MT 278 (2006).

3. I-151 passed, I-153 passed, and C-43 did not pass in November 2006.

4. Amendments to 1972 Montana Constitution document, available from the Montana Secretary of State's Office (406) 444-5346.

5. *See* Appendix A.

6. *Montana PIRG v. Johnson*, CV 03-183-M-DWM, Order at 17 (D. Mont. Mar. 28, 2005).

7. 51 MT Attorney General Opinions No. 2 (2005).

8. http://data.opi.mt.gov/bills/2007/billhtml/SB0096.htm.

9. Voter Information Pamphlets are available through the Montana Secretary of State Elections Bureau office at (406) 444-5346 and the Montana Legislative Library at (406) 444-3588. The most recent pamphlet (2006) is available online at http://sos.mt.gov/ELB/Voter_Information.asp.

APPENDIX A
Initiatives and Referendum in Montana Since 1906

The following information is compiled by the Montana Secretary of State's Elections Bureau office and is available from their office. The table lists the type of ballot issue, the date, the subject, the vote, and if passed, the chapter law number assigned.

**Initiative and Referendum Issues
Since Adoption of Constitutional Amendment, Article V,
Section I, Permitting the
Referendum and Initiative**

General Election – November 6, 1906
For 36,374   Against 6,616
Effective: December 7, 1906

**1908
November 3, 1908**

Referendum	State Bond Issue for Higher Education. No number assigned. Chapter 58, Laws of 1907	**For 24,809** Against 12,910

**1912
November 5, 1912**

Initiatives Effective: December 13, 1912

Referendum	Bond Issue for Insane Asylum. No number assigned. Chapter 144, Laws of 1911 Effective: No record of proclamation by Governor	**For 34,235** Against 30,461
IR 300-301	Organization of State Militia.	For 21,195 **Against 41,749**
I 302-303	Party Nominations by Direct Vote.	**For 46,473** Against 12,879
I 304-305	Limiting Campaign Expenses of Public Candidates.	**For 44,337** Against 13,645
I 306-307	Popular Referendum for Election of Senators.	**For 45,620** Against 12,442
I 308-309	Direct Presidential Preference Primary.	**For 46,241** Against 12,144

(continued)

1914
November 3, 1914

Referendum	Levy for Support of Educational Institutions. No number assigned. Chapter 117 Laws of 1913	For 28,703 **Against 46,265**
IR 6	Establishing Athletic Commission.	For 34,440 **Against 42,581**
I 7	Workmen's Compensation.	For 36,979 **Against 44,275**
I 8	"Farm Loan Bill" Relating to Investment of Permanent State Funds.	**For 45,162** Against 27,780
I 9	Consolidation of State Institutions of Higher Education	For 30,465 **Against 46,311**

1916
November 7, 1916

Referendum	Bond Issue for Twine Factory at State Prison. No number assigned. Chapter 106, Laws of 1915	For 68,059 **Against 79,158**
R 10	Prohibition. Effective December 31, 1918 by proclamation dated Dec. 4, 1916	**For 102,776** Against 73,890
I 11	Establishing Athletic Commission.	For 72,162 **Against 76,510**

1918
November 5, 1918

I 12	An Act Authorizing and Regulating the Practice of Chiropractors.	**For 46,302** Against 39,320
Referendum	Terminal Elevator Bonds.	**For 54,215** Against 29,630

1920
November 2, 1920

IR 13	To Provide for Direct Nominations of Public Office Candidates.	For 60,483 **Against 77,549**
R 14	Establishing Athletic Commission.	**For 82,827** Against 65,928

(continued)

APPENDIX A (continued)

IR 15	To Amend Direct Primaries Law.	For 66,131 **Against 74,079**
IR 16	Repeal of Presidential Preferential Primaries Law.	For 60,793 **Against 80,023**
I 17	To Provide a New Workmen's Compensation Law. *Withdrawal petitions left initiative petition signatures insufficient.*	
I 18	1 1/2 Mills Levy for Maintenance of University.	**For 82,669** Against 71,169
I 19	$5,000,000 Bonds for State Educational Institutions Buildings.	**For 90,441** Against 66,237
I 20	$20,000,000 Bond Issue for Reclamation of Arid Lands.(NOTE: referred to as referendum in Official Election Returns)	For 68,785 **Against 76,949**
I 21	Special Method of Tax Collection. *Insufficient number of signatures to place measure on ballot*	
I 22	Special Metals Tax. *Insufficient number of signatures to place measure on ballot.*	
R 23	$14,000,000 Bond Issue for Highways.(Note: referred to as initiative in Official Election Returns)	For 55,276 **Against 89,828**
I 24	Providing for County Free Hospitals. *Insufficient number of signatures to place measure on ballot.*	

1922
November 7, 1922

R 25	Soldiers' Compensation.	**For 67,463** Against 62,100
I 26	Pari-Mutuels.	For 60,057 **Against 66,363**

1924
November 4, 1924

R 27	Repeal of Presidential Primary Law.	**For 77,948** Against 57,540
I 28	Metal Mines Tax.	**For 87,790** Against 65,742

(continued)

1926
November 2, 1926

R 29	Five-Mills Levy for Maintenance of Public Elementary and High Schools.	For 53,143 **Against 86,897**
I 30	Relating to Repeal of State's Intoxicating Liquor Laws.	**For 83,231** Against 72,982
I 31	3 Cent Gasoline Tax for Good Roads.	**For 114,763** Against 42,232

1928
December 3, 1928

I 32	For Adoption and Enforcement of the Federal Prohibition Laws.	For 68,431 **Against 80,619**

1930
November 4, 1930

R 33	Bond Issue for State Institutions.	**For 77,761** Against 58,312
R 34	Levy For University, Agricultural Experiment Stations and Extension Service.	**For 70,548** Against 61,207

1931
May 5, 1931 Special Election

R 35	State Highway Treasury Anticipation Debenture Act of 1931.	**For 60,075** Against 21,256

1936
November 3, 1936

IR 36	Requiring Certificates of Good Health before Issuance of Marriage Licenses.	For 54,368 **Against 96,647**
IR 37	Providing for State Insurance of Public Buildings.	For 67,067 **Against 84,245**
I 38	State Liquor Control Act of Montana. *Held invalid by Supreme Court on grounds that two petitions could not be certified as one because text of proposed law differed on each petition. Injunction issued on October 6, 1936 restraining secretary of state from certifying the initiative to county clerks (Ford v. Mitchell 103 Mont 99)*	

(continued)

APPENDIX A (continued)

I 39	Licensing and Classification of Chain Stores. *Supreme Court held that title and legend of Act were not descriptive, thus ballot did not comply with law. Injunction issued on October 8, 1936, restraining the secretary of state from certifying the initiative to county clerks. (Sawyer Stores, Inc., v Mitchell Et. Al 103 Mont. 148)*	

1938
November 8, 1938

IR 40	Regulating, Licensing and Authorizing Sale of Liquor at Retail.	**For 113,332** Against 68,685
I 41	State Highway Treasury Anticipation Debentures Act of 1938.	**For 126,247** Against 32,134

1940
November 5, 1940

R 42	Three and One-Half Mills Levy University of Montana.	**For 58,968** Against 52,998
R 43	State Hospital for Insane $500,000 Bond Issue.	**For 75,824** Against 38,249
I 44	Montana State College Bonds.	For 51,921 **Against 57,197**

1942
November 3, 1942

R 45	Montana State College Bonds $690,000.	For 28,664 **Against 56,509**
R 46	Northern Montana College Educational Bonds $350,000.	For 25,027 **Against 58,921**

1944
November 7, 1944

R 47	State Highway Treasury Anticipation Debenture Act of 1943. *Supreme Court issued injunction on May 19, 1943, enjoining the election. (Burgan & Walker v. State Highway Commission, 114 Mont. 459)*	
I 48	Defining Osteopathy–Authorizing and Regulating Practice of Osteopathic Physicians and Surgeons.	For 72,206 **Against 108,882**

1945
June 5, 1945 special election

R 49	State Highway Treasury Anticipation.	**For 38,756** Against 8,326

(continued)

	1946 **November 5, 1946**	
R 50	Hospital for Insane Bond Issue $2,000,000.	**For 90,360** Against 19,268

	1948 **November 2, 1948**	
R 51	University of Montana Levy.	**For 77,820** Against 50,167
R 52	University of Montana Building Bonds for Construction and Equipping Necessary Buildings.	**For 75,601** Against 49,621

	1950 **November 7, 1950**	
R 53	Slot Machines.	For 55,348 **Against** **140,309**
I 54	Military Honorarium.	**For 108,251** Against 75,411

	1952 **November 4, 1952**	
I 55	Tax on Gasoline.	For 76,627 **Against** **102,455**

	1954 **November 2, 1954**	
R 56	Presidential Primary Law.	**For 99,337** Against 44,884
R 57	Montana State Hospital Bond Issue $2,000,000.	**For 143,587** Against 20,759
R 58	Bond Issue $1,500,000 Montana Training School.	**For 131,400** Against 25,982

	1958 **November 4, 1958**	
IR 59	Liquor Tax.	**For 100,383** Against 85,742

(continued)

APPENDIX A (continued)

R 60	Bond Issue and Tax Levy for University of Montana of $10,000,000. *Held unconstitutional-District Court permanent injunction enjoining secretary of state from placing measure on ballot affirmed by Supreme Court July 22,1958.* *(Mornga v. Murray 134 Mont. 92)*	
R 61	Six Mills Levy for Support, Maintenance and Improvement of University of Montana.	**For 89,251** Against 84,002

1960
November 8, 1960

R 62	Prison Bond Issue.	For 78,291 **Against** **120,749**

1964

I 63	To Legalize Gambling. *Held unconstitutional. Supreme Court issued injunction on July 24, 1964,* *restraining SOS from placing measure on ballot* *(state ex res.Steen v Murray 144 Mont. 61)*	

1966
November 8, 1966

LR 64	Relating to Tobacco Tax for Purpose of Financing the Cost of Construction and Remodeling State Buildings. Effective November 8, 1966 by Governor's proclamation dated December 6, 1966	**For 107,208** Against 92,619

1968
November 5, 1968

R 65	To Continue 6-mill Tax Levy for Support of University System.	**For 127,625** Against 89,396
I 66	To Reduce Taxable Valuation of Certain Personal Property, Including Stocks of Merchandise.	For 70,497 **Against** **158,191**

1970
November 3, 1970

R 67	Whether the Legislature Should Call a Constitutional Convention. Effective November 20, 1970 by governor's proclamation	**For 133,482** Against 72,643

1971
November 2, 1971 special election

R 68	Methods of Taxation–Sales Tax or Increased Income Tax.	For 66,967 **Against** **154,680**

(continued)

1974

R 69	Referring House Joint Resolution No. 4 Laws of Montana 1974, Ratifying the Proposed Amendment to the US Constitution Relating to Equal Rights on Account of Sex, to a Vote of the People. *Certified to the governor August 23, 1974-Secretary of State restrained and enjoined from placing on ballot, August 30, 1974, State of Montana ex re Robin Hatch v. Frank Murray, 526 P2nd 1369.*	

1976
November 2, 1976

R 70	State Funding to Public Library Federations with a One Mill Levy on all Taxable Property.	For 109,792 **Against 176,568**
I 71	Requiring Legislative Approval of Any Nuclear Facility Licensed under the Montana Major Facility Siting Act.	For 120,557 **Against 175,925**
I 72	To Provide Property Tax Relief for Owner-Occupied Homesteads.	**For 204,532** Against 83,611
I 73	Montana Recall and Advisory Recall Act.	**For 155,899** Against 115,702

1978
November 7, 1978

LR 74	To Raise the Legal Drinking Age to Nineteen.	**For 207,476** Against 65,196
LR 75	To Continue 6-mill Tax Levy for Support of University System.	**For 181,920** Against 88,641
	Chapter 343 Senate Bill 403, Laws of 1977 enacted: An act to generally revise the laws implementing the constitutional right of the people to petition for initiative and referendum on statewide issues; amending sections 23-2704, 23-2803, 23-3326, and 89-2330.3, RCM 1947; and repealing sections 37-104.4, 37-104.5, 37-104.6, 37-104.7, 37-104.8, 37-104.9, 37-104.10 37-105 through 37-110, and 37-201 through 37-203, RCM 1947	
IR 76	To Revise and Clarify the Montana Economic Land Development Act. *Insufficient number of signatures filed to place measure on ballot.*	
IR 77	Establishing Energy Emergency Powers for the Governor. *Insufficient number of signatures filed to place measure on ballot.*	
IR 78	Amending Montana Recall and Advisory Recall Act, Initiative No 73. *Insufficient number if signatures filed to place measure on ballot.*	

(continued)

APPENDIX A (continued)

I 79	Allowing Cities, Towns or Counties to Adopt Obscenity Ordinances on Resolutions More Restrictive than State Law.	**For 139,763** Against 125,475
I 80	Empowering Montana Voters to Approve or Reject Any Proposed Nuclear Power Facility Certified under the Montana Major Facility Siting Act.	**For 177,778** Against 95,179
I 81	Authorizing Grocery Stores and Drug Stores to Sell Table Wine for Off-Premises Consumption.	**For 169,069** Against 112,195
I 82	Providing for a Replacement Tax for Property Now Levied on Habitable Property. *Insufficient number of signatures to place measure on ballot.*	

1980
November 4, 1980

I 83	Proposing a Second Veterans Home within the Department of Institutions Located at Twin Bridges. *Insufficient number of signatures filed to place measure on ballot.*	
I 84	Forbidding the Disposal of Radioactive Waste Material within the State of Montana.	For 172,796 Against 172,173 Recount: **For 172,909** Against 172,493
I 85	Requiring Public Disclosure of Money Spent to Influence Action of Public Official. (Lobbyist Disclosure)	**For 259,698** Against 76,358
I 86	Proposing To Change the Montana Income Tax Structure that Tax Brackets, Exemptions, Standard Deductions, and Minimum Filing Requirements be Adjusted to Prevent Increase Due Solely to Inflation.	**For 233,497** Against 102,635
I 87	Montana Litter Control And Recycling Act.	For 100,761 **Against 248,928**
I 88	Assisting Employees and Communities Affected by Business Closings and Large Scale Layoffs. *Insufficient number of signatures filed to place measure on ballot.*	

1982

LR 89	Removing the Prohibition of Disposal of Certain Radioactive Materials in Montana Enacted by I 84. Chapter 612, House Bill 652, Laws of 1981	For 70,375 **Against 222,210**
I 90	Community Stabilization Act-Requiring Certain Business to Provide Advance Notice of Major Employee Layoffs, Severance Payments and a Fund to Assist Affected Employees and Communities. *Insufficient number of signatures filed to place measure on ballot.*	

(continued)

I 91	Opposing the Placement of MX Missiles in Montana.	**For 168,594** Against 125,092
I 92	Expanding Gambling and Creating a State Gaming Commission. Expansion of Authorized Gambling to Include Blackjack, Punchboards and Certain Electronic or Mechanical Gambling Devices, etc.	For 115,297 **Against 191,334**
I 93	Milk Price Decontrol-Decontrol of the Wholesale and Retail Price of Milk. *Insufficient number of signatures filed to place measure on ballot.*	
I 94	Beer and Wine License Quota System. Abolishing the Quota System on Beer and Wine Licenses for Restaurants and Prepared Food Businesses.	For 121,078 **Against 182,724**
I 95	Invest Coal Tax-Investing Part of The Coal Severance Tax Permanent Trust Fund in the Montana Economy and Creating a Montana Economic Development Fund.	**For 207,629** Against 84,875

1984

I 96	Milk Price Decontrol-to Abolish the State Board of Milk Control and Eliminate State Control of the Price of Milk.	**For 145,342** **Against 222,200**
I 97	For Allowing the Practice of Denturity.	**For 194,285** Against 171,448
I 98	Declaring that the People of Montana Call for Immediate Steps Leading toward Nuclear Disarmament. *Insufficient number of signatures filed to place measure on ballot.*	
I 99	Regarding a Balanced Federal Budget. *MEASURE DROPPED BY SPONSORS BEFORE COMPLETING PROCESS FOR APPROVAL*	

1986

LR 100	To Establish a State Lottery and Provide for Its Administration. Chapter 669, House Bill 945, Laws of 1985	**For 216,706** Against 97,459
I 101	Investing of Portion of Coal Tax Trust in Montana Agriculture. *Insufficient number of signatures filed to place measure on ballot.*	
I 102	Divestiture of Public Funds. *Insufficient number of signature filed to place measure on ballot.*	
I 103	Celebrating March 19, the Birthday of Charles M Russell as a Legal Holiday Every 5 years. *MEASURE DROPPED BY SPONSORS BEFORE COMPLETING PROCESS FOR APPROVAL*	
I 104	Milk Price Decontrol-Decontrol of the Wholesale, Jobber, and Retail Prices of Milk.	**For 153,293** **Against 160,835**

(continued)

APPENDIX A (continued)

I 105	Limitation of Property Taxes to 1986 Levels.	**For 166,694** Against 136,904

1988

LR 106	Giving the Legislature Authority to Levy Up to 6 Mills for the Montana University System.	**For 227,638** Against 127,259
I 107	Prohibiting Parking Meters. *SPONSOR DIED BEFORE FINAL APPROVAL OF PETITION WAS ISSUED (SEE I 109).*	
I 108	Extending the Terms of the Two Temporary Associate Justice Positions of the Montana Supreme Court and Extending the Terms of the Two Temporary Associate Justice Positions of the Montana Supreme Court an Additional Eight Years, until January 1997. *Insufficient number of signatures filed to place measure on ballot.*	
I 109	Prohibiting Parking Meters. *Insufficient number of signatures filed to place measure on ballot.*	
I 110	Repealing the Montana Seatbelt Use Act.	For 155,481 **Against 211,090**
I 111	Raising the State Minimum Wage. *Insufficient number of signatures filed to place measure on ballot.*	
I 112	Licensing Massage Therapists. *SPONSORS WITHDREW PETITION.*	
I 113	Requiring Refundable Deposits on All Beverage Containers Sold in Montana.	For 78,509 **Against 287,461**
I 114	Repealing the Montana Seatbelt Use Act. *SPONSOR FAILED TO FILE FINAL COPY OF INITIATIVE.*	

1990

I 115	To Increase the Cigarette and Tobacco Sales Tax.	For: 130,707 **Against 188,732**
I 116	Require Voter Approval of Enactment of Sales Tax. *Insufficient number of signatures filed to place measure on ballot.*	

1992 Primary

LR 109	2 Mill Levy Funding Vo-tech Centers.	For 76,546 **Against 133,841**
LR 110	Treasure State Endowment Fund-Creating This Fund to Provide Local Governments Coal Severance Tax Trust Fund Interest for Water, Sewer, Solid Waste, and Bridge Projects.	**For 132,820** Against: 79,562

(continued)

| I 117 | School Base Budget.
WITHDRAWN BY SPONSOR. | |

1992 General

| None | Not applicable. | |

1993 (June 8, special election)

| LR 111 | Sales Tax | |

1994

I 118	Revising Campaign Finance Laws. (Jonathan Motl)	**For 200,679** Against 129,983
I 119	Revising Recall Act. (Gary Marbut) *Insufficient number of signatures filed to place measure on ballot.*	
I 120	Prohibit Corporate Spending on Ballot Issues. (Jonathan Motl) *Insufficient number of signatures filed to place measure on ballot.*	
IR 112	Repeal HB671. (sales tax) (Rob Natelson)	Approve HB 671: 83,813 **Reject HB 671: 246,368**

1996

I 121	Increase Minimum Wage. (MontCEL)	For 175,769 **Against 227,975**
I 122	Water Quality. (National Wildlife Federation–Tom France)	For 175,534 **Against 230,283**
I 123	Anti-Intimidation Act of 1996.	**For 200,682** Against 180,295
I 124	Pop-Tax Trust Fund for Programs under the Montana Older Americans Act. (Evelyn Havskjold) *Insufficient number of signatures filed to place measure on ballot.*	
I 125	Corporate Contributions to Ballot Measures. (Jonathan Motl) I 125 ruled unconstitutional, *Montana Chamber of Commerce vs. Argenbright, 226 F. 3d 1049 (9th Cir. 2000)*	For 201, 186 Against 183,114
I 126	Duties of Departments Regarding Records. (Alvin Birkholz) *Insufficient number of signatures filed to place measure on ballot.*	
I 127	Stopping and Parking Vehicle Limitations. (Alvin Birkholz) *Insufficient number of signatures filed to place measure on ballot.*	

(continued)

APPENDIX A (continued)

I 128	Qualifications, Powers, and Duties of Game Wardens. (Alvin Birkholz) *Insufficient number of signatures filed to place measure on ballot.*	
I 129	Government Disclosure. (Alvin Birkholz) *Insufficient number of signatures filed to place measure on ballot.*	
I 130	Establish Office of State Court Auditor. (Alvin Birkholz) *Insufficient number of signatures filed to place measure on ballot.*	
I 131	Restrictions on Fishing Methods. (Alvin Birkholz) *Insufficient number of signatures filed to place measure on ballot.*	
I 132	Term Limits. (Fred Thomas-Montanans for Term Limitation)	For 172,911 **Against 207,508**

1998

I 133	Repeal the Montana State Lottery Act of 1985. (David Ewer) *Insufficient number of signatures filed to place measure on ballot.*	
I 134	Repeal the Montana Retail Motor Fuel Marketing Act. (Jack Gunderson).	**For 172,081** Against 146,629
I 135	Revising DUI laws and Sale of Alcohol. (Sharon Snell) *Insufficient number of signatures filed to place measure on ballot.*	
I 136	Revising Outfitter and Hunting Licensing. (Brad Molnar)	For 141,425 **Against 180,280**
I 137	Prohibit Cyanide Process Open Pit Gold and Silver Mining. (MEIC)	**For 169,991** Against 155,034
I 138	Electric Utility Restructuring. (MEIC) *Insufficient number of signatures filed to place measure on ballot.*	
I 139	Requiring the State to Acquire all Water Rights Owned by Montana Power Company on May 1, 1997 in Connection with Its Power Generation Dams. (Russell B. Hill) *Insufficient number of signatures filed to place measure on ballot.*	
I 140	Requiring the State to Acquire Water Rights Exceeding 4,000 Acre-feet that are Connected with Power Generation Dams Sold between May 1997 and July 2004. (Russell B. Hill) *Insufficient number of signatures filed to place measure on ballot.*	
LR 113	Continue the Authority for the Tax Levy for the Support of the Montana University System for 10 Years. (SB133)	**For 199,871** Against 125,656

(continued)

IR 114	Repeal HB 575, Corporate Contributions to Ballot Issues. (Jonathan Motl) *HB 575 was ruled unconstitutional, so IR 114 was moot.*	**Approve HB 575: 161,476** Reject HB 575: 144,425

2000

I 141	Delete Requirement of SSI Number on Certain Recreational Licenses. (Gary Marbut) *Insufficient number of signatures filed to place measure on ballot.*	
I 142	Game Farm Reform. (Stan Frasier) *WITHDRAWN AND REFILED AS I 143.*	
I 143	Game Farm Reform. (Stan Frasier)	**For 204,282** Against 193,079
LR 115	Revising Taxation of Certain Vehicles. (HB540)	**For 228,737** Against 168,396
LR 116	Repealing State Inheritance Taxes. (HB7)	**For 265,951** Against 126,274

2002

I 144	Replace plurality voting with instant runoff voting. (Matthew Singer) *WITHDRAWN BY SPONSOR.*	
I 145	Montana Hydroelectric Security Act: To create a public power commission to purchase or condemn hydroelectric dams whose acquisition it determines to be in the public interest. (Sen. Ken Toole)	For 103,742 **Against 221,999**
I 146	To dedicate 49 percent of Montana's yearly tobacco settlement funds for tobacco disease prevention and expanding access to health insurance programs. (Alliance for a Healthy Montana)	**For 209,638** Against 113,065
IR 117	To reject HB 474, a bill to change provisions of the deregulation of the electricity industry. (Rep. Michelle Lee)	Approve HB 474 116,370 **Reject HB 474: 177,966**

2004

I 147	Allow open-pit mining for gold or silver using heap leaching or vat leaching with cyanide ore-processing reagents.	For 185,974 **Against 257,280**
I 148	Montana Medical Marijuana Act.	**For 276,042** Against 170,579
I 149	The 2004 Healthy Kids, Healthy Montana Tobacco Tax Increase Act.	**For 282,448** Against 163,626
I 150	Montana public power board. *Insufficient number of signatures filed to place measure on ballot.*	

(continued)

APPENDIX A (continued)

2006

I 151	Raising the state minimum wage to the greater of either $6.15 an hour or the federal minimum wage, plus an annual cost-of-living adjustment.	**For 285,535** Against 107,294
I 152	Protect private property rights. *WITHDRAWN BY SPONSOR AND RESUBMITTED AS I-154.*	
I 153	Prohibiting certain former state officials and staff from becoming licensed lobbyists within 24 months following their departure from state government.	**For 288,098** Against 93,291
I 154	Protect private property rights. *Decertified by Supreme Court, Montanans for Justice v. State, 2006 MT 277, 10/26/2006.*	

APPENDIX B
Research Tools

Voter Information Pamphlets

The Montana Secretary of State Elections Bureau office prepares a pamphlet to be sent by county election administrators to all households with active registered voters. The pamphlet is also available at all voting precincts. Starting in 2006, these voter information pamphlets are online at http://sos.mt.gov/ELB/Voter_Information.asp. The Secretary of State's office has a complete run of the voter pamphlets from 1920 to 2006, and the Montana Legislative Library contains paper copies of the pamphlets from 1972 to 2006.

The voter information pamphlet contains, for each ballot issue appearing on the ballot, the ballot title, fiscal statement, if applicable, complete text of the issue, form in which the issue will appear on the ballot, arguments for and against the issue and the rebuttal arguments. The names of the members of the committees who draft the arguments and rebuttals are also included. Other additional information for voters is also usually included in the pamphlet.

Almanacs and Encyclopedias

Barone, Michael. *The Almanac of American Politics.* Chicago: University of Chicago Press, 2006.

> This source features in-depth profiles and photographs of every governor and member of Congress, as well as insightful narratives for each state and congressional district. Also includes district maps, information on campaign expenditures, voting records, and census data.

The Encyclopedia of Public Choice. Norwell, MA: Kluwer Academic Publishers, 2004.

The Hutchinson Encyclopedia of Modern Political Biography. Oxford, England: Helicon Pub., 2004.

"Referendum." *West's Encyclopedia of American Law*. (2nd ed.), vol. 8 (2005): 264-265. General background information on the history and operation of the referendum. The referendum, along with the initiative, are two forms of direct legislation adopted by many states during the direct democracy movement of the early twentieth century. Referendum allows the people to state their opinion on laws that have been enacted by the legislature, and the initiative allows the people to propose their own laws.

Waters, Dane. *Initiative and Referendum Almanac*. Carolina Academic Press, 2003.

Annotated Codes

The **Montana Code Annotated** (MCA) is produced biennially by Montana Legislative Services Division, Capitol Rm. 110, Helena, MT 59620. Ballot issues are specifically addressed at MCA Title 13, Chapter 27, available online at http://data.opi.mt.gov/bills/mca_toc/index.htm. Part 1 contains general provisions such as initiative and referendum procedures, time for filing, penalties for violations, etc. Part 2 addresses the form of petitions. Submission and processing of petitions is the focus of Part 3 and involves tabulations of signatures by the Secretary of State and review of the ballots by the Attorney General's office. Part 4 of Title 13, Chapter 27 contains the provisions for the voter informational pamphlets previously discussed. In addition, Part 5 contains the statutes pertaining to the election procedure which falls under the purview of the Secretary of State.

Periodicals and Periodicals Indexes

The Montana Legislative Reference Center (leglib@mt.gov) maintains **hard copy subject files** of initiative and referendum issues in general, and Montana specifically since 1979. These files contain newspaper clippings, articles from both state and national publications, and legislatively produced documents relating to the topic. These subject files are searchable via the library's in-house database and use the same subject headings as those utilized for bill drafting by Montana Legislative Services. The reference center also has Montana **newspaper clips**, **indexed articles** from Montana and national articles, and **legislative staff memos** on the topic of initiative and referendum that are accessible via its in-house database.

Internet Resources

Montana Secretary of State, at http://sos.mt.gov/ELB/index.asp. The Secretary of State's election staff is responsible for interpreting state election laws and ensuring that they are implemented uniformly throughout the state. It also qualifies candidates for the ballot; qualifies initiatives and referendums for the ballot; certifies the language and form of the ballot; publishes the official state voter information pamphlet; conducts the official canvass of election results; and trains local election officials.

Montana Legislature, at http://www.leg.mt.us. Information on Montana's ballot measures http://leg.mt.gov/css/research/information/ballot_measures.asp. Contains names, numbers, and votes on all ballot measures from 1981 to 2006. See also the Montana Legislative Reference Catalog at http://leg.mt.gov/css/research/library/default.asp where one can search and find a number of reference books on the topic of initiative and referendum.

APPENDIX C Selected Bibliography

General Background Materials

Bone, Hugh. *The Initiative and Referendum.* New York: National Municipal League, 1975.

> Includes an analysis of the history of I&R in each state. Also includes chapters on the constitutional initiative, the theory of direct legislation, the uses of popular lawmaking, and some constitutional and practical questions. Although old, the material in this book is still relevant for background purposes in researching I&R.

Braunstein, Richard. *Initiative and Referendum Voting: Governing Through Direct Democracy.* New York: LFB Scholarly Pub., 2004.

> Addresses ballot issue politics in the United States In 1898, South Dakota became the first state in the nation to adopt initiative and referendum voting. Early twentieth century reformers believed that the legislative process had failed to live up to the expectation of representative governance. This book attempts to address the considerable gaps in our understanding of how the institutional dynamics of initiative and referendum voting drive outcomes in elections.

Broder, David. *Democracy Derailed: Initiative Campaigns and the Power of Money.* New York: Harcourt, 2000.

> A new form of government is sweeping across America: the initiative process, available in half the states and hundreds of cities. Where once most state laws were passed by legislatures, now voters decide directly on such explosive issues as drugs, affirmative action, casino gambling, assisted suicide, and human rights. Ostensibly driven by public opinion, the initiative process is, in reality, manipulated by moneyed interests, often funded by out-of-state millionaires pursuing their own agendas. In this highly controversial book David Broder tells how this revolution came about.

Durban, Thomas. *Initiative, Referendum, and Recall by Citizen Petition.* Washington, D.C.: Congressional Research Service, 1993.

> This report analyzes the concepts of state initiatives, referenda, and recalls as used in the various states and concentrates on these areas utilizing database searches in each state. Quite a comprehensive analysis.

Initiative and referendum in the 21st century: Final report and recommendations of the NCSL I&R Task Force: Washington, D.C.: National Conference of State Legislatures, 2003.

Piott, Steven L. *Giving Voters a Voice: The Origins of the Initiative and Referendum in America.* Columbia: University of Missouri Press, 2003.

> Although the initiative and referendum are generally regarded as key elements of progressive reform, Piott demonstrates that both were actually the culmination of a broad-based movement launched in the 1890s by a number of long-forgotten individuals. Piott examines 16 states that adopted measures between 1898 and 1918.

Montana Resources

Constitution of the State of Montana: As adopted by the Constitutional Convention, March 22, 1972, and as ratified by the people, June 6, 1972; Referendum No. 68. Indianapolis, IN: Allen Smith Company, 1972.

> Probably the most important referendum in Montana history, the voters of the state adopted a new state Constitution in 1972. Article II, Section 10's right of privacy provision–The right of individual privacy is essential to the well-being of a free society and shall not be infringed without the showing of a compelling state interest–is one of the strongest in the nation and the subject of much debate in the state.
> The Montana Secretary of State's Office has compiled two large lists of information relating to the initiative and referendum process in Montana. One (contained in Appendix A of this article) is a summary of all referenda and initiatives in the state since they were permitted in 1906. The other is a list of the amendments to the Montana Constitution since 1972. This list includes all amendments proposed by petition or the legislature whether or not they were adopted. Call the Montana Secretary of State's Election Office at (406) 444-5346 to receive copies of these very helpful lists.

Voter's Information Pamphlets. Available in the Montana Legislative Reference Center or the Montana Secretary of State's Office.

> The voter information pamphlet contains, for each ballot issue appearing on the ballot, the ballot title, fiscal statement, if applicable, complete text of the issue, form in which the issue will appear on the ballot, arguments for and against the issue and the rebuttal arguments.

Waldron, Ellis. *Atlas of Montana Elections, 1889-1976.* Missoula, MT: University of Montana, 1978.

> Includes a great deal of ballot information up to 1976.

CONTACT INFORMATION FOR MONTANA RESOURCES

The **Montana Secretary of State's Election Bureau** office is the "official" source of initiative and referendum materials in Montana. Write the Elections Bureau at P.O. Box 202801, Helena, MT 59620-2801, e-mail soselection@mt.gov, or call (406) 444-5346.

The **Montana Legislative Reference Center**, home to the ballot measure drafters, has copies of all documentation relating to proposed ballot measures, including the initial request, subsequent correspondence, and the actual text of the measures. Write the Montana Legislative Reference Center at State Capitol, Rm. 10, P.O. Box 210706, Helena, MT 59620-1706, e-mail leglib@mt.gov, or call (406) 444-3588 for more information.

The **Montana Historical Society** also has copies of older archived materials related to Montana's initiative and referendum process. Write to the Montana Historical Society at 225 N. Roberts, P.O. Box 210201, Helena, MT 59620-1201, e-mail kbjork@mt.gov, or call (406) 444-7428 for assistance.

Researching the Initiative and Referendum Process in Nebraska

Patrick J. Charles

INTRODUCTION

Nebraska has a rich history regarding the initiative and referendum process and there has been quite a lot written about it.[1] The "initiative" is the first power reserved by the people and is found in Article III, § 2 of the Nebraska Constitution. In Nebraska, an initiative is defined as a petition in which the voters can potentially create new laws or amend the Nebraska Constitution. The initiative process allows the people to amend the Nebraska Constitution and enact laws separate and independent from the Nebraska Legislature.

The second power reserved by the people is the "referendum" and it is found in Article III, § 3 of the Nebraska Constitution. In Nebraska, a referendum is defined as a petition in which the voters can strike down or repeal an existing statute. In Nebraska, the referendum can only be used to repeal laws passed within the most recent legislative session.[2]

Initiatives can address almost any issue; however, they cannot interfere with the Legislature's ability to raise revenue. Initiatives can only deal with a single subject as mandated by Art. III, § 2 of the Nebraska Constitution. Additionally, there are restrictions in place to provide that the same or similar initiative petitions cannot be submitted within a three-year period. These restrictions to the initiative process have been the subject of much controversy and the Nebraska Supreme Court recently visited these issues in *State ex rel. Lemon v. Gale*, 272 Neb. 295, 721 N.W.2d 347 (2006).

This article is meant to be a research guide for those interested in researching statewide initiatives and referendums in Nebraska. This guide will give a brief history of the initiative and referendum process in Nebraska. Following that there will be a step-by-step description of the initiative and referendum process in Nebraska. Included in this will be a description of the major parties involved in the initiative and referendum process in Nebraska. The final part will describe the various sources one would consult when researching initiatives and referendums in Nebraska. Appendix A includes citations to the Nebraska Constitution and Nebraska Revised Statutes that directly or indirectly affect the initiative and referendum process in Nebraska. Appendix B includes a selective bibliography of books and articles specific to the initiative and referendum process in Nebraska. Appendix C includes a list of major cases which have analyzed initiative and referendum issues in Nebraska.

HISTORY OF THE INITIATIVE AND REFERENDUM PROCESS IN NEBRASKA

In 1897, Nebraska became the first state to authorize initiatives and popular referendums by permitting cities to put the procedures in their charters; however, it wasn't until 1907 when the cities of Lincoln and Omaha enabled the initiative and referendum process.[3] In 1912, Nebraska allowed citizens to use initiatives and referendums on a statewide level.[4] At that time the Populist Party in Nebraska was at its zenith and four sections dealing with initiatives and referendums were adopted by constitutional amendment by nearly a thirteen to one margin.[5]

From 1914-2006, the voters of Nebraska have voted on sixty-three (63) initiative and referendum measures and have only adopted twenty-two (22) measures for a passage rate of 35%.[6] Perhaps the most famous Nebraska initiative was the 1934 passage of an initiative measure intended to amend the Nebraska Constitution and create the Nebraska Unicameral Legislature. This initiative abolished Nebraska's two-chambered Legislature and created the Unicameral Legislature.

The initiative and referendum have made the people co-equal with the Legislature when it comes to creating new legislation and, as a result, this has caused some animosity on the part of the Legislature towards the initiative and referendum process. Through the years, the Legislature has attempted to restrict or limit the initiative and referendum process.[7] The Nebraska Supreme Court has allowed the Nebraska Legislature to enact some laws to facilitate the initiative and referendum process, and the Legislature may enact reasonable legislation to prevent fraud or to render intelligible the purpose of the proposed law or constitutional amendment; however, legislation that would obstruct, hamper or render ineffective initiatives and referendums are unconstitutional.[8]

PROCEDURE IN NEBRASKA

Filing

Sponsors who have an idea for an initiative or referendum measure must deliver to the Secretary of State a statement of the object of the petition and the text of the measure, along with the names and addresses of every person, association or corporation sponsoring the petition.[9] Once the Secretary of State receives this information, it is sent to the Revisor of Statutes. Within ten (10) days after submission by the Secretary of State, the Revisor of Statutes must prepare a written review of the petition and can suggest changes to form and draftsmanship.[10] If there are any suggested changes by the Revisor of Statutes, the Secretary of State then informs the sponsor and they may accept or reject the Revisor's changes. These suggested changes are kept confidential for five (5) days after receipt by the sponsor.[11]

After the changes are made, then the Secretary of State must provide the sponsor with five (5) camera ready copies within five (5) days. It is the sponsor's responsibility to print the petitions to be circulated. Neb. Rev. Stat. §§ 32-1401 to -1411 (2004) provides initiative and referendum forms.

Sponsors may also be subject to the campaign finance provisions of the Nebraska Political Accountability and Disclosure Act.[12]

Circulation of the Petition for Signatures

After the sponsors have the petitions, the next step involves gathering signatures. The required number of signatures is based on the number of registered voters at the filing deadline. The required number of signatures is also contingent upon the type of measure on the ballot. For an initiative to propose a law, it must be signed by seven percent (7%) of the registered voters in the state.[13] For an initiative to amend the constitution, it must be signed by ten percent (10%) of the registered voters in the state.[14] For a referendum petition, the required number of signatures is five percent (5%) of the registered voters in the state.[15] For a referendum to suspend a law from taking effect, ten percent (10%) of registered voters in the state must sign the petition.[16]

In addition to the signature requirement, there is a distribution requirement for initiatives and referendums. Signatures must be collected from five percent (5%) of the registered voters of each of two-fifths (38 of 93) of the counties in the state.[17]

Submitting the Petition

Nebraska requires the petitions be filed at least four (4) months prior to the general election at which the proposal would be submitted for the voters. After the requisite number of signatures is gathered by the sponsor, the sponsor submits the signed petitions to the Secretary of State for verification.

Verification of the Signatures

Signatures are verified by the Secretary of State with the aid of the county election commissioners and county clerks.[18] Upon receipt of the petitions, the county officials compare the signatures with the voter registration records. For those signatures not found in the voter registration records and determined to be invalid, the county official must submit a written certification of the reasons for the invalidation for each signature.[19] Within forty (40) days, the county officials must return the verified petitions and certifications to the Secretary of State.

Certification

The Secretary of State then totals the valid signatures and determines if all the constitutional and statutory requirements have been met. If all the requirements are met, then the measure is certified to appear on the general election ballot.[20]

Pre-Election Period

When an initiative or referendum is certified by the Secretary of State, the Secretary of State provides a copy of the measure to the Nebraska Attorney General. The Attorney General then writes, in no more than one hundred (100) words, a ballot title for the measure and files this with the Secretary of State.[21] Any person who is not satisfied with the ballot title written by the Attorney General may, within ten (10) days after the ballot title is filed, appeal to the District Court asking the court to create a different ballot title.[22] The District Court will examine the ballot title, hear arguments and render a decision by September 1 prior to the general election.

Ballot titles for initiatives must clearly state that voters are voting either "For" the measure or "Against" the measure.[23] Ballot titles for referendums must clearly state that voters are voting either to "Retain" the measure or "Repeal" the measure.[24] After the ballot title's language is finalized, it is delivered to the Secretary of State. The Secretary of State then assigns a number to the measure. From 1986 onwards, initiatives and referendums have been numbered consecutively beginning with 400.[25] All initiatives and referendums are submitted in a strictly nonpartisan manner without any indication they have been endorsed by any political party.[26]

The Secretary of State then gives this information to county election commissioners or county clerks so that they may place them on the official ballots.[27]

Prior to the election, the Secretary of State is required to notify the voters of the existence of the ballot measures via three (3) different methods. The first method of notification is through the publication of an informational pamphlet on all the initiative and referendum measures on the ballot.[28] The Secretary of State writes, in no more than two hundred fifty (250) words, the arguments for and against each measure.[29] The information may be provided by sponsors, opponents or other interest parties of each measure. These informational pamphlets are then distributed by the Secretary of State to county election commissioners or county clerks throughout the state at least six (6) weeks prior to the general election.[30] The Secretary of State's second method of notification is to hold at least one (1) public hearing in each Congressional District in order to elicit public comment on the measures.[31] These hearings must be widely publicized and held at least eight (8) weeks prior to the general election. The final method of notification required of the Secretary of State is the publication of the ballot title and the entire text of each measure in all legal newspapers in the state once each week for three (3) consecutive weeks immediately prior to the general election.[32]

Election

In order for a measure to pass it must have a majority of votes, as well as at least thirty-five percent (35%) of the votes cast in that general election.[33]

Post-Election Period

After the general election, initiative and referendum votes are counted by the county election commissioners or county clerks and these results are sent to the Secretary of State.

On the fourth Monday after the election, the State Canvassing Board must certify the statewide results of the election regarding the ballot measures.[34] The State Canvassing Board then forwards the results to the Governor. The Governor shall issue a proclamation declaring that the voters have approved (or denied) the initiative or referendum. If two (2) or more conflicting measures pass, the Governor shall proclaim which is paramount in accordance with Neb. Rev. Stat. § 32-1416.[35] The proclamation and results are forwarded to the Secretary of State for publication.[36]

MAJOR PARTIES INVOLVED IN NEBRASKA'S INITIATIVE AND REFERENDUM PROCESS

Sponsors of the Initiative and Referendum Petition: Sponsors can be any person, association or organization. There is no Nebraska residency requirement to sponsor an initiative or referendum petition. Because of this, there have sometimes been critical advertising campaigns done by opponents of a particular initiative or referendum if it was sponsored by an out-of-state organization.

Nebraska Secretary of State: The Secretary of State is probably the most important entity in the entire initiative and referendum process. The Nebraska Secretary of State receives the object statement of the petitions from the sponsors; provides the Revisor of Statutes with the language of petition; provides the sponsors with the final language of petition before signatures are gathered; verifies the signatures on the petitions; publishes the informational pamphlets on initiatives and referendums; holds public hearings on initiatives and referendums; publishes the full text of each initiative and referendum in legal newspapers; forwards the language of the initiatives and referendums to the county election commissioners and county clerks to be placed on the ballot for the general election; and makes sure that every measure approved by the voters is printed with the general laws.

Revisor of Statutes: The Revisor of Statutes has the duty of reviewing initiative and referendum petitions when they are initially submitted to the Secretary of State by the sponsors.

Circulators of the Initiative and Referendum Petition: There is no residency requirement for circulators of initiative and referendum petitions.[37] Circulators may circulate an initiative or referendum petition anywhere throughout the state. Nebraska allows circulators to be paid; however, the paid circulator must use a form that discloses that the circulator is being paid to gather signatures.[38] Circulators must sign an affidavit stating that the signatures were gathered and witnessed by the circulator.

Signers of the Initiative and Referendum Petition: Signers are the people who actually sign the initiative or referendum petition. Signers must be registered voters of Nebraska on or before the date on which the petition is required to be filed with the Secretary of State.[39]

State Canvassing Board: The State Canvassing Board certifies the state-wide results of ballot measures. The State Canvassing Board consists of the Governor, Attorney General, Auditor, Treasurer and Secretary of State.

County Election Commissioners and County Clerks: County election commissioners and county clerks put the initiative and referendum measures on the local ballots. In addition, county election commission-ers and county clerks count the ballots after the election and forward the results to the State Canvassing Board.

Nebraska Accountability and Disclosure Commission: The Nebraska Accountability and Disclosure Commission is an independent adminis-trative agency that is responsible for enforcing the campaign finance provisions of the Nebraska Political Accountability and Disclosure Act. Under the act, ballot question committees are required to disclose re-ceipts and expenditures. A ballot question includes any initiative or refer-endum. A ballot question committee is any combination of two or more individuals that receives contributions or makes expenditures of more than $5,000 during a calendar year to support or oppose the qualifica-tion, passage, or defeat of a ballot question.[40]

Nebraska Attorney General: The Attorney General writes the ballot title for each measure. Additionally, the Attorney General issues Attorney General Opinions given at the request of a public official interpreting an administrative, statutory or constitutional provision. There are many Attorney General Opinions that discuss various aspects of the initiative and referendum process in Nebraska.

Nebraska District Court: The Nebraska District Court may be asked by any person dissatisfied with a ballot title written by the Attorney Gen-eral to come up with a ballot title that is sufficient and fair. The District Court also has the jurisdiction to hear cases where the Secretary of State has refused to place on the ballot an initiative or referendum measure.[41]

Nebraska Governor: The Governor issues a proclamation declaring that the voters have approved (or denied) an initiative or referendum measure. The Governor also issues a proclamation declaring a paramount initiative or referendum measure in situations where two (2) or more conflicting measures pass in the same election.

SOURCES AVAILABLE FOR INITIATIVE
AND REFERENDUM RESEARCH IN NEBRASKA

Nebraska Secretary of State's Web site, at http://www.sos.state.ne.us/elec/.

This site is the best source of information for current and recent successful and unsuccessful initiative and referendum measures.

This Web site contains PDF copies of the informational pamphlets on the initiative and referendum measures from the 2000, 2004 and 2006 general elections. Prior informational pamphlets can be obtained by contacting the Secretary of State's office or the Nebraska State Archives.

Beginning in 2006, the Secretary of State makes available the initiatives petition filing list which provides access to the petitions that have been filed for that particular election. This list links to PDF copies of the sponsor's sworn statements, the object statements, the sworn list of the sponsors of the petition, the final language of the measures, and the names and addresses of the sponsors.

According to *Schedule 34-4* from the Nebraska Records Management Division of the Office of the Secretary of State, the historical files of initiative and referendum records is to be retained permanently or transferred to the Nebraska State Archives at the Nebraska Historical Society after sixteen (16) years. The historical file includes: a sample of a petition; contributors and contribution reports; listing of circulators; administrative correspondence; District Court hearing files, orders and transcripts; certification of results; Secretary of State press releases and news clippings; copy of Governor's post-election proclamations.

This site also provides a PDF copy of a step-by-step guide for initiative and referendum sponsors entitled, *How to Use the Initiative and Referendum Process in Nebraska*. This guide is available at http://www.sos.state.ne.us/elec/pdf/ir_pamphlet.pdf.

Nebraska Accountability and Disclosure Commission's Web site, at http://nadc.nol.org.

This Web site includes the Nebraska Accountability and Disclosure Commission statutes, as well as the Commission's rules and regulations.

In addition, the site contains a very useful publication entitled, *Ballot Question Committee Treasurer's Guide*. This guide is available at http://nadc.nol.org/cf/ballot_questions_guide.html.

The Commission's site includes the campaign statements filed with the Commission by ballot question committees. Campaign statements disclose the amount and sources of contributions to the committee and the amount purposes of expenditures by the committee. The site also includes Reports of Contributions filed with the Commission by corporations, unions and by industry, trade or professional associations. Reports of Contributions disclose contributions and expenditures made to support or oppose ballot questions. In addition, advisory opinions, forms, instructional materials and a list of committees can be accessed on the Commission's site.

Nebraska Attorney General's Web site, at http://www.ago.state.ne.us/.

This Web site has a fully-searchable database of Nebraska Attorney General Opinions from January, 1981 to the present. Prior opinions can be found by contacting the Attorney General's Office or by checking the Nebraska State Law Library or the state's two academic law libraries. In addition, Nebraska Attorney General Opinions are available electronically on the following subscription databases: Casemaker (1997-present), Westlaw (NE-AG database from 1976-present) and LexisNexis (NE Attorney General opinions database from January, 1970-present).

Nebraska Governor's Web site, at http://www.gov.state.ne.us/proclamations/.

This Web site contains current proclamations as well as proclamations going back to 2005.

Nebraska State Historical Society

Messages and Proclamations of the Governors of Nebraska, 1854-1941 was published by the Nebraska State Historical Society in 1941 and contains proclamations from Nebraska Governors from 1854 to 1941.

Nebraska State Archives, at http://www.nebraskahistory.org/lib-arch/research/public/state.htm.

The Nebraska State Archives at the Nebraska Historical Society houses the initiative and referendum petition records from 1885 to 1988. In addition, the Nebraska State Archives at the Nebraska Historical Society has initiative and referendum proclamations that were issued by the various Governors.

This is the best source for researching prior successful and unsuccessful referendum and initiative measures in Nebraska.

The Nebraska *Legislative Journal*

The Nebraska *Legislative Journal* contains copies of the Secretary of State's election results for the general elections. The *Legislative Journal* is compiled under the authority of the Clerk of the Legislature and is available in print. The *Legislative Journal* for the current legislature is available at http://nebraskalegislature.gov/web/public/lj. Electronic access to prior editions of the *Legislative Journal* going back to 1999 are available using the Bill Finder feature on the Unicameral Legislature's Web site at http://uniweb.legislature.ne.gov/Apps/BillFinder/finder.php.

Nebraska District Court

The Nebraska District Court may be asked by any person dissatisfied with a ballot title written by the Attorney General to come up with a ballot title that is sufficient and fair. To locate the court file, contact the Lancaster County District Court Clerk to locate the file. The Secretary of State also has a copy of the District Court's file along with transcripts in the historical file.

NOTES

1. Steven L. Piott, *Giving Voters a Voice: The Origins of the Initiative and Referendum in America* 242 (University of Missouri Press 2003); Robert D. Miewald & Peter J. Longo, *The Nebraska Constitution: A Reference Guide* (Greenwood Press 1993); Don Stenberg, *Preserving the Democratic Legacy of the American Frontier: Limiting Regulation of the People's Initiative and Referendum Process, in The Battle Over Citizen Lawmaking* 217 (M. Dane Waters ed., Carolina Academic Press 2001); David Schmidt, *Citizen Lawmakers: The Ballot Initiative Revolution* (Temple University Press 1989); David A. Rahm, Note, *Citizens Versus Legislators–The Continuing Fight to Ensure the Rights of Initiative and Referendum in Nebraska: State ex rel. Stenberg v. Beermann*, 26 Creighton L. Rev. 195 (1992).

2. Neb. Const. art. III, § 3; Neb. Rev. Stat. § 32-1407(3) (2004).

3. Steven L. Piott, *Giving Voters a Voice: The Origins of the Initiative and Referendum in America* 244 (University of Missouri Press 2003).

4. Neb. Const. art. III, §§ 1-4.

5. David D. Schmidt, *Citizen Lawmakers: The Ballot Initiative Revolution* 249 (1989).

6. Clerk of the Legislature, *Nebraska Blue Book 2004-05*, 269-70 (2005).

7. For a discussion of this *see* David A. Rahm, Note, *Citizens Versus Legislators–The Continuing Fight to Ensure the Rights of Initiative and Referendum in Nebraska: State ex rel. Stenberg v. Beermann*, 26 Creighton L. Rev. 195 (1992).

8. *State ex rel. Ayres v. Amsberry*, 104 Neb. 273, 274, 177 N.W. 179, 180 (1920).

9. Neb. Rev. Stat. § 32-1405(1) (2004).

10. Neb. Rev. Stat. § 32-1405(2) (2004).

11. Neb. Rev. Stat. § 32-1405(2).

12. Neb. Rev. Stat. §§ 49-1401 to -14,139 (2004 & Supp. 2005).

13. Neb. Const. art. III, § 2.

14. Neb. Const. art. III, § 2.

15. Neb. Const. art. III, § 3.

16. Neb. Const. art. III, § 3.

17. Neb. Const. art. III, § 2.

18. Neb. Rev. Stat. § 32-1409 (2004).

19. Neb. Rev. Stat. § 32-1409(2).

20. Neb. Rev. Stat. § 32-1409(3).

21. Neb. Rev. Stat. § 32-1410(1) (2004).

22. Neb. Rev. Stat. § 32-1410(3) (2004).

23. Neb. Rev. Stat. § 32-1410(1).

24. Neb. Rev. Stat. § 32-1410(2) (2004).

25. Neb. Rev. Stat. § 32-1411(1) (2004).

26. Neb. Const. art. III, § 4; Neb. Rev. Stat. § 32-1411(2) (2004).

27. Neb. Rev. Stat. § 32-1411(3) (2004).

28. Neb. Rev. Stat. § 32-1405.01(1) (2004).

29. Neb. Rev. Stat. § 32-1405.01(2) (2004).

30. Neb. Rev. Stat. § 32-1405.01(3) (2004).

31. Neb. Rev. Stat. § 32-1405.02 (2004).

32. Neb. Rev. Stat. § 32-1413 (2004).

33. Neb. Const. art. III, § 4.

34. Neb. Rev. Stat. §§ 32-1037, -1414 (2004).

35. If two or more conflicting constitutional amendments or laws are approved in the same election, the measures receiving the greatest number of affirmative votes shall be paramount.

36. Neb. Rev. Stat. § 32-1415 (2004).

37. *Bernbeck v. Moore*, 126 F.3d 1114 (8th Cir. 1997).

38. Neb. Rev. Stat. § 32-628(2) (2004).

39. Neb. Rev. Stat. §§ 32-1037, -1404 (2004).

40. Neb. Rev. Stat. §§ 49-1406, -1409.

41. Neb. Rev. Stat. § 32-1412 (2004).

APPENDIX A
CITATIONS TO THE NEBRASKA CONSTITUTION AND THE NEBRASKA REVISED STATUTES FOR THE INITIATIVE & REFERENDUM PROCESS

Nebraska Constitution

Neb. Const. art. III, § 2.

This discusses the initiative process and initiative requirements in Nebraska.

Article III § 2:

The first power reserved by the people is the initiative whereby laws may be enacted and constitutional amendments adopted by the people independently of the Legislature. This power may be invoked by petition wherein the proposed measure shall be set forth at length. If the petition be for the enactment of a law, it shall be signed by seven percent of the registered voters of the state, and if the petition be for the amendment of the Constitution, the petition therefore shall be signed by ten percent of such registered voters. In all cases the registered voters signing such petition shall be so distributed as to include five percent of the registered voters of each of two-fifths of the counties of the state, and when thus signed, the petition shall be filed with the Secretary of State who shall submit the measure thus proposed to the electors of the state at the first general election held not less than four months after such petition shall have been filed. The same measure, either in form or in essential substance, shall not be submitted to the people by initiative petition, either affirmatively or negatively, more often than once in three years. If conflicting measures submitted to the people at the same election be approved, the one receiving the highest number of affirmative votes shall thereby become law as to all conflicting provisions. The constitutional limitations as to the scope and subject matter of statutes enacted by the Legislature shall apply to those enacted by the initiative. Initiative measures shall contain only one subject.

Neb. Const. art. III, § 3.

This discusses the referendum process and referendum requirements in Nebraska.

Article III § 3:

The second power reserved is the referendum which may be invoked, by petition, against any act or part of an act of the Legislature, except those making appropriations for the expense of the state government or a state institution existing at the time of the passage of such act. Petitions invoking the referendum shall be signed by not less than five percent of the registered voters of the state, distributed as required for initiative petitions, and filed in the office of the Secretary of State within ninety days after the Legislature at which the act sought to be referred was passed shall have adjourned sine die or for more than ninety days. Each such petition shall set out the title of the act against which the referendum is invoked and, in addition thereto, when only a portion of the act is sought to be referred, the number of the section or sections or portion of sections of the act designating such portion. No more than one act or portion of an act of the Legislature shall be the subject of each referendum petition. When the referendum is thus invoked, the Secretary of State shall refer the same to the electors for approval or rejection at the first general election to be held not less than thirty days after the filing of such petition.

When the referendum is invoked as to any act or part of act, other than emergency acts or those for the immediate preservation of the public peace, health, or safety, by petition signed by not less than ten percent of the registered voters of the state distributed as aforesaid, it shall suspend the taking effect of such act or part of act until the same has been approved by the electors of the state.

APPENDIX A (continued)

Neb. Const. art. III, § 4.

This discusses the number of signatures required, the number of votes cast in order for a measure to pass and authorizing the legislature to enact laws to facilitate the initiative and referendum process.

Article III § 4:

The whole number of votes cast for Governor at the general election next preceding the filing of an initiative or referendum petition shall be the basis on which the number of signatures to such petition shall be computed. The veto power of the Governor shall not extend to measures initiated by or referred to the people. A measure initiated shall become a law or part of the Constitution, as the case may be, when a majority of the votes cast thereon, and not less than thirty-five per cent of the total vote cast at the election at which the same was submitted, are cast in favor thereof, and shall take effect upon proclamation by the Governor which shall be made within ten days after the official canvass of such votes. The vote upon initiative and referendum measures shall be returned and canvassed in the manner prescribed for the canvass of votes for president. The method of submitting and adopting amendments to the Constitution provided by this section shall be supplementary to the method prescribed in the article of this Constitution, entitled, "Amendments" and the latter shall in no case be construed to conflict herewith. The provisions with respect to the initiative and referendum shall be self-executing, but legislation may be enacted to facilitate their operation. All propositions submitted in pursuance hereof shall be submitted in a non-partisan manner and without any indication or suggestion on the ballot that they have been approved or endorsed by any political party or organization. Only the title or proper descriptive words of measures shall be printed on the ballot and when two or more measures have the same title they shall be numbered consecutively in the order of filing with the Secretary of State and the number shall be followed by the name of the first petitioner on the corresponding petition.

Nebraska Revised Statutes

Neb. Rev. Stat. §§ 32-1401 to -1417 (2004).

These sections discuss the initiative and referendum process on a statewide level in Nebraska.

Neb. Rev. Stat. §§ 18-2501 to -2538 (1997 & Supp. 2005).

These sections discuss the initiative and referendum process for Nebraska cities and other municipal subdivisions.

Neb. Rev. Stat. §§ 32-628 to -632 (2004 & Supp. 2005).

These sections discuss the requirements for petitions and gathering signatures.

Neb. Rev. Stat. §§ 49-101 to -14.141 (2004 & Supp. 2005).

This is the Nebraska Political Accountability and Disclosure Act which are Nebraska's campaign finance statutes.

APPENDIX B
SELECTIVE NEBRASKA INITIATIVE & REFERENDUM BIBLIOGRAPHY

Thomas E. Cronin, *Direct Democracy: The Politics of Initiative, Referendum and Recall* (Harvard University Press 1989).

> Cronin, a political scientist, examines the use of initiatives, referendums and other forms of direct democracy in the United States.

Nebraska Accountability and Disclosure Commission, *Ballot Question Committee Treasurers' Guide* (Nebraska Accountability and Disclosure Commission 2003).

> This seventeen page pamphlet published by the Nebraska Accountability and Disclosure Commission provides assistance to initiative and referendum petition sponsors in complying with provisions of the Nebraska Political Accountability and Disclosure Act that pertain to campaign finance practices.

Nebraska Office of the Secretary of State, *How to Use the Initiative and Referendum Process in Nebraska* (Nebraska Office of the Secretary of State 2004).

> This twelve page pamphlet published by the Nebraska Secretary of State provides the basic information on the rules and procedures for those wishing to use the initiative or referendum process in Nebraska.

Steven L. Piott, *Giving Voters a Voice: The Origins of the Initiative and Referendum in America* (University of Missouri Press 2003).

> Piott's book examines the history of initiatives and referendums in sixteen different states. Of particular interest to Nebraska researchers is the chapter which discusses the early history of initiatives and referendums in Nebraska.

Robert D. Miewald & Peter J. Longo, *The Nebraska Constitution: A Reference Guide* (Greenwood Press 1993).

> This comprehensive guide to the Nebraska Constitution provides an article by article historical and legal analysis of the Nebraska Constitution. Of particular interest is the chapter which discusses Article III, sections 2 through 4, the provisions relating to initiatives and referendums.

David A. Rahm, Note, *Citizens Versus Legislators–The Continuing Fight to Ensure the Rights of Initiative and Referendum in Nebraska: State ex rel. Stenberg v. Beermann*, 26 Creighton L. Rev. 195 (1992).

> This law review case note examines the history of the initiative and referendum process in Nebraska. It also looks at recent legislative attempts to restrict the initiative and referendum process and the Nebraska Supreme Court's response to these legislative restrictions.

David Schmidt, *Citizen Lawmakers: The Ballot Initiative Revolution* (Temple University Press 1989).

> Schmidt's book provides a comprehensive history of initiatives and referendums in Nebraska, as well as other states. In addition, this book provides guidance for initiative and referendum organizers.

M. Dane Waters, *Initiative and Referendum Almanac* (Carolina Academic Press 2003).

> This book is written by Dane Waters,President of the Initiative and Referendum Institute at the University of Southern California. It is the most complete and comprehensive history of the initiative and referendum process in the United States.

The Battle Over Citizen Lawmaking: An In-Depth Review of the Growing Trend to Regulate the People's Tool of Self-Government: The Initiative and Referendum Process (M. Dane Waters ed., Carolina Academic Press 2001).

APPENDIX B (continued)

This book presents a series of articles promoting the idea that legislatures throughout the country are damaging the initiative and referendum process by imposing undue and un-necessary restrictions. Of particular interest to Nebraska researchers is former Nebraska Attorney General Don Stenberg's chapter entitled, "Preserving The Democratic Legacy of the American Frontier: Limiting Regulation of the People's Initiative and Referendum Process."

Nebraska Records Management Division, *Schedule 34-4 Secretary of State Elections Division* (Nebraska Office of Secretary of State 2004).

This nine page pamphlet from the Records Management Division of the Nebraska Secretary of State provides the policies and procedures relating to the retention of initiative and refer-endum records in Nebraska.

APPENDIX C
MAJOR NEBRASKA STATE & FEDERAL CASES

West Topics & Key Numbers

Constitutional Law 9-9(.5)

Elections 175, 184 and 189

Nebraska Cases Discussing the Initiative Process

Bernbeck v. Moore, 126 F.3d 1114 (8th Cir. 1997).
This Eighth Circuit case discusses the constitutionality of statutory requirements relating to initiative circulators.

Dobrovolny v. Moore, 126 F.3d 1111 (8th Cir. 1997).
This Eighth Circuit case discusses the constitutionality of statutory requirements relating to initiative signatures.

Duggan v. Beermann, 245 Neb. 907, 515 N.W.2d 788 (1994).
This Nebraska Supreme Court case discusses the constitutionality of statutory requirements relating to initiative signatures.

Loontjer v. Robinson, 266 Neb. 902, 670 N.W.2d 301 (2003).
This Nebraska Supreme Court case discusses the scope and meaning of the "single subject" requirement for initiative petitions.

State ex rel. Bellino v. Moore, 254 Neb. 385, 576 N.W.2d 793 (1998).
This Nebraska Supreme Court case discusses the constitutionality of statutory requirements relating to initiative signatures.

State ex rel. Brant v. Beermann, 217 Neb. 632, 350 N.W.2d 18 (1984).
This Nebraska Supreme Court case discusses the subject matter of initiative petitions.

State ex rel. Labedz v. Beermann, 229 Neb. 657, 428 N.W.2d 608 (1988).
This Nebraska Supreme Court case discusses the process of challenging initiative petitions.

State ex rel. Lemon v. Gale, 272 Neb. 295, 721 N.W.2d 347 (2006).
This Nebraska Supreme Court case discusses the scope and meaning of the resubmission clause to the Nebraska Constitution relating to initiative petitions.

State ex rel. Morris v. Marsh, 183 Neb. 521, 162 N.W.2d 262 (1968).
This Nebraska Supreme Court case discusses the statutory requirements relating to initiative circulators.

State ex rel. Stenberg v. Beermann, 240 Neb. 754, 485 N.W.2d 151 (1992).
This Nebraska Supreme Court case discusses the constitutionality of statutory requirements relating to initiative circulators.

State ex rel. Winter v. Swanson, 138 Neb. 597, 294 N.W. 200 (1940)
This Nebraska Supreme Court case discusses the power of the legislature to enact laws facilitating the operation of the initiative process.

Nebraska Cases Discussing the Referendum Process

Klosterman v. Marsh, 180 Neb. 506, 143 N.W.2d 744 (1966).
This Nebraska Supreme Court case discusses the type of legislation in which a referendum may be invoked.

Lawrence v. Beermann, 192 Neb. 507, 222 N.W.2d 809 (1974).
This Nebraska Supreme Court case discusses the constitutional provisions excepting appropriations bills from referendum petitions.

Ponylake School Dist. 30 v. State Committee for Reorganization of School Districts, 271 Neb. 173, 710 N.W.2d 609 (2006).
This Nebraska Supreme Court case discusses the right of voters to conduct a referendum.

State ex rel. Ayres v. Amsberry, 104 Neb. 273, 177 N.W. 179 (1920).
This Nebraska Supreme Court case discusses the legislature's power to prevent fraud in the collection of signatures in referendum petitions.

State ex rel.Stenberg v. Moore, 251 Neb. 598, 558 N.W.2d 794 (1997).
This Nebraska Supreme Court case discusses the requirements of the explanatory statement relating to referendum petitions.

Researching Initiatives and Referenda: A Guide for Nevada

Thomas R. Boone

INTRODUCTION

The initiative and referendum (I&R) petition processes in Nevada serve distinct purposes. Initiatives allow voters to create new state statutes, amend existing statutes and amend the state constitution. Referenda, however, provide voters the opportunity to approve or disapprove existing legislation.

Performing legal research in Nevada can be a frustrating experience. Until the last decade or so, the population of the state remained quite low. As a result, few publishers created legal research materials for a market as small as Nevada. Naturally, I&R resources are few and far between, being limited mainly to government information published on the Internet.

HISTORY OF I&R IN NEVADA

Neither the initiative nor the referendum was included in the Nevada Constitution when first enacted in 1865.[1] As with many other states, however, both processes were added later as a result of the Progressive Movement of the late 1800s and early 1900s.[2]

Specifically, the referendum process was added to the state constitution in 1904.[3] The action has been used infrequently in Nevada and can only be used for legislative actions, not administrative ones. One unique aspect of Nevada's referendum procedures is the fact that once a statute has been approved through statewide referendum, the legislature cannot repeal or amend the statute. Instead, such changes can only be made through another voter referendum or initiative petition. Abortion rights activists took advantage of this requirement in 1990 by petitioning for a statewide referendum on Nevada's abortion statute. The referendum passed, meaning that even if the U.S. Supreme Court overturns *Roe v. Wade* at some point in the future, Nevada's statute will remain on the books unless another referendum petition process is completed and the State's voters overturn the law.[4]

The initiative process was added in 1912.[5] It was first used in the 1918 election to pass the State's alcohol prohibition statute.[6] The initiative process has been used more frequently than that for referenda, most frequently to amend the State constitution. Recent topics of ballot initiatives include medical marijuana (legalized in 1998) and same sex marriage (banned in 2000).[7] The 2006 election cycle resulted in significant media coverage for Nevada's initiative procedures, as heated court battles ensued over petitions concerning government spending and eminent domain.[8] Eventually, the Nevada Supreme Court threw out one of the measures and significantly limited the other.[9]

STATEWIDE INITIATIVE PROCESS

The first steps in Nevada's process for creating an initiative to propose or amend a state statute or to amend the state constitution are identical. First, a copy of the petition along with a 200-word description of the petition's effect must be filed with the Secretary of State's office.[10] For inclusion on the ballot, the petition must then be signed by enough registered voters to equal 10% of the votes cast in the previous general election.[11] This 10% requirement must be met in 75% of the state's counties, a provision that prevents a heavily populated county such as Clark or Washoe from single-handedly getting an initiative on the ballot.[12]

Following a petition's circulation for signatures, the parties must submit the initiative petition to the County Clerk or Registrar in the county in which it was circulated, and all documents must be submitted simultaneously. Within 4 days of receiving the petitions, the County Clerk or Registrar must add up the number of signatures on the petition and submit the total to the Secretary of State. Based on these figures, the Secretary of State determines if the petition has the minimum number of required signatures. If it falls short, the Secretary of State notifies those submitting the petition that no additional action will be undertaken on the initiative.[13] If, however, the petition does have the necessary signatures, the County Clerk or Registrar verifies the signatures by taking a random sample of 500 or 5% of the signatures (whichever is greater). Following verification, the County Clerk or Registrar forwards the results back to the Secretary of State.[14]

At this point the procedure differs depending upon the type of initiative. For petitions proposing a new state statute or an amendment to an existing statute, the Secretary of State sends the initiative to the state legislature as soon as the new session begins. The legislature has 40 days to either enact or reject the exact language of the submitted petition. If the legislature passes the petition and the Governor signs it, it becomes law. If, however, the legislature rejects the petition or fails to act on it within the 40 day period, the Secretary of State will place the proposed legislation on the ballot for the next general election. If the legislature wishes to propose separate legislation on the same subject, and the

governor approves the proposal, it will appear on the ballot along with
the original petition. In the event that both of the ballot measures pass,
the one receiving more total votes will become law.[15]

For petitions proposing an amendment to the Nevada Constitution,
the Secretary of State does not submit the initiative to the legislature,
but instead places the petition on the ballot for the next general election
immediately following the signature verification process. If the petition
passes, the Secretary resubmits the identical petition for inclusion on the
ballot for the following election. When the proposed amendment passes
for the second time, it is enacted. If the petition fails at either election,
however, no further action is taken.[16]

STATEWIDE REFERENDUM PROCESS

The procedures for referendum petitions in Nevada are nearly identical
to those for initiatives. A copy of the petition and a 200-word description
must be filed with the Secretary of State, and enough signatures of
registered voters must be gathered to equal 10% of the total votes cast in
the last general election (though only 10% total for the entire state, not
the 75% of counties required for initiative petitions).[17] In addition, the
County Clerk or Registrar verifies referendum petition signatures in the
exact same manner as for initiatives.[18]

If a referendum petition has a sufficient number of signatures, the
Secretary of State places it on the ballot for the next general election. If
approved, the statute involved remains in effect. If disapproved, the
statute becomes immediately void.[19]

RESEARCHING I&R IN NEVADA

Until the last decade or so, Nevada had an extremely low population
compared to most states. As a result, few legal publishers developed
research materials for the state, and state government did little to make
up the difference. As a result, little information exists for research into
Nevada I&R. What little does exist is limited to information published
by government agencies on the Internet. What follows below is an
overview of resources related to performing research about initiatives
and referenda in Nevada. When you need something not available from
the materials listed, the best option is to contact the Legislative Counsel
Bureau Research Library in Carson City at (775) 684-6827.

PRIMARY LAW

Constitution of the State of Nevada

The procedures for initiatives and referenda petitions are established in Article 19 of the State Constitution. The sections provide basic guidelines for each type of petition, including the required number of signatures.

Nevada Revised Statutes (NRS)

Chapter 295 of the NRS provides more of the specific details of Nevada I&R, outlining the specific procedures to be followed by the Secretary of State and county clerks. In addition, chapter 293 of the NRS contains statutes regarding various types of petitions which include those circulated in the I&R process.

Nevada Administrative Code (NAC)

Chapter 295 of the NAC consists of only two regulations dealing with initiatives and referenda, but the first of these is extremely important as it outlines the specific requirements for the documents of petition used in I&R campaigns.

STATE GOVERNMENT WEB SITES

Nevada Secretary of State, Elections Division, at http://www.sos. state.nv.us/nvelection/.

The Elections Division portion of this Web site features the *State of Nevada Initiative and Referendum Guide.* Published every two years, this guide provides step-by-step guides to citizens about Nevada I&R procedures, including the exact number of required signatures for petitions based upon the previous general election and specific due dates for different stages of the process. The guide also includes all pertinent sections of the Nevada Constitution, NRS, and NAC, along with sample blank petition forms. The Secretary of State Web site also has the complete text of all circulating I&R petitions for the last two general elections, dating back to 2004. In addition, the site contains Campaign Contributions and Expense Reports that include information concerning contributions made by and to candidates and political action committees (PAC) among others. The information concerning PACs includes contributions to I&R campaigns.

Vote Nevada–A Guide to Nevada Elections, at http://www.leg.state. nv.us/lcb/research/elecinfo.cfm.
This Web site is actually part of the Nevada Legislature Web site, maintained by the Legislative Counsel Bureau's Research Division. The site provides a great deal of information concerning elections in Nevada, including information on candidates and coverage of primary and general election results. Some of its I&R information duplicates that found on the Secretary of State Web site, including information on ballot questions from the most recent election and the text of recent circulating petitions. The most valuable information found here, however, is the full text of ballot questions for every general election in Nevada dating back to 1942.

A Political History of Nevada, 1996, at http://dmla.clan.lib.nv.us/ docs/nsla/archives/political/main.htm.
This book, published online by the Nevada State Library and Archives, contains a chapter titled "Questions on the Ballot," authored by Robert Erickson, Research Director at the time for Nevada's Legislative Counsel Bureau. The chapter outlines the state's I&R procedures as of 1996, and provides a list of ballot questions put before Nevada voters since I&R was first adopted.

NOTES

1. Eleanore Bushnell & Don W. Driggs, *The Nevada Constitution: Origin and Growth*, 48 (6th ed., U. Nev. Press, 1984).
2. Michael W. Bowers, *The Nevada State Constitution: A Reference Guide* 145 (Greenwood Press, 1993).
3. *Id.*
4. *Id.*
5. Bushnell & Driggs, *The Nevada Constitution* at 48.
6. *Initiative & Referendum Institute, Nevada*, http://www.iandrinstitute.org/ Nevada.htm.
7. *Id.*
8. Sean Whaley & Molly Ball, *Initiative rulings up, down*, Las Vegas Rev.-J. A4 (Sept. 9, 2006).
9. *Nevadans for Nev. v. Beers*, 142 P. 3d 339 (Nev. 2006); *Nevadans for the Prot. of Prop. Rights, Inc. v. Heller*, 141 P. 3d 1235 (Nev. 2006).
10. Nev. Const. art. 19, § 2(3).

11. Nev. Const. art. 19 § 2(2).
12. Bushnell & Driggs, *The Nevada Constitution* at 48.
13. Nev. Rev. Stat. § 293.1276 (2006).
14. Nev. Rev. Stat. § 293.1277 (2006).
15. Nev. Const. art. 19, § 2(3).
16. Nev. Const. art. 19, § 2(4).
17. Nev. Const. art. 19, § 1(1); Nev. Const. art. 19, § 1(2).
18. Nev. Rev. Stat. § 293.1276 (2006).
19. Nev. Const. art. 19, § 1(3).

Powers Reserved to the People: A Guide for Researching Initiatives and Referendums in North Dakota

Rhonda R. Schwartz

You are the people. It is for you to say what questions you want to vote on, which to adopt, and which to reject. There is no sense in preventing yourselves from doing what you want to do.[1]

INTRODUCTION

The right of the people in North Dakota to initiate or refer laws is guaranteed by Article III of the North Dakota Constitution. Article III provides, in part, that

> [T]he people reserve the power to propose and enact laws by the initiative, including the call for a constitutional convention; to approve or reject legislative Acts, or parts thereof, by the referendum; to propose and adopt constitutional amendments by the initiative; and to recall certain elected officials.

The purpose of this guide is to assist those who are researching initiatives and referendums in North Dakota. After a brief overview of initiatives and referendums, the guide begins with a short history of initiatives and referendums in North Dakota; continues with the current petition process and recall practices in North Dakota; includes selected statutes and case law; provides annotations for selected secondary materials; provides selected LexisNexis and Westlaw databases; and ends with selected Web sites.

OVERVIEW OF INITIATIVES AND REFERENDUMS

The Initiative and Referendum Institute in Washington D.C., a non-profit educational organization, provides helpful factsheets about the initiative and referendum process at its Web site.[2] Factsheet One is particularly useful for an initial overview of the terminology: "In many states, citizens have the ability to adopt laws or to amend the state constitution. This is commonly referred to as the Initiative process. In many of the same states, as well as others, the citizens have the ability to reject laws or amendments proposed by the state legislature. This process is commonly referred to as the Referendum process."[3] Although there is no national initiative process in the United States, 24 states have either a direct or indirect initiative process. The direct initiative is "when constitutional amendments or statutes proposed by the people are directly placed on the ballot and then submitted to the people for their approval or rejection (the state legislature has no role in this process)."[4] The indirect initiative, on the other hand, is "when statutes or amendments proposed by the people through a petition must first be submitted to the state legislature during a regular legislative session. If a legislature fails to approve the statute or amendment or it amends the proposal in a manner that is not acceptable to the proponents of the proposal, the proponents may proceed to collect the additional signatures, if required, to have the original proposal submitted to the voters."[5]

Just as there is no national initiative process in the United States, there is no national referendum process. However, 49 states have either a popular or legislative form of referendum. Popular referendum is "when the people have the power to refer, through a petition, specific legislation that was enacted by their legislature for the people to wither accept or reject."[6] Legislative referendum on the other hand, is "when the state legislature, an elected official, state appointed constitutional revision commission or other governmental agency or department submits propositions (constitutional amendments, statutes, bond issues, etc.) to the people for their approval or rejection."[7]

HISTORY OF INITIATIVES AND REFERENDUMS IN NORTH DAKOTA

Lars A. Ueland is often regarded as the "father" of the North Dakota initiative process. Both David Schmidt, in *Citizen Lawmakers: The Ballot Initiative Revolution*,[8] and M. Dane Waters, in *Initiative and Referendum Almanac*,[9] refer to Ueland as such. Lars Ueland was born in Wisconsin in 1855 and educated at Iowa's Luther College.[10] He homesteaded in Edgeley, North Dakota in 1887, and farmed in North Dakota for over twenty years. His strong interest in public affairs led him to organize a local unit of the Farmers' Alliance, an agrarian protest movement that fought against those who supported out-of-state corporate interests. Those interests were backed by Alexander McKenzie, the long-time leader of the North Dakota Republican party, the dominant political party. As a Republican himself (and later a Populist, then a Democrat), Ueland was elected to the first Legislative Assembly of North Dakota, serving in the winter of 1889-1890. He chose not to run for a second term, fearing that the Republican stronghold was not conducive to the reforms he and the Alliance favored.[11]

By 1892, Ueland had severed his ties with the Republican Party and had joined forces with the new People's Populist party and supported their platform which included the initiative and referendum. In 1896, Ueland was elected to the executive committee of the National Direct Legislation League, a league formed at the People's Party National Convention in St. Louis. The National Direct Legislation League functioned as an information bureau for issues regarding direct legislation.[12]

In 1902, Mrs. Katherine King of McKenzie organized the North Dakota Referendum League, an affiliate of the People's Sovereignty League of America. Mrs. King has been referred to as the "mother" of the North Dakota initiative process by both David Schmidt and M. Dane Waters. The North Dakota Referendum League functioned as an information bureau for the direct legislation movement in North Dakota. Mrs. King's League "won passage of Ueland's I&R bill through both houses of the legislature in 1907, despite opposition from Prohibitionists who feared the possibility of an initiative to repeal the state's anti-liquor amendment."[13]

The 1907 concurrent resolution, H.B. No. 26, was for an amendment to the North Dakota Constitution providing for the initiative and referendum.[14] Because the initiative and referendum amendment needed to be approved by the legislature in two successive sessions, the next year found Ueland out advocating for his cause. In an address delivered on January 13, 1908, in Valley City, North Dakota, Ueland provided his listeners with a brief overview of the origins of the initiative and referendum in Switzerland.[15] He acknowledged the objections that some might have to direct legislation: people will not vote; people are not intelligent enough; people are too anxious to vote; people might be corrupt; and the constitution should be stable.[16] Ueland addressed each concern, remarking, for example, about a stable constitution:

> Some say we want a stable and safe constitution. Yes, but that does not mean a stationary one. Large bodies move slowly. People are naturally conservative. They progress only gradually, and that constitution is most stable and safe that just keeps pace with them.[17]

Ueland sounded the rallying cry in Valley City:

> Think what a spectacle it is for the farmers of North Dakota, with such an overwhelming majority as they have, to ask meekly, please Mr. Representative, please Mr. Politician, may we not get a little law against the corporations, just a little; or please, Mr.

Representative, we humbly petition, can we have just a very small appropriation for the farming interest! More sensible it would be for the farmers to insist on getting the initiative and referendum, and then to say to their representatives: 'Do our bidding, and if you can't or won't, we will help ourselves to what we want.'[18]

Despite Ueland's efforts, the Legislative Assembly did not follow through in 1909 as needed, and the initiative effort failed. Nevertheless, both Ueland and King persevered, and in 1911 and 1913, the Legislative Assembly approved the initiative. In 1914, the voters of North Dakota also expressed their approval.

Two years later, North Dakota voters then tried, unsuccessfully, to use the initiative.

The first attempt to use the initiative in this state, the initiative of an amendment to the state constitution in 1916, ended in failure when the state Supreme Court declared the initiative on amendments not self-executing. However, the Non-Partisan League in 1918 initiated seven amendments to the Constitution, among them two amendments which made the initiative much easier to use, and this time the Supreme Court reversed its 1916 decision and declared the initiative on amendments measure self-executory. The League Amendments were adopted.[19]

M. Dane Waters briefly describes the Non-Partisan League in his *Initiative and Referendum Almanac*:

The watershed event in North Dakota's century of statehood was the agrarian revolt of 1915-1916, which spawned the Non-Partisan League, one of the most successful state-level reform organizations in the nation's history. In that revolt . . . farmers united against an unresponsive state government controlled by banks, railroads, and big grain dealers. The League put seven constitutional amendments on the 1918 ballot. All seven passed by similar majorities of about 58 percent.[20]

One of the two 1918 amendments changed the signature requirement for initiating a statutory measure from 10% of the voters in half of the counties to a flat 10,000 and to 7,000 for referring legislative actions. In addition, the amendment provided that initiated measures could go directly to a vote of the people, thereby changing the initiative process from indirect to direct.[21] The other 1918 amendment changed the signature requirement for initiating constitutional amendments from 25% of the voters in half the counties to a flat 20,000. In addition, the amendment provided that constitutional amendments could be submitted to the people by a simple majority vote in one legislative session rather the voters or the legislature approving the measure for a second time, as was previously required.[22] In 1978, the signature requirement was changed to 2% for statutory measures and to 4% for constitutional amendments.[23]

NO VOTER REGISTRATION IN NORTH DAKOTA

When researching the initiative and referendum, it is important to note that North Dakota is the only state in the nation without voter registration. The North Dakota Legislative Assembly enacted a bill in 1895 requiring voter registration, but in 1951 was the first state to abolish it. There were several later attempts to pass legislation requiring registration, but all proved unsuccessful. According to the Secretary of State's Web site,[24] the fact that North Dakota is a rural state with close community ties reduces the need for voter registration:

> North Dakota's system of voting, and lack of voter registration, is rooted in its rural character by providing small precincts. Establishing relatively small precincts is intended to ensure that election boards know the voters who come to the polls to vote on Election Day and can easily detect those who should not be voting in the precinct.[25]

Because there is no voter registration in North Dakota, the state is exempt from the National Voter Registration Act of 1993. The state is also exempt from several provisions of the 2002 Help America Vote Act (HAVA), including the implementation of a centralized voter registration system, the implementation of certain provisional voting requirements, and the voter identification requirements.[26]

The North Dakota Century Code does, however, include provisions for both the qualifications of electors and the approved forms of identification for voting purposes. The section of the North Dakota Century Code that provides for the qualifications of electors was amended in 2003, with new provisions added regarding college students, members of the armed forces, and temporary employment. North Dakota Century

Code section 16.1-01-04 currently provides, in part, for the qualifications of electors:

> (1) Every citizen of the United states who is eighteen years or older; a resident of this state; and has resided in the precinct at least thirty days next preceding any election, except as otherwise provided in regard to residency in chapter 16.1-14, is a qualified elector. (2) For the purposed of this title, every qualified elector may have only one residence, shown by an actual fixed permanent dwelling, establishment, or any other abode.

The section of the North Dakota Century Code providing for identification for voting purposes was amended in 2005. In addition to providing for challenges, verifications, and directing voters to the proper precincts, North Dakota Century Code section 16.1-05-07 now provides:

> Before delivering a ballot to an individual according to section 16.1-13-22, the poll clerks shall request the individual to show identification which includes the individual's residential address and date of birth. The identification may include: (a) An official form of identification issued by the state; (b) An official form of identification issued by a tribal government; (c) A form of identification prescribed by the secretary of state; or (d) A combination of any of the forms of identification under subdivisions a through c.

In addition, in 2003 a new chapter of the North Dakota Century Code was created. The new chapter, 16.1-02, provides for a permanent central voter file. North Dakota Century Code section 16.1-02-01 provides, in part:

> A permanent, centralized electronic data base of voters, to be known as the central voter file, is established with the offices of the secretary of state and county auditors linked together by a centralized statewide system . . . The central voter file must be accessible by the secretary of state and all county auditors for purposes of preventing and determining voter fraud, making changes and updating the central voter file, and generating information, including pollbooks, reports, inquiries, forms, and voter lists.

Several amendments to chapter 16.1-02 were passed in 2005, along with significant election reform legislation, to make the North Dakota election laws HAVA compliant where applicable. North Dakota retained its paper ballot optical scan voting system as well, utilizing Auto-MARK, the system preferred by representatives of North Dakota's disabilities communities.

Also of note, North Dakota municipalities may require voter registration. North Dakota Century Code section 40-21-10 provides:

> The governing body of any city may require the registration of voters in any election held or conducted within the municipality at such time and place or places as the governing body may designate.

Presently only one North Dakota city, Medora, registers its voters for city elections.

THE PETITION PROCESS IN NORTH DAKOTA

The petition process, as it is called in North Dakota, refers to both the initiative and referendum procedure. The office of the North Dakota Secretary of State provides a pamphlet entitled, *2005-2007 Initiating and Referring Law in North Dakota*, available at www.nd.gov/sos/ electvote/elections/measures.html. This pamphlet provides information about the current procedures of the petition process described below and provides helpful definitions of the terminology used in the process. Although the signatures needed for initiatives and referendums are gathered on petitions, the terms "petition" and "measure" are often used interchangeably (as in initiated petition/initiated measure and referral petition/referred measure). Once an initiative or referendum has been placed on the ballot, however, it is referred to as a "measure."

The petition process can be utilized to propose a statutory initiative, a constitutional initiative, or a referred measure (also called a referral initiative or referral drive). The statutory initiative petition process is used to amend or enact a law in the North Dakota Century Code. The constitutional initiative petition process is used to amend or enact a new portion of the North Dakota Constitution. The referred measure petition process is used to refer legislation passed by the Legislative Assembly to a vote of the people of North Dakota.

The election laws for North Dakota are found in Chapter 16.1 of the North Dakota Century Code. North Dakota Century Code section-16.1-01-09 provides for initiative and referendum petitions, and includes a form for petitions. Before a petition can circulate for signatures, the proponent of the petition first submits a request to the Secretary of State for approval of the petition. The petition must include a sponsoring committee, composed of twenty-five or more qualified North Dakota voters, whose names and addresses must appear on the petition. The sponsoring committee members complete an affidavit, a sworn statement stating that the member is a qualified North Dakota voter and has agreed to be on the sponsoring committee. This affidavit, known as the Signature Form, must be notarized. In addition, one member of the sponsoring committee must act as chair.

With all the needed signatures in place and notarized, the Secretary of State drafts a concise statement of the petition and presents it to the Attorney General for approval or disapproval. If approved, the statement is affixed to the petition before it is circulated to the general population for signatures and is called the "ballot title." The Secretary of State and the Attorney General have between five to seven business days to draft the ballot title. The ballot title, which represents the substance of the measure, appears on the petition immediately before the full text of the measure. If the petition is a referral petition, the petitioner must collect and file the required numbers of signatures within ninety days after the legislation is filed with the Secretary of State.

Gathering signatures is the next step in the petition process. The North Dakota Constitution Article III, Section 4 provides:

> The petition may be submitted to the secretary of state if signed by electors equal in number to two percent of the resident population of the state at the last federal decennial census.

The population of North Dakota at the last federal decennial census, in 2000, was 642,200.

The signature requirement for referral petitions is 2% of the resident population; for statutory initiatives, 2% is also required; and for constitutional initiatives, 4% of the resident population is required. All those who sign petitions must be qualified voters and must sign in the presence of those who circulate the petitions. In addition, the circulator, who must also be a qualified voter, must sign an affidavit affirming that petition was signed in his or her presence and that those who signed are (to the best of the circulator's knowledge) qualified voters.

The deadline to file an initiative petition and submit the signatures to the Secretary of State is no later than one year from the date the petition was approved for circulation. The deadline to file a referendum petition is within ninety days after the legislation that is being referred was signed by the Governor and filed with the Secretary of State.

In 2005, a new section was added to the North Dakota Century Code relating to the estimated fiscal impacts of initiated measures. Section 16.1-01-17 provides, in part:

> At least ninety days before a statewide election at which an initiated measure will be voted upon, the legislative council shall coordinate the determination of the estimated fiscal impact of the initiated measure . . . [t]he legislative council shall hold hearings, receive public testimony, and gather information on the estimated fiscal impact of the measure . . . At least thirty days prior to the public vote on the measure, the legislative council shall submit a statement of the estimated fiscal impact of the measure to the secretary of state.

The Secretary of State must then include a notice as to where copies of the fiscal impact statement can be obtained. If voters approve the initiated measure, a comparison must be made (within thirty days of the close of the complete fiscal year after the effective date) between the estimated and the actual fiscal impact of the measure.

Two initiated measures were on the ballot for the general election in November, 2006, an initiated constitutional measure relating to the taking of private property and an initiated measure relating to child custody and support. In accordance with North Dakota Century Code section 16.1-01-17, the North Dakota Legislative Council coordinated the estimated fiscal impact of the measures. For the taking of private property initiative, the North Dakota Department of Transportation and the Department of Commerce presented information and provided fiscal impact statement. For the parenting plans and child custody and support initiative, the North Dakota Supreme Court and the Department of Human Services presented information and provided fiscal impact statements.

RECALL IN NORTH DAKOTA

Article III of the North Dakota Constitution provides, in part, that "the people reserve the power to . . . recall certain elected officials." *Governing North Dakota, 2005-2005* provides a brief overview of recall in North Dakota at page 51:

> North Dakota is one of a dozen states providing for a procedure to force public officials to stand for election before their term are up. If citizens gather signatures equal to 25% of the vote last cast for

governor, they can force any elected judge, legislator, state executive, or county official to stand for election immediately. The 1989
legislature extended the recall to include all locally-elected officials
and provided that petitions bear the signatures of 25% of the
number of votes cast for the office in the last election. Once such
petitions are filed, a special election must be held within 60 days.

Although recall is rarely used, North Dakota was the first state to
recall its governor. In 1921, Governor Lynn Frasier was recalled, along
with the Attorney General and the Commissioner of Agriculture and
Labor. For more information, see Theodore Sharpe's *Recall* in the
Selected Annotated Bibliography *infra*.

SELECTED NORTH DAKOTA CENTURY CODE STATUTES

The following selected statutes from the North Dakota Century Code
are provisions relating to initiatives and referendums.
Estimated Fiscal Impact of an Initiated Measure
    N.D. Cent. Code § 16.1-01-17 (Supp. 2005)
Initiative or Referendum Petitions–Signature–Form–Circulation
    N.D. Cent. Code § 16.1-01-09 (2004 & Supp. 2005)
Permanent Central Voter File
    N.D. Cent. Code § 16.1-02-01 (2004)
Poll Clerks to Check Identification and Verify Eligibility
    N.D. Cent. Code § 16.1-05-07 (2004 & Supp. 2005)
Qualifications of Electors
    N.D. Cent. Code § 16.1-01-04 (2004)
Recall Petitions–Signature–Form–Circulation
    N.D. Cent. Code § 16.1-01-09.1 (2004 & Supp. 2005)
Registration of Voters [Municipalities]
    N.D. Cent. Code § 40-21-10 (2006)

SELECTED CASE LAW

The following list provides selected North Dakota case law related to
initiative and referendum issues.
Bolinske v. North Dakota State Fair Ass'n., 522 N.W.2d 426 (N.D. 1994).
    Right to circulate petition at state fair not hampered.
Coghlan v. Cuskelly, 62 N.D. 275, 244 N.W. 39 (1932).
    Withdrawal of signed recall petition.

Dawson v. Meier, 78 N.W. 2d 420 (N.D. 1956).
Validity of signature on petition and failure to add date.
Dawson v. Tobin, 74 N.D. 713, 24 N.W. 2d 737 (1946).
Statutes in conflict with amendments relating to initiative and referendum inoperative.
Hernett v. Meier, 173 N.W. 2d 907 (N.D. 1970).
Validity of signature on petition and date of affidavit.
Husebye v. Jaeger, 534 N.W. 2d 811 (N.D. 1995).
Constitutionality of period for submission of petitions.
Initiative and Referendum Institute v. Jaeger, 241 F. 3d 614 (8th Cir. 2001).
Affirmed district court's ruling upholding state law that prohibits paying circulators on a per-signature basis and requires that circulators be eligible North Dakota voters.
Municipal Servs. Corp. v. Kusler, 490 N.W. 2d 700 (N.D. 1992).
Adequacy of ballot title.
Nelson v. Gass, 27 N.D. 357, 146 N.W. 537 (1914).
The place of residency for purposes of voting.
Pelkey v. City of Fargo, 453 N.W. 2d 801 (N.D. 1990).
The power to initiate and refer relating to local laws and ordinances.
Schumacher v. Byrne, 61 N.D. 220, 237 N.W. 741 (1931).
Liberal construction of statute to facilitate circulation of petitions.
State ex rel. Frazier v. Hall, 50 N.D. 659, 197 N.W. 687 (1924).
Governor Frazier had power to accelerate election.
State ex rel. Langer v. Olson, 44 N.D. 614, 176 N.W. 528 (1920).
Legislative power vested in people through initiative and referendum.
State ex rel. Linde v. Hall, 35 N.D. 34, 159 N.W. 281 (1916).
Initiative on amendments not self-executing.
State ex rel. Twichell v. Hall, 44 N.D. 459, 171 N.W. 213 (1918).
Initiative on amendments self-executing.
Sunbehm Gas, Inc. v. Conrad, 310 N.W. 2d 766 (N.D. 1981).
Powers reserved to the people and terminology.
Wood v. Byrne, 60 N.D. 1, 232 N.W. 303 (1931).
Liberal construction of statute to facilitate circulation of petitions.

SELECTED SECONDARY MATERIALS

Secondary materials such as texts, treatises, and dissertations provide the researcher with valuable background information on initiatives and referendums.

Anderson, Raymond V. *Adoption and Operation of Initiative and Referendum in North Dakota* (Ph. D. Dissertation, University of Minnesota, 1962).
A comprehensive study of the initiative and referendum beginning with prestatehood Dakota Territory days. The goal of the study was "to determine the degree to which the arguments advanced by the advocates and opponents of direct legislation are adequate or inadequate to explain the operation of direct legislation in North Dakota."

Beard, Charles A. and Birl E. Schultz. *Documents on the State-Wide Initiative, Referendum and Recall.* New York: The Macmillan Co., 1912.
Includes the text of five concurrent resolutions and bills relating to the initiative, referendum, and recall from the 1911 session laws, the Law of North Dakota, that were passed at the 1911 session and were referred to the 1913 session for adoption or rejection. The adopted resolutions were then met with voter approval in the 1914 election. (L. A. Ueland and Katherine King, discussed above, were instrumental in getting the legislative approval in 1911 and 1913.)

Book of the States. Lexington, KY: Council of State Governments, 1935–.
An annual reference book, the 2006 edition (volume 38) contains approximately 200 tables with 50-state comparative data. See in particular Chapter Six, "Elections and Ethics," Tables 6.9 through 6.18, dealing with initiatives and referendums, and Tables 6.19 through 6.21, dealing with recalls. In Table 6.11, "State Initiatives: Requesting Permission to Circulate a Petition," the text notes, on page 309, that "[i]n some states, a list of financial contributors and the amount of their contributions must be submitted to the specified state officer with whom the petition is filed. In North Dakota, must report any contribution and/or expenditures in excess of $100. Must also report the gross total of all contributions received and gross totals of all expenditures made. Must give total cash on hand in the filer's account at the start and close of a reporting period."

Broder, David S. *Democracy Derailed: Initiative Campaigns and the Power of Money.* New York: Harcourt, Inc., 2000.
Washington Post journalist Broder provides a history of the initiative, from its Populist and Progressive movement days, to the present day. Broder then cautions that the initiative campaigns and the "power of money" threaten the representative form of government in the United States. He concedes, however, that some legislators support the initiative, noting on page 205, that North Dakotan "John

[*sic*] Donso . . . strongly supported the initiative process, saying it had 'made the legislature more responsive,' without weakening its legitimacy in the eyes of the public . . . 'People in North Dakota trust the legislature.'"

Butler, David and Austin Ranney, eds. *Referendums: A Comparative Study of Practice and Theory.* Washington, D.C.: American Enterprise Institute for Public Policy Research, 1978.
This resource provides a comparative study of the referendum in Switzerland, the United States, Australia, France, Scandinavia, Ireland, and the United Kingdom. See Chapter Four, Table 4.1 "Adoption of Legislative Initiative and Referendum in the United States, by State," detailing South Dakota as the first state in 1898, and North Dakota as the nineteenth state, in 1914.

Cree, Nathan. *Direct Legislation by the People.* Chicago: A. C. McClurg and Co., 1892.
Cree proposed modes of direct legislation which were modification of the Swiss initiative and referendum. Includes overview of the history of the Swiss initiative and referendum.

Cronin, Thomas E. *Direct Democracy: The Politics of Initiative, Referendum, and Recall.* Cambridge, Mass.: Harvard University Press, 1989.
Note in particular the perspectives on the politics of the recall; North Dakota recalled its Governor in 1921.

Ellis, Richard J. *Democratic Delusions: The Initiative Process in America.* Lawrence, KS: University Press of Kansas, 2002.
For a discussion of North Dakota's prohibition on per-signature payments in the initiative process, see generally Chapter Three, "The Business of Signatures," and specifically pages 70-71.

Erickson, Nels. *The Gentleman from North Dakota, Lynn J, Frazier.* Bismarck, ND: State Historical Society of North Dakota, 1986.
A brief biography of the twelfth governor of North Dakota, Lynn Frazier, who served from 1917 until his recall in 1921. For more on Frazier's recall, see Theodore Sharpe's *Recall,* this bibliography.

Eriksmoen, Curtis. ed. *North Dakota Centennial Blue Book, 1889-1989.* Bismarck, ND: Published by Legislative Authority, 1989.
First published in 1889 as a guidebook for North Dakota legislators, the *North Dakota Centennial Bluebook,* from page 8, is "a comprehensive

chronicle of the people who have served in the legislative, executive and judicial branches of state government . . . This book is an introduction to North Dakota; an encyclopedic history of this state's people and government." See in particular Section Six, North Dakota Legislature and Election Issues, "Measures Before the Voters," for a multi-page listing of constitutional, initiated, and referred measures from 1889 to 1987.

For a brief history of the *North Dakota Blue Book*, a continuing publication, see the "Editorial Notes and Acknowledgements" in the *North Dakota Blue Book, 2003-2005*.

Geelan, Agnes. *The Dakota Maverick: The Political Life of William Langer, Also Known as "Wild Bill" Langer*. Fargo, ND: Kaye's Printing Co., 1975.

A political biography of William Langer, an early member of the Nonpartisan League and later a member of the Independent Voters Association. Langer served as Governor of North Dakota from 1933-34 and from 1937-38. (He was removed from office in 1934 on fraud and conspiracy charges and was later acquitted.) Langer then served in the U.S. Senate from 1940 until his death in 1959.

Governing North Dakota. Grand Forks, ND: Bureau of Governmental Affairs, University of North Dakota, 19—.

A biennial publication, with information about the legislative, executive, and judicial branches of North Dakota state government. Also includes information about political parties, county and city governments, townships, schools, special districts, and government finances. See in particular, Chapter Six, on elections and voting: "State Election System Welcomes Everyone Who Wants to Participate."

Journal: North Dakota Constitutional Convention. Bismarck, ND: The Convention, 1972.

The journal of the 1971-72 North Dakota Constitutional Convention. The convention delegates proposed a new constitution, with four alternate propositions to certain sections. The new constitution was defeated by the voters on April 28, 1972, with the result that the alternative propositions were ineffective.

Magleby, David B. *Direct Legislation: Voting on Ballot Propositions in the United States*. Baltimore: The Johns Hopkins University Press, 1984.

See in particular Chapter Three, Table 3.2 "Stringency of Signature Requirements and Number of Initiatives and Referendums Qualifying for Ballot, 1950-80," indicating that North Dakota was the heaviest user of direct legislation during that time period, with 67 proposals. See also Chapter Four, Table 4.3 "Statutory and Constitutional Initiatives Proposed and Approved by Voters for All States, 1898-1979," indicating that North Dakota had 41% of its statutory initiatives approved (55 of 135) and 60% of its constitutional initiatives approved (18 of 30) during that time period.

Matsusaka, John G. *For the Many or the Few: The Initiative, Public Policy, and American Democracy.* Chicago: University of Chicago Press, 2004.

For specific North Dakota information on the initiative, see Appendix 1, Table A1.1 "Initiative Provision, Signature Collection, Approval, and Amendment Provisions as of 2003;" Table A1.2 "Initiative Restrictions as of 2003;" and Table A1.3 "Changes in Initiative Provisions over Time."

Omdahl, Lloyd B. *Fraud-Free Elections are Possible Without Voter Registration: A Report on North Dakota's Experience.* Grand Forks, ND: Bureau of Governmental Affairs, University of North Dakota, 1971.

Omdahl concludes, on page 20, that "[i]t is hardly likely that the people of North Dakota are any more honest or dishonest than people anywhere else in the United States. What works in North Dakota, as dependent on voter integrity as it is, will very likely work in most other comparable areas of the country. The era of election frauds of the latter half of the last century that first spawned registration laws is over. The rise of an affluent middle class that values its vote more dearly than money or patronage has made votes too expensive to purchase. Consequently, there are neither buyers nor sellers in the voter markets in the 1970s."

Omdahl, Lloyd B., ed. *Vote of the People: A Brief History and Compilation of All Measures Submitted to a Vote of the People of North Dakota from Statehood Through, 1966.* Grand Forks, ND: Bureau of Governmental Affairs, University of North Dakota, 1968.

This resource lists the amendments to the North Dakota Constitution and the measures initiated and referred by the people from 1889 through, 1968, listing the total vote for, the total vote against, and the result. The first measure, in 1889, regarding the adoption of the Constitution for the new state of North Dakota, was adopted with a vote of 27,441 for and 8,107 against. In 1914, the measure giving the electorate the power to initiate statutory measures and to refer acts of the legislature was adopted with a vote of 48,783 for and 19,964 against. In addition, the measure providing for initiative petitions for constitutional amendments was adopted with a vote of 43,111 for and 21,815 against. Also in 1914, the measure extending the right to vote to women was defeated, with a vote of 40,209 for and 49,348 against. In 1919, the measure to establish the bank of North Dakota and designate it as the official depository of all public funds was adopted with a vote of 61,495 for and 48,239 against. The last measure listed in the addendum to this resource, the 1968 referred measure to repeal the prohibition against farming by corporations, was defeated with a vote of 53, 938 for and 171,321 against.

Later editions of *Vote of the People* extend the compilation through, 1974, 1980, 1984, 1987, and 1989.

Robbins, James W. *A Consideration and Analysis of Initiated and Referred Legislation Submitted to the Electorate of North Dakota from 1940 to 1958.* (unpublished M.A. Thesis, University of North Dakota, 1959).

This thesis provides a study of direct legislation in North Dakota for a specific during a specific time frame, 1940 to 1958. Along with the Selke thesis, *infra*, it provides a good introduction to the initiative and referendum in North Dakota.

Schmidt, David D. *Citizen Lawmakers: The Ballot Initiative Revolution.* Philadelphia: Temple University Press, 1989.

For a discussion of the history of the initiative and a brief discussion North Dakota's farm-aid initiative that established a state bank, a state-owned grain elevator, and a farm tax to insure crops against weather damage, see Chapter One, "History." For a discussion of taxes and the use of the initiative, including North Dakota's, 1980 initiative to double the state tax on oil production, see Chapter Six, "Tax Revolt: Conservatives Take the Initiative." For a state-by-state history of the initiative process, see Appendix II, "Development of the Initiative." The section on North Dakota's history includes a discussion on the state bank (in 1921, voters defeated an initiative that would have abolished the state bank; in 1922, voters approved an initiative that had the effect of allowing the bank to make additional farm loans). For a summary of local initiatives and referendum procedures, see Appendix IV, "Petitioning: A State-by-State Guide to Rights and Requirements." The section on North Dakota notes that initiative ordinances and referendums are allowed in those North Dakota cities with either commission or home rule charter forms of government.

Selke, Albert G. *A History of the Initiative in North Dakota.* (unpublished M.A. Thesis, University of North Dakota, 1940).
Provides a good history of the initiative in North Dakota. Includes a description of a 1932 initiated measure, an amendment to the constitution to move the state capitol from Bismarck to Jamestown. The old capitol building had burned in December, 1930, and proponents of the measure argued that Jamestown was nearer to the geopolitical and population center of the state.

Sharpe, Theodore C. *Recall.* Grand Forks, ND: Bureau of Governmental Affairs, University of North Dakota, 1971.
Includes a discussion, at page 3, of the first state governor ever to be recalled: "In 1921 in North Dakota, however, the Governor, Attorney General, and Commissioner of Agriculture were removed in one fell swoop . . . The Nonpartisan League (NPL), established in 1915, advocated a platform calling for state ownership of mills, elevators, hail insurance and other socialistically-orientated programs. Frazier was elected Governor in 1916, along with an almost complete sweep of lesser officers supported by the League. In 1920 the power and prestige of the NPL began to decline. Also in 1920, the people of North Dakota, at the behest of the NPL, ratified the thirty-third amendment to the state constitution providing for recall of any elected official. One year later Governor Frazier was recalled and R. A. Nestos was elected to the governorship." Frazier was elected to the U.S. Senate in 1922, but lost both his membership in the Republican party and his seniority when he supported Robert LaFollette for President in 1924.

Smith, Daniel A. and Caroline Tolbert. *Educated by Initiative: The Effects of Direct Democracy on Citizens and Political Organizations in the American States.* Ann Arbor: University of Michigan Press, 2004.
One of Smith and Tolbert's conclusions is that those states in which citizens can directly participate in policy decisions, via the initiative, have corresponding higher levels of civic engagement among its citizens. Smith and Tolbert use Robert Putman's (author of *Bowling Alone: The Collapse and Revival of American Community*, 2003) measure of social capital as a proxy for civic engagement. Putnam's social capital index ranked the states, with North Dakota among those

ranking highest in social capital (along with Minnesota, Montana, Nebraska, South Dakota, and Vermont).

Townley, Arthur C. *Address of A.C. Townley, President of the National Non-Partisan League: at the Farmers and Workers Conference, held at St. Paul, Sept. 18, 19, and 20, 1917.* St. Paul, Minn.: National Non-Partisan League, 1917.

Arthur Townley, a flax farmer from Beach, North Dakota, and friend Fred Wood of Deering, founded the Non-Partisan League (NPL) in 1915, advocating state control of mills, grain elevators, and banks. The NPL spread throughout the Progressive Era and was a national organization for a brief period.

Waters, M. Dane. *Initiative and Referendum Almanac.* Durham, NC: Carolina Academic Press, 2003.

This is an indispensable resource for research on the initiative and referendum. The *Almanac* provides a comprehensive look at the following: The History of the Initiative and Referendum Process in the United States (Chapter One); Comparison of Statewide Initiative Processes (Chapter Two); I & R in American Cities: Basic Patterns (Chapter Three, by J. G. Matsusaka); State-by-State History and Overview (Chapter Four); Common Questions Regarding the Initiative Process (Chapter Five); The Courts and the Initiative Process (Chapter Six, by K. P. Miller); Legislative Attempts to Regulate the Initiative and Referendum Process (Chapter Seven); Polling (Chapter Eight); A sampling of Issues Brought Forth through the Initiative and Referendum Process (Chapter Nine); and The Issue of a National Initiative Process (Chapter Ten, by D. Polhill).

The *Almanac* lists, on page 8, the five states with the highest number of statewide initiatives on the ballot from 1904 to 2002. North Dakota is one of the five states (along with Oregon, California, Colorado, and Arizona). From 1904 to 2002, there were 168 statewide initiatives proposed and 76 adopted in North Dakota. The passage rate in North Dakota was 45%, the highest passage rate among the five states.

ADDITIONAL SELECTED SECONDARY MATERIALS

These additional secondary sources, such as legal encyclopedias, legal periodicals, and A.L.R. annotations, also help the researcher to learn more about a particular area of the law. The following selected materials provide an indication of their usefulness to the researcher.

Alexander J. Bott, *North Dakota's New Election Code*, 57 N.D. L. Rev. 427 (1981).
This article discusses the election code that became law in 1981; the new code did not require registration of voters.

Rebekah K. Browder, *Internet Voting with Initiatives and Referendums: Stumbling Towards Direct Democracy*, 29 Seattle U. L. Rev. 485 (2005).
This article explores the initiative and referendum process and the impact of Internet voting on that process.

William H. Dane, Jr., J. D., *Residence of Students for Voting Purposes*, 44 A. L.R.3d 797 (1972).
This annotation addresses the question of where a student resides for the purpose of voting.

W. J. Dunn, *State Voting Rights of Residents of Federal Military Establishments*, 34 A.L.R.2d 1193 (1954).
This annotation discusses residents of military establishments located within particular states and their rights to vote in state elections.

William B. Fisch, *Constitutional Referendum in the United States of America*, 54 Am. J. Comp. L. 485 (2006).
This article provides an overview of direct democracy and constitution-making, first at the federal level, and then at the state level over the past two centuries.

Beth B. Holliday, "Initiative and Referendum." 42 *American Jurisprudence 2d* §§ 1–53 (2000 & Supp. 2006).
This encyclopedia article provides an excellent introduction to initiatives and referendums. The article provides references to other useful secondary resources as well as extensive footnotes to case law.

Thad Kousser and Matthew D. McCubbins, *Social Choice, Crypto-Initiatives, and Policymaking by Direct Democracy*, 78 S. Cal. L. Rev. 949 (2005).
This article examines "crypto-initiatives," initiatives that use direct democracy as an instrument to achieve nonpolicy-related goals, and suggests that such initiatives seldom improve the public's welfare. The defense of marriage initiative is discussed (North Dakota was one of eleven states that passed defense of marriage initiatives in November, 2004).

Robin Miller, J. D., *Validity, Construction, and Application of State Criminal Disenfranchisement Provisions*, 10 A.L.R.6th 31 (2006).
This annotation discusses the denial of the right to vote, or to register to vote, based on a conviction of a criminal offense.

Lloyd B. Omdahl, *The Case for Constitutional Revision in North Dakota*, 48 N.D. L. Rev. 197 (1971-1972).
This article details several weaknesses in the Constitution of North Dakota and argues for a consensus to modernize the document.

B. C. Ricketts, *Construction and Application of Constitutional or Statutory Provisions Expressly Excepting Certain Laws from Referendum*. 100 A.L.R.2d 314 (1965).
This annotation discusses cases and the use of the referendum and its exceptions.

Corpus Juris Secundum, 82 C. J. S. *Statutes* §§ 108–144 (1999 & Supp. 2006).
This *Corpus Juris Secundum* encyclopedia article provides a good introduction to initiatives and referendums. The article includes numerous references to additional secondary sources and includes extensive footnotes to case law.

Glen Staszewski, *The Bait-and-Switch in Direct Democracy*, 2006 Wis. L. Rev. 17 (2006).
Using the 2004 Michigan constitutional amendment to prohibit same -sex marriages as a recent and controversial example, this article argues that the judiciary should adopt interpretive canons able to narrowly construe ambiguous ballot measures as appropriate.

Jay M. Zitter, J. D., *Constitutionality of State and Local Recall Provisions*, 13 A.L.R.6th 661 (2006).
This annotation discusses the constitutionality of the recall of state and local officials in particular state and federal cases.

Jay M. Zitter, J. D., *Sufficiency of Technical and Procedural Aspects of Recall Petitions*, 116 A.L.R.5th 1 (2004).
This annotation discusses under what circumstances a petition for the recall of local or state officials have been held valid.

Jay M. Zitter, J. D., *Validity, Construction, and Application of State Statutory Voting Offenses*, 5 A.L.R.6th 1 (2005).

This annotation discusses statues that criminalize voting offenses.

Boyd L. Wright, *The Legislative/Administrative Dichotomy and the Use of the Initiative and Referendum in a North Dakota Home Rule City*, 51 N.D. L. Rev. 855 (1974-1975).
This article analyzes six measures submitted to the voters of Minot, North Dakota to see if any of the measures were administrative in nature, and therefore, not subject to the initiative or referendum.

SELECTED LEXISNEXIS AND WESTLAW DATABASES

LexisNexis (a Reed Elsevier division) and Westlaw (Thomson West) are two premier, fee-based, legal research databases. Below are selected databases that might prove helpful to the researcher.

LexisNexis Selected Library and File Names
Bills (full text): ND; NDTEXT
Cases (state): ND; NDCTS
Cases (state and federal): ND; NDMEGA
Constitution: ND; NDCNST
Law Review: ND; NDAKLR
Statutes: ND; CODE

Westlaw Selected Database Identifiers
Bills (full text): ND-BILLTXT
Cases (state): ND-CS
Cases (state and federal): ND-CS-ALL
Law Review: NDLR
Statutes (annotated): ND-ST-ANN

SELECTED WEB SITES

The following Web sites were selected to provide useful information for the researcher. The emphasis is on North Dakota sites.

Initiative & Referendum Institute, at http://www.iandrinstitute.org.
The Initiative & Referendum Institute is an educational and research organization committed to the study of the initiative and referendum process. The Institute is affiliated with the University of Southern

California-Caltech Center for the Study of Law and Politics. This Web site is recommended as one of the best online resources for information about initiative and referendum processes in all fifty states.

For North Dakota, the site includes a history of the initiative and referendum process; indicates which processes are available in North Dakota (the initiative, the popular referendum, and the legislative referendum); provides information on the elections; provides an initiative historical listing; provides the basic steps to undertake an initiative campaign in North Dakota; provides relevant constitutional and statutory provisions; and provides links to the North Dakota Secretary of State's initiative and referendum history and election results.

League of Women Voters, at http://www.lwv.org.

The League of Women Voters is a nonpartisan political organization; its mission is to educate citizens and to impact public policies. The site includes links to projects (e.g., openness in government), to actions (e.g., election reform), to voter information searchable by state (e.g., voter registration).

National Conference of State Legislators, at http://www.ncsl.org.

The National Conference of State Legislators (NCSL) is a bipartisan organization; its mission is to provide research and technical assistance for the legislators and staffs of all fifty states. In addition, the NCSL advocates for state interests before both Congress and the federal agencies. The site includes state legislature internet links, with links to all state legislatures, searchable by content area, e.g., bills, constitution, issue reports, legislators, etc. The site also includes a ballot measures database, searchable by state, topic area, year, election, and measure type.

North Dakota Century Code, at http://www.legis.nd.gov/information/ statutes/cent-code.html.

The North Dakota Century Code at this site includes all statutory changes made by the 59th (2005) Legislative Assembly, which adjourned on Saturday, April 23, 2005.

North Dakota Constitution, at http://www.legis.nd.gov/information/ statutes/const-laws.html.

The Constitution of North Dakota is available as a PDF document at this site.

North Dakota Governor, at http://governor.state.nd.us.
This site includes Executive Orders and Proclamations, the Governor's Initiatives, the Executive Budget for 2007-2009, and links to boards and commissions (e.g., the Board of Higher Education, the Library Coordinating Council, the State Gaming Commission).

North Dakota Legislative Assembly, at http://www.legis.nd.gov/assembly.
This site provides information about organizational sessions, orientation sessions, the Senate, the House, the legislative districts, statutory memberships, legislative deadlines, legislation and effective dates, and audio and video sessions for the 54th (1995) through the 59th (2005) Legislative Assemblies. The 60th Legislative Assembly convened January 3, 2007, with information added as available.

North Dakota Legislative Council, at http://www.legis.nd.gov/council.
This site provides an overview of the Legislative Council, and provides links to committee minutes, committee documents, interim information, and links to the biennial reports of the Legislative Council since, 1999.

North Dakota Mill and Elevator Association, at http://www.ndmill.com.
The North Dakota Mill and Elevator Association is the only state-owned milling facility in the United States. The Nonpartisan League placed seven constitutional amendment initiatives on the 1918 ballot, including one to authorize the state, counties, and cities to engage in business activities. The initiative passed and the North Dakota Mill and Elevator Association was created in 1919 for the purpose of encouraging and promoting agriculture, commerce and industry.

North Dakota Secretary of State, at http://www.nd.gov/sos.
An excellent source of information about the initiative and referendum process in North Dakota. From the homepage, follow this path: select the "Elections and Voting" link; the "Elections–Details for Election Administration, Running for Office, and Initiated Measures" link; and then the "Ballot Measures" link. From this point, the following documents are available: Ballot Measure Filing Deadlines and Signature Requirements; Ballot Measures to be Considered; Pending Measures; Initiating and Referring Law in North Dakota (a PDF document); and History of Initiative and Referendum in North Dakota.
The "History of Initiative and Referendum in North Dakota" document begins with the following historical detail: "Since the adoption of the North Dakota Constitution on October 1, 1889, four types of questions

have been submitted to the electorate for approval or rejection: (1) Amendments to the Constitution as proposed by the Legislative Assembly or as proposed by the people through a petition procedure. (2) Statutory proposals initiated by the people through a petition procedure. (3) Acts of the Legislative Assembly referred to the electorate by a petition procedure. (4) A proposed new constitution, with four alternate propositions to certain sections, submitted by a constitutional convention. (April 28, 1972)."

North Dakota Session Laws, at http://www.legis.nd.gov/information/statutes/session-laws.html.

The Laws of North Dakota, the session laws, from 1997 through 2005 are available at this site.

North Dakota State Bank, at http://www.banknd.nd.gov.

The Bank of North Dakota is the only state-owned bank in the United States. The Nonpartisan League placed seven constitutional amendment initiatives on the 1918 ballot, including one to authorize the state, counties, and cities to engage in business activities. The initiative passed and the North Dakota State Bank, along with the North Dakota Mill and Elevator Association, were created in 1919. The bank's mission, like that of the state mill, is to encourage and promote agriculture, commerce, and industry in North Dakota.

North Dakota State Government, at www.nd.gov.

The official portal for North Dakota state government, with links to business, education, government, living, state facts, tourist information, working, and directories for agencies, forms, and online services.

North Dakota Supreme Court, at http://www.court.state.nd.us.

This site provides opinions from 1967 forward, searchable by citation, by topic, by justice, and by trial judge. Among other helpful information provided is a Guide to the North Dakota Judicial System, a Judicial System Glossary, a Juror's Handbook, and a directory of North Dakota lawyers.

NOTES

1. L. A. Ueland, *Majority Rule: or, The Initiative and Referendum*, Address, Valley City, North Dakota, Jan. 13, 1908.

2. Initiative and Referendum Institute, at http://iandrinstitute.org (accessed Dec. 30, 2006).

3. Ibid.

4. Ibid.

5. Ibid.

6. Ibid.

7. Ibid.

8. Schmidt, David D. *Citizen Lawmakers: The Ballot Initiative Revolution.* Philadelphia: Temple University Press, 1989.

9. Waters, M. Dane. *Initiative and Referendum Almanac.* Durham, NC: Carolina Academic Press, 2003.

10. Anderson, Raymond V. *Adoption and Operation of Initiative and Referendum in North Dakota* (Ph.D. Dissertation, University of Minnesota, 1962) at 29.

11. Ibid. at 35-36.

12. Ibid. at 48.

13. Waters, M. Dane. *Initiative and Referendum Almanac.* Durham, NC: Carolina Academic Press, 2003, at 317.

14. 1907 N.D. Laws 451.

15. L. A. Ueland, *Majority Rule: or, The Initiative and Referendum*, Address, Valley City, North Dakota, Jan. 13, 1908, at 3.

16. Ibid. at 13-15.

17. Ibid. at 15-16.

18. Ibid. at 23.

19. Selke, Albert G. *A History of the Initiative in North Dakota.* (unpublished M.A. Thesis, University of North Dakota, 1940) at 113.

20. Waters, M. Dane. *Initiative and Referendum Almanac.* Durham, NC: Carolina Academic Press, 2003, at 317.

21. Ibid. at 318.

22. Ibid.

23. Matsusaka, John G. *For the Many or the Few: The Initiative, Public Policy, and American Democracy.* Chicago: University of Chicago Press, 2004, at 157-158.

24. ND Secretary of State, at http://www.nd.gov/sos (accessed Dec. 30, 2006).

25. Ibid.

26. North Dakota State HAVA Plan 2004, at http://www.nd.gov/hava/documents.

Researching Initiatives and Referenda: A Guide for Ohio

Sara A. Sampson

INTRODUCTION

The Ohio Constitution gives the Ohio General Assembly the power to legislate, but reserves the right to "adopt or reject" laws and to adopt constitutional amendments.[1] The adoption of laws or constitutional

amendments is called initiative and the rejection of laws is called referendum. Together, this is the I&R process. The initiative may be used to
propose or enact legislation or to amend the constitution. The referendum
may be used to repeal legislation before it becomes effective.

There are limitations on the I&R power. The voters may not enact
non-uniform tax laws through I&R.[2] Also, any legislation that goes into
effect immediately after being signed by the Governor is not subject to
referendum. This includes any emergency legislation, tax levies, and
current appropriations for state government and institutions.[3]

HISTORICAL BACKGROUND

Neither of Ohio's first two constitutions contained any mechanism
for its citizens to directly enact or change legislation. The General
Assembly could put the question of a constitutional convention to the
voters, but the voters could not convene such a convention on their
own.[4] Long time supporters of governmental reforms such as I&R tried
to convince the General Assembly to put constitutional amendments
concerning these issues on the ballot, but they had been unsuccessful.
Once they decided to push for a constitutional convention instead, they
were successful. When Ohio held a constitutional convention in 1912,
Herbert Bigelow, a Cincinnati minister who had run the Direct Legislation League, was elected president of the convention. Instead of proposing
a new constitution, the convention proposed forty-two amendments,
including I&R. The voters approved the I&R amendments.[5]

Ohio's voters have been active in proposing amendments and legislation. In the decade following the creation of I&R, women's suffrage,
regulation of alcohol, and home rule issues dominated the I&R process.
In the 2005 election, five constitutional amendments were proposed by
initiative, four concerned elections and one was a bond issue.

THE INITIATIVE PROCESS

Ohio voters may propose constitutional amendments or new laws
through initiative petitions. To begin this process, one thousand registered
voters must sign an initial petition. This serves as notice that the group
intends to circulate more petitions to place the matter on the ballot.

Ohio Revised Code § 3519.05 sets forth the strict requirement for the
format of these initial petitions and the petitions that eventually will be

more widely circulated. There are also strict requirements for who circulates the petition, who signs petitions (including the distribution of signatures from around the state), and how they are signed.

These petitions are submitted, along with a summary of the proposed changes to Ohio law, to the Attorney General ("AG"). If the AG finds that the summary is "fair and truthful," he or she will forward the proposal to the Ohio Ballot Board.[6]

This board then determines if the proposal contains only one law or amendment. If it does, the OBO sends the proposal back to the AG, who then files it with the Secretary of State ("SOS"). If the proposal contains more than one law or amendment, the OBO divides the proposal, the petitioners must write new summaries and re-submit the proposal to the AG.[7]

Once the initial petitions are verified by the SOS, the group may circulate the petitions. To place a proposed constitutional amendment on the ballot, ten percent of electors must sign the petition;[8] to place a proposed new law on the ballot, three percent of electors must sign the petition.[9]

If the SOS determines that there are enough valid signatures on the petition by sending the petitions to the county boards of elections for verification, the proposed amendment or legislation appears on the ballot.

A simple majority of votes is needed for the proposed amendment to pass.[10] If a simple majority of the voters vote in favor of the new law, it is submitted to the General Assembly, where it is treated like any other bill. If the General Assembly fails to enact the measure within four months, another set of petitions may be submitted to the SOS to place the measure on the ballot.[11] A simple majority of the votes cast then determines whether the law is enacted.[12]

THE REFERENDUM PROCESS

To begin the referendum process, the petitioners must file with both the AG and the SOS (1) an initial petition signed by a thousand qualified electors, (2) a summary of the proposal, and (3) the text of the law to be repealed. The AG reviews the summary and determines whether it is "fair and truthful," while the SOS verifies the signatures and compares the text of the law submitted to the official copy on file.[13]

Once the AG and SOS certify the measure, the petitioners may begin circulating petitions to get the measure on the ballot. These petitions must also follow the strict requirements of Ohio law. These requirements include who circulates the petition, who signs petitions (including the

distribution of signatures from around the state), and how they are
signed.[14] These petitions must be verified by the SOS as having the
signatures of six percent of the electorate within ninety days of the law's
enactment for the measure to appear on the ballot.[15] The SOS's verification
immediately prevents the law from going into effect. A simple majority
of the votes cast is the final determination of whether the law goes
into effect.[16]

RESEARCHING I&R

Locating official documents concerning I&R is not difficult because
there is not much to find. These documents may be supplemented with
secondary sources such as newspapers, reports, and Web sites concerning
the issue.[17]

Official documents are available from the SOS. A summary of the
initiatives and referenda proposed in Ohio since 1912 is available on the
SOS's Web site; this list does not contain the text of the proposed
legislation or constitutional amendment.[18] From 1998 forward, the
ballot language, which includes (1) the summaries of the proposals, and
(2) the text of the arguments pro and con are available on the SOS's
Web site.[19] For earlier ballot language, contact the SOS's election
division.[20] Successful I&R proposals are available in legislative materials
including Ohio session laws and the Constitution. *Ohio Election Statistics*
is a biennial publication of the SOS, which includes the results for I&R
at the county and state level. These are available back to at least 1893.
Many libraries in Ohio as well as a few university libraries throughout
the country have these reports. Recent results are also available on the
SOS's Web site.[21]

The availability and quality of secondary sources varies widely.
Some proposals such as 2004's Issue One generated many reports, news
accounts and court opinions,[22] while other issues generate very few.

To research the specific requirements of I&R processes, turn to
Chapter 3519 of the Ohio Revised Code, which sets forth the specific
I&R procedures. Novices may want to begin with the SOS's summary
of I&R requirements[23] because it provides a broad overview with references to the code sections for each step in the process. Many of Ohio's
election laws, including the I&R provisions, were amended in 2006 by
Am.Sub.H.B. 3, so it is important to check the last update of any
secondary source used. The resources listed below provide information
to help understand the current I&R process and its history.

OHIO I&R MATERIALS

Almanacs and Encyclopedias

56 Ohio Jur. 3d Initiative and Referendum §§ 1-52 (2003).

> These sections of Ohio Jurisprudence provide a detailed summary of the law including citations to primary authority. Although written for a legally trained audience, those familiar with the I&R process will benefit from the practical tips on navigating the process and advice to attorneys assisting groups wishing to file I&R petitions.

M. Dane Waters, *Initiative and Referendum Almanac* (Carolina Academic Press, 2003).

> Contains a wealth of information on I&R for all fifty states. The Ohio section contains a brief history of the adoption and use of I&R, statistics on I&R usage and a list of proposed I&R from 1912 to 1998. The summary of I&R procedures should not be relied upon due to the many changes in the I&R process since the book was published.

Constitution and Codes

Ohio Revised Code

> Title 35 includes the majority of the code relating to elections. The I&R process is contained in Chapter 3519. To find laws that were enacted through the initiative process, it is best to begin with one of the lists of I&R proposals available from the SOS's Web site or the *Initiative and Referendum Almanac* to determine the subject matter and, perhaps, a code section. The Revised Code is available online from Anderson Publishing.[24]
> The Ohio Revised Code Annotated has references to primary law such as related code sections and court opinions and attorney general opinions interpreting and applying statutory law and secondary sources such as law review articles, legal encyclopedias. Ohio has two annotated codes: (1) *Page's Ohio Revised Code* published by LexisNexis and available on Lexis.com, and (2) *Baldwin's Ohio Revised Code* published by West and available on Westlaw.

Ohio Constitution

Article I, section 1 sets forth detailed procedures for I&R, which are amplified by the Ohio Revised Code. The constitution is available in the Ohio Revised Code as explained above and from the General Assembly's Web site.[25]

Internet Resources

Ohio Secretary of State, at www.sos.state.oh.us/sos.
Ohio's SOS provides a wealth of I&R information on its Web site. A list of proposed I&R including a summary and the outcome from 1912 to the present is available. Election Statistics, including those from I&R (listed as statewide issues), is available from 1940. The site also includes a summary of the procedures necessary to get I&R on the ballot and the forms necessary for those wishing to circulate petitions.[26]

Ohio League of Women Voters, at http://www.lwvohio.org/.
During an election, the league provides a web page for each state-wide issue (I&R) with the text of the proposed legislation or amendment and links to voter educational resources. These include arguments for and against the proposal and advocacy and non-partisan Web sites. This is a good way to find Web sites of groups supporting or opposing specific I&R proposals. Recent versions of these Web sites have been archived by Smart Voter.[27]

Election Law@Moritz, at http://moritzlaw.osu.edu/electionlaw.
This non-partisan institute studies national election law issues, but covers important Ohio issues. During elections, it may follow selected state-wide issues, including I&R. When it does, it provides links to newspaper stories and selected Web sites as well as analysis and commentary.

Equal Vote, at http://moritzlaw.osu.edu/blogs/tokaji.
Authored by Ohio State University College of Law Professor Dan Tokaji, Equal Vote also covers national election law issues, including Ohio issues. In the past, he has covered developments in Ohio state-wide issues, including links to primary documents and in depth analysis and commentary. Archives back to February, 2004 are available and are searchable.

Legislative Service Commission, at http://www.lsc.state.oh.us/.
This legislative agency is tasked with providing research services to the Ohio General Assembly. They produce research reports pursuant to statutes and legislator request. The full-text of selected reports is searchable. Reports related to I&R include *How an Issue Becomes a Statewide Ballot*,[28] and *Some Suggestions on How to Approach the Constitution*.[29]

Law Reviews and Other Periodicals

Searching the full-text of law review databases or periodical indexes can lead to high-quality, in-depth articles on either the I&R process or on specific ballot measures.[30] The articles listed below focus on the I&R process or history in Ohio. As with any secondary source, be sure to update with primary law sources before relying on them.

Richard A. Chesley, Student Note, *Current Use of the Initiative and Referendum in Ohio and Other States* 53 U. Cinn. L. Rev. 541 (1984).
Provides a succinct summary of the creation of I&R in Ohio and the impact of I&R on taxation in Ohio.

Jefferson B. Fordham & Arthur J. Prendergast, Jr., *The Initiative and Referendum at the Municipal Level in Ohio*, 20 U. Cinn. L. Rev. 313 (1951).
Although somewhat dated, this article provides a nice history of I&R at the municipal level in Ohio.

Jefferson B. Fordham & J. Russell Leach, *The Initiative and Referendum in Ohio*, 20 Ohio St. L.J. 495 (1950).
This companion piece to *The Initiative and Referendum at the Municipal Level in Ohio* is also outdated, so don't rely on the description of I&R process, but provides a through overview of I&R history with citations to many primary and other secondary sources.

NOTES

1. Ohio Const. art. II, § 1.
2. Ohio Const. art. II, § 1e.
3. Ohio Const. art. II, § 1d.
4. Ohio Constitution of 1802 art. VII, § 5; Ohio Constituion of 1851 art. XVI, § 1.

5. Barbara A. Terzian, Ohio's Constitutional Conventions and Constitutions, in *The History of Ohio Law* vol. 1 40-87 (Michael Les Benedict & John F. Winkler, eds., Ohio University Press, 2004).

6. Ohio Rev. Code § 3519.01(A).

7. *Id.*

8. Ohio Const. art. II, § 1a.

9. Ohio Const. art. II, § 1b.

10. *Id.*

11. *Id.*

12. *Id.*

13. Ohio Rev. Code § 3519.01(B).

14. Ohio Rev. Code § 3519.05.

15. Ohio Const. art. II, § 1c.

16. *Id.*

17. For example, the Ohio League of Women Voters created and maintained a webpage with links to official and advocacy information about 2004's statewide initiative concerning gay marriage. The page is archived at http://www.smartvoter. org/2004/11/02/oh/state/issue/1/.

18. A summary from 1912 through 1997 is available at http://www.sos.state. oh.us/sos/ElectionsVoter/issueHist.pdf and a summary from 1998 to present is maintained by the SOS's office at http://www.sos.state.oh.us/sos/ElectionsVoter/histCompare. aspx?Section=393. Steven H. Steinglass & Gino J. Scarselli, *The Ohio State Constitution: A Reference Guide* (Praeger, 2004) contains a listing of proposed constitutional amendments, including those proposed through the initiative process, from 1803 until 2004 and the statewide vote tally for each proposal.

19. Each year's initiatives and referenda are summarized in a PDF. From this page http://www.sos.state.oh.us/sos/ElectionsVoter/histCompare.aspx?Section=393, click the "Read More" link.

20. Currently, the Secretary of State's telephone number is (614) 466-2585.

21. http://www.sos.state.oh.us/sos/ElectionsVoter/electionResults.aspx.

22. *Ohio v. Carswell*, 2005-Ohio-6547 (12th D. Ohio), appeal accepted for review by 2006-Ohio-1967, 846 N.E. 2d 533 (2006).

23. http://www.sos.state.oh.us/sos/ElectionsVoter/OhioElections.aspx?Section=2.

24. http://onlinedocs.andersonpublishing.com.

25. http://www.legislature.state.oh.us/constitution.cfm.

26. http://www.sos.state.oh.us/sos/ElectionsVoter/OhioElections.aspx?Section=2.

27. http://www.smartvoter.org/.

28. http://www.lsc.state.oh.us/membersonly/126ballotissue.pdf.

29. http://www.lsc.state.oh.us/membersonly/124ohioconstitution.pdf.

30. For example, this law review article examines why a particular state imitative failed: Tamara Karel, Student Author, *The Failure of Ohio's Drug Treatment Initiative*, 51 Clev. St. L. Rev. 203 (2004).

Researching Initiatives and Referenda: A Guide for Oklahoma

Patricia R. Monk

INTRODUCTION

Researching initiatives and referendums in Oklahoma requires looking at Oklahoma history, becoming familiar with the constitutional and statutory requirements and procedures, and finding pertinent print and Web resources.

HISTORICAL BACKGROUND

The Oklahoma Constitution was the first state constitution to include direct initiative and popular referendum provisions for statutes and constitutional amendments as originally written in 1907.[1] Between 1889 and 1906, Congress considered thirty-one bills for either single or joint statehood for Indian Territory and Oklahoma Territory. Congress rejected an Indian state to be called Sequoyah in 1905 despite promises in the Atoka Treaty. President Theodore Roosevelt signed the Oklahoma Enabling Act creating one state in 1906 which required that the "constitution shall be republican in form." Although delegates to the Oklahoma Constitutional Convention in 1906-1907 feared that Oklahoma would not be admitted as a state due to opposition to the initiative and referendum as expressed by President Theodore Roosevelt's Secretary of War William Howard Taft and U.S. Attorney General Charles Bonaparte, they voted 80 to 5 to include both provisions in the Oklahoma Constitution. However, the Constitutional Convention stopped short of making the direct initiative and popular referendum self enacting so that statutes had to be passed later.[2]

Theodore Sturgis founded the Oklahoma Territory's Direct Legislation League in 1899, part of a nation wide movement centered in the western states that advocated direct democracy. In 1906 the League had written commitments from 102 of the 112 delegates to Oklahoma's Constitutional Convention to include the initiative and referendum in the Oklahoma Constitution. The delegates from Oklahoma Territory and the Indian Territory consisted of 99 Progressive/Populist Democrats, 12 Republicans, and 1 Independent who voted with the Democrats. William "Alfalfa Bill" Murray was elected President of the Constitutional Convention with the help of 34 Sequoyah supporters from Indian Territory and 34 Farmer's Union men from Oklahoma Territory.[3]

> "Alfalfa Bill" Murray demonstrated his distrust of the legislature by saying:
>
> We should adopt the initiative and referendum, patterned after the law in force in the Republic of Switzerland and the State of Oregon. The only argument offered against this system is that the people are not conservative, while the history of the optional power shows that the people are more conservative than reform leaders. The fact that the people have this power will prevent bribery of the members of the Legislature.[4]

Charles Haskell, lawyer and railroad supporter turned Progressive, helped "Alfalfa Bill" Murray run the Constitutional Convention. Charles Haskell was instrumental in laying the ground work for state wide prohibition in the Oklahoma Constitution and keeping women's suffrage out of the Oklahoma Constitution. The Progressive Movement stood for the support of the initiative and referendum, agrarian democratic interests, labor unions, direct election of senators, prohibition, and women's suffrage. The Progressive Movement and the Oklahoma Constitution opposed monopolies, trusts, and the railroads. Voters passed the Oklahoma Constitution by a vote of 180,333 to 73,059 or 71% and elected Charles Haskell the first governor. On November 16, 1907, President Theodore Roosevelt signed the proclamation bringing Oklahoma into the union as the forty-sixth state.

THE INITIATIVE AND REFERENDUM PROCESS IN OKLAHOMA

The Oklahoma Constitution, Article 5, sections 1-8; the Oklahoma Constitution, Article 24, sections 1-3; and Oklahoma Statutes, Title 34 provide for direct initiatives for statutes and constitutional amendments and popular referendums on legislative statutes "except as to laws necessary for the immediate preservation of the public peace, health, or safety" and for the legislative to refer statutes and constitutional amendments to the voters for approval. By passing "emergency" statutes, the Oklahoma legislature ensures that they are not subject to a referendum, which requires the signatures of 5% of the voters. These "emergency" statutes are subject to an initiative petition which requires the signature of 8% of the voters who voted in the last election for the state office which received the highest number of votes.

After the proponents of an initiative or referendum draft the petition, they file it with the Secretary of State and the Attorney General. Not more than three proponents can be listed on an initiative or referendum petition. A referendum petition must be filed within 90 days of the end of the legislative session which enacted the statute. The number of voters required to sign an initiative petition to propose a statute is 8% of the highest number of voters voting in the last election for a state office. The percentage is 15% to propose an amendment to the Oklahoma Constitution, while a referendum petition requires 5%. The state office receiving the highest number of votes is usually the governor.

Ninety days after the initiative or referendum petition's filing, the signed copies must be filed with the Secretary of State for counting. The Secretary of State publishes the count which starts a ten day period during which protests to the petition or objections to the count may be filed with the Oklahoma Supreme Court under Okla. St. Ann. tit. 34, §8. The Supreme Court will hear arguments with dispatch and issue a final order.

The proponents' suggested ballot title is reviewed by the Attorney General. The suggested ballot title cannot exceed 200 words and must be written to the eighth grade reading level. If the ballot title is defective the Attorney General will re-write it and return it to the Secretary of State. A re-write can be appealed to the Supreme Court, if there is no appeal or if the ballot title meets requirements, the Secretary of State notifies the Governor, the Election Board, and the proponents. The Governor issues a proclamation giving the substance of the measure and the date of the election. The state question must be published by the Secretary of State not less than 5 days prior to the election in two newspapers of general state circulation and in one newspaper in each county. Publication of the state question includes publishing "a copy of all ballots on initiated and referred questions, measures, and constitutional amendments, and an explanation how to vote for or against propositions."

LOCATING PRIMARY OKLAHOMA MATERIALS

For measures that are approved, the Secretary of State binds together the measure, sheets of signatures, affidavits, and a certified copy of the governor's proclamation and keeps them for two years after the measure was filed with the Secretary of State or for two years after a final Supreme Court decision. After two years, the Secretary of State may "dispose of the material in cooperation with the Archives and Records Commission." The initiative and referendum petitions provide the names and addresses of no more than three proponents.

Unfortunately, Oklahoma only requires by statute Okla. St. Ann. tit. 34, §17 (West, 2006) the publication in newspapers not less than five days before the election "a copy of all ballots on initiated and referred questions, measures, and constitutional amendments, and an explanation how to vote for or against propositions." Preferable for an informed citizenry and for research is a publication like the *California General Election Official Voter Information Guide*, available at http://www.voterguide.ss.ca.gov/, which provides the title and summary, analysis, arguments and rebuttals, fiscal impact, and the complete text of the proposed initiative laws. California also provides help in drafting the initiative if the proponents desire assistance but Oklahoma does not.

SECONDARY OKLAHOMA MATERIALS

Depending on the subject of the initiative, constitutional amendment, or referendum, information may be found in newspapers, magazines, law reviews, political science journals, state historical journals, political pamphlets or newspapers, and legislative publications as well as the occasional thesis, dissertation, or book. Much of the information may be distributed in pamphlet form or in political newspapers in print or on the Web so that the information is often ephemeral.

John F. Cooper, *The Citizen Initiative Petition to Amend State Constitutions: A Concept Whose Time Has Passed, or A Vigorous Component of Participatory Democracy at the State Level?* 28 N.M. L. Rev. 227 (1998).
  A former Oklahoma Assistant Attorney General and present Professor of Law at Stetson University College of Law, the author uses Oklahoma and Florida examples to illustrate his points. He gives the constitutional history of the initiative petition and defends the initiative petition as a method of reform.

Oklahoma Family Policy Council. *The 2006 Oklahoma Voters' Guide*, available at http://0000952.previewcoxhosting.com/voters_guide.htm.
  Provides information on the four state questions as well as major federal, state, and judicial candidates on the November 7, 2006 General Election ballot.

James D. Gordon and David B. Magleby, *Pre-Election Judicial Review of Initiatives and Referendums*, 64 Notre Dame L. Rev. 298 (1989).
  This article finds pre-election review of substantive law to violate ripeness requirements, to be issuing an advisory opinion, to constitute judicial interference with the legislative process, and to void the policy of avoiding unnecessary constitutional questions. Review of procedural requirements and subject matter limitations is appropriate.

Charles N. Haskell, *Governor Haskell Tells of Two Conventions*, 14
Chronicles of Oklahoma 189 (June, 1936), available at http://digital.
library.okstate.edu/Chronicles/v014p189.html.
    Charles N. Haskell recalls the Sequoyah Constitutional Convention
    in Indian Territory where he was a delegate and later the Oklahoma
    Constitutional Convention where he was a delegate.

Robert Henry, *Deliberations About Democracy: Revolutions, Republicanism, and Reform*, 34 Willamette L. Rev. 533 (1998).
    The author is a U.S. Circuit Judge with the United States Court of
    Appeals for the Tenth Circuit, was formerly Attorney General of
    Oklahoma, 1987-1991; and was Dean and Professor of Law at
    Oklahoma City University, 1991-1994. The history of Oklahoma, the
    tension between democracy and republicanism, and suggested
    reforms of the initiative process are all discussed.

J. Michael Medina, *The Emergency Clause and the Referendum in
Oklahoma: Current Status and Needed Reform*, 43 Okla. L. Rev. 401
(1990).
    Initiatives are more numerous than referendums because so many
    laws are passed as emergency laws which mean that the initiative
    must be used rather than the referendum.

Oklahoma Secretary of State at http://www.sos.state.ok.us.
    The Secretary of State gives information on the "Initiative and Ref-
    erendum Process" at www.sos.state.ok.us/exec_legis/Singature_
    requirements.htm. A "Brief of Petition Process" at www.sos.state.ok.us/
    exec_legis/brief_of_petition_process.htm outlines the steps for a state
    wide petition and referendum. State Questions can be searched by
    State Question Number or by keyword at http://www.sos.state.ok.us/
    exec_legis/Initiatives_and_Referendums.asp. Proposed State Questions
    are available at http://www.sos.state.ok.us/exec_legis/SQ_Proposed.
    asp. At www.sos.state.ok.us/exec_legis/InitListAll.asp the Secretary
    of State provides a table with each State Question, beginning with State
    Question 27, available as a PDF document, the type of question–
    whether an initiative, referendum or legislative, the "Resolution or Bill
    Number" if a proposed statute was referred for a vote of the people by
    the legislature, the "subject matter," and the "disposition"–whether
    abandoned, whether an election occurred, or the election returns.

M. Sean Radcliffe, Student Author, *Pre-Election Review of Initiative Petitions: An Unreasonable Limitation on Political Speech*, 30 Tulsa L.J. 425 (1994).
The author advocates that the Supreme Court return to judicial restraint and not thwart direct democracy. He contends an initiative petition should only be reviewed after it has become law.

West's Oklahoma Statues Annotated

Appendix, *Initiative and Referendum*, Okla. St. Ann. tit. 34, (West, 2006) has a list of all the "State Questions" labeled with either the "Initiative" number or "Referendum" number; the "Subject Matter;" "Disposition" such as "rejected," "no election held," "petition failed," "petition not filed," "approved," or "abandoned;" and if passed the *West's Oklahoma Statutes Annotated* cite based on records supplied by the Secretary of State.
West's Annotated Oklahoma Statutes is perhaps the most helpful unofficial source with its "Historical and Statutory Notes," "Cross References," "Law Review and Journal Commentaries," "Library References," and "Notes of Decisions" for the Oklahoma Constitution, Article 5 covering "Initiative and Referendum," Article 24 covering "Constitutional Amendments," Title 34 covering "Initiative and Referendum," and for any initiative or constitutional amendment that has passed and become a statute or part of the constitution.

NOTES

1. John F. Cooper, *The Citizen Initiative Petition to Amend State Constitutions: A Concept Whose Time Has Passed, or a Vigorous Component of Participatory Democracy at the State Level?* 28 N.M. L. Rev. 227, 228 (1998).
2. Robert Henry, *Deliberations About Democracy: Revolutions, Republicanism, and Reform*, 34 Willamette L. Rev. 533, 544 (1998).
3. William H. Murray, The Constitutional Convention, 9 Chronicles of Oklahoma 126. 134 (1931), available at http://digital.library.okstate.edu/chronicles/v009/v009p126.html.
4. Cooper, supran. 1, at 229.

Researching Oregon Initiatives and Referendums

Beth Williams
David Dames

How would you like to live in a state where the people can do and enact laws for the common good, which their Legislature has failed to enact for them, where they can nullify any obnoxious measure passed by the Legislature, where they can nominate and elect, or defeat for public office, any man regardless of his party strength, and can recall any public officer, Supreme Judge included, whose acts they do not approve; a state where the party boss has been put out of business; a state in short where the people rule . . . Such a state is Oregon.

Allen H. Eaton, *The Oregon System* (1912).

INTRODUCTION

If the states really are "laboratories of democracy,"[1] then some of Oregon's most daring experiments have been possible because of its initiative and referendum (I&R) process. For instance, in the past fifteen years, Oregon voters have used initiatives to take on issues of local and national controversy that legislators might not have been willing to consider. Oregon voters passed initiatives allowing the use of medicinal marijuana,[2] approving the practice of doctor-assisted suicide,[3] establishing a system that gives property rights priority over environmental and land use regulations,[4] and, like voters in ten other states in November, 2004, restricting the state's definition of marriage.[5] In 1998 Oregon voters even used the initiative process to change the way they vote. Taking the baton from elected officials who had made limited progress with the issue, Oregon voters decided that they would, henceforward, vote only by mail.[6]

In fact, the people of Oregon may enjoy the democratic powers of the initiative and referendum process more than the people of any other state. According to the Initiative & Referendum Institute, as of 2006, Oregon held the records for initiatives on a single ballot (27 in 1912) and average number of initiatives per general election (6.6).[7] The ballot in the November, 2006 election was typical in that it contained 10 voter-sponsored initiatives. In the same election, 155 proposed initiatives did not make it onto the ballot.[8] As a result of this heavy use of direct democracy, any visitor to downtown Portland can tell when there is an upcoming election, because there will be many young men and women in Pioneer Courthouse Square, in the South Park blocks, in front of the Multnomah County Library, and in front of the Multnomah County Courthouse, all trying to gather signatures for their petitions.

In response to this prolific use of the initiative and referendum process, there are a few good resources for information regarding both the initiative and referendum process, and specific initiatives and referendums. Most notable is the information offered on the Web sites of the Oregon Secretary of State and the City Club of Portland. These and other resources are described more fully below.

HISTORY OF THE OREGON SYSTEM

Direct democracy through initiative and referendum was for years commonly called the "Oregon System."[9] And the story of Oregon's adoption of that system is, in no small way, the story of William Simon U'Ren.[10] U'Ren–known as "the father of the Oregon system"–was a miner, a newspaper editor, a Democratic Party worker, a practicing member of the Colorado Bar, and a sugar plantation foreman before moving to Oregon in 1889.[11] Soon after arriving in Oregon, he became involved in progressive politics. U'Ren spearheaded the Direct Legislation League, which was born out of the populist movement in Oregon in reaction to widespread belief that Oregon's political institutions were corrupt.[12]

After much effort, and several dramatic attempts at passage, the addition of the initiative and referendum process to Oregon's constitution was introduced in the 1899 legislative session as Joint Resolution #1 and passed easily.[13] On June 2, 1902 the voters ratified the constitutional amendment by a vote of 62,024 to 5,668.[14] The new version read: "The people reserve to themselves the initiative power, which is to propose laws and amendments to the Constitution, and enact or reject them at an election independently of the Legislative Assembly."[15]

BASICS OF OREGON'S I&R PROCESS

Oregon's constitution permits direct initiatives, popular referendums, and legislative referendums,[16] and the constitution can be amended by initiative and referendum.[17] However, the constitution specifically restricts proposed measures to "one subject only and matters properly connected therewith."[18]

To begin the process, a prospective petition is filed with the Secretary of State, accompanied by a statement of sponsorship signed by at least 25 "electors," i.e., eligible voters.[19] The Secretary of State's Office then sends a copy to the Attorney General's Office to draft the ballot title.[20] Oregon law requires the Secretary of State to "provide reasonable statewide notice of having received the draft ballot title" in order to receive written commentary from the public.[21] At nearly every stage of the process, Oregon citizens receive notice of the initiative or referendum petition, and they retain the right to make public comments that are retained by the Secretary of State's Office.

The Oregon Constitution explicitly requires that, in order to qualify for the ballot, initiative petitions must gather signatures equal to "six percent of the total number of votes cast for all candidates for Governor" in the preceding gubernatorial election.[22] By the same measure, initiative amendments to the constitution require eight percent, and referendum petitions require four percent.[23] If the Secretary of State verifies these signatures as timely filed, the initiative or referendum measure is certified to appear on the next general election ballot.[24] Of particular interest to researchers is the Oregon law requiring the Secretary of State to retain for six years all signature sheets of filed initiative or referendum petitions, along with copies of the proposed measures. If a measure is ultimately approved by the voters, a copy of it and the Governor's proclamation declaring the measure approved are retained as a permanent public record.[25]

It should be remembered, however, that the life of a ballot measure in Oregon is not always so neat and tidy. Because initiatives and referendums often deal with controversial subjects, they are routinely subject to legal challenges. Any voter can challenge an election decision by a state or local official or administrator.[26] And a voter who comments on a proposed initiative or referendum may challenge the Attorney General's title for and summary of the proposed measure in the Oregon Supreme Court.[27] Although proposed ballot measures cannot be KeyCited or Shepardized, an action challenging the title and summary of a measure will appear in that measure's record in the Secretary of State's initiative, referendum, and referral database described below. This is just one of several valuable resources for researching Oregon I&R.

RESEARCH RESOURCES

There are five categories of research resources below. The first is a description of official sources of I&R information available in Oregon's published session laws and annotated codes. The second lists selected Web sites where a good deal of information related to recent initiatives and referendums may be found. The third provides a list of selected documents that provide histories and overviews of I&R in Oregon. Fourth, there is a list of state agencies that collect records relevant to Oregon's I&R process. Contact information for these organizations is included as well, since it is likely that they will need to be consulted when undertaking an extensive research project. Finally, a list of selected Oregon libraries with related print resources is also included.

Oregon Session Laws and Statutory Codes

A good place to begin researching the history of Oregon laws passed or introduced by the initiative and referendum process is the most recent edition of Oregon's published session laws, *Oregon Laws and Memorials and Resolutions*. This set is also known as *Oregon Laws*, and it is published every two years and supplemented with advance sheets. Though a fair number of resources are described below containing both historical and current lists of Oregon initiatives and referendums, the information contained in *Oregon Laws* has the benefit of being both official and easy to use.

For example, volume 1 of *2005 Oregon Laws* contains a list of the votes on statewide ballot measures in the primary, general, and special elections during the prior two years. The list includes the ballot title and number and the outcome on the vote–all extremely useful information for researchers. In addition, volume 3 contains a table of ballot measures adopted at the most recent general election, along with their effective date–again, particularly useful information readily available from an official source. *Oregon Laws* is available in print, on microfiche in many libraries, on Hein Online for those organizations with a subscription, and selectively available on the Web at http://www.leg.state.or.us/bills_laws/.[28]

When searching for information about a particular ballot measure from a known time period, simply consult the volumes of *Oregon Laws* that were published immediately subsequent to that election. This will provide the ballot measure number–akin to the process of finding a bill number for laws introduced in the more conventional way–possession of which will help in using many of the additional resources described in the lists below. Alternatively, one can simply browse the lists available in *Oregon Laws* to find out which laws were proposed and passed via the Oregon System.

Oregon laws concerning the I&R processes itself may be searched using either *West's Oregon Revised Statutes Annotated* or the Oregon Legislative Council Committee's *Oregon Revised Statutes*. Both publishers include "Initiative and Referendum" as a subject heading in their general indexes. Unfortunately, that subject heading does not include cross-references to the substantive laws passed *by* the I&R process, and the set does not index ballot measures either by popular name (i.e., ballot title) or by ballot measure number. Therefore, researching the codified versions of laws that began as initiatives and referendums when only the popular ballot title or number is known requires interim steps. If the I&R subject is known, then these subject indexes may be more useful, though that will not always be the most efficient way to find the appropriate code sections for statutes passed by initiative or referendum.

Note also that the *Oregon Revised Statutes*, the official State Code which includes the Oregon Constitution, is annotated. The annotations include notes of decisions, law review citations, Attorney General Opinions, and cross-references to related statutes. The cross-references do not include substantive laws passed by the initiative and referendum process. Researchers may access the official annotations to the *Oregon Revised Code* on the Web at http://www.leg.state.or.us/ors/annos/home.html.

Internet Resources

The sites listed below are notable for their primary documents and explanatory statements of individual initiatives and referendums–specifically, the primary documents available through the Secretary of State's initiative, referendum, and referral database, and the summaries of ballot measures available from the City Club of Portland. These sites also offer a few good materials on Oregon I&R as a whole, such as the Secretary of State's initiative and referendum manuals. The types of documents one can expect to find on these sites–e.g., ballot text, analysis, newspaper articles, and fiscal impact statements–are highlighted within the annotations below for ease of use.

City Club of Portland, at http://www.pdxcityclub.org.
  "The City Club of Portland is a non-profit, nonpartisan education and research based civic organization dedicated to community service, public affairs, and leadership development." Their research **Reports & Resolutions** are a goldmine for researchers interested in Oregon I&R. These reports are usually a thorough **analysis** of a particular

initiative or referendum, including the **measure text** as it will appear on the ballot, **background information, arguments both for and against** the measure, a fairly lengthy **discussion**, and a **conclusion and recommendation**. The Web site permits searching these documents by keyword or by subject all the way back to 1920, available at http://www.pdxcityclub.org/cgi/search_research.pl. Only citations are available through the 1994 election. From 1996 on, though, some full text reports are available, and from 2001 forward all reports are available for free in PDF format. Reports not available online may be purchased through the organization, and many are available at libraries throughout Oregon (see list *infra*).

Oregon Blue Book, at http://bluebook.state.or.us.
The Oregon Blue Book is "the official state directory and fact book about all levels of government in Oregon." The Oregon Elections Process and History page provides several links to current and historical election information—notably, a **brief introduction** to the Oregon I&R system and a **comprehensive list of election results** for initiatives, referendums and recalls, from 1902 to the present, available at http://bluebook.state.or.us/state/elections/elections.htm. (The page with these results is the same as the one linked to from the Secretary of State's Elections Division page mentioned below.)

Oregon Legal Research Guide, at http://lawlib.lclark.edu/research/oregonlaw.php.
Lewis & Clark Law School's Paul L. Boley Law Library publishes an online legal research guide on Oregon law, including a section on Statewide Ballot Measures. This section concisely provides links to many of the pages mentioned here.

Oregon Secretary of State, at http://www.sos.state.or.us/.
The Web site of Oregon's Secretary of State provides a wealth of information on Oregon I&R, and is an ideal starting point for research on this subject. The Elections Division page contains a link to an Initiative, Referendum and Referral page, available at http://www.sos.state.or.us/elections/other.info/irr.htm. This page organizes recent **signature verification results**, the **administrative rules** for signature verification, **a FAQ** regarding referendum petitions, a summary of **historical election results** for initiatives and referendums, and an extensive list of the official State, County and District **I&R Manuals**

and Forms, including state and country initiative and referendum manuals, and a district manual with sections on initiatives and referendums. The manuals are available in PDF format, and the forms are available as fillable PDFs and Word documents.

These are all very helpful resources, but the best feature of this page is the **searchable database** of initiatives and referendums, available at http://egov.sos.state.or.us/elec/web_irr_search.search_form. The database permits searching by keyword, petition status (i.e., active, qualified to ballot, rejected or withdrawn), and measure type for any election year from 1998 through 2008. The only drawback to this database is that it will only search one election year at a time. However, if the year is the only criteria selected, it will present an exhaustive list of proposed measures from that year. The search results often contain **detailed petitioner information** and **PDF versions of the original paperwork** impacting the life of the measure, for example, draft ballot title, certified ballot title, and any comments that may have been submitted.

The Secretary of State also provides electronic versions of the **Voters' Guides** from 1995 through the present, available at http://www.sos. state.or.us/elections/other.info/stelec.htm. These Guides contain the **ballot title, text, explanatory statements, arguments in favor, arguments in opposition,** and **legislative argument in support,** if any. PDF files of the printed Voters' Pamphlets are also available for recent elections, from the May, 2004 primary election to the present.

Oregon State Legislature, Committee Services Office, at http:// www.leg.state.or.us/comm/commsrvs/.

The Committee Services Office is a unit of Oregon's Legislative Administration, providing research on issues and measures, and legislative oversight assistance to members of the Senate and House of Representatives. Of primary interest to I&R researchers are the Committee Services Office's **Legislative Issues Briefs,** available at http://www.leg.state.or.us/comm/commsrvs/issue_briefs.htm. Briefs from 1995-2002 are included. These briefs were written in response to a legislator's request for information. Although some of the briefs available on this Web site concern specific ballot measures, most of them are referred to by popular subject name only, regardless of whether they include information on a specific ballot measure. Very similar **topical Background Briefs** from 2003 and 2004, also by the Committee Services Office, are available at http://www.leg.state.or.

us/comm/commsrvs/comm_srvs_pubs.htm. Of particular interest is the 2004 brief on the initiative and referendum process itself.

Selected Bibliography

The materials listed below offer good histories and overviews of the initiative and referendum process in Oregon. However, one should be careful to combine them with more current materials if they are being used for an overview of the current process–Oregon's procedures for initiatives and referendums are subject to change and have certainly changed over time.

Paul Thomas Culbertson, *A History of the Initiative and Referendum in Oregon* (unpublished Ph.D. dissertation, University of Oregon, 1941) (at University of Oregon Knight Library).
    Culbertson's doctoral thesis in history at the University of Oregon is a behemoth at five hundred and forty-four pages. Despite its unwieldy size, this book is particularly useful for those researching the historical and political context of older Oregon initiatives and referendums. In addition, the bibliography is an invaluable comprehensive list of a variety of historical resources.

City Club of Portland, *The Initiative and Referendum in Oregon* (City Club of Portland, 1996) (available at http://www.pdxcityclub.org/pdf/ Initiative_Referendum_1996.pdf).
    The City Club's seventy-six page report on the statewide I&R system in Oregon is both a concise history and a careful analysis of contemporary trends impacting the citizens of the state. The report concludes that several remedial measures should be undertaken in order to restore the Oregon system to its role of dealing with matters of fundamental law, rather than bypassing the legislature to enact budgetary and other statutory decisions into the Oregon Constitution. The report includes several appendices, including a substantial bibliography, and an annotated list of changes in Oregon's I&R process from 1902 to 1995. Note also that the City Club regularly has published reports on proposed ballot measures since the 1920s, as discussed above. A brief update to this report is available at http://www.pdxcityclub.org/research/ documents/InitiativeandReferendumcharge_2005.pdf, and a completely revised version is expected soon.

Carlton B. Grew, *Governing by Initiative: The Rise and Fall–and Rise Again–of Oregon's Initiative Ballot Measure*, 61 Or. St. B. Bull. 9 (2000).
This short article provides an analysis of the effect on, and role of, attorneys in Oregon's I&R system from the perspective of a practicing member of the Oregon State Bar. Grew cites to then-recent case law, and provides an outline of the initiative and referendum process and its effect on the state's constitutional landscape and the practice of law in Oregon. This article is a good place to start for a brief overview of the Oregon I&R system.

Cody Hoesley, *Reforming Direct Democracy: Lessons from Oregon*, 93 Cal. L. Rev. 1191 (2005).
This commentary provides a good overview of the current state of I&R use in this country, and a nice, brief history of the Oregon System. Emphasis is placed on recent judicial and non-judicial attempts to reform the I&R system.

Symposium, *Redirected Democracy: An Evaluation of the Initiative Process*, 34 Willamette L. Rev. 391 (1998).
The Summer-Fall, 1998 issue of the Willamette Law Review is dedicated to the issue of the initiative process in Oregon, following a symposium on Oregon I&R held at the law school in February, 1998. The texts of all five presentations given at the symposium are published in this large law review edition, in addition to three articles and eight essays–all concerning various aspects of Oregon's I&R system. Topics include statutory construction of laws proposed by initiative, budgetary concerns raised by current use of the initiative process, and the impact I&R usage has on legislative committees and the legislative process. This special issue contains significant scholarly legal literature on the topic of Oregon's I&R system.

David Schuman, *The Origin of State Constitutional Direct Democracy: William Simon U'Ren and the "Oregon System,"* 67 Temple L. Rev. 947 (1994).
This law review article provides a biographical sketch of the man responsible for bringing the initiative and referendum process to the state of Oregon: William U'Ren. In telling U'Ren's story and the story of Oregon's "Hold-up Legislature of 1897," during which the Oregon legislature was so seriously fragmented on the issue that it failed to convene, Schuman describes in detail the process by which the

Oregon Constitution was amended in 1902 to include the initiative and referendum process.

Contact Information

The following agencies and libraries collect documents related to initiatives and referendums and may be helpful when undertaking an I&R research project.

AGENCIES

Oregon Department of Justice, Attorney General
Oregon Department of Justice
1161 Court Street NE
Salem, OR 97301-4096
Phone: (503) 378-4400
Email: doj.info@state.or.us
http://www.doj.state.or.us/index.shtml

The Attorney General is responsible for drafting the titles and summaries of initiatives and referendums that reach the ballot. The Attorney General site also offers a searchable database of Attorney General Opinions at http://www.doj.state.or.us/agoffice/search.shtml. Some of these opinions relate to initiatives and referendums.

Oregon Secretary of State, Archives Division
Oregon State Archives
800 Summer St. NE
Salem, OR 97310
Phone: (503) 373-0701
Fax: (503) 373-0953
Email: reference.archives@state.or.us
http://arcweb.sos.state.or.us/

The State Archives contain records from initiatives and referendums that were adopted by the voters.

Oregon Secretary of State, Elections Division
Oregon Secretary of State, Elections Division
141 State Capitol
Salem, OR 97310

Phone: (503) 986-1518 or 1 (866) ORE-VOTES
http://www.sos.state.or.us/elections/

The Elections Division retains records from proposed initiatives and referendums that did not make the ballot for six years before destroying them, and records from initiatives and referendums that did make the ballot for four years before transferring them to the State Archives.

LIBRARIES

Boley Law Library
Lewis & Clark Law School
10015 S.W. Terwilliger Blvd.
Portland, OR 97219
Phone: (503) 768-6676
Fax: (503) 768-6671
Email: lawlib@lclark.edu
http://lawlib.lclark.edu

John E. Jaqua Law Library
1221 University of Oregon
Eugene, OR 97403-1221
Phone: (541) 346-3088
Fax: (541) 346-1669
Email: lawref@uoregon.edu
http://lawlibrary.uoregon.edu

Oregon State Library
250 Winter St. NE
Salem, OR 97301-3950
Phone: (503) 378-8800
Fax: (503) 585-8059
Email: reference@library.state.or.u
http://www.oregon.gov/OSL/

State of Oregon Law Library
1163 State Street
Salem, OR 97301-2563
Phone: (503) 986-5640
Fax: (503) 986-5623
http://www.ojd.state.or.us/library

NOTES

1. Paraphrasing Justice Brandeis' famous statement. *New State Ice Co. v. Liebmann*, 285 U.S. 262, 311 (1932).
2. Oregon Medical Marijuana Act, Or. Rev. Stat. §§475.300-346 (2005) (approved as Ballot Measure 67 (1998)).
3. The Oregon Death With Dignity Act, Or. Rev. Stat. §§127.800-127.890 (2005) (approved as Ballot Measure 16 (1994); attempted repeal of Measure 16 failed with Ballot Measure 51 (1997), which was referred to the voters from the legislature).
4. Or. Rev. Stat. §197.352 (2005) (approved as Ballot Measure 37 (2004)).
5. Or. Const. art XV, §5a. (approved as Ballot Measure 36 (2004)).
6. Or. Rev. Stat. §254.465 (2005) (approved as Ballot Measure 60 (1998)). An outline of the legislative history of the vote by mail movement in Oregon is offered by the Secretary of State. *A Brief History of Vote by Mail*, at http://www.sos.state. or.us/elections/vbm/history.html.
7. Initiative & Referendum Institute, *Initiative & Referendum Institute at the University of Southern California, Oregon*, at http://www.iandrinstitute.org/Oregon.htm.
8. The process often begins with a few alternate or competing versions of each initiative.
9. David Schuman, *The Origin of State Constitutional Direct Democracy: William Simon U'Ren and the "Oregon System,"* 67 Temple L. Rev. 947, 948 n.7 (1994).
10. Schuman offers an excellent and entertaining history of U'Ren and the origins of the Oregon System. *See generally id.* For a shorter historical overview, *see* M. Dane Waters, *Initiative and Referendum Almanac* at 357-359 (Carolina Acad. Press, 2003).
11. Oregon Historical Society, *Oregon Biographies, William S. U'Ren*, at http://www.ohs.org/education/oregonhistory/Oregon-Biographies-William-Uren.cfm; and Schuman, *supra* n. 9, at 951-2. U'Ren was so influential that a 1908 newspaper editorial "referred to 'four departments' of state government–the executive, legislative, judicial, and Mr. U'Ren, leaving open the question which exerted the most power." James D. Barnett, *The Operation of the Initiative, Referendum and Recall in Oregon* 17 (1915) (quoting The Oregonian).
12. Schuman, *supra* n. 9, at 948-952.
13. *Id.* at 955.
14. *Id.* at 956.
15. Or. Const. art. IV, § 1(2)(a).
16. Or. Const. art. IV, § 1.
17. Or. Const. art. IV, § 1(2)(a).
18. Or. Const. art. IV, § 1(2)(d).
19. Or. Rev. Stat. § 250.045 (2005).
20. Or. Rev. Stat. § 250.065 (2005).
21. Or. Rev. Stat. § 250.067 (2005).
22. Or. Const. art. IV, § 1(2)(b).
23. Or. Const. art. IV, §§ 1(2)(c) and 1(3)(b).
24. Laws regarding the gathering of signatures have changed in the past decade in response to accusations of fraud and abuse. The constitution now prohibits paying signature gatherers per signature. Or. Const. art. IV, § 1b. The legislature sets out laws directing the Secretary of State how to determine whether signatures are valid and paperwork has been filed correctly. Or. Const. art. IV, § 1(4)(a). These laws are found in the Oregon Revised Statutes in section 250. For an explanation of these requirements,

see Oregon Secretary of State, Elections Division, *2006 State Initiative and Referendum Manual* (Or. Sec. of St.), published biennially, available at http://www.sos.state. or.us/elections/publications/state_ir.pdf.

25. Or. Rev. Stat. § 250.135 (2005).

26. Or. Rev. Stat. § 246.910 (2005).

27. Or. Rev. Stat. § 250.085 (2005).

28. Note that only the ballot measures table appears to be available in the version of *Oregon Laws* published on the Oregon State Legislature Web site; strangely, the very handy list of votes on statewide measures typically found in volume 1 of *Oregon Laws* is not available on this site.

Researching Initiatives and Referendums: A Guide for South Dakota

Candice Spurlin

INTRODUCTION TO INITIATIVE AND REFERENDUM

The proponents of the initiative and referendum movement, which took root in South Dakota in the late 1800s, hoped that initiative and referendum would serve as a release valve for a frustrated public. The public was dissatisfied with legislators who were not seriously addressing popularly embraced causes such as agricultural reform. After fifteen years of annual defeats, I&R procedures were finally adopted in 1898. Adoption did not end the struggle. It would be another decade before the first measure was successfully proposed; this proposal was then defeated at the polls.[1]

In modern South Dakota politics, I&R questions are viewed by some as a means of avoiding the legislative process. Questions appear on the ballot that have never been introduced in the legislature. Social and moral questions such as video lottery, marijuana use, and abortion tend to appear or reappear on the ballot.

Concerns about I&R are currently being addressed by a temporary Constitutional Revision Commission. Since 2005, the Commission has conducted a comprehensive study of Article III §1 of the South Dakota Constitution which authorizes the I&R process.[2] Although the Commission has proposed legislative changes for the 2007 legislative session, none of the proposed changes indicate a major shift in policy, such as raising the number of signatures required for the initiative and referendum petitions; rather, the proposals include changes such as conducting public hearings to review the wording of petitions.

HISTORY OF INITIATIVE AND REFERENDUM
IN SOUTH DAKOTA

"In 1898 the people of South Dakota approved the first constitutional amendment among the several existing states that reserved to the electors legislative powers previously within the sole control of the elected assembly."[3] The State holds the distinction of being the first in the Union to provide for initiative and referendum. The constitutional amendment extended voter approval to both the state and municipal levels.[4] The amendment to Article III § 1 of the Constitution states:

> The legislative power of the state shall be vested in a Legislature which shall consist of a senate and house of representatives. However, the people expressly reserve to themselves the right to

propose measures, which shall be submitted to a vote of the electors of the state, and also the right to require that any laws which the Legislature may have enacted shall be submitted to a vote of the electors of the state before going into effect, except such laws as may be necessary for the immediate preservation of the public peace, health or safety, support of the state government and its existing public institutions. Not more than five percent of the qualified electors of the state shall be required to invoke either the initiative or the referendum.

This section shall not be construed so as to deprive the Legislature or any member thereof of the right to propose any measure. The veto power of the Executive shall not be exercised as to measures referred to a vote of the people. This section shall apply to municipalities. The enacting clause of all laws approved by vote of the electors of the state shall be: "Be it enacted by the people of South Dakota." The Legislature shall make suitable provisions for carrying into effect the provisions of this section.[5]

The amendment was proposed as a remedy for some of the problems with representative government, and the notion spread to most of the states in the western half of the country within a short time.[6] In the 1970s, South Dakota extended direct government to include counties,[7] and in certain situations school districts[8] and conservation districts[9] are also open to voter approval.

Article XXIII of the constitution was amended in 1972 to permit constitutional amendments by initiative,[10] and in 1988, voters amended Article III §1 to allow an initiative to be placed on the ballot without first submitting it to the legislature for approval.[11]

Statistical information on the Secretary of State's Web page indicates that sixteen of forty-one initiatives have passed for a 39.0% success rate, and thirty-five of forty-two referred laws have been rejected for an 83.0% success rate. Eleven constitutional amendments were initiated by the people with five of them enacted, and 207 amendments were proposed by legislators with 202 enacted, for a 51.0% success rate.[12]

BASICS OF SOUTH DAKOTA INITIATIVE AND REFERENDUM PROCESS

The constitution allows several types of ballot questions: the initiated measure, the referred law, and the initiated constitutional amendment.[13]

The constitution states that the Executive shall have no veto power over laws referred by the people.[14] The State's constitution extends authority for the initiative and referendum, while the statutory framework governs the procedures for both.[15]

The initiative petition is used to propose state statutes. The petition must be filed in the Office of the Secretary of State by the first Tuesday in May of a general election year.[16] All measures must contain the signatures of not less than five percent of the qualified electors of the state,[17] that number shall be determined by the number of votes cast for Governor in the last proceeding gubernatorial election.[18] No signatures may be obtained more than eighteen months preceding the general election that was designated at the time of filing of the petition.[19]

A referred law is a petition to prevent a measure passed by the legislature from becoming effective. The petition must be filed in the Secretary of State's office within ninety days after the adjournment of the legislature which passed the law.[20] The form of the petition shall be prescribed by the State Board of Elections and shall be signed by not less than five percent of the qualified electors of the state.[21] Any law which the legislature may have enacted, except one which may be necessary for the immediate preservation of the public peace, health, or safety, or support of the state government and its existing public institutions, is subject to referendum.[22]

Anyone proposing initiatives or initiated constitutional amendment may propose to amend, repeal, or add to provisions to the constitution. The petition must be filed containing the text of the proposed amendment and the names and addresses of its sponsors at least one year before the next general election.[23] The petition shall require the signature of at least ten percent of the total votes cast for Governor in the last gubernatorial election.[24] The proposed amendment may amend one or more articles and related subject matter in other articles.[25] No signatures may be obtained more than twenty-four months prior to the general election.[26]

All initiatives and initiated amendments to the constitution must submit a copy to the Director of the Legislative Research Council for style and form review before it can be circulated for signatures. The director has fifteen days from the date of receipt to provide written comments.[27] The Legislative Research Council archives copies of the petitions chronologically in folders which are available to the public during office hours.[28] All proposed measures may be viewed on the Secretary of State's Web page. They are accompanied by explanation pamphlets by the Attorney General, but the responsibility for publicizing them is placed on those who are sponsoring the measure.

All measures, whether initiated and referred measures or constitutional amendments, approved by a majority of all votes cast become effective the day after the completion of the official canvass of the State Canvassing Board.[29]

LOCATING DOCUMENTS

The electorate voted on eleven ballot questions in the last election: four constitutional amendments, six initiated measures and one referred law. The 2006 election demonstrates that the populist spirit continues to thrive in contemporary South Dakota politics. South Dakota has tried to make researching the I&R procedure as public friendly as possible. Information on I&Rs–both past and present–is readily accessible, since many of the state's information resources have migrated to Web sites.

The Secretary of State's Web site is the most comprehensive resource for the I&R process and procedure, as well as initial I&R research. This Web site links many electronic resources including the South Dakota Political Almanac, the current Blue Book, and individual links to past election information beginning with the 1972 election. These various resources are helpful in identifying what measures have passed over the years.

Despite this user-friendly approach, there are pitfalls in I&R research. Locating the codified version of enacted measures and amendments in the South Dakota Codified Laws is difficult. Ballot questions that have been enacted into law are not indexed by measure, nor do they appear in the Session Laws. The best way to locate that information is to use the online queries suggested in the section on South Dakota Codified Laws. Unfortunately, as is true with all South Dakota's legislation, supporting historical documents are not available for I&R issues.

For more involved research, various state departments, online resources, and resources around the state have been highlighted in this bibliography. Phone calls to governmental departments such as the Secretary of State's office and the Legislative Research Council proved helpful when compiling information for this bibliography. Reference librarians at the University of South Dakota School of Law Library, the Documents Department at the University of South Dakota and the South Dakota State Library all have access to hard copies of documents such as the Blue Book, law reviews, and some of the monographs noted in the bibliography.

INTERNET RESOURCES

South Dakota, Secretary of State, at http://www.sdsos.gov/index.shtm.
Initiative and referendum information is available at the Secretary of State's Web page at http://www.sdsos.gov/electionsvoteregistration/ electionprocess_initiativesRefsTemp.shtm. Information is indexed under the broad headings of Election Resources, Election Process, Upcoming Elections and Past Elections. Information includes a brief history of the initiative and referendum for enacting and rejecting state legislation, the types of measures that may be included on the ballot, deadlines for filing petitions, and statistics, and links to statutes and rules governing initiatives and referenda.

The Secretary of State posts the list of the ballot questions on the Upcoming Election page. The ballot questions are accompanied by the Attorney General Explanations and Pamphlets to help the voter understand the questions.

The Past Elections page, available at http://www.sdsos.gov/ electionsvoteregistration/pastelections.shtm, has an index of links to past election information. This includes a link to a graph of the number of legislative constitutional amendments, initiated constitutional amendments, initiatives, and referenda that have either passed or been defeated since 1898. That link appears at http://www.sdsos.gov/electionsvoteregistration/ electvoterpdfs/InitiativesReferendumsBallotQuestionsHistory_Barchart. pdf. The page contains a link to a file of the South Dakota Political Almanac where a list of short titles for the ballot questions and election results from 1890 to 2004 can be found. The link for this file is found at http://www.sdsos.gov/electionsvoteregistration/electvoterpdfs/ pastelections_BallotQuestions1890-2004.pdf.

Municipal and county initiative and referendum information are also located on the Secretary of State's Web page under the heading of Election Process. The page is located at http://www.sdsos.gov/ electionsvoteregistration/electionprocess_municipalIntRef.shtm. The information includes instructions for circulating petitions and when the elections must be held. The Election Resource page links to the state laws and administrative rules that apply to elections.

South Dakota Legislative Research Council, at http://legis.state.sd.us/ index.aspx.
This is the official Web site for government publications in South Dakota. The LRC e-publishes: the state code, administrative rules, and

beginning about 1996, issue memorandums concerning initiatives and referendums. Article 05:02 of the South Dakota Administrative Rules, entitled State Board of Elections, includes the forms needed for filing constitutional amendments, state legislation initiative and referendum petitions, as well as county and municipal petitions. Issue memorandums are best located using the search box on the LRC Web page and entering the search: issue memorandums initiative referendum.

Issue memorandums, codes, and administrative rules are also available in hardcopy in the documents department of South Dakota depository libraries, and prior to 1996, they are only available in depository libraries.

The South Dakota Legislative Manual, at http://www.sdsos.gov/adminservices/bluebook.shtm.

Commonly known as the **Blue Book**, is published by the Secretary of State's office every two years in accordance with South Dakota law. The Blue Book contains voting statistics for constitutional amendments, initiated measures, and referred laws–voter results are usually listed by county. Blue Books are an important resource in I&R research; however, with the exception of a few sporadic volumes throughout the series, they are not a reliable way to determine the substance of an act. With the exception of a few volumes in recent years, the typical title of an act is a disappointingly short-working-title, e.g., Suffrage. Some of the volumes prior to the 1950s and some volumes after 1990 contain the text or short explanations of the measures.

The Secretary of State's Web site links to the current Blue Book; hardback copies of prior years of the Blue Book can be located in libraries throughout the state by searching the state library catalog at http://apollo.sdln.net/F.

South Dakota Codified Laws, Thompson West 2004.

Without doing a year by year search in the Blue Book, locating which initiatives and referenda have passed and the voting statistics is difficult. Within the South Dakota Code, the information describing which measures and amendments have passed may be found in one of several places: the History, the Historical Notes, or the Commission Notes of the code section will contain the information. While the information is recorded for each measure in the notes, the researcher must know which statute to look for. Unfortunately, the measures are not cataloged under the topic of 'initiative' or 'constitutional amendment' in the index.

Westlaw electronic version of the South Dakota Codified Laws.
The most productive method for locating a referred or initiated measure is through the use of Lexis or Westlaw. To search in Westlaw, use the Credit field and enter the search "initiated," or the use the search (initiated & vote) in the Historical Notes field, or the search (referendum or referred) in the Credit field. These searches make it possible to locate which measures have passed and are current law.

SoDakLIVE, at http://www.sodaklive.com/.
Sponsored by the South Dakota State Library, this database is the South Dakota response to a nation-wide effort to retain and preserve all electronic documents for state government. The South Dakota State Library, which brought the project live in 2002, has taken the leadership to preserve state documents through the use of technology. The project continues to harvest and add older documents as they become available from state agencies.

Using the search engine for SoDakLIVE to locate government documents which pertain to initiatives and referenda produces a large result of documents that vary greatly in terms of their importance. Documents are harvested from all the departments of the executive branch, the unified judicial system, and the legislature, so narrowing the search can be accomplished through choosing a particular department or by adding terms.

GENERAL BACKGROUND MATERIALS

Braunstein, Rich. *Initiative and Referendum Voting: Governing through Direct Democracy in the United States*. New York: LFB Scholarly Publishing, 2004.
This volume has already been described in another portion of this article, but is included here because the book contains excellent background on South Dakota's interest in the initiative and referendum. The book notes that the initiative and referendum represent "the character of South Dakota voters and their desire to be intimately involved in governing processes,"[30] and they remain an important part of the populist spirit of current South Dakota politics.

Clem, Alan L. *South Dakota Political Almanac: A presentation and analysis of election statistics, 1889-1960* (Report/Governmental

Research Bureau, State University of South Dakota) Vermillion [S.D.] Dakota Press [c1969].

This volume contains valuable information regarding the general elections between 1889 and 1968. Information of value to the I&R researcher may be found at table 6 which records the voter turnout and approval rate in the general elections; table 7 which lists the results of the elections on state constitutional amendments and initiated and referred law, and chapter III which documents the measures on the ballot in each general election by listing the measure with a short title. Electronic links to these tables are located on the South Dakota Secretary of State's Web site [the links are noted under Internet Resources, *supra*].

Jorgensen, Delores A. *South Dakota Legal Research* Guide 2nd ed. (NY: William Hein & Co., Inc.) 1999.

Pages 81-82 outline a brief description of the direct democracy process in South Dakota. The author cites pertinent constitutional and statutory citations for initiatives and referenda.

Lowe, Chip J. *Restrictions on Initiative and Referendum Powers in South Dakota*, S.D. L. Rev. 28 (1982): 53-87.

This article discusses the legal parameters of initiative and referendum and explains that the courts are called upon to referee the extent to which the electorate may exercise these parameters. The writer concludes that the courts are invariably put in the uncomfortable position of "second guessing the decisions of the lawmaking body which are objectionable to the minority of the voters."[31]

Ortbahn, David L. *Initiative and referendum*. South Dakota Legislative Research Council, (Issue Memorandum 98-10), 1998.

This issue memorandum is a backward-look at one century of South Dakota's experience with the initiative and referendum process. The memorandum concludes that the initiative and referendum measure "have served their intended purpose in this state," while other states may be questioning the processes in their states and the ease with which special interests use them to avoid the legislative process.[32] The voters in the 2006 election in South Dakota voted on eleven measures, a larger than usual number with a number of special interest topics. This memorandum is available electronically at http://legis. state.sd.us/IssueMemos/IssueMemos/im98-10.pdf.

Tiffany, B. E. *Initiative and referendum in South Dakota.* Vermillion, South Dakota: University of South Dakota Thesis (M.A. History and Political Science), 1919.
This thesis explains how South Dakota, after a decade and a half of education on the direct legislation principle, was finally able to convince the voters that something needed to be done to combat the "boss ridden political parties refus[al] to listen to the demands of the discontented masses.[33]

NOTES

1. *See* Rich Braunstein, *Initiative and Referendum Voting: Governing through Direct Democracy in the United States* 40-41 (LFB Scholarly Publishing, 2004).
2. South Dakota Legislature, *Constitutional Revision Commission,* http://legis. state.sd.us/interim/2005/CRC.pdf.
3. Chip J. Lowe, *Restrictions on Initiative and Referendum Powers in South Dakota,* 28 S.D. L. Rev. 53, (1982).
4. S.D.Codified.Laws § 9-20 (2004).
5. S.D. Const. art. III § 1.
6. Lowe, *supra* n. 3, at 53-54.
7. S.D.Codified.Laws § 7-18A (2004).
8. S.D.Codified.Laws § 13-6-41 to 49 (2004).
9. S.D.Codified.Laws § 38-8A-12 to 12.2 (2004).
10. S.D. Const. art. XXIII (amended, 1972). "A proposed amendment may amend one or more articles and related subject matter in other articles…"
11. 1987 S.D. Laws ch. 1. The 1987 proposal, approved on November 8, 1988, deleted a provision requiring the Legislature to enact proposed measures and made minor changes in phraseology.
12. *See* South Dakota Secretary of State, State of South Dakota, *Initiatives and Referendums,* at http://www.sdsos.gov/electionsvoteregistration/electionprocess_ initiativesRefsTemp.shtm. (Statistics as of the 2004 election.)
13. *Id.* (A general description of each type of ballot question is given.)
14. S.D. Const. art. III § 1.
15. *See generally,* S.D.Codified.Laws § § 2-1, 9-20 (2004).
16. S.D.Codified.Laws § 2-1-2 (2006 Supp).
17. S.D.Codified.Laws § 2-1-1 (2004).
18. S.D.Codified.Laws § 2-1-5 (2004).
19. S.D.Codified.Laws § 2-1-6.2 (2004).
20. S.D.Codified.Laws § 2-1-4 (2004).
21. S.D.Codified.Laws § § 2-1-3, 2-1-5 (2004).
22. S.D.Codified.Laws § § 2-1-3.
23. S.D. Const. art. XXIII § 1.
24. *Id.*
25. *Id.*
26. S.D.Codified.Laws § 2-1-6.2 (2004).
27. S.D.Codified.Laws § 12-13-25 (2004).

28. Telephone interview by Candice Spurlin with James Fry, South Dakota LRC Director (Oct. 16, 2006).

29. S.D.Codified.Laws § 2-1-12 (2004).

30. Braunstein, *supra* n. 1 at 42.

31. Lowe, supra n. 3 at 86.

32. David L. Ortbahn, *Initiative and referendum* South Dakota Legislative Research Council (Issue Memorandum 98-10) 7 1998, also available at http://legis.state.sd.us/IssueMemos/IssueMemos/im98-10.pdf.

33. B. E. Tiffany, *Initiative and referendum in South Dakota* 43 (Vermillion, South Dakota: University of South Dakota Thesis [M.A. History and Political Science] 1919).

Utah Initiatives and Referenda: A Research Guide

Connie Strittmatter

INTRODUCTION

The initiative process allows individuals to create and submit proposed legislation directly to the citizens for a popular vote, thus by-passing the state legislature. If the initiative receives the majority of the vote, it becomes law. This proactive approach insures that individuals in a given state are able to have an active voice in its legal system and are not restricted by a legislature's reluctance to enact a law. Conversely, the referendum process is reactive. When a legislature passes a law, citizens may attempt to veto the legislation by placing it on the ballot and submitting the law to a vote by the people. If voters pass the referendum, then the law is repealed.

In Utah, the right to initiate new laws and veto recently passed legislation is guaranteed in the constitution.[1] Citizens can submit a law to be voted on by the people through direct and indirect initiatives or repeal an enacted law through the referenda. The goal of this article is to provide insight into this area of research. Part one will provide a history of initiatives and referenda in Utah. It is followed by an explanation of the process in part two. The final section provides a list of primary and secondary sources to consult when researching this topic.

UTAH INITIATIVE AND REFERENDUM HISTORY

In 1899, Utah became the second state in the nation to provide the power of legislation to its citizens.[2] As progressive as this may sound, it took another 18 years before the legislature enacted implementing laws that would bring this right into fruition. Even then, the laws that were passed in 1917 were not in the spirit of the initiative and referendum process. In order to sign a petition, a citizen had to sign in the presence of an official who could administer an oath.This inhibited the ability to obtain signatures because petitions could not be circulated. In addition, sponsors submitting applications for petitions were required to pay a $10 fee for services performed by the Secretary of State as well as printing costs for petition copies and $0.50 for every 100 circulation sheets issued.[4] It wasn't until after the Second World War that the laws were eased and in 1960 the first initiative was passed.[5] However, the laws became more stringent in 1998 when pro-hunting groups lobbied the Legislature to amend the constitution and laws to require any initiative involving the protection of animals to be passed by a supermajority (two-thirds vote) rather than a simple majority.[6] To date, only four initiatives have passed and become law in Utah.[7]

UTAH'S INITIATIVE AND REFERENDUM PROCESS

The process of placing an initiative or referendum on the ballot begins with an application filed with the Lieutenant Governor's office. The application must be sponsored by five Utah residents who have voted in a general election within the last three years. It contains a copy of the proposed law and a statement indicating whether individuals gathering signatures for the petition will receive payment for their services.[8] An initiative application can be filed at any time but must be qualified within one year of submitting the application.[9]

The Lieutenant Governor reviews the initiative application and may reject it if the proposed law is unconstitutional, nonsensical, impassable or substantially similar to an initiative that had been submitted within two preceding years.[10] If the application is accepted, it is submitted to the Governor's Office of Planning and Budgeting who prepares a financial impact statement.[11] Once the financial impact statement is released, the sponsors of the initiative must hold seven public hearings throughout designated areas in Utah.[12] It is only after the hearings are held that the sponsors may circulate the petitions packets. If it is a direct initiative, sponsors must obtain legal signatures that meet two requirements. First, signatures must equal ten percent of all votes cast statewide in the previous gubernatorial election.[13] For example, in the 2004 election, there were 942,010 votes cast for the Utah Governor's race. For an initiative to be placed on the ballot between 2004 and 2008, sponsors would need to obtain 94,201 signatures.[14] The second part of the statute requires sponsors to obtain signatures equaling at least ten percent of the votes cast for the governor's race in at least 26 Senate districts.[15] This is intended to insure that there is support for the initiative throughout the entire state, not just in one or two Senate districts.

To qualify the initiative petition for placement on the ballot, sponsors must deliver the initiative packet to the clerk of the court in the county where the signatures were collected by the June 1 before the regular election. The clerk of the court will verify the signatures by determining whether the signer is a Utah resident at least 18 years of age and a registered voter. Once the names are certified, it is delivered to the Lieutenant Governor who determines whether the petition received the required number of signatures and declares the initiative either sufficient or insufficient.[16]

If the initiative is sufficient, the Lieutenant Governor delivers a copy of the proposed law to the Office of Legislative Research and General Counsel who titles the initiative, gives it a number and an impartial title summarizing the initiative. It is then returned to the Lieutenant Governor who then sends it to the county clerk to be printed on the ballot.[17] After the election when the votes are certified, the Governor declares a proclamation that states the total number of votes for and against each initiative. Each one that receives the required number of votes becomes law in Utah.[18] The initiative becomes effective law either five days after the official date of the governor's proclamation or the date specified in the initiative.[19] The Governor may not veto an initiative. However, an approved initiative may be amended by the Legislature.

The indirect initiative process is similar to the direct initiative process with the following exceptions:

- Indirect initiatives only require legal signatures equal to five percent of the votes cast in the last gubernatorial election and legal signatures equaling five percent of the votes cast in at least 26 Senate districts.[20]
- Indirect initiative packets must be submitted to the county clerk by November 15 for verification rather than June 1 deadline for direct initiative packets.[21]
- Once the signatures are obtained, the proposed legislation is sent to the Legislature who can either pass or reject the initiative: it may not amend it.[22] If the initiative is passed, it becomes law and the effective date is 60 days after the Legislature adjourns during the session that it enacted the law or on the effective date included in the proposed law if it was passed by a two-thirds majority of each house.[23]
- If the initiative is rejected by the Legislature, the sponsors may obtain the remaining legal signatures needed to meet the ten percent requirement to place it on the ballot as a direct initiative.[24]

The referendum application process is nearly identical to that of the initiative process. The major differences are that referendum applications:

- Must be submitted within five calendar days after the end of the legislative session in which the law was enacted.[25]
- May not be submitted if the law was passed by two-thirds of each house of the Legislature.[26]
- Requires ten percent of the votes from 15 Senate districts instead of the 26 required for initiatives.[27]
- Must be delivered to the county clerk within forty days of the end of the legislative session.[28]

SOURCES FOR INFORMATION ABOUT UTAH INITIATIVES AND REFERENDA

Secondary Sources

There are a limited number of secondary sources that discuss Utah's initiative and referendum process. Some resources that can be consulted are discussed below.

Citizen Participation and Elections in *A Citizen's Guide to Utah State Government* (Office of Legislative Research and General Counsel, 2005).

This chapter discusses citizen participation in Utah elections and provides detailed information on registering to vote and voting processes, duties and obligations of political parties, the initiative and referendum process, lobbying and lobbyist regulations and a political history of Utah's Legislature and Governor's Office. Although this chapter is not dedicated exclusively to the initiative and referendum process, it provides valuable information on the topic and should be consulted when researching initiatives and referenda. In clear and concise language, it explains the laws governing the direct and indirect initiative and referendum process for state laws as well as county and city ordinances. It also outlines the information provided on ballot measures that appear in the voter information pamphlet. This book is available at several public and university libraries in Utah and can be purchased from Utah's Legislative Printing Office for a nominal fee.

Patton W. David. *The Initiatives and Referendum Process in Utah*, at http://www.imakenews.com/cppa/e_article000594636.cfm?x=b11, 0,w.

The first half of Patton's article is a general overview of the initiative and referendum process that is not specific to Utah. It discusses the evolution of the process and outlines the arguments for and against the use of initiatives and referenda. The second half of the article explores Utah's experience with ballot measures. He outlines the initiative and referendum procedures governing the process and lists some of the major issues that have appeared on the ballot. This is not a comprehensive list of propositions and it does contain some errors. The 2004 constitutional amendment banning gay marriage was passed. It was also not an initiative.[29] In 1999, an indirect initiative proposing that English should be the official language of Utah was sent to the legislature and defeated, but was passed in 2000 as a direct initiative.[30] The strength of this article is the clear explanation of the Utah initiative and referendum process.

Primary Sources

Voter Information Pamphlets (Office of the Lieutenant Governor)

By law, the Lieutenant Governor is responsible for informing voters on the issues and candidates in an election. For each election, a Voter Information Pamphlet is published. This pamphlet is probably the most valuable resource for locating the text of initiatives and referenda. It provides not only the text of the initiative or referendum, but it also provides arguments supporting and opposing the measure as well as rebuttal arguments. Each argument includes the author's name and title, which is helpful in identifying groups and organizations supporting or opposing the measure. If there is a referendum on the ballot, the vote cast by the Legislature is included.[31]

The publicity pamphlets are mailed to state residents, placed in newspapers for general circulation, and made available to each county clerk for free distribution and placement at polling locations.[32]

Voter Information Pamphlets can be obtained from the following resources:

- The current pamphlet is available on the Lieutenant Governor's Web site at http://elections.utah.gov/VoterInformationPamphlet2006.html.
- Older print copies can be found at Utah State Library (1980-2000, 2006) and University of Utah Libraries (1988-2006).
- The Utah History Research Center housed in the Rio Grand Train Depot in Salt Lake City is a research facility operated by the Utah State Archives. They have two archival series that can be useful when researching initiatives and referenda that are described below. They provide telephone and email reference services and will conduct approximately 30 minutes of research upon request. Their Web site can be found at http://historyresearch.utah.gov/.
- Utah State Archives and Records Service, *Elections Office, Voter Information Pamphlets Series, 21810.* This series contains voter

information pamphlets ongoing from 1975. Information can be found at http://historyresearch.utah.gov/inventories/21810.html.

- Utah State Archives and Records Service, *Secretary of State, Elections Papers 1851-1976 Series 364.* This series contains selected initiative petitions and returns from 1934-1956. They are on microform, but the detailed inventory guide is very useful in locating the reel, box and folder containing the information needed. A description of this series can be found at http://historyresearch. utah.gov/inventories/364.html and the Document Container List/ Inventory guide is accessible at http://historyresearch.utah.gov/ inventories/pdf/364.pdf.

Utah Lieutenant Governor, at http://elections.utah.gov/index.html.

The Lieutenant Governor's Office Web site provides information on Utah initiatives and referenda and is a suitable place to start when researching current measures. It links to a page titled *Constitutional Amendments, Initiatives and Referendum* at http://elections.utah.gov/ propositionsinitiativesreferendums.html. From this page, researchers can access the results of the initiatives and referendum that have appeared on the ballot since 1960. The information is limited as it provides a brief title of the initiative, the year it appeared on the ballot, and whether it was passed or defeated. Researchers can also link to a list of measures currently in circulation. This site also provides information on the initiative and referendum process, an online application to submit a measure, a list of currently scheduled public hearings, and the signature requirements needed to qualify an initiative or referendum.

From the main Lieutenant Governor's page, under the heading *Voter Information,* researchers can view the current voter information pamphlet and election results from 1982. The format for the election results vary and the information presented is not always consistent. Initiative and referendum information is not listed from 1990-1994. It should also be noted that the term "proposition," which is used in several election results, does not refer to initiatives and referenda, but rather constitutional amendments. Overall, this site is useful and should be consulted.

Utah Code Annotated

The laws describing the statewide and local initiative and referendum process can be found in Title 20 Chapter 7 of the *Utah Code Annotated.*

The index contains the following subject headings related to this topic:

- Initiatives–Statewide
- Initiatives–Local
- Referenda–Statewide
- Referenda–Local

Unfortunately, these subject headings refer only to the laws governing the process and not to the statutes that have been passed through initiatives. A researcher would need to know the topic of the passed initiatives to locate where it is codified. The table below provides the statutory cites for the four initiatives that have passed in Utah.

Utah Code Citations for Passed Initiatives

Year Passed	Initiative Topic	Utah Code Citation
1960	Establishment of Merit System for Deputy Sheriffs	17-30-1 through 17-30-23
1976	Freedom from Compulsory Fluoridation and Medication Act	19-4-11 through 19-4-111.2*
2000	Utah Property Protection Act	24-1-1 through 24-1-15; 23-20-1; 32A-13-103; 41-6a-211; 53A-16-101; 58-37-13; 58-37a-6; 58-37c-15; 58-37d-7; 59-14-207; 76-3-501; 76-10-16-3.5; 76-10-1908; 76-10-11-7; 76-10-1108
2000	English as the Official Language of Utah	63-15-1.5

* These statutes are the most comparable to the passed initiative that the author could locate in the Utah Code Annotated.

CONCLUSION

Utah is not a state that passes many initiatives and referenda as evidenced by the four that have been passed since their establishment in 1899. As a result, there is not a large body of literature on this topic. With the lack of secondary and electronic sources available, researchers must rely heavily on primary and print resources. Fortunately, these are relatively easy to obtain and provide the necessary information needed.

Researchers should have success when attempting to locate information on Utah initiatives and referenda.

NOTES

1. Utah Const. art. VI, § 1(2)(a)(i).
2. *Initiative and Referendum Almanac* 400 (M. Dane Waters ed., Carolina Academic Press 2003).
3. 1917 Utah Laws ch. 56 § 8.
4. 1917 Utah Laws ch. 56 § 13. This practice continued through 1987 when the service fees were $50, the sponsor paid printing costs for petition copies, and $5 for every 100 circulation sheets. This was repealed by 1987 Utah Laws ch. 145 § 4. Currently, the Lieutenant Governor provides a copy of the initiative petition and signature sheet to the sponsors who are then responsible for printing additional copies. Utah Code Ann. § 20A-7-204 (Lexis 2003).
5. *Initiative and Referendum Almanac* 400 (M. Dane Waters ed., Carolina Academic Press 2003).
6. 1998 Utah Laws S.J.R.10 § 1.
7. Lieutenant Governor, State of Utah. *Other Elections Information*, at http:// elections.utah.gov/ResultsofUTInitiativesandReferendums2004.htm.
8. Utah Code Ann. § 20A-7-202 (Lexis 2003).
9. *Id.*
10. Utah Code Ann. § 20A-7-202 (Lexis 2003).
11. Utah Code Ann. § 20A-7-202.5 (Lexis 2003).
12. Utah Code Ann. § 20A-7-204.1 (Lexis 2003).
13. Utah Code Ann. § 20A-7-201 (Lexis 2003).
14. Lieutenant Governor, State of Utah. *Other Elections Information* http://elections. utah.gov/signature_nos.htm.
15. *Id.* Utah Code Ann. § 20A-7-201 (Lexis 2003). For example, of the 94, 201 signatures required to place an initiative on the ballot, 1,651 signatures would need to be from Senate District 1 (There were 16,510 votes cast in the gubernatorial election), 3,017 signatures would need to be from Senate District 2 (There were 30,170 votes cast in the gubernatorial election) and so forth.
16. Utah Code Ann. § 20A-7-206 (Lexis 2003) Utah Code Ann. § 20A-7-207 (Lexis 2003).
17. Utah Code Ann. § 20A-7-209 (Lexis 2003).
18. Utah Code Ann. § 20A-7-211 (Lexis 2003).
19. Utah Code Ann. § 20A-7-212 (Lexis 2003).
20. Utah Code Ann. § 20A-7-201 (Lexis 2003).
21. Utah Code Ann. § 20A-7-206 (Lexis 2003).
22. Utah Code Ann. § 20A-7-201 (Lexis 2003).
23. Utah Code Ann. § 20A-7-712 (Lexis 2003).
24. Utah Code Ann. § 20A-7-208 (Lexis 2003).
25. Utah Code Ann. § 20A-7-302 (Lexis 2003).
26. Utah Code Ann. § 20A-7-102 (Lexis 2003).
27. Utah Code Ann. § 20A-7-301 (Lexis 2003).
28. Utah Code Ann. § 20A-7-306 (Lexis 2003).

29. Utah Const. art. I, § 29.
30. Utah Code Ann. 63-13-1.5 (Lexis 2004).
31. Utah Code Ann. § 20A-7-702 (Lexis 2003).
32. *Id.;* Utah History Research Center, *Elections Office, Voter Information Pamphlets,* at http://historyresearch.utah.gov/inventories/21810.html.

Researching Washington State Initiatives and Referendums

Beth Williams

INTRODUCTION

This guide is meant to assist researchers interested in Washington statewide initiatives and referendums ("I&R"). First, by way of background, a brief history of the origins of I&R in Washington is provided, along with a short description of the mechanics of how an initiative or referendum gets on the ballot in Washington. However, this is primarily meant to be a practical research guide, and not a review of the vast scholarship on this subject.[1] For this reason, the substance of this article is the material contained under the heading "Research Resources." There is a particular emphasis here on resources available on the Internet, and an annotated list of Web sites of particular interest and importance for research purposes is provided. Finally, an annotated bibliography of selected secondary resources in print is also included.

BRIEF HISTORY OF I&R IN WASHINGTON

The Washington Constitution did not originally contain provisions permitting direct legislation.[2] However, like most states that ultimately embraced the I&R movement, Washington's story of how the initiative and referendum came to be is generally attributed to the Progressive Movement of the late nineteenth century.[3]

Several disparate Washington groups–including trade unionists, farmers, and urban progressives–came together out of a general distrust of government to create the Direct Legislation League of Washington in 1907.[4] Following the success of other Western I&R campaigns in South Dakota and Oregon, the Direct Legislation League pushed the I&R measure through the Washington legislation in 1911.[5] The people of the State of Washington quickly adopted the State's seventh constitutional amendment in 1912 with a vote of 110,110 in favor and 43,905 against.[6] The amendment added the following language:

> [B]ut the people reserve to themselves the power to propose bills, law and enact or reject the same at polls, independent of the legis- lature, and also reserve the power, at their own option, to approve or reject at the polls any item, section, or part of any bill, act or law passed by the legislature.[7]

OUTLINE OF WASHINGTON'S I&R PROCESS[8]

The I&R system in the State of Washington comprises four parts: the Initiative to the People (i.e., direct initiative); Initiative to the Legislature (i.e., indirect initiative); Referendum Measure (i.e., popular referendum); and the Referendum Bill (i.e., legislative referendum). Though the authority to exercise all initiative and referendum power is derived from the constitution, the procedures are governed by statute.[9] The statutory framework is specific about the procedures for exercising initiative and referendum powers.[10] Though broad, the initiative and referendum power in Washington is limited to subjects that are legislative in nature.[11] Notably, this power does not delegate to the people the right to amend the State constitution.[12]

The initiative is the most common way Washington citizens exercise their direct legislation power.[13] Any legal voter of the state may file an initiative or referendum measure petition, either on their own behalf or on behalf of an organization.[14] The Office of Code Revisor reviews the petition and recommends to the sponsor "such revision or alteration of the measure as may be deemed necessary and appropriate."[15] These recommendations are advisory only, and may be rejected in whole or in part by the petition sponsor.[16] In fact, this is the only drafting stage during which there is a built-in opportunity for legal advice.[17] The Office of Code Revisor then issues a Certificate of Review to the petitioner, who must re-file the petition with that Certificate in the Secretary of State's Office for assignment of a ballot measure number.[18] The Secretary of State then forwards the petition to the Office of the Attorney General, who drafts the ballot title and summary.[19]

At this stage, the sponsor is permitted to circulate petitions for signature. In the case of either the direct or indirect form of initiative, sponsors must obtain signatures equal to or exceeding eight percent of the votes cast for the office of Governor in the immediately preceding gubernatorial election; referendum measures only require signatures equal to four percent of the same.[20] If that number is met, the Secretary of State verifies the petition signatures via a statistical sampling method,[21] and issues a Certificate of Sufficiency for inclusion of the petition on the ballot.[22] In the case of an initiative to the people or a referendum measure, the petition is then placed on the ballot, accompanied by a fiscal impact statement,[23] statement of the subject of the measure, and a concise description.[24] If the petition is an initiative to the legislature, the legislature may (1) adopt the petition as proposed, (2) reject or refuse to act on the petition, or (3) approve an amended version.[25] In the second case, the legislature's failure to act triggers the measure's appearance on the next general election ballot.[26] In the third case, both the amended and the original petition will appear on the next general election ballot.[27]

RESEARCH RESOURCES

Few tasks are more challenging for the legal researcher than finding information about either a pending initiative or referendum or a law passed via that process. The trail of officially published documents is short and must often be supplemented with a diffuse collection of secondary materials. The contents below are intended to assist researchers in finding resources regarding Washington initiatives and referendums, along with detailed information on what information researchers may expect to find in those resources. The following is a list of the documents often generated in the State of Washington.

Each stage in the life of an initiative or referendum provides a finite number of officially published[28] documents. The initial stage is primarily composed of the original petition as drafted by the sponsor and the petition sponsor name(s) and contact information. The remaining official information appears in the State Voter's Pamphlet, including fiscal impact statements,[29] ballot title and explanatory statement as drafted by the Attorney General's Office,[30] and arguments for and against prepared by legislative committee members.[31] Researchers may also find some of this same information in other print materials, e.g., in the published State session laws and other legislative materials. In addition, official information may be found in various electronic resources as discussed below.

Secondary source materials are likely to be the lifeblood of any I&R research project. Newspaper articles, position papers, research reports, scholarly books and articles, and reference sources in print and online will assist in pinpointing the nature and context of initiatives and referendums. Just as there is no one resource that will answer all questions regarding initiatives and referendums, no one research method will suffice for finding information about this topic. The following tools are suggested starting points for I&R research projects that will likely branch off into as yet unmentioned locations.

Washington Session Laws and Statutory Codes

An excellent place to begin researching the history of Washington laws passed or merely introduced by the initiative and referendum process is the most recent edition of Washington's published session laws, *Session Laws of the State of Washington*. Published annually, this set contains a wealth of information for I&R researchers. Though a fair number of the electronic resources described below contain both historical and current lists of Washington initiatives and referendums, the information contained in Washington's *Session Laws* has the benefit of being official, easy to use, and often readily accessible.

A particularly rich source of I&R information is found in each annual edition of the *Session Laws*. A cumulative list called *History of State Measures* is typically found under the *Index and Tables* heading in the table of contents (and often appears towards the end of the second volume, where applicable). This list is divided into four sections: Initiatives to the People, Initiatives to the Legislature, Referendum Measures, and Referendum Bills. Each measure entry contains the following information: ballot measure number, a short statement about the subject of the measure, filing date, sponsor name(s), number of signatures gathered, date the measure was submitted to the people, and the resulting number of votes for and against. It is important to note that even ballot measures that did not pass into Washington State law are included in this extremely valuable historical list. Even-numbered year editions of the *Sessions Laws* contain complete, cumulative lists, while odd-numbered year editions merely supplement the list published in the previous annual edition. Though it may be tempting to gather this same information from a Web site like the ones provided by the I&R Institute[32] or the National Conference of State Legislators,[33] this traditional print resource is more current, more reliable, and more complete.

When searching for information about a particular ballot measure from a known time period, you may simply consult the volumes of Washington *Session Laws* that were published immediately subsequent to that election. The *Session Laws* always publish initiatives or referendums passed first, prior to all legislative bills. Simply browsing the table of contents will provide the ballot measure number, possession of which will help in using many of the additional resources described in the lists below. For example, the table of contents in the 2006 edition of the *Session Laws* begins with Chapter 1, which was *Bill No. INIT 900*, a controversial initiative that passed into law concerning performance audits of government entities.[34] Chapter number 2 of the 2006 *Session Laws* is also an initiative, while chapter number 3 begins all the legislative bills passed during that session, i.e., Chapter 3 began as *Bill No. SHB 2370*, and so on. Alternatively, one can simply browse the Chapter to Bill Table available in the *Session Laws* volumes to find out which laws were proposed and passed via a Washington initiative or referendum.

Washington law concerning the I&R processes itself may be searched using either *West's Revised Code of Washington Annotated,* or *Matthew Bender's Annotated Revised Code of Washington.* Both publishers include "Initiative and Referendum" as a subject heading in their general indexes. Unfortunately, that subject heading does not include cross-references to the substantive laws passed *by* the I&R process, and the set does not index ballot measures either by popular name (i.e., ballot title) or by ballot measure number. Therefore, researching the codified versions of laws that began as initiatives and referendums when only the popular ballot title or number is known requires interim steps. If the I&R subject is known, then the code's subject index may be more useful, though that will not always be the most efficient way to find the appropriate code sections for statutes passed by initiative or referendum.

Internet Resources

This list is a directory of major Washington Web sites containing both primary and secondary I&R materials. Organizations whose Web sites currently contain little substantive information have been excluded. Note that, though there may appear to be overlap in the kinds of information available on these sites, it is probably worthwhile to visit several of these sites when researching a particular ballot measure. The Web sites are listed below in order of importance. In the interest of convenience, I have highlighted the type of information and documents one can expect to find on each Web site. I have also included both the organization's base URL and the deep links to pages within these sites, when they may be especially helpful.

Washington Secretary of State, *at* http://www.secstate.wa.gov.
The Washington Secretary of State's Web site contains a significant amount of information on current and historical initiatives and referendums from 1996 to the present at http://www.secstate.wa.gov/ elections/initiatives/. Material available here currently includes the measure **filing date**, **names and contact information of ballot measure sponsors**, the **official ballot measure summary** and the **complete text of the measure**. In addition, this site posts **pamphlets**

on procedures for filing initiatives and referendums, **sample affidavits** for filing proposed initiatives and referendums, and a handy **initiative process checklist**. The Secretary of State's Office has also compiled **historical statistics** summarizing the outcomes of all initiatives and referendums–broken down by type–that made it to the ballot from 1914 to the present. Note, however, that only the ballot measure title and number are indicated in these statistical tables, not the full text.

This site also has one of the most valuable tools for researching past I&R ballot measures: archived **Voters' Guides** from 1997-2006, available at http://www.secstate.wa.gov/elections/voter_guides.aspx . The guides usually contain the **full text of the measure**, an **explanatory statement**, **arguments for and against the measure**, and a **fiscal impact statement**. The 2006 Guides are available in English, Spanish, and Chinese.

Washington State Legislature, *at* http://www1.leg.wa.gov/legislature. Somewhat surprisingly (since these laws are not legislatively enacted), the Washington State Legislature Web site contains the **text** of Washington initiatives and referendums from the 1997-98 biennium to the present, under the misnomer heading "Bill Information." In addition, the Web site's **topical index** includes a heading for "Initiative and Referendum" which leads to both **proposed** and, in the case of prior biennia, **past bills** affecting either previously enacted initiatives and referendums or the I&R process in general. Information about currently proposed initiatives is available at http://apps.leg.wa.gov/ billinfo/initiatives.aspx?year=2007; the 2005-2006 list is available at http://apps.leg.wa.gov/billinfo/initiatives.aspx?year=2005; and the 2003-2004 list is available at http://apps.leg.wa.gov/billinfo/initiatives. aspx?year=2003. There is also a helpful link to a **Chapter to Bill table** on this site, with links to the *Session Laws* where passed initiatives and referendums ultimately appear.

Washington Public Disclosure Commission, *at* www.pdc.wa.gov. The Public Disclosure Commission (PDC) was actually created by means of an initiative to the people (Initiative 276, codified as amended at Wash. Rev. Code § 42.17.350) "to provide timely and meaningful public access to information about the financing of political campaigns, lobbyist expenditures, and the financial affairs of public officials and candidates, and to ensure compliance with disclosure provisions, contribution limits, campaign practices and other campaign finance laws." Of particular interest to the I&R researcher are **reports** on contributions and expenditures for statewide initiative campaigns, available at http://www.pdc.wa.gov/viewreports/. The site also permits searching for and viewing PDC reports by ballot number at http://hera.pdc.wa.gov/wx/fieldsearch.asp. These reports are digital copies of original filings required under Washington's Public Disclosure Law for initiative and referendum sponsors, including **statements of monetary contributions** and **receipt and expenditure reports**.

Municipal Research and Services Center of Washington, *at* www.mrsc.org.

The Municipal Research and Services Center (MRSC) is an independent, non-profit organization that was created in 1969 "to continue programs established in 1934 under the Bureau of Governmental Research at the University of Washington." The MRSC is probably best known for and used as a free resource for the Revised Code of Washington, the Washington Administrative Code, all Washington city and county Codes, and Washington State Supreme and Appellate Court decisions. This organization also publishes **research papers** on a variety of legal topics, including initiatives and referendums. Though they are sometimes difficult to find, MRSC publishes **pages on individual initiatives,** which often include a whole host of useful information, for example, **the text** of the ballot measure, **links** to both MRSC and AWC publications concerning that measure, information about the ballot measure **sponsor(s)**, **reports published by state and local agencies**, court **decisions**, and **news stories**. Though these pages contain well-organized information, the Web site itself makes finding these pages unnecessarily difficult. The fastest way to search for these hidden gems is by running an advanced Google search for the term "Initiative" (or for a specific initiative, e.g., "I-695") and limiting the results to the domain "www.mrsc.org."

Washington Research Council, *at* http://www.researchcouncil.org.

The Washington Research Council provides nonpartisan analysis for taxpayers and lawmakers on issues affecting state and local government. They regularly draft **Policy Briefs** and more in-depth **Special Reports** on initiatives and referendums in Washington. Both resources are very useful for providing background information on proposed and historical initiatives and referendums. The Web site publishes these reports from 2002 to the present, currently available at http://www.researchcouncil.org/Main/Recent%20publications.htm.

Association of Washington Cities, *at* www.awcnet.org.
The Association of Washington Cities (AWC) was founded in 1933 as a private, non-profit, non-partisan organization representing Washington's cities and towns before the State legislature, executive branch, and regulatory agencies. The ACW Web site is a valuable resource for researchers. Their ballot measure information page, currently available by clicking on Resources >> Initiative 933, or by going to http://tinyurl.com/785mu, digests **news stories**, publishes **fact sheets**, and **links** to other resources, including Washington's Office of Financial Management **reports** on initiatives, and similar reports drafted by the Public Disclosure Commission and Attorney General's Office.

Municipal League of King County, *at* http://www.munileague.org.
The Municipal League of King County is a non-profit organization "dedicated to effective and responsive government" founded in 1910. The group evaluates candidates and ballot issues through two publications, *Issue Watch* and *Muni News*, and various reports, many of which are available on their Web site. Of primary interest to I&R researchers is the Issues Management homepage, available at http://www.munileague.org/issues/default.htm#Ballots_Issues. Here, you can link to **reports** on ballot measures from 1995 to 2007. These are primarily **position papers** and may provide excellent background material to place ballot measures in their social and political context. This page also provides **links to Voters' Pamphlets**, including guides published by the *Seattle Post-Intelligencer* and the *Seattle Times*, and **links to state newspapers** and their archives.

Washington Policy Center, *at* http://www.washingtonpolicy.org.
The Washington Policy Center describes itself as a "nonpartisan, free market think tank that publishes studies, sponsors events and conferences, and educates citizens on public policy issues facing Washington State." Though that description appears somewhat contradictory, the organization's Web site publishes **papers** and **opinion pieces/editorials** that may be of interest to I&R researchers under the tab marked Publications by Topic >> Election Laws, currently available at http://www.washingtonpolicy.org/publications_topic.html#electionlaws.

Selected Bibliography

Even, Jeffrey T. "Direct Democracy in Washington: A Discourse on the People's Powers of Initiative and Referendum." *Gonzaga Law Review* 32 (1996-1997): 247-90.

Jeffrey Even's law review article provides a practical analysis of
Washington's initiative and referendum process from the perspective
of the Washington State Office of the Attorney General. The bulk of
the article outlines the procedures for proposing and qualifying
measures for the ballot and discusses the limitations on I&R in
Washington and the scope of judicial review. This article is particularly
good at fleshing out the statutory procedures for I&R submission and
qualification, while avoiding entering the fray of I&R's legal and
political implications.

Koenig, Mark. *Do you want a Free Pony? An Analysis of the Initiative
and Referendum Process in Washington State*. Seattle, Washington:
Municipal League of King County, available at http://www.munileague.
org/issues/2002/InitiativeReportFreePony.pdf, (2002).
Drafted by the Municipal League of King County's Initiative Study
Task Force, *Do You Want a Free Pony?* analyzes Washington's current
I&R process and its use in order to determine whether that process
might be improved. The analysis highlights some of the flaws in
Washington's process, particularly as it regards the dissemination of
objective explanatory statements available to the public concerning
proposed initiatives. Though it is quite brief, this pamphlet provides a
window on the public's perception of I&R in Washington State.

League of Women Voters of Washington, *Direct Democracy: The Initiative and Referendum Process in Washington State*, available at http://
www.lwvwa.org/i&r_study/init-ref-study.pdf, (October, 2002).
The League of Women Voters' study of I&R in Washington is a very
good research paper. Longer than the Municipal League's paper described above, *Direct Democracy* discusses one of I&R's more pressing
issues: the role of money in the Washington I&R system, particularly
on the issue of paid signature gathering. The paper is also an excellent guide to the mechanics of getting an initiative on the ballot from the
petitioner's perspective. What is most surprising about this article is
the advanced level of scholarship. The sections about legal efforts to
restrict usage and constitutional issues after passage are both very
well-written explications of the law, with citations to the State Constitution, the Washington Revised Code, and specific cases. Though
there is an emphasis toward proposing changes to the current system in
the paper, this is quite an even-handed study of the subject.

Symposium, "The Initiative Process in Washington: Implications and Effects." *Seattle University Law Review* 4 (2001): 1017-1172.

The Spring 2001 issue of the *Seattle Law Review* is devoted to the issue of the initiative process in Washington. The authors of the four articles examine the constitutionality of initiatives, I&R's effect on Washington's tax system and the budgetary process, and judicial review of initiatives by Washington courts. Each author takes a decided stance on the issues—overwhelmingly in opposition to the current system—and the articles place the state of Washington's I&R system in a clear context.

NOTES

1. Though direct legislation has been the subject of more than its fair share of political science doctoral dissertations, treatment within the legal literature has been a bit spotty. In some cases, nonprofit research and civic organizations have contributed more substantive legal scholarship regarding I&R than legal scholars have. For examples, see the materials in the section labeled "Research Resources" *infra*.

2. The original text read as follows: "The legislative powers shall be vested in a senate and house of representatives, which shall be called the legislature of the State of Washington." Wash. Const. art. II, § 1 (original text). In fact, only two states' original constitutions contained provisions permitting direct legislation: Montana and Alaska.

3. For a discussion of the origins of the national movement, *see* Laura Tallian, *Direct Democracy: An Historical Analysis of the Initiative, Referendum and Recall Process* (1977). *See also* Robert F. Utter and Hugh D. Spitzer, *The Washington State Constitution: A Reference Guide* (2002) at 50, which states that Washington's original Constitutional language was "borrowed from California, Michigan and the Hill Constitution."

4. For a discussion of the Direct Legislation League of Washington's history, *see* Robert C. Benedict, *Some Aspects of the Direct Legislation Process* in *Washington State: Theory and Practice,* 1914-1973, at 70-78 (1975) (Unpublished Ph.D. dissertation, University of Washington).

5. *Id.* at 78. For more on the history of the I&R movement in Washington, *see* Waters, *supra* note 5, at 427-28.

6. Philip A. Trautman, *Initiative and Referendum in Washington: A Survey,* 49 Wash. L. Rev. 55 (1973-74) at 55, citing *Gottstein v. Lister,* 88 Wash. 462, 153 P. 595 (1915).

7. Wash. Const. art. II, § 1.

8. Two resources outline the procedures for filing and qualifying an initiative or referendum to ballot in greater detail than I will provide here. The first is an official publication drafted by the Washington Secretary of State entitled *Filing Initiatives and Referenda in Washington State, 2005-2008,* available at www.secstate.wa.gov/elections/pdf/Filing_Initiative_and_Referenda_Manual_2005-2008.pdf (also discussed in *infra*). The second is Jeffrey T. Even's excellent *Direct Democracy in Washington: A Discourse on the People's Powers of Initiative and Referendum,* 32 Gonzaga L. Rev. 247, 256-264 (1996-1997) (also discussed *infra*). Even's article includes important discussions about the limitations on the nature and scope of initiative and referendum power and the process of judicial review, the contents of which is not substantially effected by the age of the article.

9. Wash. Const. art. II, § 1(d) states that the initiative and referendum "section is self-executing, but legislation may be enacted especially to facilitate its operation."

10. *See generally* Wash. Rev. Code § 29A.72 (West, 2005).

11. *Ford v. Logan*, 79 Wash. 2d 147, 483 P.2d 1247 (Wash. 1971).

12. *Culliton v. Chase*, 174 Wash. 363, 25 P.2d 81 (Wash. 1933).

13. *See* Office of the Secretary of State, State of Washington, *Summary: State Initiatives and Referendums, 1914–2006, at* http://www.secstate.wa.gov/elections/initiatives/statistics_summary.aspx.

14. Wash. Rev. Code § 29A.72.010.

15. Wash. Rev. Code § 29A.72.020.

16. *Id.*

17. Steven William Marlowe argues that "while the drafting of proposed initiative may be somewhat improved, the lack of amendments, compromise, and broad input may lead to bad laws that tear at the fabric of society" in *Direct Democracy is Not Republican Government*, 24 Seattle U. L. Rev. 1035, 1042 (2001).

18. Wash. Rev. Code § 29A.72.020.

19. Wash. Rev. Code § 29A.72.060.

20. Wash. Rev. Code § 29A.72.150.

21. Wash. Rev. Code § 29A.72.230.

22. Wash. Rev. Code § 29A.72.250.

23. Wash. Rev. Code § 29A.72.025.

24. Wash. Rev. Code § 29A.72.050.

25. Wash. Const. art. II § 1(d).

26. Wash. Rev. Code § 29A.72.260.

27. Wash. Rev. Code § 29A.72.270.

28. By "official" I mean government documents, including documents drafted by government officials and government forms filed by petitioners or other members of the public.

29. *See* Wash. Rev. Code § 29A.72.025.

30. *See* Wash. Rev. Code § 29A.32.040.

31. *See* Wash. Rev. Code § 29A.32.060.

32. *See* http://www.iandrinstitute.org/Washington.htm >> Initiative Historical Listing.

33. *See* http://www.ncsl.org/programs/legismgt/elect/dbintro.htm.

34. INIT 900 revised Wash. Rev. Code §§ 82.08.020 and 43.88.160, added new sections to § 43.09, and added a new section to § 82.12.

Initiatives and Referenda in Wyoming

Debora Person
Tawnya Plumb

BACKGROUND AND HISTORY OF INITIATIVES
AND REFERENDA IN WYOMING

When talking about a state's statutes, we generally think of legislation drafted and introduced into the legislature by an elected representative, handled by committees, debated on the House and Senate floor, passed by Congress, and signed by the Governor. However, some states allow more direct voter participation in the process through initiatives and referenda.

The language of initiatives and referenda varies slightly from source to source. A "compulsory referendum" or "legislative amendment" is used when the state's constitution requires that certain types of questions be placed before the electorate. In addition to the compulsory referendum, there is the "legislative referendum" or "legislative statute" which allows the legislature, at their discretion, to refer a statute to the electorate. Finally, there is the "petition referendum" or "direct legislation," more commonly known as an initiative, allowing legislation to originate directly from the electorate.

Wyoming is one of 24 states that allows some form of direct legislation.[1] The extent of voter rights in enacting laws varies considerably among the states, from proposing statutes and constitutional amendments to requiring changes initiated by the people to go through the legislature or other governmental office. In Wyoming, "[t]he people may propose and enact laws by the initiative, and approve or reject acts of the legislature by the referendum."[2] Wyoming voters may initiate new legislation in the form of statutes through the initiative process, but constitutional initiatives (amendments or changes to the constitution) are not permitted.[3]

The State's initiative process is outstanding for a couple of reasons: (1) our legislature was one of the first in the nation to consider the option, (2) after its initial failure in the legislature, it was put to a popular vote and failed, and (3) at this time the process in Wyoming is the most stringent of those currently in existence in the country.

In the 1890s, Representative Tidball of Sheridan, Wyoming, was possibly the first in the nation to introduce a bill to amend the state constitution to allow for statewide initiatives and referenda. The bill did not succeed.[4] In 1911, Governor Carey's opening message to the legislature urged adoption of the constitutional amendment again. The bill had the support of the legislature but failed in the electoral vote.[5] Actually, in the popular vote the amendment passed by an overwhelming majority of 6:1, but the Wyoming Constitution required a majority of all voters casting ballots in the election (or "supermajority"). The issue arose again in the Governors' 1913 and 1965 addresses to the legislature but neither time was it acted upon.[6]

Finally, in 1967, the Wyoming legislature passed an initiative and referendum amendment, and it was ratified in an electoral vote in the 1968 general election, effective that December.[7] To date, the process has been little-used in Wyoming. According to the Wyoming Secretary of State's Office, from 1968 through 2006, 30 initiatives and referenda have been filed. Of these, eight eventually appeared on the ballot, three passing in 1992, and five have been declined by the electorate since that time. Three subjects of initiatives were passed by the Wyoming legislature before they appeared on the ballot of a general election, and one initiative is currently pending.[8]

The first successful attempt to get an initiative on the ballot was "In-Stream Flow," failing in 1981 to collect the requisite number of signatures, but qualifying in 1986 to get on the November ballot. The legislature, however, enacted the law in March of 1986, causing it to be automatically removed from the election.[9] 1992 marked the first statewide initiative placed before Wyoming voters, banning triple trailers from state highways. Two other initiatives qualified and passed that same year: term limits and regulation of railroads and hazardous materials.

Still, with only three successful initiatives in the State's history, in 1998 voters approved a legislative amendment that tightened up the signature restrictions, requiring 15% of signatures in at least 2/3 of the counties as opposed to 15% of signatures with at least one signature from 2/3 of the State's counties.[10]

Another initiative on term limits in 1996 actually did have a majority vote. Similar to the constitutional amendment 80 years earlier, it failed to pass because of Wyoming's supermajority requirement, that is, that the majority in favor of an initiative must also be a majority of the total number of people who turn out to vote in the general election. To accept an initiative, the majority vote must overcome both the negative votes and the abstentions. If ten percent of the voters in Wyoming do not vote on a given initiative, the supermajority required for that initiative to pass will be about fifty-five percent.[11] The lower the number of registered voter turn-out in an election, the higher a percentage is needed to vote for an initiative in order for it to pass. Paired with the strict signature requirement, the supermajority frustrates many initiative efforts in the state, and so it is not surprising that each has been the focus of court cases.

COURT TREATMENT

Wyoming courts are not restricted in their treatment of initiatives and referenda and hold them to the same standard they would any legislation when determining the constitutionality of the law. In fact, at this time "no state court is required to give greater deference to voter-approved laws."[12]

A 1947 case, *State ex rel Keefe v. McInerney*,[13] challenged whether only registered voters were eligible to sign initiative petitions. The court held that it was only necessary that voters be eligible or qualified to vote, not that they be registered. In *State ex rel Benham v. Cheever*,[14] signed petitions were determined to be sufficient to establish prima facie compliance with the statute for signatures and the burden was placed on the party contesting the petition to demonstrate the invalidity of signatures. Both these decisions were based on earlier versions of Wyoming Statute § 22-23-710.[15]

The Court's precedent was altered by *Thomson v. Wyoming In-Stream Flow Committee* in 1982.[16] This initiative gave the State Game and Fish Department the ability to claim water rights on behalf of fish and wildlife in an attempt to prevent future development from excessive draining of water sources. The case questioned whether the Secretary of State had the power to verify signatures on initiative petitions, arguing that in most states there is a presumption that signatures on petitions are valid registered voters. The Supreme Court instead determined that presumption of validity of signatures is not precedent in Wyoming because: (a) Wyoming's procedure did not verify that signers were qualified registered voters, and (b) the penalty for fraud is a high misdemeanor and not a sufficient deterrent.[17]

Brady v. Ohman[18] challenged Wyoming's "supermajority" requirement in federal court on the grounds that it violated equal protection and free speech rights. Since the Wyoming law essentially counts all voters who do not vote on a particular initiative as a no vote, the term limits proponents argued that the law deprived citizens of the right to abstain on an issue. The U.S. Court of Appeals for the 10th circuit rejected this argument, instead agreeing with the original trial judge that "Wyoming has a legitimate and reasonable interest in seeing that an initiative measure . . . is not enacted into law unless it is approved by a majority of those voting in the general election in which the initiated measure is being considered. If Wyoming wants to make it 'harder' rather than 'easier' to make laws by the initiated process, such is its prerogative." It was reasonable, the court concluded, for the State of Wyoming to wish to minimize "abuse of the initiated process and make it difficult for a relatively small special-interest group to enact its views into law."[19] The U.S. Supreme Court affirmed the lower court's ruling without comment.

INITIATIVE AND REFERENDUM PROCESS IN WYOMING

The process of filing initiatives and referenda in the state of Wyoming is set out in the Wyoming Statutes Annotated and the Wyoming Constitution. The process is quite detail-oriented and covers citizens' rights, the application process and review, the petition procedure and review, the ballot measure, voting, and the outcome of the initiative and referendum proposal.

Rights of Wyoming Citizens

The peoples' right in Wyoming to propose laws by initiative is established in the statutes and constitution. This right is limited to those laws that do not dedicate revenues, make or repeal appropriations, create or establish the jurisdiction of courts or court rules, enact local or special legislation, or attempt to enact that which is prohibited by the constitution. This right is also limited on an initiative that fails, as the same issue cannot be re-introduced within five years.[20]

The right of referendum to approve or reject acts of the legislature is provided by the Wyoming Statutes. The right to referendum cannot be used on acts dealing with dedications of revenue, appropriations, local or special legislation, or laws considered necessary for the preservation of public peace, health, or safety.[21]

Application Contents and Requirements

The application process for both initiatives and referenda requires the filing of an application form accompanied with a fee of $500 with the Secretary of State (Secretary).[22] The content of the application must include the initiative or referendum in bill form, a designation of three sponsors to represent all sponsors, a statement that these sponsors are qualified registered voters, and in the case of a referendum, the signatures and addresses of at least 100 qualified voters.[23] The proposed bill must limit itself to one subject, have an effective date, and contain in its title "Be it enacted by the people of the state of Wyoming: . . . "[24]

Review of Application

The contents of the application are reviewed by the Legislative Service Office, or any agency in the executive department, and comments are provided. This commentary becomes part of the public record. Within 14 calendar days, the Secretary will conference with the committee of sponsors and note any problems with format or contents of the proposed bill. The committee may choose to incorporate changes suggested, or the committee may disregard the suggestions entirely. If the bill has a fiscal impact on the state, the comments must include an estimate and explanation to be presented to the committee of sponsors at the conference. If there is disagreement between the sponsors and the Secretary of more than $25,000 on the fiscal impact statement, the comments and ballot proposition will include a range reflecting both estimates.

The committee of sponsors has five calendar days to report back to the Secretary if any amendments to the bill will be made. If amendments are made, the bill needs to be resubmitted for review and comment once again. If amendments are not made, the committee of sponsors needs to submit the names, addresses, and signatures of 100 qualified registered voters to act as sponsors to the final application.[25]

As a final act of review, the Secretary will choose to certify the application or deny with explanation within seven calendar days of receipt.[26] An initiative will be denied if the documents are not in the required form, if there is not an appropriate number of qualified registered voters as sponsors, or if the review process is not properly followed. A referendum will be denied if the application is not in the appropriate form, if there is an insufficient number of registered voters as sponsors, or if more than 90 days have expired since the act being referred was passed.[27]

Petitions

Once an application is certified, the Secretary will prepare the petitions which include a copy of the proposed bill or act to be referred, an impartial summary of the subject matter, a warning concerning signature fraud, sufficient space for signatures and addresses, and a prominently displayed statement if a paid circulator is collecting signatures. Costs for the petitions will be paid for by the sponsors. The petitions may only be circulated in person and by a sponsor or an individual designated as a circulator.[28] Any person may contest the required qualifications of a circulator (U.S. citizen and 90 day bona fide resident of Wyoming)[29] by filing a petition in the appropriate circuit court within ten days of the circulation activity.[30] Valid signatures are those from a qualified registered voter with an address listed. Signatures may be withdrawn by providing written notice to the Secretary before the petition is filed.[31] Before submitting petitions to the Secretary, the sponsor or circulator must first sign an affidavit to confirm that a valid process has been followed.[32] Petitions must be filed within 90 days for referenda and within 18 months for initiatives.[33]

To be valid, the petition filed must meet two requirements. First, the petition must be signed by qualified voters equaling 15% of those who voted in the previous general election. Second, in terms of distribution, the 15% of resident voters must come from 2/3 of the counties of the state, as determined by those who voted in the previous election.[34]

Review of Petitions

Once the petition is filed, the Secretary has 60 days to review it and determine whether or not it has been properly filed. A petition is considered improper if it contains an insufficient total number of signatures of qualified registered voters, if there is an insufficient number of signatures of qualified registered voters in at least 2/3 of the counties of the state, or if the petition was not timely filed.[35]

Ballots

If the petition is properly filed, the Secretary and Attorney General are responsible for the preparation of the ballot proposition. This proposition is to be an impartial summary of the initiative or referendum. If a fiscal note is needed, it includes the Secretary/sponsor fiscal statement along with an estimate from the State Treasurer of expected loss or gain in state funds. If these two statements differ by more the $25,000, the bill will include the fiscal range.[36] The ballot proposition, in its entirety, must be published by the Secretary in a newspaper of "general circulation" immediately preceding the general election.[37] The ballot for an initiative will be included in the first statewide election after the petition is filed, after a legislative session has convened and adjourned, and after 120 days since the adjournment of the legislature. This timing is set to allow the Attorney General to void any ballot whose content is substantially the same as a law passed by the recent legislature. The referendum will be placed on the election ballot of the first statewide general election at least 180 days after adjournment of the legislative session at which the act was passed.[38]

An initiative or referendum is successful if it is voted on by more than 50% of those voting in the general election. Following the certification of votes by the Secretary, the initiative becomes law 90 days after certification and cannot be vetoed. It also may not be repealed by the legislature within two years of its effective date, though it may be amended at any time. An act rejected by referendum becomes void 30 days after certification.[39] Once an initiative or referendum is submitted to the voters, it cannot be determined void because of the application or petition process.[40] Unsuccessful initiatives and referenda are those for which more than 50% of voters vote against it, including abstentions.[41] This completes the initiative and referendum process.

LOCAL GOVERNMENT INITIATIVES

In 1973 Wyoming enacted laws to allow for initiatives and referenda at the local government level. The statute begins, "[a]n incorporated city or town having a commission form of government may propose a municipal ordinance by an initiative petition . . . "[42] Any city or town may elect either the commission form of government or the mayor-council form. A commission form of government is run by a mayor and two commissioners, each responsible for their own departmental functions.[43] Interestingly, according to the Wyoming Association of Municipalities, the State does not have any cities or towns governed by commission, and there is no provision for petition legislation under the mayor-council form of government. Wyoming, therefore, though provided for statutorily, does not have a functional initiative and referendum process at the local level.

CONCLUSION

At this time there are some individuals calling for changes to the State's initiative process. Critics claim that current procedures make it impossible for individual volunteers to carry out a successful initiative petition and that only those initiatives with monetary backing can meet the stringent signature-gathering requirements. Proponents seem to appreciate the notion that small special-interest groups cannot pass laws without approval of the majority of the voter population. Wyoming's geography, population, and history may point to slower changes and lower usage of these democratic rights, making the future of the initiative and referendum process in Wyoming difficult to predict. However, the door has been opened, and the people have the power to make the next move.

NOTES

1. A chart of the I&R processes and requirements of all 24 states is available at http://www.iandrinstitute.org.

2. Wyo. Const. art. III, § 52(a).

3. This is not to say that registered voters in Wyoming are not given the opportunity to vote on constitutional issues. Certain issues are required by statute to be placed on the ballot, including political subdivisions of the State (Wyo. Stat. Ann. § 22-21-102(a)(i)); issuance of bonds (Wyo. Stat. Ann. § 22-21-103); acceptance of county-wide 1% sales tax (Wyo. Stat. Ann. § 39-6-412); retention of judges (Wyo. Const. art. V, § 4), and constitutional amendments (Wyo. Const. art. XX, § 1). Margaret Maier Murdock and J. Nicholas Murdock, Student Authors, *Corporate Expression in Wyoming Ballot Issues, Referenda and Initiatives: a Political and Legal Dilemma*, 14 Land & Water L. Rev. 449, 451 (1979). Proposed amendments are submitted by a 2/3 vote of each house of the legislature, or a proposed new constitution submitted by a constitutional convention may be ratified by a majority of the electors voting at the next general election (Wyo. Stat. Ann. § 22-20-101). The Secretary of State maintains two separate lists, one for Initiatives and Referenda and one for Constitutional Amendments at the Wyoming Election Division Web site, http://soswy.state.wy.us/election.

4. David D. Schmidt, *Citizen Lawmakers* 276 (Temple U. Press 1989).

5. T. A. Larson, *History of Wyoming* 322 (2d ed., U of Neb. Press 1978).

6. *Id.* at 330, 559-560.

7. Murdock, *supra* n. 3, at 454.

8. Appendix B lists initiatives and referenda filed with the Wyoming Secretary of State's Office since, 1968. For further information, there is a chart available from the Wyoming Secretary of State's Web site at http://soswy.state.wy.us/election/IRSum.pdf.

9. Schmidt, *supra* n. 4, at 277.

10. Richard J. Ellis, *Democratic Delusions: the Initiative Process in America* 73 (U. Press of Kan. 2002).

11. *Id.* at 127.

12. *Id.* at 126.

13. *State ex rel Keefe v McInerney*, 182 P.2d 28 (Wyo. 1947).

14. *State ex rel Benham v Cheever*, 257 P.2d 337 (Wyo. 1953).

15. E. George Rudolph, *Wyoming Local Government Law* 59-60 (Wyo. St. Bar, 1985).

16. *Thomson v Wyoming In-Stream Flow Committee*, 651 P. 2d 778 (Wyo. 1982).

17. Robert J. Walters, Student Author, *Administrative Law–Initiative and Referendum. Initiative Petitions in Wyoming–The Presumption of Validity and the Secretary of State's Review. Thomson v. Wyoming In-Stream Flow Committee, 651 P.2d 778 (Wyo. 1982)* 18 Land & Water L. Rev. 857, 864 (1983).

18. *Brady v Ohman*, 105 F.3d 726 (10th Cir. 1998).

19. Ellis, *supra* n. 10, at 128.

20. Wyo. Stat. Ann. § 22-24-101 (2006).

21. Wyo. Stat. Ann. § 22-24-102 (2006).

22. Wyo. Stat. Ann. § 22-24-103 (2006).

23. Wyo. Stat. Ann. § 22-24-104 (2006).

24. Wyo. Stat. Ann. § 22-24-105 (2006).

25. *Id.*

26. Wyo. Stat. Ann. § 22-24-108 (2006).

27. Wyo. Stat. Ann. § 22-24-109 (2006).

28. Wyo. Stat. Ann. § 22-24-110 (2006).

29. Wyo. Stat. Ann. § 22-24-107 (2006).

30. Wyo. Stat. Ann. § 22-24-112 (2006).

31. Wyo. Stat. Ann. § 22-24-113 (2006).

32. Wyo. Stat. Ann. § 22-24-114 (2006).

33. Wyo. Stat. Ann. § 22-24-115 (2006).

34. Wyo. Const. art III, § 52(c) (2006).

35. Wyo. Stat. Ann. § 22-24-116 (2006).

36. Wyo. Stat. Ann. § 22-24-117 (2006).

37. Wyo. Stat. Ann. § 22-24-118 (2006).

38. Wyo. Stat. Ann. § 22-24-119 (2006).

39. Wyo. Const. art III, § 52(f).

40. Wyo. Stat. Ann. § 22-24-121 (2006).

41. Wyo. Const. art III, § 52(f).

42. Wyo. Stat. Ann. §§ 22-23-101 through 22-23-1007 (2006).

43. Rudolph, *supra* n. 15 at 57. *See* Wyo. Stat. Ann. §§ 15-4-101 through 15-4-110 for statutes governing the commission form of government.

APPENDIX A
Bibliography

For further research, the materials below are likely to be most useful. The list includes the State's basic primary resources and some Wyoming-specific and general secondary works dealing with initiatives and referenda. Note that in the State's compiled statute set, successful initiatives are identified as such in both the legislative history notes and the editor's notes. The Wyoming Secretary of State's Office maintains the historical information regarding initiatives and referenda. The Office is an excellent source for answering questions and directing queries.

For researchers looking to delve more deeply into the initiative and referendum process or those wishing to expand research into a wider array of materials, we suggest a more complete review of secondary sources such as sets of legal encyclopedias (Am. Jur. 2d or C.J.S.), Legaltrac or HeinOnline journal literature, and annotated state statutes and associated case law.

Primary Law

Brady v Ohman, 105 F.3d 726 (10th Cir. 1998).
This federal case out of Wyoming challenges the State's supermajority requirement. Wyoming's strict signature requirement of 15% of qualified voters who voted in the last general election with signatures coming from 2/3 of the counties is the most frequently challenged aspect of the I&R process. The federal court determined that the State of Wyoming has the right to set the signature requirement, though it is one of the highest in the country.

Thomson v Wyoming In-Stream Flow Committee, 651 P.2d 778 (Wyo. 1982).
The Wyoming Supreme Court case challenges the process used by the Secretary of State to verify the signatures for the In-Stream Flow initiative petition. The Court determined that the Secretary must follow the process as set out in the statutes, but that verification is a necessary element because Wyoming statutes do not sufficiently require the validity of signatures as is the case in many other states.

Wyoming Statutes Annotated, (LexisNexis, 2005).
The following sections of the Wyoming statutes are relevant to the discussion on initiatives and referenda.
§§22-24-101–22-24-201: Chapter 24 of title 22 outlines the initiative and referendum process in Wyoming. These statutes are officially available in print from LexisNexis and available freely online via the Wyoming State Legislature website.
§§22-23-1001–1007: Whereas chapter 24 deals with the initiatives and referenda for the state, this set of statutes speaks to initiatives and referenda at the local level, should a Wyoming city or town select a commission form of government.

Wyoming Constitution, art. III, § 52.
Within the establishment of the legislative department, this article and section of the Wyoming Constitution briefly summarizes the initiative and referendum process.

Secondary Sources

Ellis, Richard J. 2002. *Democratic Delusions: the Initiative Process in America*. Lawrence: University Press of Kansas.
This monograph is an excellent source of information on the initiative and referendum process in general and in many cases addresses the interesting specifics of the 24 states which currently allow it.

Larson, T.A. 1978. *History of Wyoming*. Lincoln: University of Nebraska Press.
This book is a general history of the state of Wyoming written by one of the widely-accepted experts in the field of Wyoming history and politics. Professor Larson, in his discussion of Wyoming's governors and legislators, gives brief insights into the state's acceptance of initiatives, where the support originated, and its culmination into law in Wyoming.

APPENDIX A (continued)

Murdock, Margaret Maier and Murdock, J. Nicholas. 1979. Corporate Expression in Wyoming Ballot Issues, Referenda and Initiatives: a Political and Legal Dilemma. *Land & Water L. Rev.* 14: 449-489.
> Most of this comment deals specifically with the title content of corporate involvement in the initiative process, however it also has some background information and includes a number of useful cites to materials of general secondary usefulness.

Rudolph, E. George. 1985. *Wyoming Local Government Law.* Cheyenne, Wyo.: Wyoming State Bar.
> Professor Rudolph's work is specific to the workings of local government. In this sense, it is helpful for the discussion of initiatives at the local level, with discussion of a handful of court cases relevant to the I&R process.

Schmidt, David D. 1989. *Citizen Lawmakers: The Ballot Initiative Revolution.* Philadelphia: Temple University Press.
> Another excellent evaluation of the process of democratic law-making, Schmidt's book is used as the basis for the University of Southern California's Web site, Initiatives and Referendum Institute.

Walters, Robert J. 1983. Administrative Law–Initiative and Referendum. Initiative Petitions in Wyoming–The Presumption of Validity and the Secretary of State's Review. *Thomson v. Wyoming In-Stream Flow Committee,* 651 P.2d 778 (Wyo. 1982). *Land & Water L. Rev.* 18: 857-874.
> This case note has a nice discussion of the history of initiatives and referenda in Wyoming along with an in-depth discussion of the *Thomson* case that focuses on the signature verification process performed by the Secretary of State. In addition to a review of the administrative powers to make law in the form of procedures to verify petition signatures (wherein it is determined that the Secretary does not have the ability to make law as the process is clearly spelled out in the statutes), the case also clarifies a conflict between statutory and constitutional language.

Online Resources

Initiatives and Referendum Institute at the University of Southern California, at http://www. iandrinstitute.org/.
> While most of the information at this site is taken almost directly from Schmidt's *Citizen Lawmakers,* the Web site consolidates the information nicely. It contains useful charts and links directly to various state organizations like the Secretary of State's Office and Election Division who maintain the information on our state's incoming I&R.

Initiative Process, Election Administration, Wyoming Secretary of State, at http://soswy.state. wy.us/election/election.htm.
> The Wyoming Secretary of State's Election Administration website should be the first stop for learning about initiatives and referenda in the State. The *Initiatives and Referendums Summary Sheet,* available at http://soswy.state.wy.us/election/initref.htm, lists actions on all initiatives and referenda in the state. The *Initiative Process* is outlined in detail at http:// soswy.state.wy.us/election/initproc.htm and includes summaries of the relevant Wyoming statutes and constitution related to initiatives and referenda. Finally, the *2006 Initiative and Referendum Information* page at http://soswy.state.wy.us/election/2006/i-r-info. htm provides current data on the registered voter signature requirement and the filing deadline.

Wyoming State Legislature, at http://legisweb.state.wy.us/.
> This site operates as a gateway to the Wyoming statutes and constitution as well as to information about bills presented to the legislature. Access this primary law directly from http://legisweb.state.wy.us/titles/ statutes.htm. The first listing on this page provides the statutes and constitution from the Wyoming Legislative Service Office database which is

updated yearly after each legislative session. A second database, providing annotations and updated quarterly, is provided by LexisNexis.

Wyoming Legislative Service Office, at http://legisweb.state.wy.us/ leginfo/lso/lso.htm.
The Legislative Service Office functions primarily to draft legislation and conduct research for the members of congress. The office staff does have a wealth of information to share however, so they are a contact option should you have questions about initiatives and referenda.

Wyoming Association of Municipalities, at http://www.wyomuni.org/.
The Wyoming Association of Municipalities (WAM) is an excellent resource for inquiring about local legislation. WAM's publications include weekly and monthly newsletters, municipal directories, digests of legislation, and various handbooks.

APPENDIX B

Wyoming's Initiative and Referendum History

Subject	Date Filed	Outcome
Declaring gambling to be lawful	5/8/1970	Presumed failure to gather enough signatures to qualify.
Disclosing private interests by certain public officials; requiring such disclosure and providing penalties for failure to disclose and for false disclosure	7/9/1973	The initiative failed to gather enough signatures to qualify.
Relating to private ownership or possession of big and trophy game animals and importation of same into Wyoming	9/19/1973	Initiative taken up by legislature in 1975 and became WY ST 23-1-103 effectively prohibiting wild game farms.
Providing for a constitutional amendment on the general election ballot to create the office of Lt. Governor	5/14/1976	In Wyoming, the initiative process cannot be used to propose an amendment to the Wyoming Constitution.
Imposing a 23% severance tax on the value of coal produced by open mining	11/23/1976	Presumed failure to gather enough signatures to qualify.
Authorizing the issuance of malt beverage and wine permits by cities and counties to restaurants	8/31/1978	Presumed failure to gather enough signatures to qualify.
Imposing an additional 5% severance tax on the value of coal produced	9/22/1978	Presumed failure to gather enough signatures to qualify.
Preserving minimum in-stream flows	10/20/1980	The initiative failed to gather enough signatures to qualify.
Replacement of exported groundwater	6/22/1981	Presumed failure to gather enough signatures to qualify.
Public fund deposits in credit unions	3/3/1982	The initiative failed to gather enough signatures to qualify.
In-stream flow as a beneficial use of water under Wyoming law	5/23/1982	The initiative gathered enough signatures to qualify for ballot placement in the 1986 general election. However, legislation passed in 1985 was determined to be substantially the same.
Amending a constitutional provision on the initiative process and lowering the signature requirement for placement of an initiative on the general election ballot from 15% to 10%	6/16/1982	In Wyoming, the initiative process cannot be used to propose an amendment to the Wyoming Constitution.

(continued)

Subject	Date Filed	Outcome
Water storage for in-stream flows	8/22/1983	Failed to file petition by the deadline for placement on the 1984 general election ballot. The initiative later failed to gather enough signatures to qualify for the 1986 general election ballot.
Election of Public Service Commission members	7/11/1985	The initiative failed to gather enough signatures to qualify.
Link deposit program	7/15/1988	The initiative failed to gather enough signatures to qualify.
Local option gambling	7/15/1989	The initiative failed to gather enough signatures to qualify.
Prohibiting triple trailers	8/27/1990	The initiative appeared on the 1992 general election ballot and was passed: Yes votes–165,879: No votes–31,997. WY ST 31-5-1009.
Abortion restrictions	8/8/1991	The initiative appeared on the 1994 general election ballot and was defeated: Yes votes–78,978: No votes–118,760. Total votes cast - 204,025.
Term limitations	9/13/1991	The initiative appeared on the 1992 general election ballot and was passed: Yes votes–150,113: No votes–44,424. WY ST 22-5-103.
Local option gambling	10/30/1991	The initiative appeared on the 1994 general election ballot and was defeated: Yes votes–61,980; No votes–137,379. Total votes cast - 204,025.
Railway safety	10/31/1991	The initiative appeared on the 1992 general election ballot and was passed: Yes votes–130,803: No votes–52,835. WY ST 37-9-1201.
Invest in Wyoming	5/17/1993	The initiative appeared on the 1994 general election ballot and was defeated: Yes votes–75,547: No votes–114,273. Total votes cast–204,025.
Legislative accountability	8/19/1993	The initiative failed to gather enough signatures to qualify.
Term limits	3/14/1995	The referendum appeared on the 1996 general election ballot and was defeated: Yes votes–104,544; No votes–90,138. Total votes cast–215,844.
Term limits	7/5/1995	The initiative appeared on the 1996 general election ballot and was defeated: Yes votes–105,093; No votes–89,018. Total votes cast–215,844.
Denturity – establishing professional licensure of denturists	4/18/1997	The initiative failed to gather enough signatures to qualify.
Ethics in government	9/3/1997	The initiative failed to gather enough signatures to qualify.
Surface owners' accommodation for oil/gas	5/14/2004	Legislature passed similar legislation in SF 60 on 2/24/05. Initiative was withdrawn.
Food tax exemption	5/19/2005	The initiative failed to gather enough signatures to qualify. A two-year food tax exemption was adopted by the 2006 legislature however.
Denturism: a denture care choice alternative	12/2006	Certified for circulation. If signatures are gathered and qualify, initiative will appear on the 2008 general election ballot.

Index

Page numbers followed by an *n* or *f* indicate notes or figures.

Academic Search Primer, 169
Adams, Swann v. , 65,76*n*
Address of A.C. Townley, President of the National Non-Partisan League, 249
Administrative Law–Initiative and Referendum, 329*n*,332
Adoption and Operation of Initiative and Referendum in North Dakota, 243,256*n*
Adoption of Initiative and Referendum in Arkansas: The Roles of George W. Donaghy and William Jennings Bryan, 43
Adoption of Zoning Ordinance or Amendment Thereto as Subject of Referendum, 43
Advisory initiatives, Illinois, 91-92
Advisory Opinion to the Attorney General re Florida Marriage Protection Amendment, 77*n*
AG, Schulman v. , 127
ago.state.ma.us/, 121,125
ago.state.ne.us/, 214
Alaska
  history of I&R in, 16
  I&R process in, 16-17
  initiative process and, 13*n*
  researching I&R law regarding, 17-19
  summary/introduction to, 15
Alaska Statutes, 18
Alaska's Consitutional Convention, 18-19

Alaska's History of Ballot Issues and Petitions, 18
Alcohol sales, 135*n*
The Almanac of American Politics, 200
Almanacs, 4-6,104-105,128-129, 134*n*,200-201,261
Amending the Arkansas Constitution by the Initiative Process, 40,49*n*
America: History and Life, 169
American Jurisprudence, 4-5,105,250
American Law Reports, 5
America's Newspapers, 169
Amsberry, State ex rel. Ayres v. , 221
Anderson, Barbara, 131,133*n*
Anderson, Melissa Cully, 40
Anderson, Raymond V., 243,256*n*
Animal protection, 43-44
Annotated codes, 8
  Maine, 105
  Missouri, 168
  Montana, 201
  Oklahoma, 271
  Oregon, 278
  Utah, 305-306
  Wyoming, 331
arcweb.sos.state.or.us/, 283-284
Are Coloradans Fit to make their own Laws? A Common-Sense Primer on the Initiative Process, 58
Arizona
  history of I&R in, 22
  I&R process in, 22-24

initiative process and, 13*n*
introduction to, 21-22
researching I&R law regarding,
      24-29
summary, 21
Arizona Capitol Times, 27
Arizona Daily Star, 27
Arizona Republic, 27
*The Arizona State Constitution: A
      Reference Guide*, 26
Arkansas
   case law regarding, 35-37
   history of I&R in, 32-33
   initiative process and, 13*n*
   Internet resources regarding, 47-49
   introduction to, 31-32
   LexisNexis/Westlaw databases
         regarding, 46
   post 1910 events in, 33-35
   secondary materials regarding,
         38-46
   statutes regarding, 37-38
   summary, 31
*The Arkansas Ballot Initiative: an
      Overview and Some Thoughts
      on Reform*, 41
Arkansas Constitution, 47
The Arkansas Democrat-Gazette, 44
Arkansas Ethics Commission, 47
The Arkansas Gazette, 33,49*n*
Arkansas General Assembly, 47
Arkansas Governor, 47
*Arkansas Light and Power Co., Terral
      v.*, 36
Arkansas State Government, 47
Arkansas Supreme Court, 47-48
arkansasethics.com, 47
arkleg.state.ar.us, 47
Arnold, E.R., 32
Article III, South Dakota, 288-289
Article XLVIII
   defined, 116
   Massachusetts, 122
Article XXIII, South Dakota, 289
Association of Washington Cities, 317

Atlantic Digest, 106
Atlas of Montana Elections, 203
Attorney General
   defined, 116
   role of. *see specific states*
Augustus, Edward, 134*n*
awcnet.org, 317
azcapitoltimes.com/, 27
azcentral.com/news/election/ballot/
      ballot.html, 27
azleg.state.az.us/, 25
azpbs.org/horizon/index.asp, 27
azsos.gov/, 24-25
azstarnet.com/, 27

Baily, Douglas, 19
*The Bait-and-Switch in Direct
      Democracy*, 251
Ball, Molly, 228*n*
Ballot Initiative Strategy Center, 10
Ballot Measures, 48
Ballot Measures Preview 2006, 29*n*
Ballot Proposal Analyses, 54
Ballot Question Committee, defined,
      116
*Ballot Question Committee
      Treasurer's Guide*, 214,219
ballot.org, 10
Bangor Daily News, 106
banknd.nd.gov, 255
Barone, Michael, 200
*The Battle Over Citizen Lawmaking:
      An In-Depth Review of the
      Growing Trend to Regulate
      the People's Tool of
      Self-Government: The
      Initiative and Referendum
      Process*, 12-13,13*n*,215*n*,219
"Bay Stater", 114,115
*"Be it enacted by the people of the
      state of Alaska..." A
      Practitioner's Guide to
      Alaska's Initiative Law*, 19
Beard, Charles A., 38,243

Beermann, Duggan v. , 220
Beermann, Lawrence v. , 221
Beermann, State ex rel. Brant v. , 220
Beermann, State ex rel. Labedz v. , 220
Beermann, State ex rel. Stenberg v. ,
    215*n*,216*n*,221
Beers, Nevadans for Nev. v. , 228*n*
Benedict, Robert C., 319*n*
Bernbeck v. Moore, 216*n*,220
*Bess v. Ulmer–The Supreme Court
    Stumbles and the Subsistence
    Amendment Falls*, 19
Beverage container deposit bill, 100
Bill No. INIT 900, Washington,
    313-314
Binding initiatives, Illinois, 92-93
Black, Cochran v. , 36
Black, J. William, 110*n*
Black's Law Dictionary, 13*n*
Bloomekatz, Ari, 132*n*
Blue Book, 54-55,216*n*,
    244-245,279,291,293
bluebook.state.or.us, 279
Boise Public Library, 85,86
boisepubliclibrary.org, 86
Boley Law Library, 284
*Bolinske v. North Dakota State Fair
    Ass'n*, 241
Bonaparte, Charles, 266
Bone, Hugh, 202
Book of States, 38,86,243
The Boston Globe, 7,132,132*n*,134*n*
Bott, Alexander J., 250
Bottle Bill, 100
Bradeis (Justice), 285*n*
Bradley, M. Katheryn, 19
Brady v. Ohman, 324,330*n*,331
Brantley, Howie v. , 148
Braunstein, Rich, 11,202,294,296*n*,
    297*n*
Bresler, Kenneth, 130
Brickhouse, Ben B., 33
Brickhouse v. Hill, 33-34,42,49*n*
A Brief History of Vote by Mail, 285*n*
Broder, David, 202,243-244

Browder, Rebekah K., 250
Bryon, Williams Jennings, 32-33,43
Bureau of Archives and Record
    Management, Florida, 74
Burlison, James, 176*n*
Bushnell, Eleanore, 228*n*
Butler, David, 38,244
Byrne, Schumacher v. , 242
Byrne, Wood v. , 242

Cady, Blake, M.D., 130
California, initiative process and, 13*n*
*California General Election Official
    Voter Information Guide*, 268
*Camden Community Development
    Corp. v. Sutton*, 37
Campaign finance disclosure. *see*
    Disclosure records
Campaign Fun With Tax Cuts, 132*n*
Campbell, Henry M., 144
Carpenter, Thomas M., 41
*The Case for Consitutional Revision in
    North Dakota*, 251
Cavanaugh v. State, 61*n*
cde.state.co.us/stateinfo/, 59
Celebrating Prop 2 1/2,131,133*n*
*Cenarrusa, Dredge Mining
    Control-Yes!, Inc. v.* , 83
Center for Leadership Studies,
    128-129
Certificates of Review, Idaho, 84
*Character or Subject Matter of
    Ordinance Within Operation
    of Initiative and Referendum
    Provisions*, 46
Chase, Culliton v. , 320*n*
Chase, Edward E., 108-109,112*n*
Cheever, State ex rel. Benham v. ,
    324,329*n*
Chesley, Richard A., 263
Chicago Tribune, 7
Citizen Initiated Legislation, 107
*The Citizen Initiative Petition to
    Amend State Constitutions: A*

*Concept Whose Time Has
Passed, or A Vigorous
Component of Participatory
Democracy at the State
Level?*, 269,271n
*Citizen Initiatives in Florida: An
Analysis of Florida's
Constitutional Initiative
Process, Issues, and
Alternatives*, 75
*Citizen Lawmakers: The Ballot
Initiative Revolution*,
12,40,49n,174-175,176n,
216n,219,233,247-248,256n,
329n,332
Citizen Participation and Elections,
303
Citizens for Limited Taxation, 117,131
*A Citizen's Guide to Utah State
Government*, 303
Citizen's Research Council of
Michigan, 144
*Citizens Versus Legislators–The
Continuing Fight to Ensure
the Rights of Initiative and
Referendum in Nebraska*,
215n,216n,219
City Club of Portland, 278-279,281
*City of Boise City v. Keep the
Commandments Coalition*, 83
City of Coeur d'Alene, Gumprecht v.,
83
City of Fargo, Pelkey v., 242
*Clark, Term Limits Leadership
Council, Inc. v.*, 152
Clem, Alan L., 294-295
Cloning, 167
Cochran v. Black, 36
Coghlan v. Cuskelly, 241
Collins, Richard B., 56,58,61n
Colorado
    bibliography of state-specific
        material regarding, 56-58
    history of I&R in, 52
    I&R process in, 53-54

initiative process and, 13n
introduction to, 51-52
research contacts regarding, 58-60
researching I&R law regarding,
    54-56
summary, 51
Colorado Ballot Proposal Information,
56
Colorado Historical Society, 58
Colorado Joint Legislative Library,
    55,58
The Colorado Lawyer, 55
Colorado Legislative Council, 52,56
Colorado Office of Legislative Legal
    Services, 56-57
Colorado Session Laws, 55
Colorado State Archives, 55,59
*The Colorado State Constitution: A
    Reference Guide*, 58,61n
Colorado State Publications Library,
    55,59
Colorado Supreme Court Library,
    55,59
colorado.edu/law/lawlib/, 60
colorado.gov/dpa/doit/archives/, 59
coloradohistory.org/chs_library/library
    .htm, 58
Coming to Grips with the Grass Roots,
135n
Committee Services Office, Oregon,
    280-281
Commonwealth, defined, 116
Concerned Citizens for S.A.F.E.T.Y.,
126
Conrad, Sunbehm Gas, Inc. v., 242
*A Consideration and Analysis of
    Initiated and Referred
    Legislation Submitted to the
    Electorate of North Dakota
    from 1940 to 1958*, 247
*Constitutional Amendments, Initiatives
    and Referendum*, 305
Constitution of the State of Montana,
203
Constitutional amendments

defined, 116,178
Illinois, 91
initiatives and, 3-4
Constitutional convention, defined,
    178,183
Constitutional Convention of 1917,
    defined, 116
Constitutional initiative, defined, 183
*Constitutional Law–First Amendment
    Rights of Direct Democracy
    Participants versus the
    State's Interest in Regulating
    the Election Process*, 45
*Constitutional Politics in the States:
    Contemporary Controversies
    and Historical Patterns*, 40
*Constitutional Referendum in the
    United States of America*,
    250
Constitutional Revision Commission,
    296n
*Constitutional Validity of State or
    Local Regulation of
    Contributions by or to
    Political Action Committees*,
    43
*Construction and Application of
    Constitutional or Statutory
    Provisions Expressly
    Excepting Certain Laws from
    Referendum*, 251
Cooper, John, F., 269,271n
*Corporate Expression in Wyoming
    Ballot Issues, Referenda and
    Initiatives: a Political and
    Legal Dilemma*, 329n,332
Corpus Juris Secundrum, 41
Corpus Juris Secundum, 105,251
Cotton, Thomas B., 41
Council of State Governments, 86,170
County Election
    Commissioners/Clerks,
    Nebraska, 212
*County Government Law: A Reference
    Guide*, 94

Courts, role of. *see specific states*
courts.state.ar.us/courts/sc.html,
    47-48
court.state.nd.us, 255
*The Cow Says Moo, the Duck Says
    Quack, and the Dog Says
    Vote! The Use of the
    Initiative to Promote Animal
    Protection*, 43-44
crcmich.org, 144
Cree, Nathan, 244
Cronin, Thomas E., 11,38,219,244
csg.org, 170
Culbertson, Paul Thomas, 281
Culliton v. Chase, 320n
Current Law Index, 6
*Current Use of the Initiative and
    Referendum in Ohio and
    Other States*, 263
Curtis, Lukins v. , 84
Cuskelly, Coghlan v. , 241

*The Dakota Maverick: The Political
    Life of William Langer, Also
    Known as "Wild Bill"
    Langer*, 245
D'Alembert, Talbot, 74,76n
Dalton, Cornelius, 129,133n
Dane, William H., Jr., 250
Daniels, May v. , 45-46
data.opi.mt.gov, 185n
Dauer, Manning J., 74,76n,77n
David, Patton W., 303-304
Davies, Bernita J., 94
Davis, Cyrus W., 99
Dawson v. Meier, 242
Dawson v. Tobin, 242
Death with dignity, 285n
*The Debates in the Massachusetts
    Constitutional Convention*,
    126,133n
*Debates of the Constitutional
    Convention of 1917*, 133n

*Deliberations About Democracy:
    Revolutions, Republicanism,
    and Reform*, 270,271*n*
Delort, Mathias W., 94
*Democracy Derailed: Initiative
    Campaigns and the Power of
    Money*, 202,243-244
*Democratic Delusions: The Initiative
    Process in America*,
    11-12,244,329*n*,331
Democratic Party, 99
Denison, David, 135*n*
Denver Bar Association, 55
The Denver Post, 7
Denver Public Library, 55,59
Denver University Law Review, 55
denverlibrary.org, 59
The Detroit News, 7
*Digest of Initiated and Referred
    Constitutional and Statutory
    Amendments Since 1912*,
    52,60*n*
Digests, 8-9
    regarding Missouri, 168-169
*Direct Democracy: An Historical
    Analysis of the Initiative,
    Referendum and Recall
    Process*, 319*n*
*Direct Democracy and Electoral
    Reform*, 49*n*
"Direct Democracy in Washington: A
    Discourse on the People's
    Powers of Initiative and
    Referendum", 317-318
*Direct Democracy in Washington: A
    Discourse on the People's
    Powers of Initiative and
    Referendum*, 319*n*
*Direct Democracy is Not Republican
    Government*, 320*n*
*Direct Democracy: The Politics of
    Initiative, Referendum and
    Recall*, 11,38,219,244
*Direct Government in Michigan:
    Initiative, Referendum,*

    *Recall, Amendment, and
    Revision in the Michigan
    Constitution*, 143,145*n*
Direct Legislation by the People, 244
Direct Legislation League of Missouri,
    165-166
*Direct Legislation: Voting on Ballot
    Propositions in the United
    States*, 245-246
Disclosure records, 42
Division of Elections, Florida,
    66,72-73,76*n*,77*n*
dlis.dos.state.fl.us/library, 73-74
dmla.clan.lib.nv.us/, 228
*Do you want a Free Pony? An Analysis
    of the Initiative and
    Referendum Process in
    Washington State*, 318
Dobrovolny v. Moore, 220
The Docket, 55
*Documents on the State-Wide
    Initiative, Referendum and
    Recall*, 38,243
*Does Direct Democracy Threaten
    Constitutional Governance in
    Florida?*, 75
doj.state.or.us/index.shtml, 283
Donley, Dave, 19
Donoghey, George W., 32-33,43
Donovan, Clement H., 77*n*
Dorman, William E., 130
dos.state.fl.us/barm/fsa.html, 74
Dowling, Jo, 73,78*n*
Downey, Rachael, 19
*Dredge Mining Control-Yes!, Inc. v.
    Cenarrusa*, 83
Driggs, Don W., 228*n*
Duggan v. Beermann, 220
Dunn, W.J., 250
Dunning, Archibald Williams, 39
Durban, Thomas, 202

Eaton, Allen H., 274

Educated by Initiative: The Effects of Direct Democracy on Citizens and Political Organizations in the American States, 12,248-249
Education, 35
egov.sos.state.or.us/, 280
Election Contests in Missouri, 174
Election Law, 94
Election Law @ Moritz, 262
election.dos.state.fl.us/initiatives/index. shtml, 70,72,76n
Elections Division, Massachusetts, 124
elections.colorado.gov/, 55,57,58
elections.utah.gov/, 304,305,307n
Ellis, Richard J., 11-12,244,329n,331
The Emergency Clause and the Referendum in Oklahoma: Current Status and Needed Reform, 270
Enabling Act of 1910, 22
The Encyclopedia of Public Choice, 200
Encyclopedias, 4-6
    regarding Arkansas, 41
    regarding Maine, 104-105
    regarding Michigan, 143-144,146n
    regarding Missouri, 168-169
    regarding Montana, 200-201
    regarding Ohio, 261
Equal Vote, 262
Erickson, Nels, 244
Eriksmoen, Curtis, 244-245
Estes, Andrea, 132n,135n
Estimated Fiscal Impact of an Initiated Measure, 241
Even, Jeffrey T., 317-318,319n
Evolution, 35
Executive, Legislative, and Judicial Power Over Direct Legislation in Arizona, 27-28
Expanded Academic, 6
Experience With The Initiative and Referendum, 110n

The Failure of Ohio's Drug Treatment Initiative, 264n
Fair Ballot Access Act, 171
Fall Ballot Measures, 110n,185n
Falsification, in Arkansas, 37
Famous Firsts in Massachusetts, 133n
The Farmer's Almanac, 128,134n
Federation of Labor, 99
Fees, see *specific states*
FIEC. *see* Financial Impact Estimating Conference
Filing Initiatives and Referenda in Washington State, 2005-2008, 319n
Financial Impact Estimating Conference, 68-69
Fine v. Firestone, 66-67,77n
Firestone, Fine v. , 66-67,77n
Fisch, William B., 250
Fischer, Victor, 18-19
Fitzgerald, William Richard, 25
Florida
    I&R process in, 64-70
    initiative process and, 13n
    introduction to, 64
    popular referendums and, 13n
    researching I&R law regarding, 70-76
    summary, 63
Florida Department of State, 73-74
Florida Public Interest Research Group, 76
The Florida State Constitution: A Reference Guide, 76n
floridapirg.org/, 76
Florida's Constitutions: The Documentary History, 70,73,78n
Florida's Politics and Government, 74,76n
For the Many or the Few: The Initiative, Public Policy, and American Democracy, 12,246,256n
Ford v. Logan, 320n

Fordham, Jefferson B., 263

*Form of Initiative Petition–Sufficiency
  of Signatures*, 37

*Form of Referendum
  Petition–Sufficiency of
  Signatures*, 37

The Frame of Government, 132n

*Fraud-Free Elections are Possible
  Without Voter Registration:
  A Report on North Dakota's
  Experience*, 246

Fredette, Kenneth Wade, 109

Froelich, Kurt P., 94

Fry, James, 297n

*The Future of Initiative and
  Referendum in Missouri*,
  172-173

*The Future of Initiatives and
  Referendum in Missouri*,
  176n

Gaffney, Edward McGlynn, 39

Gale, State ex rel. Lemon v., 206,220

Garrett, Elizabeth, 42

Garriga, Mark, 158-159,160n

Gass, Nelson v., 242

Geelan, Agnes, 245

General Court of Massachusetts,
  116,126

*General Election Tabulations:
  Referendum Questions*, 111n

*General Laws of the State of
  Mississippi*, 157

*The Gentleman from North Dakota,
  Lynn J. Frazier*, 244

*Giving Voters a Voice: Origins of the
  Initiative and Referendum in
  America*, 39,174,202,215n,
  219

*Giving Voters a Voice: The Struggle
  for Initiative and Referendum
  in Missouri*, 174,176n

Goldberg, Marissa, 134n

Gonzaga Law Review, 317-318,319n

Goodman, Barbara B., 94

Gordon, James D., 269

Gossman, Barbara F., 143

*Governing by Initiative: The Rise and
  Fall–and Rise Again–of
  Oregon's Initiative Ballot
  Measure*, 282

Governing North Dakota, 240,245

Government and Politics in Florida,
  74,76n

The Government of Missouri, 173

Government Publications, 59,60

*Governor Haskell Tells of Two
  Conventions*, 270

governor.arkansas.gov/, 47

governor.nd.us, 253

Governors' participation. *see specific
  states*

gov.state.ak.us/ltgov/elections/, 17,18

gov.state.ne.us/proclamations/, 214

Grant, Meyer v., 61n

Greenlee v. Munn, 37

Gregg v. Hartwick, 36

Gregs v. Hartwick, 37

Grew, Carlton B., 282

Grossman, Barbara F., 146n

*Group to Back Healthcare Law's
  Implementation*, 132n

Gumprecht v. City of Coeur d'Alene,
  83

Hall, State ex rel. Frazier v., 242

Hall, State ex rel. Linde v., 242

Hall, State ex rel. Twichell v., 242

*The Handbook of Massachusetts Legal
  Research*, 129

Handson, Fred, 133n

Hanson v. Hodges, 36

Hargrove, Michelle, 19

Harris, Marvis, 33

Hartwick, Gregg v., 36

Hartwick, Gregs v., 37

Haskell, Charles, 267,270

HAVA. *see* Help America Vote Act

The Florida State Constitution: A Reference Guide, 74
Heller, Nevadans for the Prot. of Prop rights, Inc. v. , 228*n*
Helman, Scott, 135*n*
Help America Vote Act, 236-237
Henke's California Law Guide, 13*n*
Henry, Robert, 270,271*n*
Henson, Stilley v. , 36
Hernett v. Meier, 242
Hill, Brickhouse v. , 33-34,42,49*n*
The History of Ohio Law, 264*n*
History of Successful Ballot Initiatives-Massachusetts, 130
A History of the Initiative and Referendum in Oregon, 281
A History of the Initiative in North Dakota, 248,256*n*
A History of the Operation of the Initiative and Referendum in Maine from 1907-1951, 108-109,112*n*
History of Wyoming, 329*n*,331
history.denverlibrary.org/, 59
historyresearch.utah.gov/, 305,308*n*
Hodges, Hanson v., 36
Hodges, Tomlinson Bros. v. , 36
Hodgkinson, Randall L., 27-28
Hoesley, Cody, 282
Holliday, Beth B., 4-5,42,250
Home Rule and Intergovernmental Cooperation and Conflict in Municipal Law and Practice in Illinois, 94
Horizon, 27
Hosack, Marsha, 75
House and Senate Documents, Massachusetts, 126
How to Use the Initiative and Referendum Process in Nebraska, 213,219
Howie v. Brantley, 148
Huckshorn, Robert J., 74,76*n*
Husebye v. Jaeger, 242

The Hutchinson Encyclopedia of Modern Political Biography, 200

I&R law, *see also specific states*
definitions, 3-4
introduction to, 1-3
research tools for, 4-13
summary, 1
iandrinstitute.org, 9,13*n*, 28,48,57-58,77*n*,85,110*n*, 145,156,158,170,228*n*, 252-253,256*n*,329*n*,332
icpsr.umich.edu, 144-145
Idaho
history of I&R in, 80-81,82
initiative process and, 13*n*
introduction to, 79-80
researching I&R law regarding, 81-87
summary, 79
Idaho Attorney General, 86
Idaho Legislative Reference Library, 87
Idaho State Historical Society, 85,87
Idaho State Law Library, 87
Idaho Statesman, 85
idahohistory.net, 87
idsos.state.id.us/elect/inits/inithist.htm, 81
If the Citizens Speak, Listen: Idaho's Local Initiative Process, 83
ilga.gov/commission/lrb_home.html, 95
Illinois
advisory initiatives & referenda in, 91-92
bibliography/useful contacts regarding, 93-95
binding initiatives & referenda in, 92-93
initiative process and, 13*n*
overview of I&R in, 90-91
popular referendums and, 13*n*
summary, 89

Illinois Freedom of Information Act, 93
Illinois Legal Research Guide, 94
Illinois Legislative Council, 95
Illinois Legislative Reference Bureau, 95
Illinois Municipal Code, 92
The Illinois Municipal Code, 96*n*
Illinois State Bar Association, 94
ILP. *see Index to legal Periodicals and Books*
Imaging, in Arkansas, 37
imakenews.com/, 303-304
In re Municipal Suffrage to Women, 118,128,133*n*,134*n*
In Whose Court is the Ball? The Scope of the People's Power of Direct Legislation, 41
Index to Legal Periodicals, 169
Index to Legal Periodicals and Books, 6-7
Index to Legal Periodicals and LegalTrac, 169
Indirect initiative, 3,302
Initiating and Referring Law in North Dakota, 238-240
"Initiative, Referendum & Recall Handbook", 24
Initiative, Referendum and Recall by Citizen Petition, 202
Initiative, Referendum and Recall Information, 17
Initiative & Referendum Institute, 9,48
"Initiative and Referendum", 4-5
Initiative and Referendum, 42
"The Initiative and Referendum", 144
The Initiative and Referendum, 202
"Initiative and Referendum", 250
Initiative and Referendum, 295
Initiative and Referendum Almanac, 5,13*n*,17,28,41,96*n*, 104,110*n*,159,159*n*, 167,175*n*,201,219,235, 249,256*n*,261,307*n*
The Initiative and Referendum at the Municipal Level in Ohio, 263
Initiative and Referendum Database, 28

Initiative and Referendum Elections, 38
Initiative and Referendum Generally, 38
The Initiative and Referendum in Arizona, 26,29*n*
The Initiative and Referendum in Arizona: 1912-1973, 26
The Initiative and Referendum in Arkansas Come of Age, 40
The Initiative and Referendum in Maine, 109,110*n*
Initiative and Referendum in Mississippi: Dead Again?, 158-159,160*n*
The Initiative and Referendum in Missouri, 175
The Initiative and Referendum in Oregon, 281
Initiative and referendum in South Dakota, 296,297*n*
Initiative and Referendum in the 21st Century: Final Report and Recommendations of the NCSL I&R Task Force, 86
Initiative and referendum in the 21st century: Final report and recommendations of the NCSL I&R Task Force, 202
Initiative and Referendum in Washington, 319*n*
Initiative and Referendum Institute, 9,13*n*,28,57-58,77*n*,85, 145,156,162*n*,170,185*n*, 228*n*,232,252-253,256*n*, 274,329*n*,332
Initiative and Referendum Institute v. Jaeger, 242
Initiative and referendum law. *see I&R law*
Initiative and Referendum League of Maine, 99
Initiative and Referendum Petitions: A Guide for Sponsors and Canvassers, 39

Initiative and Referendum Petitions–Signature–Form Circulation, 241
Initiative and Referendum Procedures and Guidelines, 61*n*
The Initiative and Referendum Process: The Maine Experience, 109
"The Initiative and Referendum Process: The Michigan Experience", 146*n*
"The Initiative and Referendum Process: The Michigan Law Experience", 143
Initiative and Referendum Requirements, 38
Initiative and Referendum Voting: Governing through Direct Democracy in the United States, 11,202,294,296*n*
The Initiative: Citizen Law-Making, 159
Initiative Petition Process, 76*n*,77*n*
The Initiative Petition Process, 2005-2006, 121
Initiative Petitions, defined, 117
Initiative petitions, defined, 184
Initiative Process, 332
The Initiative Process, 2005-2006, 134*n*
The Initiative Process in Mississippi: An Overview, 161*n*
The Initiative Process in Missouri: A Call for Statutory Change, 173
"The Initiative Process in Washington: Implications and Effects", 318-319
Initiative referendum, defined, 183
Initiative rulings up, down, 228*n*
Initiatives, *see also specific states*
 defined, 3-4,178
 local processes for, 13*n*
 states allowing, 13*n*

The Initiatives and Referendum Process in Utah, 303-304
Initiatives and Referendums, 296*n*
"In-Stream Flow", 323,324
Intelligible, Honest, and Impartial Democracy: Making Laws at the Arkansas Ballot Box, or Why Jim Hannah and Ray Thornton were Right About May v. Daniels, 45-46
Internet resources, 9-11. *see also specific states*
Internet Voting with Initiatives and Referendums: Stumbling Towards Direct Democracy, 250
Inter-University Consortium for Political and Social Research, 144-145
isll.idaho.gov, 87
Issue: Ballot Questions, 121
issuesource.org/, 122

Jaeger, Husebye v., 242
Jaeger, Initiative and Referendum Institute v., 242
James, Steven T., 133*n*
Jameson, P.K., 75
janus.state.me.us/legs/const/, 105
John Adams, 132*n*
John C. Stennis Institute of Government, 150,156,158,160*n*,162*n*
John E. Jaqua Law Library, 284
Johnson, Montana PIRG v., 185*n*
Jorgensen, Delores A., 295
Journal: North Dakota Constitutional Convention, 245
Journal of the Senate of the State of Michigan, 141
Judicial Jurisdiction over Initiative and Referendum, 38
Judicial Review of Initiative Petitions in Florida, 76
Jumper v. McCollum, 36

Kane, Bruce, 83
Karel, Tamera, 264*n*
Karsch, Robert F., 173
Kastorf, Kurt G., 42-43
*Keep the Commandments Coalition,
City of Boise City v.* , 83
Kemper, J.R., 43
Kemper, Kurtis A., 43
Kennebec Journal, 106
Kentucky, popular referendums and, 13*n*
Kerr, Scroggins v. , 36
King, Katherine, 234
kjzz.org/news/arizona/archives/200607
/ballotmeasures, 27
Klosterman v. Marsh, 221
Koenig, Mark, 318
Kousser, Thad, 250
Krasner, Jeffrey, 132*n*
Kusler, Municipal Servs. Corp. v. , 242

Lambert, Lane, 135*n*
Larson, T.A., 329*n*,331
Lauer, T.E., 173
*Law Allowing Wine in State Food
Stores is Rejected*, 135*n*
*The Law of Initiative Referendum in
Massachusetts*, 129-130
law.du.edu/library/, 60
lawlib.lclard.edu/research/oregonlaw.
php, 279
lawlib.lclark.edu, 284
lawlibrary.uoregon.edu, 284
*Lawmakers Delay Vote on Gay
Marriage Measure*, 132*n*
Lawrence v. Beermann, 221
*$Laws for Sale$: A Study of Money in the
1994 Ballot Questions*, 133*n*
law.uidaho.edu/library, 87
Leading the Way, 129,133*n*,134*n*
League of Women Voters
Arkansas, 48
Florida, 76
Missouri, 167,171
North Dakota, 253

Ohio, 262,264*n*
Washington, 318
Ledbetter, Calvin R., Jr., 43
Legal encyclopedias. *see*
Encyclopedias
LegalTrac, 6,7
LegalTrac, 169
Legislative Council, Colorado, 53
Legislative Journal, 215
*Legislative Petitions for Initiative
Petition Amendments to the
Massachusetts Constitution,
1933 to 1992*, 133*n*
*Legislative Procedure in the General
Court of Massachusetts*, 133*n*
Legislative Procedure in the General
Court of Massachusetts,
2003, 121
Legislative Service Commission, Ohio,
263
*The Legislative/Administrative
Dichotomy and the Use of the
Initiative and Referendum in
a North Dakota Home Rule*,
252
*Legislator Again Blocks Same-Sex
Marriage Ban*, 135*n*
Legislators' Handbook, Maine, 111*n*
legislature.idaho.gov/research/
referencelibrary.htm, 87
legislature.mi.gov, 142
Legislatures. *see also specific states*
initiatives and, 3-4
referendums and, 4
unicameral, 207
legis.nd.gov/, 253,254,255
legis.state.sd.us/, 296*n*,297*n*
legis.state.us/index.aspx, 292-293
legisweb.state.wy.us/, 332,333
leg.mt.us, 201
leg.state.nv.us/lcb/research/elecinfo.
cfm, 228
leg.state.or.us/bills_laws/, 277
leg.state.or.us/comm/commsrvs/,
280-281

Lehigh, Scot, 132*n*
Leland Stanford Junior University, 41
*Lemond, Summit Mall Company, LLC
    v.* , 37
Leshy, John D., 26
Lewiston Sun Journal, 106
LexisNexis, 46,252,331
libraries.maine.edu/, 112*n*
library.du.edu/, 60
Liebert, Tobe, 13*n*
Liehmann, New State Ice Co. v. , 285*n*
lifegoeson.com/departments/archives/
    archives.html, 95
*Limitations on Initiative and
    Referendum*, 41
Limits v. President of the Senate, 128
Little, Joseph W., 75
llrx.com, 10
Lobbying on a Shoe String, 129
Local initiative processes, 13*n*,90,328
Local Records Act, Illinois, 93
Locklin, Vanessa, 19
Logan, Ford v. , 320*n*
*Logrolling Gets Logrolled: Same-Sex
    Marriage, Direct Democracy,
    and the Single Subject Rule*,
    42-43
Longo, Peter J., 215*n*,219
Loontjer v. Robinson, 220
The Los Angeles Times, 7
Lowe, Chip J., 295,296*n*,297*n*
lsc.state.oh.us, 263,264*n*
Lubinski, Joseph, 43-44
Lukins v. Curtis, 84
lwvfla.org/, 76
lwvmissouri.org, 171
lwvohio.org, 262
lwv.org/, 48
lwv.org, 253
lwvwa.org/, 318

Macy, J.E., 5,44-45
Magleby, David B., 245-246,269
Maine

bibliography regarding, 108-110
history of I&R in, 98-99
I&R process in, 100-104
initiative process and, 13*n*
Internet resources regarding,
    107-108
introduction to, 98
legislative history material
    regarding, 106-107
recent use of initiatives in, 100
researching I&R law regarding,
    104-106
summary, 97
*Maine Citizen's Guide to the
    Referendum Elections*, 111*n*
Maine Key Number Digest, 106
*The Maine State Constitution: A
    Reference Guide*, 109-110
Maine State Law and Legislative
    Reference Library, 100,108
maine.gov/, 107-108,111*n*,112*n*
*Maine's Constitutional Provisions for
    the Citizen Initiative and
    People's Veto*, 107,110*n*
*Maine's Statutory Provisions for the
    Citizen Initiative and
    People's Veto*, 107
Majority, defined, 34
*Majority Rule: or, the Initiative and
    Referendum*, 255*n*,256*n*
*Make Your Voice Heard: Missouri's
    Initiative Petition Process
    and the Fair Ballot Access
    Act*, 171
Mallory, Mara, 19
Marijuana, 133*n*,135*n*,224,285*n*
Marlowe, Steven William, 320*n*
Marsh, Klosterman v. , 221
Marsh, State ex rel. Morris v. , 220
Martin, Daniel W., 13*n*
Maryland
    initiative process and, 13*n*
    popular referendums and, 13*n*
Massachusetts
    Attorney General and, 125

conclusions regarding, 131-132
court decisions and, 127-128
General Court and, 126
glossary of terms regarding,
     115-117
history of I&R in, 117-119
I&R process in, 119-122
initiative process and, 13*n*
introduction to, 114-115
journal/news articles regarding,
     129-131
legal authority in, 122-123
Office of Campaign and Political
     Finance and, 125-126
reference tools for, 128-129
Secretary of the Commonwealth
     and, 124
summary, 113
Massachusetts Acts and Resolves, 126
Massachusetts Continuing Leading
     Education, 129
Massachusetts Digest 2d, 128
The Massachusetts Political Almanac,
     128-129
Massachusetts Political Almanac, 134*n*
Massachusetts Statewide Records
     Retention Schedule 06-06,
     122
mass.gov/, 125-126
Matsusaka, John G., 12,49*n*,246,256*n*
May v. Daniels, 45-46
MCA. *see* Montana Annotated Code
McCollum, Jumper v. , 36
McCubbins, Matthew D., 250
McCuen, Plugge v. , 35
McCuen, Porter v. , 35
McCullough, David, 132*n*
McDonough, John, 130,133*n*
McHargue, Daniel S., 143,145*n*
McInerney, State ex rel. Keefe v. ,
     324,329*n*
MCLE. *see* Massachusetts Continuing
     Leading Education
*Medical Marijuana-Timilty: No Stance
     Yet on Pot Question,* 133*n*

Medicinal marijuana. *see* Marijuana
Medina, J. Michael, 270
Meier, Dawson v. , 242
Meier, Hernett v. , 242
Meredith, Judith, 129
*Messages and Proclamations of the
     Governors of Nebraska,* 214
Meyer v. Grant, 61*n*
Michigan
     history of I&R in, 138
     I&R process in, 139-140,150-155
     initiative process and, 13*n*
     introduction to, 138
     researching I&R law regarding,
          140-145
     summary, 137
Michigan Compiled Laws Annotated,
     142
The Michigan Daily, 145
Michigan Department of State, 145*n*,
     146*n*
*Michigan Law and Practice
     Encyclopedia,* 143-144,146*n*
The Michigan Manual, 140-141
Michigan Public Radio, 145
michigandaily.com, 145
michigan.gov/sos, 142,145*n*,146*n*
michiganradio.org, 145
Miewald, Robert D., 215*n*,219
Miller, Robert G., 133*n*
Miller, Robin, 251
Minority rights, 35
*Minutes of the Daily Proceedings,
     Alaska Constitutional
     Convention,* 18
Mississippi
     annotated bibliography for, 157-159
     conclusions regarding, 157
     history of I&R in, 148-149
     initiative process and, 13*n*
     popular referendums and, 13*n*
     researching I&R law regarding,
          155-157
     summary, 147
Mississippi Code Annotated, 158

Mississippi Constitution, 158
Mississippi Law Research Institute,
    159
*Mississippi Official and Statistical
    Register*, 158
*The Mississippi State Constitution: A
    Reference Guide*, 159
Mississippi State University,
    150,156-157
*Mississippi's Initiative and
    Referendum: A Primer*,
    150,156-157,158,160n
Missouri
    history of I&R in, 165-166
    I&R process in, 166
    initiative process and, 13n
    initiatives in, 164-165
    introduction to, 164
    referenda in, 164-165
    relevant documents regarding,
        166-167
    research tools for, 167-170
    selected bibliography for, 172-175
    summary, 163
Missouri Code of State Regulations,
    168
Missouri Local Government, 167
Missouri Practice, 168-169
Missouri Time Limitations, 167
"Missourians Against Human
    Cloning", 167
"Missourians for Lifesaving Cures",
    167
*Missouri's Silenced Citizen
    Legislators: How the
    Initiative is Denied to
    Citizens in Fourth-Class
    Missouri Municipalities*, 173
Modersohn, Jennifer, 45
Mohl, Bruce, 135n
Molloy, Donald W., 180
Molpus, State ex rel. Moore v.,
    148-149
Montana

appointment of pro/con committees
    and, 183-184
current state of affairs in, 181
history of I&R in, 180
I&R process in, 181-183
initiative process and, 13n
initiatives/referendum since 1906,
    186-200
introduction to, 178
researching I&R law regarding,
    184-185,200-203
summary, 177
types of ballot measure in, 178-180
Montana Annotated Code, 201
Montana Historical Society,
    184-185,203
Montana Legislative Library, 184-185
Montana Major Facility Siting Act,
    180
Montana PIRG v. Johnson, 185n
Moore, Bernbeck v., 216n,220
Moore, Dobrovolny v., 220
Moore, State ex re. Bellino v., 220
Moore, State ex re. Stenberg v., 221
Moorman v. Priest, 36
moritzlaw.osu.edu/, 262
Morning Sentinel, 106
Morton, Kenneth G., 128-129,134n
*Moving the Capital: A History of
    Ballot Measures*, 19n
MRSC. *see* Municipal Research and
    Services Center of
    Washington
mrsc.org, 316
msgovt.org/policy.html, 156-157
muextension.missouri.edu/, 172
Municipal Law in Missouri, 173
Municipal League of King County,
    317
Municipal Research and Services
    Center of Washington, 316
Municipal Servs. Corp. v. Kusler, 242
munileague.org, 317,318
Munn, Greenlee v., 37
Murdock, Margaret Maier, 329n,332

Murdock, Nicholas, 329*n*,332
Murray, "Alfalfa Bill", 266-267,271*n*

NAC. *see* Nevada Administrative Code
nadc.nol.org, 213-214
National Agricultural Law Center, 48
National Conference of State
    Legislatures, 10,28,29*n*,
    49,86,171,253
National Direct Legislation League,
    234
National Voter Registration Act of
    1993, 236
nationalaglawcenter.org, 48
ncsl.org, 10,28,49,171
nd.gov, 255
nd.gov/sos/, 238
Neary, Mary Ann, 129
Nebraska
    bibliography regarding, 219-221
    citations to the constitution/revised
        statutes regarding I&R
        process, 217-218
    history of I&R in, 207
    I&R process in, 207-210
    initiative process and, 13*n*
    introduction to, 206
    major parties involved in I&R
        process in, 211-213
    researching I&R law regarding,
        213-215
    summary, 205
Nebraska Accountability and
    Disclosure Commission,
    212,213-214,219
Nebraska Blue Book, 216*n*
*The Nebraska Constitution: A
    Reference Guide*, 215*n*,219
Nebraska District Court, 215
Nebraska Records Management
    Division, 220
Nebraska State Archives, 214-215
Nebraska State Historical Society, 214
Nebraska Unicameral Legislature, 207

nebraskahistory.org/lib-arch/research/
    public/state.htm, 214-215
Neely, Alfred S., 173-174,176*n*
Nelson v. Gass, 242
Nevada
    history of I&R in, 224-225
    initiative process and, 13*n*
    initiative process in, 225-226
    Internet resources and, 227-228
    introduction to, 224
    primary law in, 227
    referendum process in, 226
    researching I&R law regarding, 226
    summary, 223
Nevada Administrative Code, 227
*The Nevada Constitution: Origin and
    Growth*, 228*n*
Nevada Revised Statutes, 227
Nevadans for Nev. v. Beers, 228*n*
*Nevadans for the Prot. of Prop rights,
    Inc. v. Heller*, 228*n*
New Mexico, popular referendums
    and, 13*n*
New State Ice Co. v. Liehmann, 285*n*
The New York Times, 7
News sources. *see* Periodicals
NewsBank, Inc., 169
Nichols, Russell, 132*n*
Niswanger, Stephen B., 45
*Nonbinding Question: Decriminalizing
    Marijuana Favored*, 135*n*
Norlin Library's Government
    Publications Department,
    54-55,59
North Dakota
    history of I&R in, 233-236
    initiative process and, 13*n*
    introduction to, 232
    overview of I&R in, 232-233
    petition process in, 238-240
    recall in, 240-241
    selected case law regarding,
        241-242
    selected century code statutes
        regarding, 241

selected secondary materials for, 242-252
summary, 231
voter registration in, 236-238
North Dakota Centennial Blue Book, 244-245
North Dakota Century Code, 253
North Dakota Legislative Council, 254
North Dakota Mill and Elevator Association, 254
North Dakota Referendum League, 234
North Dakota Session Laws, 255
North Dakota State Bank, 255
North Dakota State Fair Ass'n, Bolinske v. , 241
North Dakota's New Election Code, 250
Norway, Robert M., 76
Not in Montana: Citizens Against CI-97, 185*n*
NRS. *see* Nevada Revised Statutes
Nuclear power bans, 100

Oberholtzer, Ellis Paxson, 39
Oesterle, Dale A., 56,58,61*n*
Office of Campaign and Political Finance, Massachusetts, 125-126,134*n*
Office of Code Revisor, Washington, 311
Office of Legislative Legal Services Counsel, Colorado, 53
Office of Policy and Legal Analysis, Maine, 111*n*
The Official Massachusetts Information for Voters, 131,132*n*
The Official Returns of the Votes and Blanks Cast Upon the Nineteen Constitutional Amendments Submitted by the Constitutional Convention and Adopted at the State Election, November 5,1918, 133*n*
Ohio
history of I&R in, 258
initiative process and, 13*n*,258-259
introduction to, 257-258
referendum process in, 259-260
researching I&R law regarding, 260-263
summary, 257
Ohio Constitution, 262
Ohio Election Statistics, 260
Ohio Revised Code, 261
The Ohio State Constitution: A Reference Guide, 264*n*
Ohman, Brady v. , 324,330*n*,331
ojd.state.or.us/library, 284
Oklahoma
history of I&R in, 99,266-267
I&R process in, 267-268
initiative process and, 13*n*
introduction to, 265
researching I&R law regarding, 268-271
summary, 265
Oklahoma Family Policy Council, 269
Olson, State ex rel. Langer v. , 242
Omdahl, Lloyd B., 246-247,251
"One man, one vote", 64-65
Open Meetings Act, Illinois, 93
Opinion of the Justices to the Acting Governor, 127
Opinion of the Justices to the House of Representatives, 127-128
Oregon
history of I&R in, 99,275
I&R process in, 275-276
initiative process and, 13*n*
researching I&R law regarding, 276-284
summary, 273-274
Oregon Blue Book, 279
Oregon Department of Justice, 283
Oregon Historical Society, 285*n*

Oregon Laws and Memorials and
        Resolutions, 277-278,286n
Oregon Legal Research Guide, 279
Oregon State Legislature, 280-281
Oregon State Library, 284
The Oregon System, 274
oregon.gov/OSL/, 284
The Origin of State Constitutional
        Direct Democracy: William
        Simon U'Ren and the
        "Oregon System",
        282-283,285n
Ortbahn, David L., 295,297n
Other Elections Information, 307n
An Overview of Massachusetts
        Statewide Ballot Measures:
        1919-2004, 134n

PACs. *see* Political action committees
PAIS International, 7,169-170
Pamphlets. *see* Publicity Pamphlet;
        Voters Pamphlets
Paradise, Paplinka, 128-129,134n
Patriot Ledger, 133n,135n
Patten, Roland T., 99
PDC. *see* Public Disclosure
        Commission
pdc.wa.gov, 315-316
pdxcityclub.org, 278-279
Pelkey v. City of Fargo, 242
Pellitier, Lawrence Lee, 109,110n
Penrose Library, 60
The People Act, the Courts React: A
        Proposed Model for
        Interpreting Initiatives in
        Idaho, 82-83
People Veto's Application Packet,
        112n
People's Populist party, 234
People's Vetoes 1909, 110-111n
People's Vetoes, Maine,
        100,101,102-104,107-108
Periodicals, 6-7
    Arizona, 26-27

    Idaho, 85
    Maine, 106
    Missouri, 169-170
    Montana, 201
    Ohio, 263
    Washington, 312
Permanent Central Voter File, 241
Persily, Nathaniel, 40
Petition requirements. *see specific*
        states
Piott, Steven L., 39,174,176n,
        202,215n,219
PIRG. *see* Florida Public Interest
        Research Group
Platt, George M., 96n
Pletz, John S., 174
Plugge v. McCuen, 35
Polhill, Dennis, 58
Political action committees, 43
A *Political History of Nevada, 1996*,
        228
Poll Clerks to Check Identification and
        Verify Eligibility, 241
Poll taxes, 35
Ponylake School Dist. 30 v. State
        Committee for
        Reorganization of School
        Districts, 221
Popely, Ted, 19
Popular referendums. *see also specific*
        states
    defined, 4
    states allowing, 13n
Populist movement, 98,234
Porter v. McCuen, 35
Portland Press Herald, 106
"Power of Legislative Body to Amend,
        Repeal, or Abrogate Initiative
        or Referendum Measure, or
        to Enact Measure Defeated
        on Referendum", 5
Power of Legislative Body to Amend
        Repeal, or Abrogate Initiative
        or Referendum Measure, or

to Enact Measure Defeated on Referendum, 44-45
Power v. Robertson, 160*n*
A Practitioner's Guide to Challenging and Defending Legislatively Proposed Constitutional Amendments in Arkansas, 45
Pre-Election Judicial Review of Initiatives and Referendums, 269
Pre-Election Review of Initiative and Petitions: An Unreasonable Limitation on Political Speech, 271
Prendergast, Arthur J., Jr., 263
Preparing an Election Petition in Missouri, 172
Preserving the Democratic Legacy of the American Frontier: Limiting Regulation of the People's Initiative and Referendum Process, 215*n*
President of the Senate, Limits v., 128
Priest, Moorman v., 36
Prior Years Election Information, 57
Procedure for Circulation of Petition, 37
Progressive movement, 98,267,310
Project Vote Smart, 11,28
Proposed Amendments to the Florida Constitution and Bond Referendum, 77*n*
Proposition 2 1/2, 117,131,133*n*
ProQuest, 7
Public and Local Acts of the Legislature of the State of Michigan, 141
Public Controls and Influences, 176*n*
"*Public Controls and Influences*" *Missouri Practice: Administrative Practice and Procedure*, 173-174
Public Disclosure Commission, Washington, 315-316

Public Information Clearing Service, 75
Public Policy Questions, defined, 117
Publicity Pamphlet, Arizona, 23
The Pursuit of Popular Interest: Interpretive Dilemmas in Direct Democracy, 174

Qualifications of Electors, 241
Question 2: Multiple Listing of Candidates is Soundly Rejected, 135*n*
Question 3: Effort to Allow Child Care Union Comes Closest, 135*n*
Questions as to the Meaning of the Amendments, 130

Radcliffe, M. Sean, 271
Rahm, David A., 215*n*,216*n*,219
Ramer, Van Kleek v., 61*n*
Ramney, Austin, 38
Ranney, Austin, 244
Reaves, Robert Gibbs, 40,49*n*
Recall, 240,248
Recall Petitions–Signature–Form Circulation, 241
The Records of the Arizona Constitutional Convention of 1910, 26
Redirected Democracy: An Evaluation of the Initiative Process, 282
Rediscovering the Right to Instruct Legislators, 130
Reeves, Eugene E., 172
Referenda, 94
"Referendum", 201
Referendum Petition, defined, 117
The Referendum: The People Decide Public Policy, 175
Referendums, *see also specific states* defined, 4,178-179

Referendums: A Comparative Study of
    Practice and Theory, 38,244
Reforming Direct Democracy: Lessons
    from Oregon, 282
Registration of Voters
    [Municipalities], 241
Regulating Democracy Through
    Democracy: The Use of
    Direct-Legislation in Election
    Reform Law, 40
Religion, 35,83,118
Report of Law Research on Initiative
    and Referendum Legislation,
    159
Republican Party, 99,234
Required Attachments to Petitions, 37
Research in Illinois Law, 94
Research resources
    Alaska I&R law and, 17-19
    almanacs/encyclopedia use and,
        4-6
    Arizona I&R law and, 24-29
    Arkansas I&R law and, 35-49
    Colorado I&R law and, 54-60
    digests and, 8-9
    Florida I&R law and, 70-76
    Idaho I&R law and, 81-87
    Illinois I&R law and, 93-95
    Internet resources and, 9-11
    introduction to, 1-3
    Maine I&R law and, 104-110
    Massachusetts I&R law and,
        121-122,128-131
    Michigan I&R law and, 140-145
    Mississippi I&R law and, 155-157
    Missouri I&R law and, 166-175
    Montana I&R law and,
        184-185,200-203
    Nebraska I&R law and, 213-215
    Nevada I&R law and, 226-228
    North Dakota I&R law and,
        241-255
    Ohio I&R law and, 260-263
    Oklahoma I&R law and, 268-271
    Oregon I&R law and, 276-284
    periodicals/periodicals indexes and,
        6-7
    selected bibliography for, 11-12
    session laws/annotated codes and, 8
    South Dakota I&R law and,
        291-296
    Utah I&R law and, 303-306
    Washington I&R law and, 312-319
Research Roundup: Federal and State
    Elections Resources, 10
researchcouncil.org, 316
Researching California Ballot
    Measures, 13n
Residence of Students for Voting
    Purposes, 250
Restrictions on Initiative and
    Referendum Powers in South
    Dakota, 295,296n
Revising Statewide Initiative and
    Referendum Provisions of the
    Massachusetts Constitution,
    132n
Revisor of Statutes, Nebraska,
    207-208,211
Reynolds v. Sims, 64,76n
Rice, Tamara, 135n
Ricketts, B.C., 251
Robbins, James W., 247
Robertson, Power v. , 160n
Robertson, Stokes V., 148-149
Robinson, Loontjer v. , 220
Roe v. Wade, 224
Rooney, Francis J., 94
Roosevelt, Theodore, 266
Roskoski, Matthew, 19
Roush, Russell Brown, 26
Rudolph, E. George, 329n,330n,332
Rules of Campaign Finance &
    Disclosure, 47
Ryan, Andrew, 134n

Same-sex marriage, 42-43,127,132n,
    135n,224
Scanlon, Patrick, 133n

Schacter, Jane S., 174
Schmidt, David D., 12,40,49*n*,
174-175,176*n*,216*n*,
219,233,247-248,256*n*,
329*n*,332
Schulman v. AG, 127
Schultz, Birl E., 38,243
Schumacher v. Byrne, 242
Schuman, David, 282-283,285*n*
Scroggins v. Kerr, 36
sdsos.gov/, 293,296*n*
sdsos.gov/index.shtm, 292
Searan, Tindall v. , 35
Seattle University Law Review,
318-319
Secretary of State
Arkansas, 49
Colorado, 57,58,61*n*
Idaho, 81-82,87
Illinois, 91
Maine, 101-104,107,111*n*,112*n*
Massachusetts. *see* Secretary of the
Commonwealth
Michigan, 142
Mississippi, 155-156,161*n*
Missouri, 167,171-172
Montana, 182,184-185,201,203
Nebraska, 208-210,211,213,219
Nevada, 227-228,238-240
North Dakota, 254-255,256*n*
Ohio, 260,262,264*n*
Oklahoma, 270
Oregon, 276,279-280,283
South Dakota, 290,292,296*n*
Washington, 314-315,320*n*
Wyoming, 325-327
Secretary of the Commonwealth
defined, 117
Massachusetts, 121,124,133*n*
sec.state.ma.us/ele, 121
secstate.wa.gov, 314-315,320*n*
Selke, Albert G., 248,256*n*
Senate Bill 2251,Massachusetts, 122
Session laws, 8

*Session Laws of the State of
Washington*, 313-314
Seven Weeks to History, 132*n*
Sharpe, Theodore, 240,248
Sheppard, Steve, 45-46
Signature requirements. *see specific
states*
The Significance of the Returns, 135*n*
*Signing of Petition–Penalty for
Falsification*, 37
Silak, Cathy R., 82-83
Sims, Reynolds v. , 64,76*n*
Single subject rule
Arkansas, 42-43
Florida, 66-67
*SJC Rules That Initiative to Ban Dog
Racing Illegal*, 132*n*
smartvoter.org, 264*n*
Smith, Daniel A., 12,42,248-249
Smith, Jim, 76
*So You Want to Amend the Florida
Constitution? A Guide to
Initiative Petitions*, 76
*Social Choice, Crypto-Initiatives, and
Policymaking by Direct
Democracy*, 250
Socialist Party, 99
SoDakLIVE, 294
sodaklive.com, 294
*Some Aspects of the Direct Legislation
Process*, 319*n*
sos.arkansas.gov/, 47,49
sos.idaho.gov, 87
sos.mt.gov/, 185*n*,201
sos.state.ms.us/, 161*n*
sos.state.ne.us/elec/, 213
sos.state.nv.us/nvelection/, 227-228
sos.state.oh.us/sos, 262,264*n*
sos.state.ok.us, 270
sos.state.or.us/, 279-280,283-284
soswy.state.wy.us/, 332
South Dakota
history of I&R in, 288-289
I&R process in, 289-291
initiative process and, 13*n*

introduction to, 288
researching I&R law regarding,
    291-296
summary, 287
South Dakota Codified Laws, 293
South Dakota Legal Research Guide,
    295
South Dakota Legislative Manual, 293
South Dakota Legislative Research
    Council, 292-293
South Dakota Political Almanac: A
    presentation and analysis of
    election statistics, 1889-1960,
    294-295
Spurlin, 297*n*
St. Louis Post-Dispatch, 7,175*n*
Staszewski, Glen, 251
State, Cavanaugh v. , 61*n*
State Archives, Massachusetts, 124
State Ballot Questions Petitions, 121
State Board of Election
    Commissioners, 49
State Canvassing Board, Nebraska,
    210,212
State Committee for Reorganization of
    School Districts, Ponylake
    School Dist. 30 v. , 221
State Constitutions for the Twenty-first
    Century, 40
State ex re. Bellino v. Moore, 220
State ex rel. Ayres v. Amsberry, 221
State ex rel. Benham v. Cheever,
    324,329*n*
State ex rel. Brant v. Beermann, 220
State ex rel. Frazier v. Hall, 242
State ex rel. Keefe v. McInerney,
    324,329*n*
State ex rel. Labedz v. Beermann, 220
State ex rel. Langer v. Olson, 242
State ex rel. Lemon v. Gale, 206,220
State ex rel. Linde v. Hall, 242
State ex rel. Moore v. Molpus, 148-149
State ex rel. Morris v. Marsh, 220
State ex rel. Stenberg v. Beermann,
    215*n*,216*n*,221

State ex rel. Stenberg v. Moore, 221
State ex rel. Twichell v. Hall, 242
State ex rel. Winter v. Swanson, 221
State Library and Archives of Florida,
    73-74
State Library, Massachusetts, 126
State of Illinois Local Election
    Officials Handbook for the
    2007 Consolidated Elections,
    94
State of Oregon Law Library, 284
State Voting Rights of Residents of
    Federal Military
    Establishments, 250
state.ar.us/, 47,49
state.co.us/, 54,56-57,58,59,61*n*
state.me.us/legis/lawlib/peoplesveto.
    htm, 110-111*n*
Statewide Ballot Question Committees:
    a Listing of Committees and
    CPF ID Numbers, 125
Statewide Ballot Question Spending
    Reaches Almost $10Million,
    134*n*
Statutory initiative, defined, 183
Statutory research. *see* Research
    resources
Stem cell research, 167
Stenberg, Don, 215*n*
Stennis Institute of Government. *see*
    John C. Stennis Institute of
    Government
Stephen H. Hart Library, 55,58
Steps for Placing an Initiated Proposal
    on the Statewide Ballot, 61*n*
Stewart, Robert G., 129-130
Stilley v. Henson, 36
Structuring the Ballot Initiative:
    Procedures that Do and
    Don't Work, 56
Studies in Southern History and
    Politics, 39
Sufficiency of Technical and
    Procedural Aspects of Recall
    Petitions, 251

Summit Mall Company, LLC v. Lemond, 37
Sunbehm Gas, Inc. v. Conrad, 242
Super-majority requirements, 324-325. *see also specific states*
Supreme Judicial Court, defined, 117
A Survey of the Single Subject Rule as Applied to Statewide Initiatives, 19
Sutton, Camden Community Development Corp. v. , 37
Swann v. Adams, 65,76n
Swanson, State ex rel. Winter v. , 221

Taking Laws into Their Own Hands, 130,133n,134n
Tallian, Laura, 319n
Tarr, Alan G., 40
"Tax revolt" measures, 117,131,133n
Taxpayers' Federation of Illinois, 95
taxpayfedil.org, 95
Tearing Down Brickhouse: Could Judicial Demolition of Brickhouse v. Hill Prompt a New Arkansas Constitution?, 42
Term limits, 84,128,152,323
Term Limits Leadership Council, Inc. v. Clark, 152
Terral v. Arkansas Light and Power Co., 36
Terzian, Barbara A., 264n
The Referendum in America: Together with Some Chapters on the History of the Initiative and the Recall, 39
Thomas, David Y., 40
Thomson v. Wyoming In-Stream Flow Committee, 324,329n,331
Tiffany, B.E., 296,297n
Tindall v. Searan, 35
Tinkle, Marshall J., 109-110
Tobin, Dawson v. , 242
Tocqueville, Alexis de, 114

Todd, Charles Foster, 26,29n
Tolbert, Caroline J., 12,248-249
Tomlinson Bros. v. Hodges, 36
Townley, Arthur C., 249
Trautman, Philip A., 319n
Trends in the Use of the Initiative and Referendum in the State of Arizona, 25
Two Cheers for Popular Sovereignty and Direct Democracy: Historical Reflections, 39
2006 Initiative and Referendum: Facts and Information for the 2006 General Election, 40
The 2006 Oklahoma Voter's Guide, 269

ucblibraries.colorado.edu/norlin, 59
ucblibraries.colorado.govpubs/index.htm, 60
Ueland, Lars A., 233-235,255n,256n
Ulmer, Bess v. , 19
"Ultimate Human Life Amendment", 155
University of Colorado, 54-55,59,60
University of Colorado Law Review, 55
University of Denver, 55,60
University of Idaho Law Library, 87
University of Missouri, 172
University of South Dakota School of Law, 291
University of Southern California, 57-58,77n. *see also* Initiative and Referendum Institute
uniweb.legislature.ne.gov/, 215
U'Ren, William Simon, 275
Utah
   code citations for passed initiatives, 306f
   conclusions regarding, 306-307
   history of I&R in, 299-300
   I&R process in, 301-302
   initiative process and, 13n

introduction to, 299-300
researching I&R law regarding,
    303-306
summary, 299
Utah Code Annotated, 305-306
Utah History Research Center, 308*n*

*Validity, Construction, and
    Application of State Criminal
    Disenfranchisement
    Provisions*, 251
*Validity, Construction, and
    Application of State Statutory
    Voting Offenses*, 251
Van Eaton, Anson Eugene, 175
Van Kleek v. Ramer, 61*n*
*Veiled Political Actors and Campaign
    Disclosure Laws in Direct
    Democracy*, 42
Verification, signature. *see* Signature
    requirements
Vernon's Annotated Missouri Statutes,
    168
Vetoes, People's. *see* People's Vetoes
Vote Nevada–A Guide to Nevada
    Elections, 228
*Vote of the People: A Brief History and
    Compilation of All Measures
    Submitted to a Vote of the
    People of North Dakota
    From Statehood Through
    1966*, 246-247
Voter registration, 236-238
*Voter Registration Signature Imaging
    System*, 37
voterguide.ss.ca.gov/, 268
Voters Pamphlets,
    84,200,203,304-305,315
Votes on Initiated Bills 1910-,
    110-111*n*
*Votes on Referenda on Acts of the
    Maine Legislature 1910-*,
    110-111*n*
vote-smart.org, 11,28

Wade, Roe v., 224
Waldron, Ellis, 203
The Wall Street Journal, 7
Walters, Robert J., 329*n*,332
Washington
    history of I&R in, 310
    I&R process in, 311-312
    initiative process and, 13*n*
    introduction to, 310
    researching I&R law regarding,
        312-319
    summary, 309
Washington Policy Center, 317
Washington Public Disclosure
    Commission, 315-316
Washington Research Council, 316
*Washington State: Theory and
    Practice*, 319*n*
washingtonpolicy.org, 317
Waters, M. Dane, 5,12-13,13*n*,
    17,28,41,96*n*,104,110*n*,
    159,159*n*,160*n*,161*n*,
    167,175*n*,201,219,
    235,249,256*n*,261,307*n*
Wayne Law Review, 143
Webster, Daniel, 114
Wendt, Laurel, 94
Western Historical Manuscript
    Collection, 172
Western History and Genealogy, 59
Western History Collection, 55
Westlaw, 5,7,46,72,252,294
Westminster Law Library, 55,60
West's Analysis of American Law, 8-9
West's Encyclopedia of American Law,
    201
West's Florida Digest, 72
*West's Maine Revised Statutes
    Annotated*, 105
West's Missouri Digest, 168
West's Oklahoma Statutes Annotated,
    271
*West's Oregon Revised Statutes
    Annotated*, 278

West's Revised Code of Washington Annotated, 314
West's Smith-Hurd Illinois Compiled Statutes Annotated, 96n
Whaley, Sean, 228n
William A. Wise Law School Library, 54-55,60
Williams, Deborah L., 19
Williams, Robert F., 40
Wills, Elana Cunningham, 42
Wine Sale Question Nearing Record on Campaign Spending, 134n
Winkle, John W., III, 159
Wood, H.A., 46
Wood v. Byrne, 242
Wright, Boyd L., 252
www.1.leg.wa.gov/legislature, 315
www2state.id.us/ag, 86
www3.state.id.us/, 81
Wyoming
    conclusions regarding, 328-329
    court treatment in, 324-325

history of I&R in, 322-324,334-335
I&R process in, 325-328
initiative process and, 13n
summary, 321
Wyoming Association of Municipalities, 333
Wyoming In-Stream Flow Committee, Thomson v., 324,329n
Wyoming Legislative Service Office, 333
Wyoming Local Government Law, 329n,331,332
Wyoming Statutes Annotated, 331
wyomuni.org/, 333

Zimmerman, Joseph F., 159,175
Zitter, Jay M., 251
Zoning ordinances, 43

For Product Safety Concerns and Information please contact our EU
representative GPSR@taylorandfrancis.com
Taylor & Francis Verlag GmbH, Kaufingerstraße 24, 80331 München, Germany

www.ingramcontent.com/pod-product-compliance
Lightning Source LLC
Chambersburg PA
CBHW070545270326
41926CB00013B/2205

9 781138 969391